THE BIG BOOK OF OUTDOOR
DIY

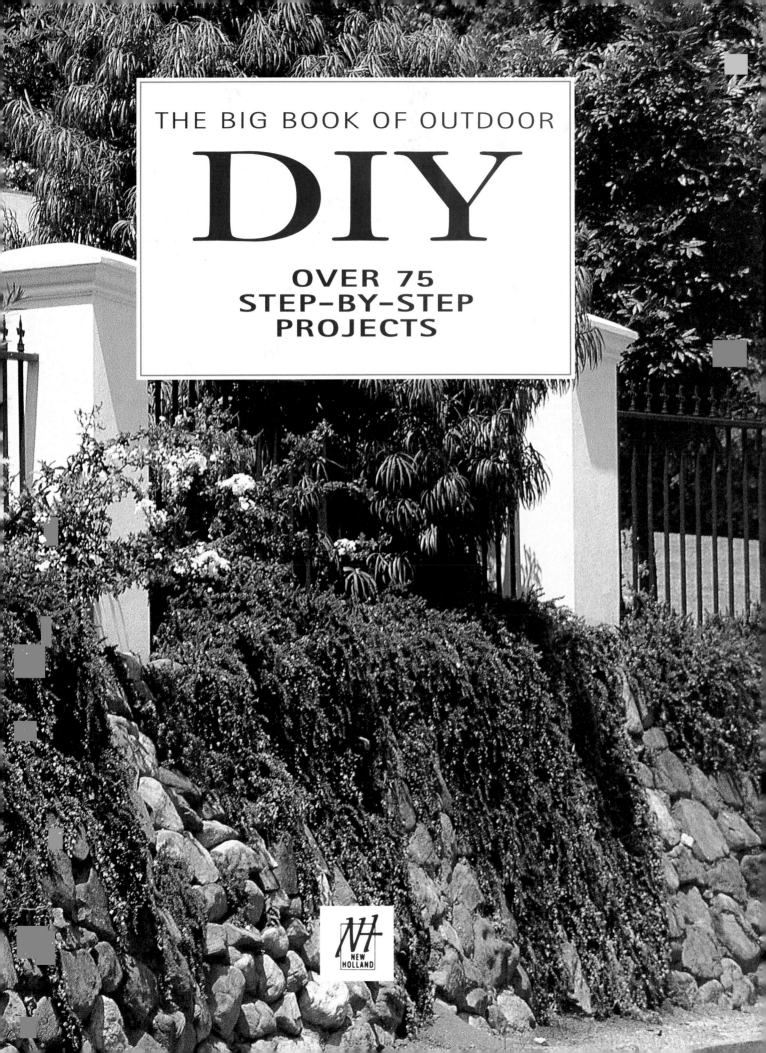

THE BIG BOOK OF OUTDOOR
DIY

OVER 75 STEP–BY–STEP PROJECTS

NEW HOLLAND

First published in 1997 by
New Holland (Publishers) Ltd
London • Cape Town • Sydney • Singapore

24 Nutford Place
London W1H 6DQ
United Kingdom

80 McKenzie Street
Cape Town 8001
South Africa

3/2 Aquatic Drive
Frenchs Forest, NSW 2086
Australia

ISBN 1 85368 693 X

Editor: Gillian Haslam
Designer: Roger Daniels
Managing Editor: Coral Walker

Printed and bound in Malaysia by Times Offset (M) Sdn. Bhd.

CONTENTS

INTRODUCTION
AND
BASIC TECHNIQUES

We have been designing, creating and developing outdoor spaces for centuries; building walls and fences; laying paths; designing courtyards and patios; adding still and flowing water features; and constructing a variety of both useful and decorative features from the materials available to us. Some of us do it ourselves, while others prefer to employ professionals to do it for them.

Much of this activity involves building and woodworking skills, and this simple, easy-to-read book offers you hands-on advice and easy-to-follow information which may be adapted to just about any environment, anywhere in the world. Whether you are starting from scratch or modifying an existing property, you will find these pages crammed with hints, inspirational ideas and useful instructions to help you do-it-yourself or simply increase your knowledge so that you can hire or contract the right person to assist you to achieve your goal.

Of course some projects may seem challenging, even daunting, but most of those illustrated here can be tackled by any DIY homeowner who is both capable and enthusiastic. A proper tool kit is important, often making light work of seemingly complicated tasks, while a knowledge of building principles and techniques is essential.

Although various building skills will help you improve your property, we all know that planting is important too; after all without flowers, shrubs and trees, what would a garden be? Although this is not a gardening book, it does give some advice and guidance which will help you plan the development of your outdoor spaces. Hundreds of full colour photographs also offer inspiration and suggest a myriad of possibilities which you can easily adapt and alter to suit your own property.

The examples shown here illustrate a wide range of types, varying not only in size and style, but in geographic location as well. The ovrall aim is to provide you with as great a cross-section of imaginative and inspirational options as possible.

Most people want a well-designed garden which incorporates walls, fences, paths, steps or patios. This may include other features and facilities where they can sit, play, entertain, or simply enjoy their little patch of nature in peace and quiet, away from neighbours and passers-by.

At the same time, designing or remodelling a garden or a part of any outdoor area presents a tremendous challenge, particularly if you have never done it before. It does take time, effort and money, but the results can be highly rewarding. Not only can you transform your property beyond all expectations, but you can also improve your lifestyle. Better still, the changes and alterations you make could increase the value of your property beyond all expectations.

With some basic knowledge of materials, tools and techniques, you will find that building your own garden features and structures in a logical and well planned manner can be one of the most rewarding and enjoyable aspects of home improvement. The next few pages will give you a good grounding in the basics of DIY so that you can tackle the projects featured later in this book with confidence.

Before you start any construction work, you will need to have a proposed layout of the garden, including a general planting plan, and a good idea

A small patio creates an ideal entertainment area.

The casual appearance of these steps and walkway conceals careful planning.

of the preferred ground surfaces and shelter possibilities. You will also need to know, more or less, how the entire outdoor area will be used. If there are specific spaces for washing lines, water features, a rose garden, greenhouse, vegetable or herb garden, seating or anything else, these must all be indicated on your plan.

Only then should you decide where the more permanent features will go. Each will have its own particular function; a factor which will help decide where the structure is to be sited. Proper planning, described in some detail over the next few pages of this book, is essential.

Walls, fences and other enclosures provide privacy. They also screen the garden from wind and noise, and, depending on the materials used, may filter sunlight. Whilst some are decorative, often visually defining a boundary or section of the garden, most are functional. Paths, steps and walkways are also practical elements

with very distinct functions, for instance steps enable us to traverse a change in level safely. They are part of what is termed the 'hard landscaping' scheme. They provide a dry, solid surface to the house and through the garden. Often linked to patios, paths and steps are an important design feature within any garden, and should therefore be planned with care and with a thought for safety, especially if children or the elderly use the garden.

Like paths and steps, patios have a hard surface, and are also part of the hard landscaping scheme. These are all elements which ideally should be tackled in the early stages of establishing any outdoor area. More than anything else, it is the patio (as well as courtyards and formal terraces) which will enable you to use the garden as an extension of your house during fine weather.

Although some people incorporate a patio when they build their house, this feature is more frequently added on

later. Walls, fences and screens also form part of the overall design, as do pergolas, arbours and gazebos which are usually built for shelter. Although the various elements are constructed at different times, they all form part of the overall plan.

When it comes to planting, or 'soft landscaping', as it is known, the secret is to consider it in the context of your overall plan. Not only do flowers provide colour and scent, but they are an integral part of the design scheme. They may be used in conjunction with other more formal features; they may also be planted alongside paths or steps, around the perimeter of a patio, or, in the case of creepers or climbers, used to create shelter over a pergola, archway or arbour.

Trees provide shade and introduce essential form to an area. They may also be used to create a backdrop for other plants or features, and as a part of the basic framework of the garden. Positioning them correctly is important.

If you are planning walls and fences around a property, large trees with sprawling root systems should not be planted near the boundary. On the other hand, shrubs and certain framework plants may be used for hedging, screenign, dividing the garden into different themed section or providing privacy as an alternative to walls and fences.

This book explores the possibilities of all these elements, from the planning stages to completion, offering a huge range of options for every type of garden, big or small. Divided into four distinct sections, it looks independently at brick, wood, stone and water features, all designed to add interest to the garden, and greatly increase the usefulness of your outdoor area.

The first section includes essential basic details on planning, design, materials, tools, construction principles and the various building techniques required to do the work yourself. You will need to refer back to these sections when tackling the projects featured further on in the book. Essential aspects are discussed here, including the role a variety of professionals may play in your project, and the possible need for plans. Building codes are discussed in some detail. There is less detail on this subject matter elsewhere, but you shoudl remember to check with your local authority if you are in any doubt as to whether you require planning permission for your garden structure. Since budget is and important factor for most people about to tackle any type of home improvement, the issue of quantifying and costing materials is discussed in all the planning sections.

Similarly, having built a solid garden wall from brick, you will hopefully have mastered the essential techniques required for bricklaying, but there are additional elements to be considered when constructing a flight of steps.

This book may be approached several ways, depending on your needs. First, browse through it and try to assimilate as much as you can. This will help you to identify just how you can improve your own particular outdoor space and what your options are. Then you can decide which jobs you feel competent to tackle yourself, and which jobs you would rather leave to the expertise of various professionals.

If you are interested in one particular section of the book, it makes sense to concentrate on that area. But do not disregard the others; by dipping into each of them, you will find you gain a much clearer insight into the possibilities for your property as a whole. You may even be inspired to tackle a completely different project to that originally envisaged.

Each of the four main parts in this book begins with an introduction and a section describing the material and the basic building techniques relating to it.

Design is also discussed in all four sections. Of course this relates to the style of structure you are planning, and also to finishing touches and design details - pillars, alcoves and niches, built-in planters and so on. Floor

Only basic skills are needed for this fence and arbour.

A simple patio is well within the skills of a beginner.

A simple timber deck with steps leading into the garden is ideal for ourdoor entertaining.

surfaces, roofing options, screening materials, lighting, seating and planting are also considered.

The construction sections focus on a range of materials, tools, methods and techniques which will show you how to tackle the project of your choice.

Although concrete and mortar are discussed in several sections, suggested ratios differ, depending on the work undertaken. Similarly, basic principles are interpreted and executed differently, depending on the project tackled. Furthermore the techniques used when tackling a brick wall, and erecting a pole structure, are quite different, simply because of the variation in materials.

If you have a particular project in mind, it is best first of all to read all you can about the specific materials you plan to use and then to study the building methods carefully. Nothing works as well as trial and error, and, unless you are familiar with construction basics, you are advised to

A pre-cast fountain forms a focal point at the end of a flagstone path.

Imaginative design transforms a rendered boundary wall with a tiled portico.

Lattice screens and a simple roof create a delightful garden structure.

practise the techniques shown photographically in the various step-by-step sections.

The projects featured in these sequences have been photographed step-by-step while in the process of being built, and they have been chosen to show generic methods, as much as the projects themselves. They show you how to form joints and connect pieces of timber, and how to lay bricks and blocks; how to erect simple timber panels which may become the walls of a shed or simple garden building.

The reason for this approach is to illustrate the various techniques as clearly as possible. The idea, too, is for readers to adapt the step-by-step building methods, and use the skills shown to build a variety of structures, including those featured as projects and plans at the back of each of the four main chapters.

A wide range of materials and methods is shown for all the projects; these include various timbers, wire mesh, both pre-cast and concrete cast in situ, bricks, stone, blocks, slabs, tiles and pavers.

Before starting your project, it is a good idea to experiment if you can. If you are working with bricks or blocks and mortar for the first time, mix a little of the cement with sand and water in ratios as described in the text, and try laying a few bricks on a solid concrete surface. Once you get the hang of using the trowel, and become familiar with handling and laying bricks, you should feel sufficiently confident to tackle the real thing.

If you are new to woodwork, use timber offcuts to try out the different tools before you get started. Drill a few holes and screw two pieces of wood together. Then practise using a saw. Once you feel confident, there will be absolutely nothing to hold you back. Ideally work with someone who has some experience; if you watch closely you may be surprised how quickly you get the hang of the different techniques and just how much you learn.

Of course many people like to design their own structures; but for those who do not have the experience, or prefer to follow plans, the book contains more than 75 detailed projects. There are full lists of materials and a brief description of the steps that should be followed during construction. The plans and projects themselves are varied, showing a number of different styles, sizes and structure types. While some are demanding, most are well within the reach of a competent handyman, including beginners with little previous building experience. All may be used as they are, or altered to suit the demands and style of your own property and its surrounding garden..

In some instances the exact materials specified may not be available. For instance a particular kind of retaining block or paver may not be manufactured in your area. Bricks, and especially blocks, may be available in a slightly different size. In most cases something similar can be substituted without any adverse effects at all. Wherever possible, alternatives are suggested. If you are confused, seek the advice of salesmen at your local garden centre or DIY store.

Timber dimensions may also differ from area to area (particularly if you are using hardwoods), but this is seldom a problem when it comes to actual construction. Slight variations are easily adapted. The exact sizes of nails and screws are also not a problem. Once you understand the principles involved, it is a reasonably simple matter to find something which will work just as well.

At the back of the book, a comprehensive glossary explains the technical terms used in building, and a list of useful addresses will help you when trying to track down more unusual materials or equipment.

Ultimately it is your own imagination and creativity which will make your DIY project special and rewarding for you. This book is packed with inspiration and information to help you transofrm your garden, however large or small, formal or informal, into a haven for relaxation, a place for entertaining or somewhere for children to play. Whatever your needs, you will find a project to suit you in the following pages. So read on, and then start building without delay.

A pre-cast fountain forms a strong focal point in an informal garden.

A simple brick path and attractive gazebo add charm to a garden.

Any project which involves the construction of a permanent feature must be well planned. If it is not, you are likely to waste time and money. You should assess your needs carefully and consider exactly what function your structure is to fulfil. You can then decide exactly where to site the feature and establish how much assistance will be required. Before you go any further, you will also need to cost the project and ensure that you are able to fund it fully. It pays to plan properly right from the start. If you are systematic and thorough, the entire project should run smoothly and you will be proud of the end result.

YOUR NEEDS

Every homeowner's needs are different, and only you can decide what will suit your own and your family's circumstances.

A major element to consider is your lifestyle. If you entertain frequently and favour the alfresco approach in good weather, you will probably need a fairly elaborate arrangement with an outdoor kitchen with storage areas. Seating and built-in tables are also options worth considering. Perhaps you and your family spend as much time as possible outdoors, soaking up the sun and enjoying the fresh air. In addition to seating and cooking facilities, you may also want to consider decorative features like planters and ponds which will improve the appearance of a patio or courtyard. Of course, a permanent masonry structure will be part of the general garden design, but it must be planned with your needs at heart, even if you decide to employ a professional to devise an outdoor scheme for you.

If you are an indoor person, but your living room overlooks a spot which will benefit from similarly ornamental features, your needs will be slightly different. For instance, you may love the sound of trickling water, in which case a fountain should be positioned so that it can be both seen and heard from inside the house.

Your children may spend more time outdoors than you do, and a little-used patio could become a favourite play area with a plant-covered pergola for shade. You could perhaps build a brick-sided sandpit at one end for toddlers, or a simple lean-to, comprising a low wall with roof sheeting, to provide an all-weather play shelter for older children. This could become a storage facility for bicycles and other recreational items.

In the garden itself, you may want features such as planters, steps, raised ponds and walled beds, depending on the layout of the area. Pergolas and solid brick arches may also be required as a part of the general design.

Do not forget to consider the utility areas, especially if you want to hide rubbish bins or if you like to pack compost into a neat enclosure.

Finally, think about any immediate needs which may change. Make absolutely certain you can adapt the plan to accommodate change.

An expansive patio, shaded by a brick-piered pergola, may be used for several activities.

CHOOSING THE RIGHT SITE

Some structures, however low or small, cannot be moved, so it is essential to make certain that they are sited correctly. Mistakes can be expensive or impossible to rectify.

The type of feature or structure you are planning to build will largely determine where it is to be located. Built-in benches, for instance, will usually be used to their full potential if constructed on a patio. Presuming that you have an established patio, or have pinpointed an area where you plan to build one, you will need to determine exactly where to place the seating. Ideally it should be reasonably sheltered from prevailing winds, and positioned to take advantage of a view, either beyond the garden or within its confines. However, you may want seating away from the house; perhaps in a rose or herb garden, or alongside a trickling stream (if you are lucky enough to have one meandering through your garden).

Similarly, a structure intended for outdoor cooking will normally be sited on a patio quite close to the house. Alternatively, you can build it up against a boundary wall which screens the site from the wind, or alongside an outbuilding which offers storage space.

The most sensible approach is to scrutinise every possible location and then look at the advantages and disadvantages of each. Make a list and note down your preferences in relation to your needs.

If you are starting from scratch, sit down with a piece of paper and a pencil and sketch some ideas. It is preferable to use graph paper to help you work to scale. Mark all the established features and buildings, trees, large rocks and even shrubs which you want to retain. Then draw in the basic framework of walls, hedges, paths and patios, and identify any definable activity centres (a utility area for washing lines, a vegetable or herb garden, an entertainment patio, play area and so on). Note the direction of prevailing winds and spots which get more than average sun or shade.

Accessibility

An important factor for any structure in the garden is accessibility which will, to a large degree, determine its usefulness. If you cannot get to a raised planter with ease, you will tend to neglect the plants and flowers growing in it; if you have to plough through shrubs to reach a seat, there is little point in having the structure, even if it has been built to capture a stunning view; if a masonry gazebo is positioned so that one has to climb a steep flight of steps to get to it, its usefulness will be limited to those who are fit enough to reach it!

Visibility

It stands to reason that a primarily decorative feature must be sited where it can be seen to best advantage. A

Built-in seating combines well with a precast table in a small, intimate outdoor eating area.

A two-tiered pond built out of facebrick is an ideal design for a sloping garden.

During the planning phase, before any major decisions are made and money is spent, it is essential to check legalities with your local council or building department. Most will require plans and specifications for any large structure, and there may be limitations in terms of what and where you may build.

If you go ahead without the necessary approval, you could find yourself having to demolish the fruits of your labour. Furthermore, there may be other penalties like a hefty fine.

Remember that a primary motivation for establishing these codes and regulations relates to safety: your local authority wants to be sure that structures are sound and will not collapse.

Although specific requirements and details will differ depending on where you live, it is possible to generalise in terms of the type of standards set internationally. Many of these relate to what may simply be considered 'good building practice'. You will find that there are various minimum requirements relating to foundations, the height of various structures, drainage and so on. There are also minimum specifications regarding materials (particularly when these are structural elements), while other rules relate to boundaries, building lines and certain zoning laws.

It is therefore is vital to find out at an early stage which building codes and regulations will affect you and the work you are planning.

If you are required to present working drawings, you will probably have to submit a site plan indicating boundaries, building lines, existing buildings and any major feature like a swimming pool, garage or shed, all clearly shown in relation to the existing structures. Proposed new work will usually be coloured on the plan. These colours are specific and must relate to the materials which are to be used (masonry, timber, concrete and so on). You may also have to indicate the contours of the site, as well as present sections and elevations to illustrate the proposed structure. Drainage installations may also have to be shown, along with any structures you wish to demolish in order to make room for the new building work.

If you plan to build on a boundary, it may be necessary to get written consent from the affected neighbours before your proposals can be considered by the authorities. If a building permit is required, you will need to pay the prescribed fee before work can begin.

Most local authorities and councils will provide a checklist of what is required; an architect or draughtsman will be familiar with these criteria.

If your house is old and you do not have the plans, consult the relevant authorities before employing somebody to draw these up from scratch. The originals will most likely be on file and you will be able to obtain copies.

Most local authorities require plans and an outline of specifications for any large structures to be constucted in the garden.

A well-constructed brick patio with walled sides offers shelter from both sun and wind.

strictly utilitarian structure, on the other hand, should be positioned out of view.

If you are building something which is practical, but will be located on a patio or near to an entrance, you will need to ensure that it is also an attractive feature. A barbecue is a good example, as frequent use tends to blacken the walls and it can become an eyesore. Siting it away from the house can be inconvenient, and even if it is linked to a patio, the cook may be left to do the dirty work alone. A little camouflage, with potted plants, clay ornaments and other weather-proof items can save the day.

Conditions

The microclimate of your garden is another important factor. Prevailing winds are an obvious consideration when siting built-in benches and other alfresco eating and cooking structures. It is preferable to chose a sheltered spot that will not become damp and cold – you will want to get maximum possible use from these features.

Planters should also be reasonably protected from wind and, in hot climates, from the sun. Take full advantage of existing walls and screens and note the spots where trees provide natural shelter.

COST

Cost is a factor that cannot be ignored, and can put a damper on any project. However, with careful planning and conscientious budgeting, you should be able to keep costs reasonable and wastage to a minimum.

The first step is to establish what kind of outlay you will have to make to be able to build the features you are planning. Try to be as accurate as possible. Avoid guesswork for even the most minor projects and gather as much information as you can.

If you already have plans, you should be able to quantify the materials required relatively easily. Otherwise, sketch the proposed structure to scale and then work out what you will need, following the detailed guidelines given on pages 34-35.

For brickwork you will need to estimate the total area, which will give an indication of the number of bricks needed. If the structure is to be rendered, the area will also determine how much cement, lime and sand will be called for; the number of bricks will be the determining factor in terms of cement, lime and sand for bricklaying. You will then need to work out what is required for the concrete foundation.

Since there is always some wastage (bricks get broken and sand blows away), you should order slightly more of each material than you think you will need. Do not forget to add this extra

A raised pond has been situated in the centre of a courtyard to create a focal point.

Paving can be laid by the DIYer, but larger structures are best done with professional help.

even a bricklayer, may be the person you require. Otherwise you may just want to employ a labourer to help you.

Before you employ anybody, find out their qualifications, check that they are properly licensed (where applicable), and ask to see examples of their work. Try to visit some sites on which they have worked and talk to the owners. Establish exactly how they plan to go about the job. If, for instance, you are hiring someone to undertake the entire operation, check whether they plan to subcontract a portion of the job (the actual building, for instance). In such a case it may be cheaper for you to consider other options.

Architect and architectural designer
An advantage of employing an architect or designer to tackle garden

amount into the initial costings. Order about 5–10% more than you have calculated and this should cover you.

If additional materials are to be used, for instance for roofing or storage areas, these must also be costed, along with any labour you are planning to employ. Professional fees (if any) should also be included.

All sorts of items can increase the costs, but if you know exactly what is required, you can budget accordingly. You may even be able to stagger the project and complete it as additional funds become available.

PROFESSIONAL ASSISTANCE
Unless you have some kind of building experience, there is a good chance you will need the assistance of at least one professional. Since plans are often required for large structures, the person who is most likely to draw these up will be a draughtsman or architect who can formalise your ideas on paper and ensure that they are acceptable to the authorities in your area. If the features you are planning are part of an integrated landscape scheme, you may decide to use the services of a landscape architect. If you feel you cannot tackle the building work yourself, a building contractor, or

Even a simple brick walkway or pergola usually requires plans before you can build.

projects is that he or she has been trained in building styles, and will be able to create an effect to blend with the existing house and outbuildings. Often a short consultation is all that is required and you can then approach a draughtsman to draw up plans. Architects will usually tackle this type of project only if they were involved with the initial design of the house. It is usually a better idea to consult a landscape architect who specialises in gardens and other outdoor areas.

Landscape architect and landscaper

The types of structures considered here are very much a part of garden design and landscaping as a whole. It is therefore advisable to seek the services of somebody who specialises in this field. Bear in mind that a landscape architect has a professional qualification, while many 'landscapers' may simply be garden specialists with varying amounts of knowledge and experience rather than formal training. Who you decide to use will depend on your needs and the abilities and expertise of the professionals available in your area.

Draughtsman

Architects and designers frequently subcontract draughtsmen to draw up their plans for them. If you know what you want, you could instead contact one directly to do the same for you. Most draughtsmen will have a good working knowledge of the materials required for your structure as well as the specifications set down by the local authority.

Make sure that you approach the right person before you go ahead and spend money on plans.

Building contractor

Usually many builders are available to undertake garden projects, but not all of them are competent. Make absolutely certain you have reliable recommendations and carefully inspect other work completed by the builder you plan to use. Also check that he is in a position to submit plans

A brick pergola and adjoining wall have been designed to match the style of the house.

to the relevant authorities on your behalf (if these are required). If he is not, the chances are that he is simply subcontracting labour and does not have an established business. Before signing any agreements, confirm whether or not the building contractor will provide all the materials; if you are able to source cheaper materials it is possible to cut costs by agreeing to a labour-only contract.

Some building companies specialise in specific types of structure, including pergolas, carports, gazebos and barbecues. If any of these features fit into your design scheme, you may want to get quotations from the companies offering them. Once again, it is advisable to check how much of the project they will complete themselves, and also to compare their quotation for labour and materials with the cost of doing the job yourself.

Subcontractor

A variety of trained workmen, including bricklayers and stonemasons, may be hired for the job. Most will charge you an hourly fee, although you may be able to set a fee for the entire project. You will have to supervise the building work yourself and it is therefore essential that you have a basic understanding of all the techniques and procedures involved in building your proposed structure.

Locating competent subcontractors can be difficult, so try to rely on referrals from friends who have recently had work done. Alternatively, check adverts in your local newspaper, but don't forget to ask for references.

It is a good idea to check the legal implications of hiring casual labour. In some areas you will need to observe certain labour regulations, and other requirements such as insurance.

A brick plinth beneath a garden lamp.

Good design is an essential element of any garden scheme. Not only must the structures you are planning blend with the architectural style of your house, but they must also suit the garden environment in which they are to be located. It is important that larger features do not block sunlight or spoil a vista, and that nothing looks like an afterthought which was built in a rush.

There are so many design options for garden structures that it can be confusing to those without expreience. But if you follow a few basic rules, and rely on common sense, you will find that it is really not that difficult to create something which is both practical and visually pleasing.

If you get stuck, reconsider the possibility of seeking professional guidance at this early stage.

DESIGN BASICS

An excellent starting point is to consider the garden as an extension of the house. Not only will this give you an idea of suitable materials for garden buildings, features and small structures of all types, but it will also guide you in terms of size, scale and proportion. It may even suggest a suitable style for your structure.

The kind of garden you have serves as a guide. If it is essentially formal, with straight lines and clearly defined beds, any new features should also be formal. An informal garden with curved

A low planter alongside the house has been rendered to match the walls of the building.

paths, natural rockeries and island beds will benefit from a less austere approach. Seating may be curved, or simply interspersed with planters to create a more harmonious effect, and ponds built in an irregular shape. The design of a structure which features straight lines and square corners, may be softened by planting or placing pots on or around it.

Balance and proportion
A variety of elements are found in outdoor areas, big and small. These range from trees, shrubs and flowers, to the vast array of structures which may be built from masonry and wood. One of the fundamental principles of good design is that balance is created between all these components. Furthermore, they must be combined so that there is harmony between what nature provides and what we are able to construct ourselves.

If there is too much brickwork and it is not softened by plants, it will tend to look out of place, incongruous and unbalanced. If any structure is not in proportion to the garden (or patio) and the house, it will look discordant; if it is simply too large, and out of proportion, it will be too dominant and will ruin the whole effect.

Contrast
Contrast is another fundamental requirement within the garden, but it should not be obtrusive or obvious. Instead, it should be used to introduce a kind of pattern and texture. There are various ways of achieving this, but one of the most obvious is to combine hard elements with soft landscaping or planting. Not only are the walls of a structure juxtaposed with natural elements found outdoors, but they can be softened further by planting along the base, or by the addition of built-in containers as part of the design.

Various structures will introduce shadows into the garden, and this in itself is a form of contrast. For instance, the beams of a pergola will create a pattern of straight lines across the ground when the sun shines, while

Built-in furniture should be in proportion with the size of the patio area.

A neat facebrick letterbox matches the style of other structures in this front garden.

a series of archways will introduce an uneven play of light and shade.

SIZE AND SCALE
Having established the importance of proportion, it follows that any structure should be designed to a suitable scale. If it is not, the scheme will lack balance and unity. Generally, the size of any design should complement the house and the garden. However, there are few unbreakable rules in garden

design, and you will need to assess how the structure you plan to build will fit into the available space you have.

It seems obvious that minimal structures fit small spaces and that you need a large property to build something on a grand scale. While this is an obvious route for most people to follow, it is also possible to create cosy corners alongside a mansion, and you may be able to build an expansive outdoor entertainment area beside a little cottage without it looking odd.

The design and style you choose for any garden structure will determine the materials required, but before you start, ensure that you can master the relevant techniques and confidently handle all the tools needed to work with the chosen materials.

The basic construction principles and methods used for the projects in this book are certainly within the capabilities of most handymen. The secret is to familiarise yourself properly with the rudiments and stick to them while you work.

THE BASICS

Common sense will tell you that all components need to be vertical and level. Supporting poles must not tilt; bricks and blocks must be laid level and square; paving must be flat and even. You may be working with the best quality materials, but if you do not ensure that your workmanship is square, level and plumb, you will not achieve the professional kind of finish that we all appreciate.

Square

If the corners of a structure are at right angles, it will be square. Of course, this principle will not be relevant if the design is acutely angled or circular, or has any curved sides, but it is often applicable when building with bricks or blocks.

When setting out a design with right-angled corners, it is simple to check that it is square by using the 3:4:5 method (see page 25). When you build up the brickwork you will need to use a builder's square, which will enable you to check constantly that the rising corners are at 90°.

Level

In brickwork, all horizontal surfaces must be absolutely level. You can ensure this by checking foundations and footings, as well as each brick course you lay, with a spirit level. If the bubble in the horizontal vial is centred, the surface is level. When using this useful tool on large surfaces (when paving or throwing a concrete slab, for instance) it is common practice to set the spirit level on a long straight-edged piece of wood.

A line level may be used to ensure that brick pillars are progressing evenly, or to check that a builder's line is correctly positioned.

A carport erected in front of a garage. Beams and crosspieces are square and level.

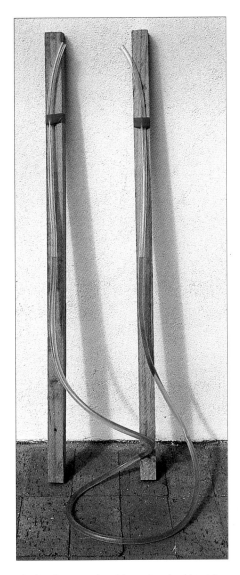

A simple water level is an invaluable aid when tackling any building project.

Paved areas should slope slightly for drainage, and you will have to take this into account. When paving, it is therefore helpful to set up a line corresponding with the slope of the finished surface. Do not rely on guesswork; instead, use a spacer block under your spirit level or straightedge to keep the angle consistent, and then set up the line. To achieve a gradient of 1 in 40, use a 25 mm (1 in) block of wood for each metre (3 ft 3 in).

You can also use a water level to set up a drainage slope, or, for that matter, to ensure that your building site is level. This method is particularly useful over a long stretch or when you need to ensure consistency around a corner.

All you need is some transparent tubing, long enough for the requirements of your project, or an ordinary hosepipe with small pieces of transparent tubing fitted in each end. Fill the tube or hosepipe with water and attach it to two pegs set in the ground at any given height.

Since water finds its own level, you will immediately see whether to remove more earth or to fill in.

A water level is also invaluable when building a structure with timber uprights. Once you have concreted the posts into the ground, use it to check that the tops are exactly level with one another. If not, simply saw off enough wood to make them the same height.

Plumb

Vertical surfaces of all walls and timber posts must also be aligned and level. A spirit level with both a vertical and a horizontal vial is most commonly used to check for plumb. Alternatively, you can use a plumb bob, which is especially useful for ensuring that the corners of brick or block pillars are straight and upright.

FOUNDATIONS

If you are building with bricks and mortar, timber or metal, all upright pillars and poles must be securely anchored or constructed on a sound footing. You will also need to dig strip foundations for any walls or screens included in your garden design, and you may have to throw a concrete slab prior to paving if the ground is unstable for building.

Minimum dimensions for foundations and footings are specified by building regulations (see page 16), although some local authorities may enforce more stringent specifications.

Concrete

A basic concrete mix consists of cement, sand, stone and water, often combined with plasticiser to make it more pliable. Use ordinary Portland cement, widely available in sealed 50 kg (112 lb) bags; clean building sand (called sharp sand in some countries), sold in bags of about 50 kg (112 lb), or supplied in bulk by the cubic metre or cubic foot; 19 mm (¾ in) or 13.2 mm (½ in) crushed stone; and, finally, potable tap water.

Dry premixed materials are also available. These are very useful for small projects, including footings for garden structures. Purchasing concrete this way, however, is more expensive than buying the constituent materials individually.

The quantities and proportions you use will depend on the work to be done. However, low-strength concrete is quite adequate for the foundation of most simple structures. If you are working with 19 mm (¾ in) stone, the recommended proportions of cement, sand and stone for hand compaction are 1:4:4, measured by volume. If you opt for a smaller 13.2 mm (½ in) stone, which is certainly easier to mix by hand, less stone should be used – alter the proportions to 1:4:3. If a stronger mix is required, a suitable ratio for the larger stone is 1:3:3, and for the smaller stone, 1:3:2. If necessary, an engineer will advise.

There is no need to measure the water to be used. Simply mix the cement and sand together until the colour is uniform; form a hollow in the middle and add a small amount of liquid at a time, shovelling from the outsides to the centre until you have a workable consistency. Add the stone last, with a little more water if the concrete is too dry.

When using a concrete mixer, load the stone first, together with some water. This prevents cement from building up around the blades of the machine. Add the cement next, and then the sand and enough water to achieve a soft, porridgey consistency.

If you are sinking metal or timber posts into the ground, these must be supported with some form of bracing to ensure that they are absolutely vertical and do not fall over. Once you have checked for plumb with a spirit level, shovel the concrete into the hole and tamp down well with the back of your shovel to compact it and expel all air bubbles.

A spirit level is used to ensure that poles are plumb.

A screen wall and pillar are constructed on a strip foundation.

Foundations for brickwork must be allowed to set before building commences. The concrete must be kept moist while it is curing – hose it lightly with water or cover it with hessian or plastic. Avoid exposure to drying winds, hot sunshine and frost. Ideally, it should be left to cure for five to seven days, although in practice building often begins a day or two after throwing the foundations.

Dimensions

The dimensions of foundations and footings will depend on your particular design, as well as on soil conditions in your garden. Nevertheless, they should always be at least 200 mm (8 in) deep, and more substantial if a heavy roof is to be incorporated. A useful rule of thumb when estimating the width of any foundation for brickwork or blockwork is that it should equal the thickness of the wall or pillar plus twice the depth of the concrete. Thus a 200 mm (8 in) deep footing for a 400 mm x 400 mm (1 ft 4 in x 1 ft 4 in) pillar should be at least 800 mm (2 ft 8 in) wide. If you are in any doubt, increase the size of the footing or seek professional advice.

While some people bed wooden poles directly in the ground, compacting around the poles to stabilise them, it is best to set them in concrete. A concrete foundation is

essential if the structure has a solid roof, as uplift (which occurs when wind gusts under the roof) could result in it collapsing if it is not securely anchored.

Metal poles should always be bedded in reasonably substantial footings at least 600 mm (2 ft) deep, while the base of precast concrete pillars should also be set in a concrete foundation.

When digging foundations for poles, it may be tempting to use a mechanical auger. However, this tool will excavate a hole which is smaller than the size recommended for foundations, and this in turn will affect the strength of the foundations. If you do use one, you will have to bore much deeper into the ground to prevent the pole from coming loose.

Above-ground anchorage

When working with wood, the most common alternative to setting the base in a concrete footing is to use metal base plates. Many people prefer above-ground anchorage as it reduces the likelihood of wood rot. Various anchor plates for posts are available off the shelf for cut timber, but you will probably have to get an engineering firm to make something to secure wooden poles, for instance sturdy galvanised iron bent in an L-shape.

Whatever form of anchorage you use, it will be necessary to throw a

foundation or slab upon which it can be fixed, unless there is already solid base. Although a concrete slab might be thinner, an acceptable minimum depth for individual footings is 200 mm (8 in). As an alternative to a conventional footing, you may prefer to use a tube form which will give you a neat finish, even if the concrete shows above ground. These are made of cardboard and are available in several sizes. If the footing extends above ground level, any visible tubing is removed once the concrete has set.

A post anchor bolted in place.

The first step in any building project is to set out the site according to the dimensions and layout of your plan.

Square and rectangular structures

Unless the design of your garden structure is to be circular or have acute or obtuse angles, you will have to ensure that each corner is exactly square. The simplest way of doing this is to use the 3:4:5 method, as shown below.

Setting out a structure such as a carport measuring 4 m x 3.5 m (13 ft x 11 ft 6 in) from outer corner to outer corner of the pillars is a relatively easy matter. The dimensions of the footings will depend on the structure itself; in this case the pillars, to be built from concrete blocks, will measure 400 mm x 400 mm (1 ft 4 in x 1 ft 4 in). To support these, foundation footings should measure 800 mm x 800 mm (2 ft 8 in x 2 ft 8 in) across, and about 300 mm (1 ft) deep. If you draw the dimensions to a smaller scale on paper first, you will see that the distances between the inner sides of the pillars will be 3.2 m (10 ft 6 in) and 2.7 m (8 ft 10 in). 200 mm (8 in) of each

footing will therefore extend beyond the framework at each corner.

Having decided on the location of the carport, knock a peg into the ground at one corner. Using a steel square or a wooden square (see page 32), measure 3.5 m (11 ft 6 in) in one direction and 4 m (13 ft) at right angles to this line. Insert a peg in the ground at each of these points. To check the angle using the 3:4:5 method, knock another peg into the ground 3 m (10 ft) from the corner on the shorter side, and then measure the distance between this peg and the one already inserted 4 m (13 ft) from the corner. It should be exactly 5 m (16 ft 4 in) away. If not, adjust the angle slightly until the measurement, and therefore the angle, is correct.

Now measure the other two sides and knock a peg into the ground where they meet. Check all the corners to ensure that each one is at 90°. To double-check them, measure the diagonals; they should be the same length and, in this case, should measure just over 5.3 m (17 ft 4 in). To work out the distance mathematically, determine the square root of (side A^2 + side

B^2), that is, $\sqrt{1(3.5^2 \text{ m}) + (4 \text{ m})^2} = 5.315$ m $\sqrt{(11 \text{ ft } 6 \text{ in})^2 + (13 \text{ ft})^2} = 17.357$ ft, or 17 ft 4¼ in).

The next step is to mark the position of all four footings. You can use lime, white cement, chalk or even flour to do this. The easiest way is to take your pegs and set up a builder's line along the perimeter of the building site, extending beyond the corners by 200 mm (8 in). Then, using the line as a guide, mark the ground 600 mm (2 ft) from each peg, in both directions. Using a builder's square for accuracy, join up the four points to form a square.

Circular designs

If your structure is to be circular, the best way to set out the site is to use a home-made compass. All you need is a couple of wooden or metal pegs and a piece of string. Knock a peg into the ground at the central point, attach the string to it and then tie the second peg to the other end, ensuring that the length of the string equals the radius of your design. Pull the string taut and mark the circumference of the circle with the second peg.

To set out for a structure, pegs were knocked into the ground at each corner and the foundation footings marked with flour. The yellow line indicates the outside edge of the structure since the foundations are 200 mm (8 in) wider than the pillars on all sides. To check for square, a red peg has been inserted as described above. A steel tape is used to check the distance between the red peg and the corner.

A facebrick pillar and screen wall match the exterior walls of the house.

BRICKS AND MORTAR

While it is quite possible to erect garden structures without using brickwork anywhere, brick and block walls, piers and pillars are feature which are often found in even the simplest designs.

The basic techniques required for bricklaying are reasonably easy to master and are shown on pages 57-61, although, as with any other building techniques, it will take practice to perfect them.

Bricks and blocks

There is a wide range of bricks and blocks available which are suitable for all kinds of garden structures. This includes facebricks, clay and concrete bricks designed to be plastered, inexpensive concrete blocks which are also plastered, and reconstituted (reconstructed) stone blocks made in imitation of natural stone. Although special tools and skills are required for cutting natural stone (see pages 181 and 189), this material is also ideal for use in the garden.

Mortar

Both bricks and blocks are bonded together with mortar to give the structure maximum strength. While a range of suitable bonding patterns may be used for garden walls, pillars and piers are most commonly built using a stretcher bond. To achieve this bond, bricks are laid lengthways and those in each successive course overlap the bricks below by half. For the mortar you will need cement, sand (sometimes referred to as soft sand) and water. Use the same Portland cement as you do for concrete. This may be mixed with ordinary building sand (to which hydrated builder's lime should be added to improve the binding and water-retentive quality of the mixture) or plaster sand (which may already contain lime). In some areas, plasticiser is used instead of lime, and some people even use liquid soap as a substitute in small projects.

Dry premixed mortar is available too, although, like premixed concrete, it is considerably more expensive.

A suitable mix for general external use is based on a cement:sand ratio of 1:4. Combine the dry materials and add water (as though you were making concrete, but without adding stone). The mixture is ready for use when it is of a uniform colour and consistency, and when you can push a brick into it end on with your hand. It should have a plastic texture and be cohesive to achieve a good bond with the bricks.

Mix only enough mortar for immediate use. After about two hours it will start to stiffen and will have to be discarded. Never try to soften it at a later stage by adding more water as this will weaken the mixture.

Bricklaying

The most important tool you will use is a trowel, essential for lifting the mortar and buttering the bricks. In addition, you will need a spirit level and a builder's square, and you should also make a gauge rod (see page 44), which is invaluable for maintaining equal courses. For cutting bricks, use the chisel end of a brick hammer, or a bolster and hefty club hammer. If you are building with facebricks, you will also need a jointing tool to finish off the brickwork.

Before attempting to lay bricks for the first time, practice using the trowel. The technique is reasonably easy to master; the secret is to ensure that the brickwork remains square, level and plumb. For this reason it is essential to make frequent use of your spirit level, square and gauge rod.

Each brick course is bedded in mortar, which will bond better if it is slightly furrowed. Butter the header (the short end) of the brick before sliding it into position; if there are any gaps showing, use the trowel to fill them with more mortar. Tap the brick gently into place with the trowel handle until it is level, and then scrape off any excess mortar.

Plaster or render

Unless pillars and piers have been built with facebricks, the surface should be plastered or rendered. Not only can a plaster finish look decorative, but it will also make the structure far more weatherproof.

Plaster or render is made in exactly the same way as mortar, but it is more important to add lime to the mixture. This helps to prevent cracking and gives the plaster or render a plastic quality, making it easier to apply. Plaster sand, which has a lime content, is therefore generally preferred.

Newly built brickwork is usually perfect for plastering; if it is at all dusty or grimy, clean it before work begins. It is also advisable to moisten the surface 24 hours before it is to be plastered or rendered to prevent too much water from being absorbed from the plaster mix.

Garage and carport walls have been plastered and painted to match the house.

Apply the plaster, or render, to the surface with a plasterer's trowel, pressing it down to ensure that it sticks. Leave it for about half an hour before scraping it to a uniform finish with a screed board; then smooth it with a wooden or steel float. Use a corner trowel to neaten the corners. Take care not to over-trowel the surface as it can bring the finer material to the surface and cause cracking. While plaster is usually 10 to 15 mm (about ½ in) thick, uneven areas may require a thicker covering. If this is necessary, apply it in two coats. Let the first set, then scratch it to provide a key for the second.

Plaster should not dry out too quickly, so keep it damp for two or three days by spraying it lightly with a hose. Once the surface has dried, you can paint it; whether you use a primer and/or sealant first depends on the paint you use and on local climatic conditions.

Plaster or render is applied to the surface with a trowel.

A simple shelter with white plastered pillars, built beside a garage.

TIMBER

The type of wood chosen will depend on what is available locally, what is required for your design, and cost – with forest depletion, the price of many woods has soared in recent years and some formerly common woods are now hard to find. Timber can be bought as poles or as cut wood (including laminated timber), both of which are suitable for a wide range of garden structures.

Cut timber

Both hardwoods (from deciduous trees) and softwoods (from conifers) may be used in the garden, although most woods must be treated in some way. A hardwood like teak is tough and will withstand most weather conditions, but few people can afford it; other less expensive hardwoods can be substituted. Suitable softwoods include redwood and various pines, but it is essential that they be treated for structural use.

Various preservatives are used, most of which are applied under extreme pressure, although different countries favour certain specific products. These include pentachlorophenol and tributyl tin oxide - both organic substances. Generally speaking, if a wood has been treated according to recognised specifications, it will be suitable for construction purposes and as durable as other materials.

If you are treating your own timber, do so before construction, and ensure that it is thoroughly dry, otherwise the chemicals will not penetrate.

Rough-cut wood may be used for structures such as carports, but it is generally better to opt for planed timber or laminated beams. Although the latter are more expensive, they are also stronger and more stable. Another advantage of using laminated wood is that it is available in much longer lengths, more than double the span of ordinary planks and beams. Cover strips (thin, flat strips of wood) or half-round strips of timber may also be useful for securing shadecloth and awning material in position and preventing it from lifting in heavy wind.

Never accept wood that is badly warped or cracked. While small knots are unavoidable in many woods, it is best to avoid boards with very large knots, as they can affect the strength of your structure.

While the roof structure of most buildings consists of a number of components (beams, trusses, rafters, battens and so on), the configuration of roofs is usually quite simple. Such a structure typically has beams supporting crosspieces or purlins, and these in turn hold up the roof sheeting. Some roof structures may also have battens, which are usually smaller than purlins.

Poles

There is a charming rusticity about pergolas built with poles. Using poles does not limit the usefulness of the structure, and they may be combined with cut timber, for example, to create a more sophisticated shelter with a solid roof structure.

Usually there is a choice between poles which have simply been debarked, and those which have been machined to a smooth surface, making them reasonably regular in size. Split poles, which are useful if you wish to incorporate railings or screen a section of the pergola, are also available commercially. Whatever you choose, it is best to opt for poles that have been treated against infestation and rot.

Traditionally, hardwood poles were dipped in or coated with creosote, a dark brown oil distilled from coal tar and considered for many years to be the best wood-preservative available. If it is not pressure-treated, though, it wears off and must be regularly reapplied. It is also toxic to plants and will cause some materials, including shadecloth, to rot.

Today, many sawmills impregnate poles with substances which enable the wood to resist pests and withstand damp conditions. One of the most common of these substances is chromated copper arsenate (CCA), a water-based preservative which usually gives wood a slight green tinge.

Poles that have not been treated should at least be coated at one end with a bituminous waterproofing compound, creosote or some other preservative which will prevent them from deteriorating too rapidly when buried in the ground.

Poles and rough-cut timber combine to create a rustic pergola in a Japanese-style garden.

Working with wood

One of the attractions of a wooden structure is that it is reasonably simple for the amateur to erect. The materials are comparatively easy to handle, and the carpentry skills involved are generally elementary. If you have an aptitude for making things and can use a drill and a saw, you are already halfway there.

You do not need an elaborate toolkit, and can even make a simple structure with hand tools alone. The minimum equipment you will need is a saw, steel tape measure, drill (an inexpensive hand drill will suffice), screwdriver, hammer, and of course the tools required to ensure that the poles, posts and beams are square, level and plumb. Power tools will, of course, simplify the task. If you do not have any tools, consider how much you will use them in future, as well as how much you can afford to spend, before going shopping.

Finishes

Most timber, especially softwood that has been cut and planed, needs additional protection if it is to look attractive and last for a reasonable length of time. While a good quality hardwood like teak will weather to a gentle grey colour without losing its strength and stability, softwoods like pine should always be varnished or painted. If you are planning to paint or seal your garden structure, ensure that the preservative you use is compatible with the finishing coat – some treatments, for instance creosote, cannot be overcoated.

Perhaps the simplest coating is a penetrating oil preservative dressing which will waterproof the wood and protect it against the weather, rot and insect attack. These dressings are easy to apply but, because they are not resistant to sunlight, have to be reapplied every six to nine months. They are also more suitable for use on hardwoods than on softwoods. Although it is not a preservative dressing as such, linseed oil will 'feed' the wood, and can be used on its own on some hardwoods.

A timber structure can easily be erected by a DIY builder.

Exterior varnish, which comes in various shades and both matt and gloss finishes, is generally UV-resistant as well as waterproof. A good quality wood varnish will last for several years.

Alternatively, you can paint the wood. There are numerous types of paint from which to choose, although the most usual kind found on outdoor structures is ordinary gloss paint, which will give you a tough, durable surface in a vast range of colours. In addition to two coats of gloss paint, you will first have to prime the wood to protect it and aid adhesion, and then give it a suitable undercoat.

OTHER MATERIALS

While brick and timber are certainly the most common materials used for the upright framework of garden structures,these are by no means the only options available to you.

Timber beams varnished for protection.

Precast concrete

A practical and attractive choice, precast concrete pillars are well suited to carports and pergolas. They are available in a variety of styles and heights, and if you wish, they may be concreted on to a precast plinth or a brick base to raise their height. These pillars usually have built-in reinforcing on to which the roof beams or poles are bolted.

Metal

Galvanised steel poles are commonly used for carports, and less frequently, for pergolas. Poles should be at least 38 mm (11½ in) in diameter, and set in substantial footings (see pages 23-24) or bolted into a base plate and post connector which has been attached to a concrete slab.

Rectangular or square aluminium tubing is sometimes used for outdoor construction. However, it is not a common do-it-yourself material.

Fibrecement

Piping made from fibrecement is a more unusual, but quite acceptable, material. It may be used in the same way as poles, with fat pipes forming the uprights, and thinner ones the crossbeams. The uprights should be reinforced and filled with concrete.

Far left: A simple carport made from fibrecement poles.
Left: An all-metal carport.
Above: Precast concrete pillars support timber beams.

SPECIAL CONNECTORS FOR POLES

A 'Log Dog' bracket connects two poles.

'Gumbou' brackets join poles at all angles.

While regular screws and bolts are universally available and easy to use, new inventions which are specifically designed for connecting logs and poles to each other and to other components often appear on the market. The most successful connectors are often patented in several countries. In spite of their effectiveness, however, a major problem with many of them is availability, as some of the smaller manufacturers are unable to fund large-scale marketing programmes – so if you are building with poles, shop around in your area.

One of the simplest methods of joining logs and poles is to use a specially formed galvanised metal cradle. For instance, 'Log Dog' (which has been patented in the USA and Australia and which is available in several other countries) is a rigid connector which will support a range of poles varying from 90 mm (3½ in) to 140 mm (5½ in) in diameter. It has claws and spikes, as well as holes for screws or nails, all of which stabilise the structure.

Pole hangers, which are screwed to the wall and have an angled base to support the pole, are particularly useful when one is

A pole hanger screwed to the wall.

attaching horizontal beams to a wall.

Other V-shaped connectors, some of which bolt together, are invaluable when assembling structures which do not meet at 90° angles. 'Gumbou', a South African invention, is a series of galvanised steel brackets which enable you to join poles at any angle. No drilling is required; the brackets, a spanner, a hammer and nails are all you need. The structure will be strong enough not to need concrete foundations – simply sink the poles into holes 800 mm (2 ft 8 in) deep, fill the holes with earth, and compact it thoroughly.

FIXING AND FASTENING

Numerous fastening aids are available, including a variety of nails, truss and joist hangers, bolts, clamps, couplings, screws and rivets. While different products are recommended for different materials, aluminium, brass, stainless steel and galvanised fastenings should be used where possible for outdoor work as they will not rust or stain wood.

Various cuphead bolts and washers, coach screws and wire nails are essential for all projects. Crosspieces and uprights are usually bolted or screwed together, although nails can also be used. Beams can be held together with clips, grips and joist hangers. Truss hangers can be used to fix beams to a wall. Uprights can be fastened to specially manufactured post anchor bases which are attached to concrete with expanding bolts or anchor bolts. Bolts and screws should be long enough to go right through the timbers they are securing. If they are

Metal poles with support brackets hold the main beams in place.

Galvanised brackets are used to secure poles and the timber roof structure.

too long, they can be cut with a hacksaw once they are in place. Spiked metal connector plates, designed to simplify the assembly of roof trusses, are also useful for joining beams when the required lengths of timber are not available.

If you wish, angle iron may be adapted for attaching pieces of timber to each other or to a wall. Clamps and

galvanised hoop iron are useful for securing the roof structure. Mild steel reinforcing rods are invaluable when building brick pillars

Tacks, wire nails or heavy duty staples are used if shadecloth is chosen to provide shelter. Special fasteners with 'teeth', similar to those used to connect roof trusses on site, are also available in some areas.

Upright poles are bolted to the main beams of this carport; purlins are slotted into notches and nailed down.

Metal has been concreted into a precast pillar to secure the overhead beams of this pergola.

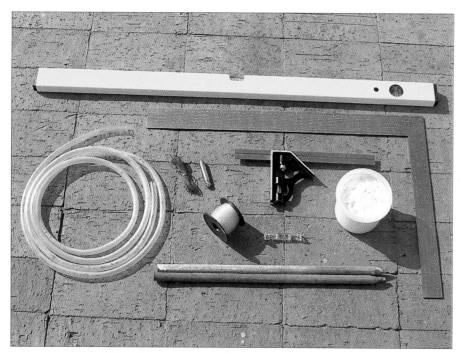

Essential tools used for setting out and levelling.

TOOLS

Do-it-yourself enthusiasts usually have a selection of tools which will be quite adequate for the projects in this book. Most are available from DIY or hardware stores, although a few will have to be made at home. If you do not want to buy new tools, they can often be hired.

Setting out and levelling

Essential equipment that you will need for setting out your site and for ensuring that your structure is square, level and plumb must be included in your basic toolkit for any building job. In addition, you will need to use a good quality retractable tape measure at all stages of the project.

Chalk is sold for setting out a site, although you could use lime or white cement instead, if you have it. Even flour can be used, and is usually the cheapest option too.

Squares are indispensable to all aspects of the building operation. A steel square and an adjustable carpenter's square are particularly useful. A home-made wooden square is practical for setting out; it can be made by nailing together three pieces of wood cut in the ratio 3:4:5 – for example, lengths of 0.9 m, 1.2 m and 1.5 m (3 ft, 4 ft and 5 ft) – to create a right-angled corner. A combination square, which incorporates a small spirit level, is handy for minor bricklaying projects and carpentry.

Pegs, used for setting out and for holding a builder's line in place, may be metal or wooden, although the latter are cheaper and are also easy to make yourself.

Builder's line or string is used for setting out, and to ensure that paving or brickwork is straight and level.

Levels are also essential for all stages of any building project, from the foundation up. They include spirit levels which are available in several lengths, home-made water levels made from transparent tubing, and line levels, which can be useful but are not essential (see pages 22-23).

Punners are ramming tools which you can make by attaching a heavy weight to the end of a pole. A punner is used instead of a compacting machine to compact earth or hardcore before paving or concreting.

Plumb bobs are for checking vertical surfaces. Simply a weight attached to a length of string, a plumb bob is not necessary for garden building projects.

Spades and shovels are used to dig foundations and mix concrete, mortar and plaster. A pick is also useful if you are excavating hard ground.

Concrete and brickwork

In addition to the basic tools used for levelling and for ensuring that the brickwork is square and plumb, there are a number of other items you cannot be without when working with concrete or bricks.

Wheelbarrows are essential to have for removing soil from the site and transporting materials, and are useful for mixing concrete and mortar.

Trowels are used for both bricklaying and plastering. Small pointing trowels are useful for neatening the joints of facebrick surfaces, and corner trowels (available for both inner and outer corners) are useful for giving plaster edges a neat finish.

Straightedges and gauge rods are simply lengths of wood, used to level concrete and to check the mortar joints between brick courses respectively. A gauge rod can easily be made by marking off a straight length of wood at intervals equal to one brick plus a 10 mm (½ in) mortar joint.

Corner blocks are used to string up a builder's line as bricklaying progresses. The line is wrapped around the block and through the slot to secure it, and the blocks are then hooked on to the ends of brickwork. They are also useful for checking levels and to help you ensure that pillars are square with one another. Corner blocks are sometimes available commercially, or they can easily be made by sawing a groove halfway through an L-shaped piece of wood.

Hammers with a chisel end (brick hammers) are used for cutting bricks.

A selection of tools used for concrete and brickwork.

lengths, there is invariably some cutting to do. While a stocky back saw or tenon saw will cope with most small jobs, a general purpose bowsaw is best for sawing logs and a hacksaw (which may also be used for cutting metal) is favoured by some do-it-yourselfers. Ripsaws, for cutting along the grain, crosscut saws which work best across the grain, smaller panel saws, which do both, and power saws are all useful.

Drills are fairly expensive, but are essential for woodwork. If you do not already own an electric drill (see page 34) and do not intend to invest in one, you could use a hand drill (a wheel brace for minor applications and a more heavy-duty bit brace are both useful) for a relatively simple construction project. Remember that you will also need the correct wood bits for the woodwork, and ordinary masonry bits for drilling into brickwork or concrete.

Screwdrivers are indispensable, and you will need the right size for the job. Sophisticated spiral ratchet screwdrivers, with different positions and a reverse action, are a worthwhile investment, but are not essential.

Alternatively, a club hammer may be used with a bolster. A rubber mallet, which looks like a hammer but has a heavy rubber-topped head, is used to tap pavers and slabs into position.

Bolsters (broad chisels) are useful for cutting bricks.

Jointing tools are not essential for garden brickwork. They are used for pointing or shaping the mortar joints in facebrick walls, but may be substituted with a piece of metal.

Mortarboards and screedboards are used by professional bricklayers and plasterers respectively to hold small quantities of mortar and plaster while they work.

Floats, made in both wood and metal, are used for smoothing plaster and the screed laid over concrete.

Woodwork
When tackling almost any type of woodwork project, there are some simple hand tools which you just cannot afford to be without. You will

also need the basic levelling tools, a good quality tape measure and a carpenter's pencil.

Saws are the first requirement in a woodworker's toolkit. However careful you are when ordering the correct

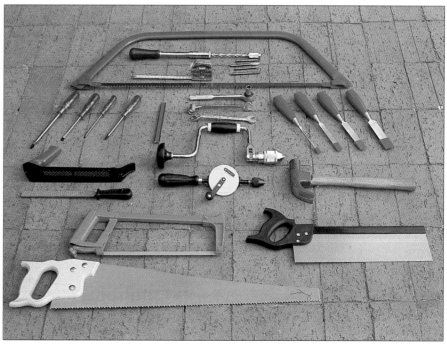
A range of tools required for woodwork, including a selection of saws and screwdrivers.

Hammers are necessary for nailing pieces of wood together. With a claw hammer you will also be able to extract nails.

Spanners are needed to tighten nuts and bolts. There are several types from which to choose.

Chisels, rasps and files are useful for shaping, planing and finishing small lengths of wood, especially when jointing beams.

Power tools

Although power tools are not an essential requirement, there is no doubt that they do take the drudgery out of many jobs. They also enable you to cope with many construction problems which hand tools simply cannot manage.

Drills will simplify most projects. For joining wood, screws are more accurate and will give a more secure grip than nails, but holes must be drilled for them.

Although a single-speed drill is the cheapest option, a two-speed or variable-speed drill is more versatile and therefore a better buy, although it will obviously cost more. An electric drill with a hammer action is useful if you need to drill into really hard materials such as concrete lintels. Cordless drills, which run on batteries, are also available.

Saws are essential for cutting wood, and power saws will speed up and streamline the job. A circular saw will make smooth perpendicular or angled cuts in most materials, while a jigsaw will cut curved lines.

Planers enable you to smooth the surface of long pieces of timber at home. They may also be used for bevelling or angling edges and for cutting simple rebates.

Sanders are useful for smoothing timber which has already been planed. A belt sander will remove material quickly and is the best tool to use for levelling planks and boards; vibrating orbital sanders are better for finishing a surface which would otherwise be sanded by hand.

Other useful power tools include compactors and plate vibrators (which compact hardcore or soil for foundations or paving); angle grinders for cutting bricks and tiles; and block splitters or masonry saws for halving some precast concrete products.

QUANTIFYING AND COSTING

Once you have chosen a design, work out the quantities of materials required, and the cost of the project.

Use working drawings (the drawings submitted to council) or do your own sketches to scale. The more detailed they are, the more accurately you can determine costs. List all the materials you will need, and increase quantities of bricks, cement and so on (including those listed for the projects in this book) by about 10% to allow for wastage and breakage.

Bricks and blocks

Although brick sizes do vary slightly, you can safely assume that 110 bricks will be sufficient for a square metre (11 ft²) of one-brick wall 222 mm (8¾ in) thick, and 55 bricks for half-brick or single walls.

To determine the number of bricks in a pillar, divide the planned height of the pillar by that of the brick plus mortar joint to assess how many courses you will need, then multiply by the number of bricks used in each course. A 2.4 m (7 ft 10 in) two-brick pillar, built with four 222 mm x 106 mm x 70 mm (8¾ in x 4 in x 2¾ in) stock bricks in each course and 10 mm (⅜ in) mortar joints, will use 120 bricks. If the structure has four pillars, you will need 480.

The number of blocks needed to build a wall or pillar depends, of course, on the size of the blocks used. The blocks used for the pergola on page 103 measure 390 mm x 190 mm x 190 mm (1 ft 3 in x 7½ in x 7½ in), and about 13 of these are required for each square metre (11 ft²) of wall. If your blocks are a different size, multiply the length (plus mortar joint) in millimetres by the height (plus mortar joint) in millimetres, and divide the result into 1,000,000 (or divide the result in square inches into 1,296 – the number of square inches in a square yard). Alternatively, calculate the surface area of your proposed wall and divide by the size of one block. Apply the same principle used for bricks to work out how many blocks you will need for pillars.

Perforated decorative screen walling blocks are usually 290 mm x 290 mm x

Useful power tools, left to right: (top) belt sander. angle grinder, planer, orbital sander; (bottom) circular saw, two drills, jigsaw.

90 mm or 100 mm (11⅜ in x 11⅜ in x 3½ in or 4 in) and you will need 11 blocks for every square metre (11 ft²). To lay a square metre (11 ft²) of brick paving you will need about 45 pavers.

Cement

You will need cement for foundations, slabs, mortar, and plaster or render.

For major building projects one would order ready-mixed concrete according to the compressive strength required, but simple mix proportions are adequate for most garden brickwork. If you use 19 mm (¾ in) stone for foundations and footings, a cement:sand:stone mix in the ratio 1:4:4 (by volume) will yield about 5¼ units of measurement; adjust the ratio to 1:4:3 for 13.2 mm (½ in) stone, though. If you are building fairly substantial walls, a slightly stronger 1:3:4 mix is recommended for the foundations. For every cubic metre (35 ft³) of foundations you will need 4½-5 bags (225-250 kg or 505-560 lb). If you are casting a concrete floor, use a 1:2:3 mix – you will need about eight bags of cement per cubic metre (35 ft³).

If mixing by hand, it is preferable to work out quantities required per bag of cement (50 kg or 112 lb), for which you will need 150 litres (33 gal) each of sand and stone (for a 1:4:4 mix). The yield will be about 205 litres (45 gal).

When mixing mortar, you can count on using one bag for every 200 bricks in a half-brick wall, or for every 150 bricks in a one-brick wall (which has a double skin of brickwork). Mix cement with sand in the ratio 1:4 (by volume), or if lime is added, 2:1:8 for cement:lime:sand. If you are using 390 mm x 190 mm x 190 mm (1 ft 3 in x 7½ in x 7½ in) blocks, a weaker 1:6 cement:sand mixture is adequate and you will need about one bag for every 100 blocks. As you will use about 12½ blocks per square metre (11 ft²) of wall, 50 kg (112 lb) of cement should be enough to build about 8 m² (86 ft²).

The same mix ratios may be used for plaster, which will then match the strength of the mortar. It should be 10-15 mm (about ½ in) thick, and you will need about 4 kg (9 lb) of cement for

every square metre (11 ft²).

Pillars are seldom left hollow, so you will need extra cement for concrete to fill in the central cavity- unless you are building solid, one-brick square piers.

Sand

Quantifying sand by volume is never very accurate because sands differ and their moisture content varies. The mass of sand per cubic metre (35 ft³) is roughly 1,350 kg (2,976 lb).

Using a 1:4 cement:sand mix for both mortar and plaster, for every 100 bricks of one-brick wall you lay you will need 100 litres (22 gal) or about 2½ 50 kg (112 lb) bags of sand. For plastering, 12 litres (2⅔ gal) or 16 kg (35 lb) will be enough for each square metre (11 ft²). If there is a lot of brickwork and you order in bulk, a cubic metre of sand (35 ft³) is enough for laying 1,000 bricks or plastering 84 m² (900 ft²) of wall. Sand is also required for foundations and concrete slabs. Work out the quantities for foundations according to the ratios already specified. For a slab, a 1:2:3 cement:sand:stone ratio is recommended. Alter this to 1:2:2 if you are working with the smaller stone. Paving bricks and blocks should be laid on a layer of building sand 25-50 mm (1-2 in) thick. At a thickness of 40 mm (1½ in) one cubic metre (35 ft³) will cover 25 m² (269 ft²). You will need slightly more to brush over the surface once paving is complete. Some people advocate brushing on a 1:6 cement: sand mix instead of pure sand.

Stone

As the vital coarse aggregate used for making concrete, stone is essential for all foundations and solid slabs. The quantity will depend partly on the size of stone you use – relevant proportions are detailed above. See the chapter on stone (pages 180-189) for further detailed information.

Binders

If you use plaster sand with a lime content for mortar and plaster, no extra lime is needed. Note that adding lime to ordinary builder's sand to improve its binding quality will give a slightly higher

yield if you use the same cement:sand mix proportions. Alternatively, add 50 ml (2 fl oz) of plasticiser to every 50 kg (112 lb) of cement. For small projects, use a tablespoon of good quality liquid soap as a substitute.

Timber

It is almost always cheaper to buy timber in standard lengths. Check what is available before designing your structure – or adapt the requirements to fit. If a number of smaller lengths are to be used (for a screen or railings, for instance), buy whatever lengths will give you the least wastage. If the lengths used in the projects are not available, buy longer pieces and cut them to size.

Roofing materials

Many roofing materials are available in only a few standard widths. Instead of cutting the sheets (which may be difficult to handle), it is usually possible to design a structure utilising the full expanse of the widths. This simplifies construction and also cuts down on time and labour.

Guttering

To ensure effective drainage, guttering is installed on structures with a solid roof covering, often on one side only, to catch the run-off from a sloping roof. Some designs include concealed gutters, adjacent to the fascia board or at the back of the structure between wall and beam. A downpipe, the length of a pillar or post, takes water from the gutter to a channel or drain. Remember to buy the correct brackets and connectors to fit these components.

Other costs

If you are planning to enlist the help of professionals or artisans, include their fee in your final costing. Rather overestimate their time, otherwise you may throw out the budget at a crucial time and jeopardise the entire project.

Budget for materials such as tiles, reinforcing and connectors, finishing touches like paint and plants, and any tools you need to buy. Add in a figure for removing excess soil and rubble.

BRICK

PART
ONE

Anyone who values an outdoor lifestyle will appreciate a well-designed garden which incorporates functional areas for entertaining, relaxing or simply sitting outside.

This does not mean that you need a large property; even a small area may be planned to meet the needs of a family that enjoys outdoor living. What you do need, though, are some permanent structures which will facilitate your lifestyle. Built-in seating, tables and barbecue structures will encourage people to spend time outdoors in good weather. A pergola or gazebo will create shelter, a sandpit will provide a place for little children to play, and raised planters, ponds, pools and fountains will all add charm and character to the outdoor space.

While many garden structures are decorative, many more are strictly utilitarian. Simple box-shaped designs, topped with a weatherproof lid, may be used to store firewood, coal or even folding outdoor furniture. A three-sided

enclosure built adjacent to a wall may house rubbish bins, and similar arrangements may be used to make compost, provided the design allows sufficient air to enter the walls.

A pond or fountain may be included in the design of a wall, while steps frequently feature planters on either side. Permanent seating is a welcome addition to any patio.

There are various materials which may be chosen to construct these features, but masonry is undoubtedly the most common, as well as the most durable. Almost all the surviving structures from the ancient world were made from masonry units of some kind, and many of those structures which have disappeared were either destroyed by warfare or demolished by man. Masonry is eminently suitable for all the structures mentioned here; not only will it last well, but it requires relatively little maintenance too.

Although the focus of this chapter is on brickwork, masonry structures take

many forms, depending on how a specific type of building is used.

Clay bricks (including American adobe mud blocks) are amongst the oldest and most universal materials available. In ancient times, they were simply left in the sun to dry; nowadays, most clay bricks are fired in huge kilns to extremely high temperatures which make them hardy and ideal for all types of building work; size, colour and finish vary from place to place. They can be used in all climatic conditions, and are available all over the world.

Concrete bricks and blocks are a more recent invention, and one which is generally less expensive than clay. Although concrete bricks, moulded to roughly the same size and shape as clay bricks, are solid, the larger blocks are hollow. This makes them easy to work with and simple to reinforce.

Another option is reconstituted or reconstructed stone, also made from concrete but moulded in imitation of natural stone. Not only is this material uniform in size (unlike stone), making it ideal for the do-it-yourself builder, but it is also generally less expensive than the real thing. Of course stone, which is classified as masonry, is perfect for garden structures, and the basic techniques and skills required for bricklaying may be adapted to stonework (see the chapter on stone for more information).

Many people who have never tried working with bricks and mortar find the prospect daunting, but the skills and techniques involved are really not hard to pick up. Learning them takes time and patience, but once you have mastered them, you are sure to find many ways of utilising your new-found abilities to add to and further improve your outdoor environment.

This chapter will help you understand what is involved, illustrating in a clear, visual manner the skills you will need to master for particular projects. At the

Simple brick pillars form the basic framework for a charming, shady arbour.

same time, it will help you to decide which tasks may be undertaken by others who may be more competent in certain other areas. For instance, you may be more than happy to undertake the physical construction work yourself, but unsure of the technicalities of drawing up plans. If you are unfit, you may prefer to hire labourers to do the more arduous tasks (for instance mixing concrete and mortar) while you tackle those jobs which require a little more expertise. Alternatively (and this is a real option for many people), you may feel your talents lie in organising a team of subcontractors and labourers who will do everything for you. Even members of your family may be prepared to help! But you will still want to be involved in the planning stages of the project, and will benefit from the many suggestions and ideas offered here.

Most of the possibilities given within the pages of this chapter are minor building projects, but there are still many potential pitfalls and possible obstacles which every do-it-yourselfer should try to avoid. Not only can these threaten to delay the building programme, but they may also add unnecessary costs. Of course, most problems can be avoided with proper planning and an understanding of what is involved. To achieve a professional finish, you should also take a logical approach and follow the project through systematically.

This section is designed to help you to complete your project successfully, regardless of the specific route you plan to take, and irrespective of how much of the physical work you intend doing yourself. Introductory sections explain basic planning skills and will help you decide what your needs and priorities are, and how best to accommodate them. A variety of suitable sites are suggested, along with guidelines that should enable you to establish which is the right location for your own brick structure. Since cost is invariably a vital factor, we suggest ways in which you can cut down on

Brick has been used to build planters, a garden seat and a simple barbecue unit.

expenditure. Refer back to pages 18-19 for information about the various professionals who may be able to help you in certain areas, and page 16 for the kinds of regulations and building codes which may affect your project.

A host of design ideas is provided and explained in layman's terms, enabling anyone to create an attractive feature which blends with their existing outdoor environment. The importance of using compatible materials is highlighted, and the relevance of harmony and balance, along with the significance of size and proportion, are considered in a straightforward manner. A breakdown of the possibilities which may be explored when using bricks and blocks of various kinds is given, and a range of style options is recommended. Since even a simple brick pergola or gazebo may incorporate a roof of some sort, numerous suitable roofing materials are assessed, as is a comprehensive range of masonry building units.

For those wanting to tackle more complicated projects, there is some basic information on extensions and additions, as well as a detailed look at what is involved in creating an outdoor kitchen or a barbecue.

The full spectrum of tools and materials required for bricklaying are itemised and some helpful hints given regarding how to assess quantities correctly. Although the emphasis in this chapter is obviously on brickwork, the preparation and use of concrete, which is essential for foundations, is also discussed briefly. Basic building methods, essential principles of construction and the best techniques are then explained.

In a separate step-by-step section, these building methods are illustrated succinctly in photographic form. The aim here is not to follow through one project as such, but to present a hands-on sample of the techniques which you will need to tackle the range of plans and projects presented later.

MATERIAL OPTIONS

There is a surprisingly wide choice of materials for garden structures which are to be built in masonry. Both clay and concrete bricks are manufactured in a range of colours and finishes, and concrete blocks are available either hollow, pierced, or in the form of reconstructed or reconstituted stone. Some types of bricks or blocks are intended to be left as they are, while others should be rendered with mortar and then painted.

In some areas clay and/or mud adobe blocks are available, and many of the structures we have suggested may also be built with natural stone.

Clay and concrete bricks

Available as facebricks for renderingor plastering, these materials are a popular choice for garden masonry structures. There is a wide range of colours and textures to choose from, which means you are sure to find something that will suit any garden environment. Brick sizes are relatively standard, differing slightly from country to country. They are relatively small and therefore easy to handle, making them the perfect choice for the first-time builder.

Your choice of brick will depend largely on the style and character of the structure you are building. The most expensive option is clay facebrick (also called facing brick) which is strong and long-lasting in all weather conditions – an important consideration in areas which experience severe frost and snow or constant sea spray. You will find, though, that specifications differ, and where conditions are harsh, it is wise to check durability factors with your supplier or manufacturer.

Concrete facebricks are also available in a range of textures and colours, although these are not as natural as the hues of clay brick.

If you plan to render the surface of your structure, it makes sense to use non-face bricks (or non-facings). These are much cheaper than facebricks, and are not intended to be left unprotected.

Concrete blocks

Standard blocks, manufactured in a reasonably wide range of sizes, are a cost-effective option. Not only are they cheaper than bricks (when compared per square metre), but these hollow units are also quicker to lay because of their size.

As ordinary concrete blocks are not particularly attractive, in most instances you will need to render (plaster) the finished surface. Another possibility is to camouflage the structure with a brick veneer, although this will involve additional work and will also increase costs because of the extra materials required.

Screen blocks

A range of attractive screen blocks with pierced patterns may be used

Attractive facebricks have been used to build an arched entrance and matching boundary wall.

within the garden. Commonly used for both boundary and screen walls, these units allow both light and air to pass through the structure. Since they are laid in a stack bond, which is not particularly strong, they are only suitable for certain applications, where intermediate piers help support them.

Pierced blocks could be used to construct a compost bin, provided the pattern of holes is not too open.

Reconstituted (reconstructed) stone blocks

Manufactured from concrete in imitation of stone, reconstituted stone blocks and smaller brick-like units are ideal for garden structures and buildings, as long as they will suit the style of your garden and existing structures. Colours and textures are chosen to blend with natural stonework, and sizes to correspond to the typical dimensions of cut stone.

An advantage of building with reconstituted stone rather than the genuine material is that these blocks are considerably easier to lay because of their regular shapes and sizes. Large jumper blocks, which are the height of two courses, are sometimes available in a variety of different sizes for authenticity.

Clay and mud blocks

Although clay blocks are fired in the same way as clay bricks, adobe blocks (or mud bricks) are manufactured in quite a different way, and are only available in some parts of the world.

Traditional adobe structures eventually deteriorate, but nowadays these blocks are stabilised with asphalt, cement or straw to prevent them crumbling and decomposing. Larger than clay bricks (and even some clay blocks), adobe blocks are solid and heavy, and therefore relatively cumbersome to work with.

Stone

The craft of stone masonry has been passed down through the ages in just about every country in the world. Whether you use cut or dressed stone

A combination of stone and brick.

Sundial on a concrete slab set on stone.

or lay irregular rocks in a random pattern, the effects attained will add charm to any garden. Stone is suitable for many garden features, although it is considerably more difficult to lay than brick and block.

Various types of stone are found in different areas; your choice will depend on availability. Refer to the chapter on stone for more details.

ROOFING POSSIBILITIES

Brick pergolas, gazebos, walkways and various garden buildings built with masonry units may incorporate simple roofs which offer some shelter from the sun, rain and wind. A shed or summerhouse will, of necessity, have a roof which provides a greater degree of protection than the average pergola.

It is not surprising that the type of roof chosen will depend largely on the degree of shelter you require from the elements. Awning material (shadecloth), for instance, will be quite adequate for a pergola which will provide shade, while a tool shed will demand something much more substantial. A gazebo traditionally incorporates a tiled or shingled roof while the covering chosen for a rustic summerhouse might be thatch, if this material is available.

As with all other materials, the type of roofing you choose must complement the materials used

elsewhere. This does not mean you necessarily have to match the roof to your house, but any new material you introduce should blend well with it.

The supporting structure of the roof will depend on what it will cover and the load it will bear; however, specific structural elements are not considered in any detail here as more substantial buildings will require greater expertise than is necessary for the projects here.

Plants

If you do not want to cover a pergola or similar overhead structure with roofing, plants should always be considered. You will find that a wide variety of climbers and creepers are suitable for this purpose. Not only will they make the structure look attractive, but flowering species will also add colour, and many types will give off a delightful fragrance as well. A pergola is an effective structure for supporting plants; if properly trained, they will soon form a charming, natural ceiling.

The types of plant you choose will depend on what is available at your garden centre, but suitable species include honeysuckle and the various jasmines. Clematis, wisteria and vines will all lose their leaves in winter, but this allows the sun to filter into an area which might otherwise become cold, damp and unusable at certain times in the year. Bear in mind that any climbing plants will take time to grow.

Awning material

Awning material is available in various guises and is a good choice for pergolas located on patios which require some shade. Although some types are water-resistant, most are not waterproof and will therefore not give any protection from the rain.

Most retractable awnings are made from canvas, which is available in many different colours, both plain and patterned (usually striped).

Shadecloth, made from a hardy acrylic material and sold in several parts of the world, is available in a variety of fashion colours as well as in green and black, the hues more commonly used for horticultural purposes. Various densities offer anything from 30% to 85% protection from the sun's rays. This material should be cut with a soldering iron to prevent it from fraying and should never be placed over timber that has been treated with creosote, as this will cause it to deteriorate.

Roofing felt

Bituminous roofing felt is a reasonably inexpensive option particularly suitable for sheds, carports and utility garden buildings. It is usually sold in rolls and nailed to plywood, hardboard, particle board, masonite or whatever other boarding has been used over the roof trusses or battens.

Although this material has a reasonably long lifespan, it may need to be resealed with a bituminous waterproofing compound from time to time. Odd holes, including those created by nails, may be sealed with bitumen paste or mastic.

Roof sheeting

A wide range of sheeting is suitable for the roofs of all kinds of garden buildings. Some types are available as flat sheets, but most are corrugated. All types are suitable for brick buildings with roofs that have a minimum pitch of 5-10˚ although cost will probably determine what you choose for a simple utility shed or animal shelter. If sheeting is used for a

A combination of reeds and plants form the roof of this simple, rendered pergola.

pitched roof, you will have to fix capping along the ridge; if it is used for a structure which abuts a building, you will need to seal the join with flashing to prevent rain and moisture from seeping through the gap. Remember too, that whatever kind of roof sheeting you are using, the sheets must overlap at the joins. Some will need to be predrilled prior to installation, although self-drilling roofing screws are usually sufficient.

One of the cheapest kinds of roof sheeting is fibreglass, which is suitable not only for a range of small garden buildings but also for open-sided structures like pergolas and carports. Lightweight and easy to handle, it is available in several different profiles and a range of translucent colours.

Polycarbonate, a smooth, synthetic material which looks like glass or perspex, is better suited to pergolas and conservatory-type extensions. It comes in flat or corrugated sheets,

and is available in the same sheet sizes as fibreglass and metal.

Another lightweight, corrugated variety of sheeting is Onduline (a trade name), which is manufactured in France from organic fibres which have been saturated in bitumen. Widely distributed, it is available in brown, black, bottle green, red and translucent, and is perfect for outbuildings and overhead structures which require a solid roof.

Both corrugated iron and aluminium sheeting (which is also used for some awnings) may be used, but the latter is a relatively expensive option, particularly for an outbuilding. Special tools are required to cut it, and because it is relatively 'soft' it is easily damaged. For this reason it is generally installed by professionals. On the other hand iron, which is available galvanised or colour-coated, is reasonably priced and particularly popular for carports.

Although heavy, fibrecement is another option which is usually relatively inexpensive. Also manufactured in a selection of profiles, it requires sturdy roof trusses and beams, depending of course where it is to be used.

Tiles and shingles

Many traditional garden buildings constructed with bricks and mortar or stone had roofs which were finished in tile or with slates or shingles. Today garden buildings of all kinds are roofed with these materials, provided that they have a minimum pitch of 15–26°; generally the rougher the finish, the greater the pitch required.

Flat slate and clay tiles, as well as shingles (made from wood, asphalt, aluminium or glass fibre) or thicker wooden shingles are perfect choices for a gazebo roof.

Ordinary tiles, made from various materials including clay, fibrecement and reconstituted stone, may be used to cover outbuildings, summerhouses, sheds and simple pitched pergolas.

Thatch

Suitable for pitched pergolas and some garden buildings, thatch requires a minimum pitch of about 45°. A popular choice for open-sided summerhouses in some hot climates, as well as in many traditional designs, it is usually installed by a skilled craftsman. If you favour this material, you will need to ensure that the roof structure is made with wooden poles rather than sawn timber.

If natural thatch is not readily available in your area, consider the option of acrylic thatch.

Reeds, bamboo and timber

Attached to the beams of a pergola, these natural materials will produce attractive dappled shadows, and provide shade as well as some shelter from wind and rain. Bamboo and reeds may be used as a ceiling, within a building (possibly a summerhouse or a shelter for entertaining) or on a patio which has a more substantial roof.

Timber is the most common of these three materials, probably because it is available everywhere. Laths may be arranged across the beams in a regular row, as closely or widely spaced as you wish. Obviously the smaller the gaps between the lengths of timber, the more shade and shelter you will have. If the laths are too close, this can make an enclosed area look dark and gloomy. As an alternative to straight laths, a pergola may be topped with latticework, which you can make yourself or buy ready made.

Where reeds and bamboo are available, these materials make charming patio roofs. If they are not readily available commercially, there may be a supplier in your area that has access to the material in the field. If you cannot track anyone down, try advertising in the classified section of your local newspaper.

In some areas you can buy bamboo in woven rolls, ready for installation. If you can't find these, string the stalks together to form your own panels or attach them directly to the pergola beams. Ideally you should use green material that has not yet dried out; this prevents unnecessary splitting and ensures that lengths fit neatly side by side. Either tie the lengths in place, or

predrill them before nailing them to the timber. Set the reeds with thick and thin ends alternating for an even finish.

LIGHTING

Although not every garden is illuminated at night, some form of exterior lighting is essential, not only for safety, but for security as well. It is dangerous if you cannot see where you are going, and if you cannot detect intruders.

It makes sense to install lighting in most garden buildings, especially if you want to make use of them in the evenings. If they are situated some distance from the house, you may require additional wiring. You can probably lay low-voltage cables and fix fittings yourself, but the actual mains connection should be installed by a registered electrician.

Patios should also be illuminated, and those which are attached to the house often make use of existing fittings. You will need good general lighting, rather than spotlights or uplighters. Where new fittings are installed, these must be suitable for outdoor use – most lighting shops have a good selection of sealed units from which to choose.

An open summerhouse has a thatched roof installed by a skilled craftsman.

A thorough knowledge and understanding of basic building principles is essential for anyone tackling a project in brick. Not only is it essential to know the correct techniques for laying bricks and ensuring they are properly bonded, but it is also important that all structures are square, level and plumb.

An experienced bricklayer knows the value of using the correct tools and appreciates the importance of working with the right concrete and mortar mixes. If your structure is to look professional, it is vital that you familiarise yourself with these elements. It is also useful to have some basic knowledge of quantifying materials, so that you can cost the project reasonably accurately and avoid the unnecessary wastage which is so often incurred when ordering is based on guesswork.

THE ESSENTIAL TOOLKIT

Although certain very specific tools are required for bricklaying, the essential toolkit is not extensive. All items are available at builders' stockists, hardware stores and major do-it-yourself outlets.

In addition to those listed below, you will need a spade to excavate the earth, possibly a shovel to mix concrete and mortar (although you can also use a spade), a pick if the ground is hard or stony, and a wheelbarrow to transport bricks, mixed materials and excess soil to and from the excavation.

If you are planning to incorporate timber seat tops or wooden lids and cupboard doors in your brick structure, you will also need a basic carpentry kit, with saws, a drill, screwdrivers and a hammer (see page 33). A combination square (also referred to as a carpenter's square) is useful.

Compactors

A punner, or ramming tool, is handy for compacting the earth or fill beneath footings. It can be made by filling an empty 5 litre paint can with concrete and inserting a pole or length of timber as a handle. The flat end of a fairly heavy round pole may be used instead, but if you need to compact a large area, it is advisable to hire a compacting machine.

Straightedge

Invaluable for extending the usefulness of a spirit level over large areas, a straightedge may be made of metal or timber. If wood is chosen, make certain it is not warped or bowed. A straightedge may also be used for compacting and smoothing concrete, for levelling mortar on a rendered surface, and as a gauge rod.

Tape measure

A good quality, retractable steel tape is the builder's best friend, as it is used from the setting-out stage, until completion of the project.

Gauge rod

An invaluable aid for keeping brick and block courses regular, a gauge rod is simply a flat, straight-edged length of timber or metal which is marked off according to the height of each course, at intervals equal to one brick or block plus a mortar joint. Some people mark their spirit level in the appropriate gauges, so they do not have to use two tools during bricklaying. The dimensions chosen will depend on the size of the masonry unit you are using as well as the thickness of the mortar joints. A foolproof method is to lay the first two courses and then to use this to guide you when marking it off.

Builder's square

One of the tools no bricklayer should be without, a builder's square is made

A selection of items required for the basic toolkit of anyone planning to tackle bricklaying.

A builder's square is an essential tool to ensure that all corners are at 90˚.

of steel and is marked off like a ruler. Considerably larger than a mathematical set square, it performs a similar function, enabling you to check that all corners are at 90˚. When setting out a structure, you may find that a builder's square is not big enough; if so, you can make a bigger one out of timber offcuts, using the 3:4:5 method (see pages 52-53). Make sure that the angle you create is correct or your structure will not be square.

Spirit level

An indispensable tool, a spirit level is used at every stage of the building process to ensure that foundations and both horizontal and vertical brick surfaces are level and plumb. Made of metal, this tool incorporates both a horizontal and a vertical vial; if the bubble is in the centre, the surface is level. When laying out a drainage slope, you can put a block of wood under one end of the level to achieve the required slope (see below). A line level, which is basically a vial without a straight-edged metal casing, may be strung onto a builder's line and used as an additional aid. It cannot be used to check for plumb.

Line and pins or corner block

A builder's line (or string) is used with wooden or metal pegs to set out the foundations for brick structures. Not only is string cheaper, but it is easier to see than a builder's line.

When laying bricks, builder's line is strung along the upper level of the course to be laid. It may be used in conjunction with metal pins, or with corner blocks (see page 47).

Alternatively, you can simply wind the line around a brick to secure it.

Trowels, mortarboards and floats

A standard bricklaying trowel is essential for laying the bricks, while a rectangular plasterer's trowel is used when rendering walls. Corner trowels useful; shaped to fit either outside or inside corners, they simplify the task of neatening the vertical edges of a rendered structure.

A mortarboard or screedboard (or hawk) is useful, but not essential. Many professionals use this tool to hold small quantities of mortar while they lay the bricks or render the surface. When working at ground level, you can simply dip into the wheelbarrow; alternatively use a flat piece of metal or board.

If the surface is to be rendered, you will need a wooden float to smooth the mortar. A steel float is not generally used for external walls.

Pointing and jointing tools

Various pointing and jointing tools are used to place mortar in the joints and

A straight-edged piece of timber, marked to indicate brick courses, is used as a gauge rod.

to rake it out, respectively. A pointing trowel (which looks like a small-scale bricklayer's trowel) is normally used to fill in small holes in the mortar. If you butter the ends of the bricks properly as you work, you should be able to manage without one.

While a narrow trowel or special jointer may be used to finish both vertical and horizontal joints, a piece of metal, cut to form a square tip, is quite adequate. Traditionally joints were finished in various ways; they could be either concave, flush, recessed to a square finish, or even jointed so that the mortar stuck out slightly. But there is an art to these techniques, and the DIY builder need do no more than rake out the excess mortar to neaten the joint.

A float is used to screed a concrete slab.

Brick-cutting tools

There are several options for cutting bricks. The simplest is a brick hammer, which has a chisel end for this purpose, although it does not always cut neatly, especially if you are not adept at handling it. A bolster or broad chisel may be used instead. Place the brick on the ground (preferably on a bed of sand) and score the surface to mark the required cutting line; place the chisel blade on the line and knock firmly with a hefty club hammer. For very hard bricks, an electrically powered angle grinder is a boon.

Block splitters and masonry saws may be used for cutting larger concrete blocks; they may be hired if you do not want to buy one.

Rubber mallet

The best tool for knocking paving bricks level, this rubber-headed hammer is also useful for tapping stubborn bricks into place.

Saws

Although not strictly part of the bricklayer's toolkit, a saw is essential if you are cutting timber to make corner blocks, straightedges and so on.

BUILDING PRINCIPLES

Any well-built brick structure will be square, level and plumb. The exceptions, of course, are curved walls and circular structures, in which case there will obviously be no need to aim for right-angled corners.

Square

It stands to reason that any rectangular (or square) structure must have right-angled corners. If it does not, you will end up with crooked walls and a structure which is skew. For this reason it is essential not only to set out the structure correctly (see below and page 52) but also to use a builder's square to check the corners regularly as brickwork progresses. Never rely on your own judgement. Your workmanship may look absolutely square to you, but even the slightest inaccuracies can make a difference.

Level and plumb

Horizontal surfaces must be level, and vertical surfaces plumb. To ensure that they are, it is essential to check them at every stage. Make sure that the excavation is level, the foundation slab is absolutely flat, and the brickwork is even. It is vital not to rely on guesswork, otherwise you will have problems and may find yourself having to demolish what you have built.

The most common, and certainly the most versatile, tool used for this purpose is a spirit level. It will enable you to check both horizontal and vertical surfaces, at all stages and in all positions. For instance, as brickwork progresses, you can use a

A brick hammer is used to halve a brick.

An angle grinder is useful for cutting bricks.

A bolster and club hammer used together.

spirit level to check the upper surface of the bricks. By setting it on a straight-edged length of timber, you can check that two corners are at the same height. You can also check the vertical sides of the bricks, to ensure that the wall of brickwork is rising square and true, and you can use it on the diagonal to make sure the vertical surface is even.

A spirit level is an essential tool to ensure that brickwork is level and plumb.

A builder's line can also be used to keep brick courses level. Hooked onto the corner of the brickwork with a corner block, or attached by sticking special pins into the mortar, it creates a constant guide at whichever level you set it at. On a large expanse of wall, it may be used in conjunction with a line level.

Although corner blocks are sometimes available commercially, they are easily and quickly made with offcuts of wood. You will need two blocks of wood approximately 100 mm x 50 mm x 50 mm. Cut a section out of each to form a chunky L-shape, and then saw half-way through the foot of the L to create a slot which will hold the line in place. Wind the line around the base of the foot and draw it through the slot. The block is then hooked onto the corner of the brickwork at the correct height, and the line stretched to the opposite corner where it is attached to a second corner block.

Although a plumb bob may be used to check vertical surfaces at corners,

few people bother with this tool. It is really only useful on a large expanse of wall, such as a multi-storey building.

Bonding

It is vital that all bricks are properly bonded so that the walls of the structure are strong and form a solid mass. This ensures that the load is distributed laterally, along the entire

length of the wall. If the brickwork is not bonded, the vertical joints (or perpends) will be in a straight line and the load will not be distributed at all.

There are various ways of bonding brickwork, and several different patterns. The simplest, which is also the most common, is known as stretcher (or running) bond.

Stretcher bond brickwork is achieved by laying bricks so that they overlap those in the course below by half. Not only is the result attractive, but it is incredibly strong as well. It is also the only structurally sound bond which can be used to build a half-brick wall (comprising a single skin of brickwork), and the most economical when a cavity wall (with two rows of parallel brickwork) is constructed. It is the obvious choice when building a wall which is to be rendered, since there is little point in creating a pattern which will not be visible. When a one-brick wall is built in facebrick, any of the other options may be used, as you will find that the patterns created are quite different to stretcher bond.

English bond, believed to be the strongest of all bonds, is created by laying alternate courses of headers and stretchers. A course of headers is laid across a double skin of brickwork, where each brick is placed at right angles to the main run of bricks, exposing just the end, or header, on the outer wall.

Corner blocks, easily made from blocks of wood, help keep brick courses straight.

English garden wall bond is a variation of ordinary English bond and consists of a header course followed by three to five stretcher courses.

Flemish bond consists of alternating headers and pairs of stretchers in the same course. The headers in the second course are centred over the stretchers of the first, and vice versa.

Flemish garden wall bond consists of a header followed by two or three pairs of stretchers in the same course.

MATERIALS

The basic ingredients of all masonry work are the same. You will need bricks, blocks or stone, as well as mortar made with cement, sand and water (and sometimes lime or plasticiser to bind the units together). You will also need concrete foundations or footings, made with cement, sand, a coarse aggregate and water. Metal reinforcement may be used in the foundations or between the brickwork. Timber may be required for

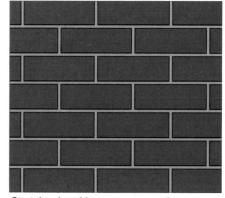

Stretcher bond is a common option.

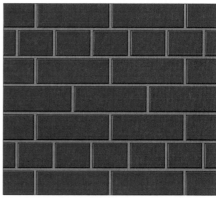

English bond, probably the strongest bond.

English garden wall bond.

Flemish bond has headers and stretchers.

A single or half-brick wall constructed using a stretcher bond pattern.

seating, storage and cupboards, as well as for formwork when pouring or casting concrete slabs.

Bricks and blocks

Made from clay, concrete or calcium silicate, bricks and blocks are available in a range of reasonably standard sizes, depending on where they are made. Your choice depends on what kind of structure you are building and whether it is to be rendered and painted or left with the brick showing.

Although reconstituted (reconstructed) stone blocks are solid, many other concrete blocks are hollow. Bricks, on the other hand, may have an indent (or a frog) in one face, or they may have two or three holes in them. Paving bricks are generally solid and flat. Both frogs and holes will aid the bonding, and these two characteristics are formed as a result of different methods of manufacturing – indented bricks are moulded, while the holes are caused by a more modern process of extrusion.

In addition to standard bricks and blocks, bricks shaped in various ways are available for finishing walls and other brickwork. Pavers, of course, may be used to top a table or the working surface of a barbecue or outdoor bar structure, while bullnosed bricks (which are rounded along one side or at one end) may be used to finish ends neatly. They are also useful for laying around ponds and other decorative features. Various coping (or capping) bricks are also available.

The quality of bricks does vary. For instance, those manufactured for general building work that is to be rendered may deteriorate if they are not coated with mortar. You will also find that there is some variation in the size and finish of different facebricks.

Apart from the bricks chosen to build your structure, you may decide to use firebricks on the cooking surface of a barbecue and tough engineering or exposure-grade bricks where walls are likely to be exposed to constant damp. If necessary, seek professional advice.

Bricks are available in a variety of shapes and sizes for paving and construction work.

Cement

Ordinary Portland cement, suitable for most concrete and mortar work, is used internationally. Sold in sealed 50 kg (and sometimes 25 kg or 40 kg) pockets or bags, it should be stored in a waterproof place, preferably above the ground and covered with plastic sheeting. If cement gets wet, it will become lumpy and unusable. Unless you are involved in a major building project, do not buy more cement than you can use within three months.

Sand

Sold in volume or in open bags (usually containing 25 kg or 50 kg), sand must be of a good quality and suitable for building. The best sands are evenly graded, containing particles of various sizes. Sand that does not contain sufficient fine material ('fines') tends to produce a weak, porous surface layer if it is used for concrete. If sand is too fine, mortar tends to rise to the surface of the concrete. If the particles are mostly the same size, the concrete is difficult to work with.

If sand is graded as 'soft' and 'sharp', you should use the soft sand for bricklaying and the coarser sharp sand for concrete. If plaster sand is available, this contains lime and is suitable for mortar to be used for both bricklaying and rendering. Otherwise it is usually best to add your own lime or plasticiser (see page 50).

Concrete blocks are laid with mortar in the same way as clay bricks.

For very large jobs it is advisable to order ready-mixed concrete, delivered in a truck.

Although the source of sand is not necessarily a foolproof guide, river sand is generally clean, and it often contains hard, rounded particles which increase the workability of concrete.

A disadvantage is that the fine particles have sometimes been washed out by the river water. Beach sand tends to be poorly graded, and it usually contains shell particles and salt. If it has been properly washed and graded by the supplier, it may be suitable for building use. Fine, wind-blown sands from desert areas and mine-dump sand (which is also too fine and uniform in particle size) should be avoided. You may find a blended sand which contains some clay, making the mortar easier to work.

Aggregate (crushed stone)

The coarse aggregate which is used to give bulk to concrete may be in the form of gravel, natural pebbles or crushed stone. Although its properties have less effect on the characteristics of the concrete than the properties of the sand used, aggregate is usually screened to what is known as single sizes. The common size for DIY

projects is 19 or 20 mm aggregate. Smaller 13.2 mm stone is easier to work with, but you will need to add more cement to the mixture.

Like sand, aggregate is sold in bags or by volume from builders' suppliers or transport companies.

Premixed and ready-mixed concrete

Although premixed materials, packaged dry in bags, are suitable only for very small jobs, ready-mixed concrete, delivered by volume in special trucks, is only appropriate for larger projects . You will, however, be assured of the exact strength of the concrete as the mixes are determined scientifically.

Lime

Available at the same outlets that supply cement, loosely bagged sand and aggregate, hydrated builder's lime improves the cohesiveness and water-retention qualities of fresh mortar. Available in 25 kg bags or pockets, it is a particularly useful additive if the sand is coarse or lacks very fine particles. Adding lime is also a good precaution to take against the mortar cracking.

Agricultural lime, road lime and quicklime (calcium oxide) are not suitable for brickwork.

Plasticiser

Plasticiser can be added to mortar to make it more workable, although it has no bonding function. Usually 50 ml of the liquid is added to every 50 kg of

Small quantities of concrete may be mixed on site in a wheelbarrow.

cement, but check the manufacturer's instructions beforehand.

Water
A safe rule of thumb when mixing both concrete and mortar is to use only water which is good enough to drink. If sea water is used, white powdery deposits tend to form on the surface. If the water is contaminated in any way, with chemicals, for instance, this could have an adverse effect on the cement.

Reinforcing
It is unlikely that you will have to reinforce the concrete footings of a garden structure. If you do, you will probably be acting on the advice and specifications of an engineer. Light mesh or a grid of steel rods may be required in the foundation trench, or you may have to set vertical steel bars into the concrete. These will then be built into the wall or pillars.

The most common form of reinforcing incorporated into brickwork is a wire mesh available in rolls which is laid over the horizontal plane of every fourth or fifth course. This is effective for reinforcing the upper surface of small openings left in walls, for example over storage compartments. It is not a substitute for a lintel.

Timber
Any wood used for an outdoor project must be sound and durable. Generally, hardwood (from broadleafed tree

Various types of timber are suitable for garden projects.

species) is preferable. However some softwoods (from conifers and pines) are very suitable. In areas where it is available, redwood is a favourite for use in the garden.

Whatever your choice, make sure that the timber has been properly processed or pressure-treated with preservatives, preferably at the sawmill. Some types of timber (in particular teak and balau) will weather well in the open air, but most require some kind of weatherproof sealant to ensure that they will be able to withstand the elements over an

extended period of time. See pages 108-111 for more information.

QUANTIFYING AND COSTING
The quantity of materials required will have a direct bearing on the cost of any structure. Of course, if you choose to build one of the projects that follow, you can simply take the list of materials and work out what these items will cost you. Otherwise you will have to do some mathematical calculations first.

The easiest way to cost the materials

Hoop-iron reinforcing, set in a footing, will help strengthen a pillar.

Steel reinforcing laid in the foundation trench of a substantial wall.

required to build a structure is to work out exactly how many bricks will be needed. You can then establish how much cement, sand and lime is needed for the mortar. It is simple to determine the materials required for the footings and foundations, provided you have accurate dimensions.

Foundations and footings

The quantities and proportions of the cement, sand and aggregate required to make concrete for footings is dependent on the type of structure you are building. The larger it is, in terms of both area and height, the bigger the footings will have to be, and the stronger the concrete mix should be. However, low-strength concrete is quite adequate for the footings of the simple structures featured here. If you are working with 19 mm aggregate, the recommended proportions of cement, sand and crushed stone for hand compaction are 1:4:4. In areas where a good quality gravel is available, the preferred ratio is 1:3:6. If a stronger mix is required, alter these ratios to 1:3:3 (with crushed stone) or 1:2:3 (with gravel).

Local building regulations give minimum specifications for footings, including the necessary depth below the frostline where relevant. If you are uncertain, check these before you start building. As a guide, smaller structures may be built on footings which are between 100 mm and 150 mm thick; higher, more substantial walls will require a footing of at least 200 mm.

Once you have determined the dimensions relevant to your project, work out the volume of concrete required by multiplying the length x width x thickness or height. If you are using a 1:4:4 mix, you will need 4½–5 bags (225–250 kg) of cement for every cubic metre; for a 1:2:3 mix you will need eight bags (or 400 kg) for each cubic metre. Once you know how much cement is required, you can calculate how much sand and aggregate is needed.

Bricks and blocks

Usually the quickest way to work out brick quantities is to work out the total wall area of whatever you are building. For every square metre of half-brick wall you will need 50–55 bricks (depending on their size); for a one-brick wall you will need to double that number. To work out the number of blocks required, divide the wall area by the area of the side of one block.

When building smaller features, you can also draw the design to scale and establish how many bricks there will be in the first course of each section or side of the structure. Determine the height of the structure and divide this by the height of your bricks plus a mortar joint; this will give you the number of courses required for the vertical face. Repeat this process for every wall face in the design.

Mortar

When mixing mortar for bricklaying in the ratio 1:4 cement to sand, you can count on using 50 kg of cement for every 200 bricks laid in a half-brick wall, and the same amount for every 150 laid in a one-brick wall. Mortar works out at about 1 cubic metre per 1 000 bricks. When using larger blocks, the quantities vary; the larger the block, the less cement you will need per square metre. You will need 50 kg cement to lay a hundred 390 mm x 190 mm x 190 mm blocks, and the same amount of cement to lay about fifty 190 mm x 90 mm x 90 mm blocks. If you are planning to add lime, add 25 kg for every 50 kg of cement.

SETTING OUT

It is absolutely essential to set out the position of any structure correctly. Some helpful pointers are given on page 56, including the useful 3:4:5 method of checking that corners are all kept at 90˚. While a builder's square is a reliable guide, it is easy to make a mistake and very useful to double-check the layout using this method. Another way to check that the layout is square is to measure diagonally between opposite corners. If you have set out the structure correctly, the two measurements will be the same.

If a structure is to be built on a patio where a slight drainage slope is required, you can set this out with a

For a project to run smoothly, it is essential to plan and quantify materials carefully.

Use a straightedge to scrape and smooth wet concrete.

Concrete must set thoroughly before bricklaying starts.

spirit level, one end of which should be set on a small block of wood. The height of the block of wood will depend on the slope required. For a 1:50 slope, which is the minimum requirement, a 40 mm thick block placed under a 2 m long straightedge will do the trick. Place a spirit level on the straightedge, and position the block under one end of the timber. Then mark the slope with pegs.

If you want to level a slope, the simplest method is with a water level (see page 23). Consisting simply of a length of transparent tubing (or garden hose with a piece of clear tubing pushed into either end), this homemade tool works on the principle that water finds its own level. Tie one end to a stake and knock this into the ground at the highest point or get a partner to hold it in place. Fill the tube with water before attaching it to a second stake, which should be positioned at the lowest point. Mark off the water level on both stakes, then measure the distance between this mark and the ground at the lowest stake. Then dig out the earth at the first stake to the same depth.

BUILDING TECHNIQUES
The basic techniques required for building outdoor brick structures are illustrated on pages 57-67. Once you have familiarised yourself with them and had some practice, you will find that they really are not difficult at all.

Working with concrete
Although the principles of mixing concrete are simple, this can be backbreaking work, especially if you mix by hand. If there is a reasonable quantity of concrete to be used, it is advisable to hire a concrete mixer. You will, in any case, have to mix in batches, measuring out each one carefully. Use the same container (a large bucket or a clean 25 litre drum) for measuring all the materials.

Mixing
If you are mixing by hand, work on a hard, clean surface. Never mix directly on the ground as soil can contaminate the concrete and moisture will be absorbed from the mixture. If you mix on asphalt or paving of any sort, hose the area down immediately to prevent the concrete from drying and staining the surface.

First combine the sand and cement until you get a uniform colour, then make a small crater in the centre and add water gradually, shovelling the dry materials into the centre at the same time. Take care not to add too much water, or you will wash the cement and sand from the heap. When the mix is soft and smooth, rather like thin porridge, you can add the crushed stone or gravel. Some builders prefer to mix all the dry materials first.

When using a concrete mixer, load the coarse aggregate first with a little bit of water and run the machine for a few minutes. This prevents the mix from building up on the blades. Add the sand next, and then the cement.

Placing
It is good practice to dampen the foundation trench before placing or pouring the concrete, to prevent absorption of water from the mix into the soil. Pour the concrete out of a wheelbarrow, or shovel it into the trench. Tamp it down with the back of a spade, then use a straightedge to compact and level it. Start with a chopping motion and then use a sawing movement to finish. Stop when water starts to come to the surface.

Setting and curing
Concrete footings must be left to set, at least overnight, but preferably for several days before building on them. In cold weather, protect them from frost by covering them with sacking or plastic. In very hot weather, sprinkle or spray a little water on the surface from time to time to keep it moist.

A corner block is in place to ensure that bricks are laid correctly.

mortar set on the concrete foundation. Make sure that the concrete is clean and has not accumulated sand and garden debris. Use the trowel to place a sausage of mortar on the foundation and make furrows in it with the pointed tip. Then slide the first brick into position. Now butter the end of your second brick, and slide this into place.

If you watch the professionals at work, you will see that they build up the corners of a wall first, stepping the brickwork back by half a brick at each course. This is known as racking back and it helps ensure that the structure is kept square. Use a spirit level (set on a straight-edged length of timber if it is too short) to check that opposite corners are level. Then string a builder's line between the two corners as a guide to laying the bricks in between. Use a gauge rod to check that each course is equal in height.

The hardening of the concrete is the result of a chemical reaction between the cement and water. Although it continues to cure over a period of years, it gains most of its strength in the first 28 days.

Bricklaying

The most important tool you will have to learn to use is a bricklayer's trowel. Once you have mastered the technique of buttering the ends and sides of bricks with the trowel, you will be well on your way. The other vital aspect is to ensure that each and every brick you lay is level and plumb. A spirit level will enable you to do this; just make certain that the bubble in the vial is always centred.

Mortar for bricklaying is mixed in the same way as concrete, except that aggregate is not added. If lime is used, add it with the cement and sand.

Once you know which bond you wish to use (see pages 47-48), you can get started. The first course is laid on

Rendering

If you are not using facebricks, you will probably want to render the surface once the brickwork is complete. Mortar is used, usually mixed in the same ratio as the bricklaying mortar so that the two are compatible. To make mortar more pliable, plasticiser or lime

Butter mortar onto one end of the brick before putting it in place.

A metal pointing tool is used to scrape out the joints of brickwork.

is usually added to the mixture. The addition of a bonding agent will also help the mortar stick to the surface.

If the brick surface absorbs too much water from the fresh render, the mortar will be weakened; spray some water evenly onto the brickwork the day before you are going to start work. If it has been raining, allow the walls to become surface-dry before applying the mortar. Remember that cracking is more likely if the mortar is applied in hot sun or strong wind conditions.

Once the mixture is ready, apply it to the surface using a rectangular plasterer's trowel; press it down firmly to ensure good adhesion. It needs to set for about an hour before you can scrape the surface with a straightedge or a screed board. Once you have a reasonably level surface, smooth it out further with a wooden float.

Mortar used to render walls must not be allowed to dry out too quickly, otherwise it will not cure properly and it may crack. To prevent this, dampen the surface by hosing with a gentle spray several times a day over a two- or three-day period. It is important to ensure that the spray is really fine, otherwise it could damage the finish.

Paved surfaces

If your work tops and garden tables are to have decorative paving, you will

A normal mortar mix is used to render brickwork which is to be painted.

usually lay the pavers in mortar in exactly the same way as any other bricks or blocks. On the other hand, when paving the fire bed of a barbecue structure, lay the pavers on sand, and butt them up against one another in order to form a completely solid base for the fire. Clay bricks have been fired at very high temperatures and will not be damaged by the fire of the barbecue; however, mortar or plain concrete bases will tend to crack.

USEFUL TERMS

Aggregate Although sand is the fine aggregate added to both mortar and concrete, this term also describes the coarse aggregate added to concrete. This may be gravel or crushed stone, depending on what is available. In Britain, all-in aggregate (or hoggin) is a mixture of sand and gravel which is mixed with cement to make concrete. In South Africa, all-in aggregate is an inferior material which should be avoided.
Bond The arrangement of bricks to ensure that they overlap and therefore bind together to form a solid, stable mass. Various patterns may be formed, some of

which, if laid in facebrick, can create a decorative effect.
Buttering Method used to apply mortar to the ends or sides of bricks during the bricklaying process.
Course A complete row of laid bricks. Several courses form a wall or part of another brick structure.
Excavation The foundation trench.
Footing Projecting concrete course at the foot of a wall, pillar or pier.
Foundation The concrete base on which brickwork rests.
Jointing Method used to finish off and neaten the joints in brickwork when

facebricks have been used.
Lap The amount a brick overlaps the bricks in the course below.
Header The short end of a brick. A header course features the end of the brick on the outside of the wall.
Perpend The vertical joints in brickwork.
Pointing Filling in joints with mortar.
Racking back Method of building up the brickwork at the corners and ends of walls.
Reinforcing Metal mesh or rods built into concrete and brickwork to strengthen it.
Stretcher The long side or face of a brick. A stretcher course features the long side of the brick on the outside of the wall.

In the following pages, important building principles and basic bricklaying techniques are outlined, along with a description of the materials and tools you will need to build a brick structure in your garden. These instructions show step-by-step how to employ the various skills, starting with a section which illustrates clearly how to set out any project. To make the building process more realistic, step-by-step photographs show several specific brick features being built.

One series of pictures follows construction of a simple barbecue unit which incorporates a very basic storage area.

The second shows how seating, tables, planters and a storage box are assembled. These structures are not presented as projects, and no materials lists are given. Instead, the focus is on the procedures followed and techniques used. Once you have mastered them, you should be able to tackle any outdoor brick project featured in this book.

You will see how the principles previously explained are put into practice; how single and double walls are built, corners constructed and pillars incorporated into a design. You will also be shown how the various tools are used.

Shuttering is used to create a working surface alongside the fire bed of the barbecue, and the same project also demonstrates how to create an opening in any brick structure. Weep holes are left in the planters, illustrating a simple drainage method.

BUILDING METHODS: SETTING OUT

The first step in any outdoor building project is to set out the site correctly. You will need to decide exactly where the structure is to be located, according to the dimensions and layout of your plan, and then you will have to mark it out, clearly showing where foundation trenches must be dug. The foundations are always slightly larger than the structure itself, an important point to remember when setting out any project.

One of the advantages of building smaller garden features is that, because of their size, it is usually easy to double-check the layout. A good way to do this is to lay out loose bricks to check the area to be excavated and ensure that the design will fit the area intended for construction. If

there is a problem, it is much easier to sort it out now than when the bricks have been mortared.

Most structures tackled by DIY builders are square or rectangular in shape, so all the angles where walls meet one another will be 90°. Occasionally a design may feature acute or obtuse angles or gently curved lines.

The simplest way to check that corners are square (or at 90°) is to use the 3:4:5 method. What this means is that the length of the shortest side of the triangle must be equal to three units of measurement, the adjacent short side must be four, and the line which joins the two ends must be five units in length. If the structure is large enough, these may

be units of 3 m, 4 m and 5 m respectively; a much smaller unit may be 300 mm, 400 mm and 500 mm units. Any other multiples will also work, for instance 600 mm, 800 mm and 1 m.

You can set out a circular structure by making a basic compass with pegs and string. Knock one peg into the central point, attach string to it, and then rotate the string, marking a ring of points around the circumference. The most important thing to remember is that the length of the string must equal the radius of your circle.

Once the layout has been pegged, mark the position of the foundations or footings with dry cement, lime, chalk or even ordinary cake flour; the latter is usually the cheapest option.

The 3:4:5 method checks for square.

Use a peg and string for circles.

Check the layout with loose bricks.

Anyone who wants to build a simple brick barbecue in the garden or on a patio will find these step-by-step instructions invaluable. It does not matter whether you want to copy the design, adapt it, or simply to use the various basic building skills which are illustrated; this helpful guide will enable you to create a special structure of which you can be proud.

Various elements are covered, from foundation to finishes. The aim is to give a broad indication of what is involved when building a structure which will be used for cooking and storage. The inclusion of a solid, paved working top will increase the versatility of the design.

The fire bed featured here is sunken, and surrounded by brickwork on three sides. This means there is no need to use shuttering or any other form of reinforcing to create the cooking surface. Instead, a basic brick box is constructed and filled with soil removed from the foundation trenches. This is then compacted, topped with sand and paved with clay bricks.

Since many barbecue designs feature a storage area for firewood, coal and other items below the cooking area, the step-by-step project also includes

instructions which will enable you to tackle this design variation. The upper surface of the storage area forms a table for preparing food which is to be cooked on the barbecue or for serving, and a similar surface may be built as the fire bed itself. In this event, the most important element is the shuttering which is provided to support the surface during construction.

If a chimney of some kind is to be built, shuttering will also be necessary to support the front wall. Although the central cavity will be left open, the essential principles are the same.

This particular barbecue design measures 1.85 m x 710 mm and is 950 mm above the ground. There is a generous fire surface with dimensions based on the average metal drum, so often cut in half lengthwise for use by the outdoor cook. A 920 mm x 600 mm grid will slot in and cover this area.

MATERIALS

Facebricks are used for building because they are a low-maintenance option for any structure which is to be used for cooking. Matching paving bricks are laid in the fire bed, forming the exposed working surface, and they

are also used to finish the inside of the storage compartment.

If you decide to follow the design exactly, you will need 270 facebricks and 58 matching pavers (not allowing for wastage).

The shuttering used here is permanent, but it is not intended to be seen after completion of the structure. For this reason, relatively thin 10 mm x 150 mm wide fibrecement boards are placed over the opening to cover it. Once the surface is paved, this material is not visible. Any other slim board (or even metal) may be used, but it should be weatherproof. Concrete cast in situ and concrete lintels are not suitable.

FOUNDATIONS

As this is not a heavy structure, a foundation of 100–150 mm is ample; use a 1:4:4 or 1:3:6 concrete mix, depending on soil conditions and the aggregate available in your area.

When laying out the structure (see facing page), make sure that the foundations are about 100 mm wider than the brickwork on all sides. If the structure is to be built alongside paving laid previously, the foundation may be flush with the existing bricks.

| 1 | Decide where the barbecue structure is to be located and peg it out with string as described on page 56. Make sure that all the measurements are accurate, and use a steel builder's square to ensure that the corners are at right angles.

| 2 | The area pegged out here is adjacent to existing paving and measures 2.05 m x 810 mm. You can remove the pegs and string before you dig the foundations, provided that you mark the perimeter of the proposed trench with chalk, cement or flour first.

| 3 | If the area where you are building is lawned you may be able to use the grass elsewhere in the garden. Use the sharp end of a spade to cut into the turf, then dig out the sods neatly and carefully. Keep any excess soil on one side.

4 Bricks placed on edge are useful to indicate the upper level of your concrete. Place a spirit level across the bricks and check that the base of the trench is level. If you want a deeper foundation, use pegs, marked to the correct height.

5 Now mix concrete following the instructions given on page 53. Moisten the soil in the trench to prevent the water from the fresh mix from being absorbed into the ground. Transport the mixture in a wheelbarrow and tip it out into the trench.

6 The concrete should be level with the top of the bricks (or pegs). Level it off roughly with the back of your spade or shovel, and then neaten with a straight-edged piece of timber, using a sawing movement. Use a chopping motion to compact.

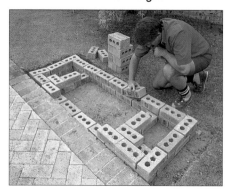

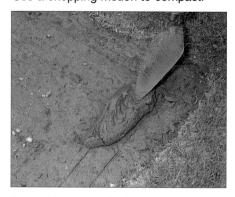

7 Once the concrete has set, lay out the bricks without mortar, positioning them correctly on the slab. Now is the time to make any minor alterations, for instance if you are not happy with the design or find that too many half bricks are needed.

8 Use a square to check that all four corners of the proposed structure are at 90°. Use a pencil or chalk to mark the position of the bricks on the concrete. Although you will have to recheck the angles later, this does help ensure accuracy.

9 Mix mortar in the ratio 1:4 (cement:sand), adding lime or plasticiser if required. Lay a sausage of mortar 10–15 mm thick where the first brick is to be laid. Use the tip of your trowel to make a jagged furrow along the centre of it.

10 Now you can bed the first brick in mortar. If it has obliterated the line you made on the concrete, use a steel square and the tip of the trowel to mark exactly where the brick should be positioned. Press the brick firmly into place and tap with the trowel.

11 It is essential that the first brick is flat and level, as you will use this surface to gauge the alignment of other bricks. Set the spirit level across the brick and check that the bubble in the vial is centred, tapping lightly with the handle of the trowel if it is not.

12 Check with the spirit level again, this time along the length of the brick. If the bubble in the vial is not centred, tap the brick gently with the trowel handle; alternatively, remove a little of the mortar from underneath the brick and check again.

13 Once the first brick is in place, you can butter one end of each consecutive brick to be laid. Trowel on a wedge of mortar and spread it across the end. Then use the pointed tip of your bricklaying trowel to make furrows to aid bonding.

14 Put a little more mortar onto the slab, at right angles to the first brick you laid, and create a furrow in it as before. Slide the second brick into place, allowing the mortar on the end to form a joint. Push it firmly into the mortar and tap with the trowel handle.

15 You will not be able to tell whether or not it is perfectly level unless you use the correct tools. Place the spirit level across the upper surface of the two bricks and continue tapping gently with the trowel until the bubble is centred.

16 It is essential that all the corners of the structure are at right angles. Even if you have followed all the previous guidelines, use a steel builder's square to check the angle again now, before the mortar sets. Then lay your next brick.

17 You can lay the first course of the side wall, but do not lay the front wall until the first corner has been built up. This is the best way to ensure that the structure will be straight and square. Put mortar on the trowel and smooth it onto the bricks.

18 Lay the first brick of the second course at the corner, pushing it firmly into the furrowed mortar. Use the spirit level frequently to check that the upper surface is flat. As you work, make sure that the textured face of each brick is on the outside.

19 The surface which will form the outside walls must also be flat and plumb. Do not forget to use the spirit level vertically to ensure that the ends of the bricks are properly aligned. Tap the first brick in the second course outwards if it is not in line vertically.

20 Continue to build up the corner, checking all surfaces regularly. Even if both horizontal and vertical surfaces are flat, level and plumb, it pays to double-check across the diagonal. You can use a straightedge of any sort to do this.

21 The side walls are only three bricks long. Leave the middle brick out of the second course and lay a brick at the corner of the back wall. Check from corner to corner, across the full length of this section of wall before filling in to complete the course.

22 Scrape any excess mortar off the bricks with the trowel as you work. When using facebricks, it is much easier to keep the surface clean than to try to remove surplus mortar at a later stage. Do not waste what is scraped off; you can use it all.

23 Even though you are buttering the end of the bricks, you will find that there are a few gaps in the joints which need to be filled as you work. Lift a little of the mortar onto the trowel, and, using a chopping movement, point (or fill) these joints.

24 Now you can move to the opposite side of the structure and lay the first course at the corner. Once a few of the bricks are in place, string a line between the two corners, making certain that it is level with the upper surface of the bricks.

25 Then lay the course of bricks which will form the front wall of the barbecue and contain the fire bed. The line you have set up will enable you to make certain that it is absolutely straight; take care not to let any of the bricks touch it or push it out of place.

26 Continue building up the walls, using the bricks at each corner as a guide. If these are level with each other, you will find it easier to ensure that the course as a whole is level. It pays to be meticulous. Tap any uneven bricks with the trowel handle.

27 Once you have laid the first couple of courses at the front of the structure, lay the internal walls which will divide the cooking surface from the storage area. The position of these walls will depend on the design of your barbecue.

28 This design features a relatively wide fire bed, with storage space on one side only. A double brick wall on the other side provides a narrow serving area and will enable you to step the brickwork so that it provides a support for the grid.

29 Decide on the best position for the cooking grid. You will need to support it with metal (inserted into the mortar during bricklaying), or by stepping the brickwork. Lay the bricks at this level slightly off the edge of the wall below, so forming a narrow shelf.

30 Lay the bricks in the same way for the outside wall. This will result in a thicker mortar joint at this level, but it will not be obvious in the overall effect. The overlap should be equal on both sides, and just wide enough to support the grid.

31 Use a long spirit level to check that the bricks are level. If your spirit level is too short to span the gap, set it on a straight-edged piece of timber. Do not rely on your own judgement; if the bricks are not level the grid will wobble.

32 Now complete the brickwork, continually checking both the horizontal and vertical surfaces. Here the front wall is built up two courses for the storage area and seven for the fire bed. You may also create a second step for the grid if you wish.

33 Once most of the brickwork is complete, but before you lay the pavers on the upper surface, fill the central cavity with broken bricks, crushed stone or sand. You can also use the soil which was excavated from the foundation trench.

34 Use a punner or solid pole to compact the fill in layers and make certain there are no voids. This is especially important if you are using rubble which is not regular in shape and size. Hosing the fill gently with water also aids compaction.

35 Cut the shuttering to size. Here, 150 mm wide lengths of fibrecement are abutted to form a solid surface which will support the paving bricks. Brace the shuttering from underneath with timber. This can be removed once the mortar has set.

36 Matching pavers may now be laid in mortar, over the shuttering, to create a serving or working surface. Lay the first two at opposite corners and use the spirit level to check that they are level with one another before laying the balance.

37 Lay pavers over the entire upper surface, allowing those along the back wall to form a slight, decorative lip if you wish. Butter the ends of the bricks and use a trowel to fill in any open joints. Use a jointing tool to neaten the joints.

38 The pavers which are to form the fire bed are laid on sand rather than in mortar. Shovel a 25 mm layer of soft building sand over the fill, then smooth and level it with a straightedge. Abut the bricks and use a rubber mallet to level.

39 Use mortar to fill in around the edges of the pavers and keep them in place. Brush sand over the surface so that it fills the joints. Finally, use a piece of metal to rake out any excess mortar from the joints in the walls to give a nice, neat finish.

Brick features may be built as individual units or as part of a more elaborate plan. These step-by-step instructions will enable you to do either. You can copy the versatile design shown here, which incorporates ample seating, storage, built-in table tops and stepped planters, or construct any one of these features on its own. Alternatively, you can use the ideas and techniques demonstrated here to create your own design.

For those wanting to duplicate the design, the layout includes a 3.8 m long, 106 mm wide, half-brick wall which has three supporting 350 mm x 350 mm piers. This was included to shield a driveway from view and at the same time add privacy to the area. It is also used as the backrest to the bench which is set in front of it. The seat itself is constructed with six lengths of 70 mm wide timber which rest on three supporting piers, built to five courses above what will be the finished floor surface of the patio.

Tables are incorporated at both ends of the 2.3 m long bench; one measures 450 mm x 450 mm, while the other is only 450 mm x 220 mm, but quite adequate for drinks, plates and so on. Two planters, built to different heights

(one three courses high and the other five courses) are built at one end of the bench. The inside measurements of these are about 560 mm x 220 mm and 450 mm x 220 mm respectively. The storage box, which doubles as a second seating structure, is slightly wider than the bench (1.5 m x 700 mm), so that it can be used to store cushions and other bulky items. The lid, made with exterior plywood and planks, is hinged to an existing wall.

Since structures may be built on both strip and slab foundations (see page 118), both types are illustrated, along with an invaluable hint which will provide essential drainage in the base of a brick planter.

Most of the brickwork involves building single (or half-brick) walls, although construction of the central pier supporting the bench shows how the thicker one-brick wall is built.

MATERIALS

Although facebricks are used to construct all these features, part of the planter walls are rendered to blend with the exterior of the house. The tables and upper edge of the planters are topped with matching paving bricks,

providing a smooth and attractive surface. If you decide to copy the design, you will need about 300 facebricks and 13 pavers for the bench, storage box, tables and planters. An additional 300 will be required to build the 1.8 m high wall.

Various types of timber may be used for the seats, although you must be sure that it is suitable for outdoor use and will withstand weathering. Most types should be treated against infestation and sealed in some way (see page 51).

The interior walls of the planters are sealed with a bitumen-based product to prevent future discolouration caused by constant moisture.

FOUNDATIONS

Relatively small, 100–150 mm thick foundations are quite adequate for the smaller features. Foundations for the wall should be thicker (at least 200 mm thick); check whether your local authority has minimum requirements or guidelines for the area you live in.

When mixing the concrete, use a 1:4:4 or 1:3:6 concrete mix, depending on soil conditions and the aggregate available in your area.

1 Use a retractable steel tape and a builder's square to set out the foundation trenches as described on page 56. Make sure that they are about 100 mm wider on all sides than the structure itself. Peg out the area with long nails and string.

2 Before you begin to excavate the foundation trenches, mark the area pegged out with chalk, lime, cement or flour. Then remove the nails (or pegs) and string. This shows the layout of the screen wall and three supporting piers.

3 Dig the foundation trench for the wall and piers to a depth of at least 200 mm. Remove all vegetation and keep the ground surface as flat and even as you can, as this will enable you to cast an even slab to support the brickwork.

4 Mark out and dig the rest of the trenches to a depth of 150 mm. Strip foundations may be laid for the storage box structure, rather than throwing a solid slab. Make sure these are at least 100–200 mm wider than the walls will be.

5 Use a straightedge set on bricks, together with a spirit level, to determine where the upper surface of the concrete will be. The bricks are then left in position, as a permanent and failsafe guide.There is no need to remove them from the trench.

6 Once all the trenches have been dug and levelled, mix concrete as described on page 53 and transport it in a wheelbarrow. To prevent water from being drawn out of the fresh concrete, moisten the soil before shovelling the concrete into place.

7 If you need to step the concrete slightly at any point, use loosely laid bricks to hold the wet mixture in place while it sets. Here the bench and table foundation is higher than that cast for the wall and piers. Compact and level the concrete thoroughly.

8 When building planters, it is vital to provide drainage of some sort. A simple solution is to position several bricks at the base of the structure before placing the concrete. For larger planters, simply throw strip foundations, leaving the centre open.

9 When the concrete has set, but is not yet hard, remove the bricks. If you leave them for too long, you will have to chip them out with a chisel; to prevent this happening, wiggle the bricks from time to time while the concrete is setting.

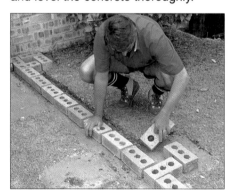

10 Remove the bricks used to step the foundation and leave the concrete to set thoroughly, at least overnight. Before you start laying the bricks, set them out on the foundations, without any mortar, to check the layout you have planned.

11 This shows the position of the central pier which will support the timber used to create seating. Because it is stepped above the first course of the wall, one extra brick will be needed alongside the wall to support it.

12 A section of the wall is included in the design at one end. If you are not building a screen wall, the back of the structure will simply be lower, in keeping with height of the planters and table, and the pier will not be included.

13 The storage box and adjacent table area are set out against an existing wall and pillar. Every site will differ and there is no reason that these features should not be free-standing. Alternatively, you could build a low wall behind the box to form a backrest.

14 Mark the position of the loose bricks with chalk or pencil, then remove them. Mix mortar in the required ratio and start laying the bricks at any one of the corners, as described in steps 9–16 on page 58. Make sure the first brick is level.

15 The first course must also be square. Use the correct tools to check the angles and to make absolutely sure that the upper surface of the first course is flat and level. To do this, set the spirit level at various angles along the tops of the bricks.

16 Do not assume that any existing walls or features are square and plumb. Rather check your own brickwork regularly. If the walls of this storage box are not laid accurately, you will have problems fitting the lid at a later stage.

17 There are various ways to build pillars and piers. This 340 mm x 340 mm pillar is constructed with four bricks, so that it can bond with the half brick wall. Lay the first course of bricks on a bed of mortar and use a spirit level to check that they are flat.

18 You can leave the central core hollow, or, if the pillar is relatively high, insert a reinforcing rod through the centre and fill the hollow with mortar or a weak concrete mix, This pillar is built with a half brick in the centre, making it reasonably solid.

19 Make sure that the brickwork is square before you go any further. Here, the wall continues from the pillar. This will ensure that the bricks bond well, but the effect of a running stretcher bond will be interrupted by a half brick at times.

20 Continue to lay the first course of all the features. The configuration of the table follows a paving stack bond at this stage; the next course will be laid so that all the bricks in this part of the structure bond properly and do not fall over.

21 Once the first course of bricks is in place, you can start laying the next course, preferably at a corner. If there is a wide expanse of wall, use a spirit level to align this first, and then use it as a datum point for the rest of brickwork at this level.

22 Then move to the next corner, align the two outside bricks, and string a builder's line at the correct height. Then lay bricks between the corners to complete the course. Be sure to bond the bricks to form a half-brick wall in stretcher bond.

23 When you lay the second course of the table adjoining the planters, you will need to cut some of the bricks to ensure the structure is properly bonded. You cannot just lay them in the opposite direction as there will be a gap through the middle.

24 The central pier which will form a support for the bench must also be built using stretcher bond, even though this little wall is only five courses high. Lay the first brick of the second course across the front of the two parallel bricks in the first course.

25 Knock the bricks into place with the handle of the trowel and then check the corners again with the builder's square. Use the spirit level to make sure the brickwork at each end is properly aligned with the central pier. It will be difficult to rectify faults later.

26 It is important to create weepholes at the base of the wall to allow water to drain from the patio. The simplest method is to leave some of the vertical joints unmortared. These holes will be just above ground level once paving is laid.

27 Use a pin and builder's line to keep the courses straight. Push the pin into the wet mortar one course below the one you are laying, and pull the line around the corner at an angle. Wind the line around a loose brick to keep it in place at the other end.

28 Even if you are buttering one end of each brick (see step 13 on page 59), you will find that you need to add mortar to some of the joints. Put a little mortar on the trowel and cut gently into the joint with the edge of the tool, tapping it slightly.

29 The stepped planters are built up three and five courses above the eventual level of the paved patio. The supporting pier for the bench is one course lower than the table surface which is incorporated alongside the two planters.

30 When creating a solid brick surface, a good tip from the professionals is to lay the outside bricks before filling in the centre. This helps to keep the vertical surfaces plumb. Take care not to shift the outer bricks when you lay those in the middle.

31 Follow the same procedure when building the larger table adjacent to the wall at the other end. Make sure that each course bonds with the one beneath it, and finish the table area one course higher than the supporting pier for the bench.

32 Continue building the screen wall to the required height. You will need to string a line along the entire length of the wall to keep the brick courses straight. It is a good idea to use a gauge rod now and then to check that all the joints are even.

33 If any portion of the brickwork is to be rendered, this can be done once the mortar used to lay the bricks has set. Mix a new batch of mortar and lay it onto your surface with a plasterer's trowel, applying enough pressure to make it stick to the bricks.

34 The render should be between 10 mm and 15 mm thick. Leave it while it begins to set, then, after about an hour, use a straight-edged length of wood or a spirit level to scrape and smooth the surface. Accuracy is not important.

35 Once the surface is reasonably smooth, use a wooden float to create a more even finish. Use an even pressure and a regular wrist movement, but do not over-trowel or the finer material will come to the surface and may cause cracking.

36 The next step is to finish table tops and all other exposed horizontal brick surfaces with pavers. Where the rendered surface meets a facebrick wall, you should use the spirit level to ensure that the pavers are level on the vertical plane.

37 Once the first paver is in position, you can lay the rest of the bricks around the lip of the higher planter and on the surface of the smaller table top. Bed the pavers in mortar and butter one side and one end before pushing into place.

38 Then lay paving bricks around the top of the lower planter, first filling in any holes with mortar. Place a sausage of mortar on the upper surface and create a slight furrow with the trowel in exactly the same way as you would to lay ordinary bricks.

39 Place the first paving brick in position and check that it is level. Butter the end of the second paver and push it into place. Then use your spirit level again, and tap any uneven bricks with a rubber mallet until they are absolutely flat and level.

40 When you have completed the planters and the mortar is well set, paint a bitumen-based sealant on the inside surface. This will prevent moisture from affecting the outer skin of the brickwork. When the bitumen is dry, fill the box with soil and plant.

41 When finishing off the table top positioned in the corner between old and new walls, lay the first brick at the outer corner and ensure that both the horizontal and the vertical surfaces are plumb. Make sure that the joints are neat and tidy.

42 Place an even bed of mortar on the upper surface of the brickwork. Then butter the sides of the bricks as you lay the outer row. Knock each one gently into place with a mallet and check that they are all level with one another.

43 Butter both the length and the top of each of the bricks laid on the inner row of the table top. There will be a slight gap between the edge of the pavers and the wall. This can be filled with mortar, using a trowel to make sure that it is level with the pavers.

44 Once the table top is complete, you may find that some of the joints need to be filled (or pointed). It will also be necessary to neaten the joints with a special trowel or jointer. Those without specialist tools could use a piece of metal instead.

45 Make the seat for the bench by screwing four 450 mm x 70 mm x 45 mm wide slats across six 2.5 m lengths. Position them so that there is one short piece on either side of the central brick pier, and one on the inside of each of the end piers.

46 The back rest is made with four 70 mm wide lengths of timber which are screwed to the wall. This will prevent a textured facebrick finish from scraping against you or damaging clothing. It also creates the impression of more substantial built-in furniture.

47 Make the storage box lid from a 1.5 m x 710 mm sheet of exterior plywood and nine 1.5 m x 70 mm wide slats. Cut five shallow channels across the width of the slats. Glue them to one side of the plywood then, working from the other side, tack the slats down.

48 Glue and screw four slats, 700 mm long and 20 mm thick, across the board, using 50 mm long screws to secure each of the nine seating slats. Screw brass hinges to the lid, then attach it to the wall with appropriate screws and Rawl plugs.

PILLARS

Free-standing block and concrete block pillars and piers have various uses, including acting as supports for basic pergolas or arbours, as posts for gates and driveways entrances, as bases for sundials or bird baths and as essential uprights which form the supporting structures for carports. Intermediate or end piers are put in free-standing brick walls for essential additional support. Building a pillar or pier is relatively easy once you have acquired the basic skills of bricklaying and understood the basic method of construction.

FOUNDATION

The minimum foundation depth for a brick pillar is 200 mm (8 in) although it may be advisable to make it as deep as 600 mm (2 ft), depending on its height and the weight it will carry.

The concrete mix used for a small pad foundation of this kind should be the standard 1:2½:3½ mix. This mixture was used for the pillar in the following step-by-step project since it was less than a metre (3 ft 3 in) high and its purpose was to be decorative rather than supportive.

REINFORCING

Some pillars must be built to take a considerable load. For this reason both reinforcing rods and a strong mortar mix should be used in their construction.

Of course, any roof structure must also be securely fixed to a pillar and metal reinforcement should be built into the final five courses.

When building brick piers and pillars, it is usually advisable to incorporate vertical metal reinforcing rods. One or two rods are set in the centre of the foundation and propped up with timber while the concrete dries. The bricks are then laid around the rods, and additional mortar is used to fill in the central cavity as you work. It is advisable to let the mortar set for seven days if the pillar is to support a roof or covering of some sort.

When building tall pillars or piers, embed a starter rod in the foundation and tie more reinforcing rods to it with galvanized wire.

BUILDING PILLARS AND PIERS

It is best to make free-standing pillars out of an even number of bricks, whether they are solid or hollow, and to make them square. Intermediate or end piers in walls can be an odd number of brick sizes a hollow square pier, with sides the width of three bricks, is a popular choice in half-brick walls, for example.

With piers in or on walls, there is a choice between bonding the brickwork of the pier to the bonding system of the actual wall, or cutting bricks in half in alternate courses and leaving a vertical joint at the sides of the pier and then reinforcing the horizontal courses with expanded metal or wall ties.

Leaving a vertical joint has the advantage that it can be used to create

Left: Brick pillars have been used to support a wooden pergola over a patio. The same technique could also be used for a carport.

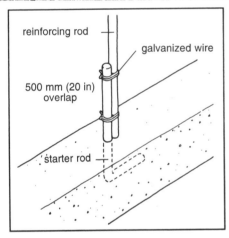

reinforcing rod

galvanized wire

500 mm (20 in) overlap

starter rod

Above: In long high walls like this one movement joints and supporting piers need to be placed at regular intervals.

Right: The brickwork of the pier has been bonded to the half-brick wall.

Below: Expanded metal used to reinforce the joint between piers and wall.

Bottom left: Movement or control joint. Half of the metal strip has been greased to prevent a bond.

Left: 'Starter rod' reinforcement is required for tall pillars and piers. The starter rod is concreted in place.

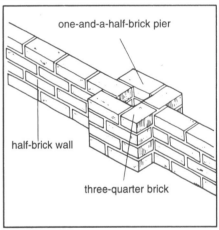

one-and-a-half-brick pier

half-brick wall

three-quarter brick

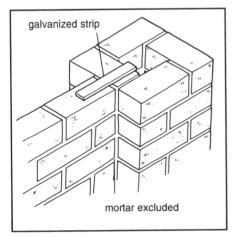

galvanized strip

mortar excluded

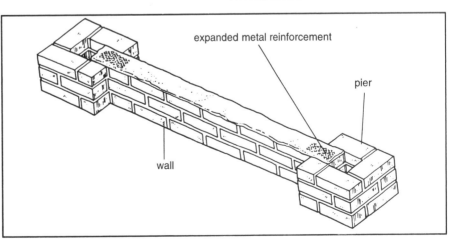

expanded metal reinforcement

pier

wall

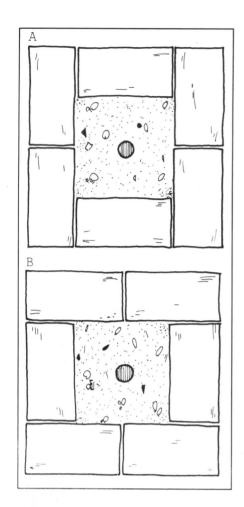
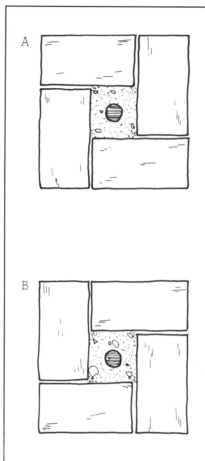
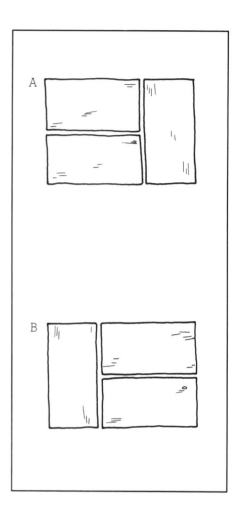

Left: The diagram shows the brick courses for pillars and piers. Lay one course as in A, one as in B, one as in A and so on until the full height of the pillar is achieved. This ensures proper bonding.

a movement (or 'control') joint in longer walls. Here, mortar is left out of the vertical joint and a flat strip of galvanized metal laid in the horizontal joints with one half of it lightly greased. This allows the wall to expand and contract along its length but supports it in a sideways direction. The sides of the otherwise open vertical joint are filled with non-setting mastic.

Step-by-step pillar
For a hollow pillar, 900 mm (3 ft) high (minus brick pavers), with a foundation 600 x 400 mm (2 ft x 16 in) and 110 mm (4¹/₂ in) deep,you will need:

Foundation
10 kg or ¹/₅ bag (22 lb) cement
25 kg or ¹/₂ cu ft (55 lb) sand
40 kg or 1 cu ft (66 lb) aggregate

Brickwork
50 bricks
5 brick pavers
10 kg (22 lb) cement
40 kg or 1 cu ft (88 lb) builder's sand
5 kg (11 lb) lime
OR 10 ml (¹/₃ fl oz) plasticizer
Metal reinforcing rod, about 1 m
 (3ft 3 in) long

Render
8 kg (18 lb) cement
48 kg or 1¹/₄ cu ft (106 lb) builder's
 sand
4 kg (9 lb) lime
OR 8 ml (¹/₄ fl oz) plasticizer

1 An area of 600 x 600 mm (2 ft sq) must be excavated for a free-standing four-brick course pillar, but this pier is attached to the wall and was built at the same time. Lay the foundation first and allow it to dry. Set out the first course of bricks without mortar.
2 Ensure the corners of the pillar are at exactly 90° to each other. Once you have laid the first course, check the corners with a builder's square and the height with a gauge rod. Use a spirit

Left: The piers blend well with the wall.

level to ensure each course is level.
3 A reinforcing rod is inserted into the still-wet mortar which has been poured into the central cavity of the pier. The top of the rod extends to the finished level of the wall and the pier. To keep it from falling over, prop up the rod with timber and continue to work around it.
4 The completed pillar is bonded to the wall and could be used as a support for a gate. Both the pillar and the wall have been rendered (pargeted) and then washed with diluted paint. Brick pavers are used to top the pillars.

ARCHES

While solid walls provide privacy and protection, arches at entrances can add visual interest to the garden.

Location

Arches may be introduced in several ways – to frame an entrance, add interest to a wall or to provide a framework for climbers. It is not usually advisable to construct a single arch – unless it has a sense of purpose it will simply look out of place. So, decide whether your arch will bridge a functional opening, separate sections of the plot or offer support for plants.

Construction

Building an archway is a project that needs to be tackled very carefully, particularly if it is to span a wide opening. The most common method is to work with a supporting formwork (also called former or a turning-piece), which is cut in the shape of a semicircle or, where a less pronounced effect is desired, as a smaller segment of a circle (a segmental arch).

A semicircular arch is simpler to set out and to build – a segmental arch means some geometrical drawing and the wall bricks on either side have to be shaped to take the first arch bricks (which will not be horizontal). The formwork may be made up of two pieces of chipboard or plywood nailed together, but separated with blocks of wood around the edges. This is positioned where the arch is to be constructed, and bricks are laid over it.

Formwork for semicircular arches

The formula for setting out an arch in a semicircle is simple: half the span of the opening equals the rise of the arch.

The base of the completed formwork must be equal in width to the span and must line up with (and therefore mark) the baseline of the rise.

Below: An arch built into a wall is an unusual way to frame features such as this gargoyle fountain.

To draw the shape, lay your board flat on the ground and mark out a semicircle with a pencil attached to a piece of string, measuring the rise as half the width of the span. Cut out the shape with a jigsaw and then use it as a template to cut a second piece.

Now lay one cut-out piece of board flat and line the inside edges with blocks of wood, approximately the same thickness (less the thickness of the boards) as the wall. Cover with the second piece of board and nail this to each block; then turn over the board

pronounced curve. When making the formwork for such an arch, include a little extra below the baseline of the rise, for ease of handling.

Decide on the height of the riser, which should not be less than a sixth of the span (for the purpose of this explanation, 900 mm [3 ft]). Lay out the board and draw a straight 900 mm (3 ft) baseline from A to B (see diagram). Mark the centre point and draw a second line at right angles through it. Measure the height of your rise (150 mm [6 in]) from the same centre point and mark C. Draw a line from A to C, bisect and draw another perpendicular line through the new centre point. The point at which it intersects your original perpendicular line, E, is the base point for drawing a segment of the circle, using the method for semicircular arches.

Note that if the rise had been 250 mm (10 in) to F, G would then mark the base point for drawing the circle.

Building the arch

While the construction of an arch may seem like a formidable task, it is possible for a novice bricklayer to master the skills required by following a few basic rules.

Once the formwork has been made, place it in position in the wall opening, supported by a timber framework constructed from pieces of wood at least 100 x 50 mm (4 x 2 in). Pairs of wedges are placed under the frame to ensure that the formwork is absolutely level at the correct height (these also help when removing the formwork once the arch has been built).

If the former has not been marked with the brick positions before putting it in place, these can be marked by laying the bricks 'dry' with wedges in between to represent the mortar courses. If you are continuing upwards with the wall over the arch, check with a gauge rod that the top of the keystone will line up with the first full course of bricks.

It is best to build up the arch evenly from both sides to prevent it being pushed out of position as you lay the bricks, check that they are in the correct place (i.e. lined up with the marks on the former) and use a spirit level (or straightedge) to ensure that

Above: A striking arch which adds visual interest to the gate while providing a framework for the plants to grow over. Right: This diagram shows how to set out a segmental arch geometrically.

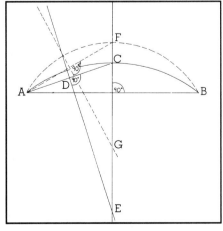

and attached blocks, and nail on the remaining board. Cover the edge with hardboard, nailing to secure it firmly.

Formwork for segmental arches

While designed along the same principles as a semicircular arch, a segmental arch gives a less

1

2

3

4

5

6

each face of the arch is level with the faces of the former.

The last block to go into place is the 'keystone' at the very top. Make sure this is firmly in place and leave the mortar to dry for at least three days before removing the former.

Step-by-step arch
To make the formwork, you will need:

1,200 mm (3 ft 11 in) chipboard
50 mm (2 in) square wood, cut into a 1.2 m (4 ft) length
Strip of hardboard, whose width equals the thickness of the arch and whose length is 1:6 times the arch width
75 mm (3 in) wire nails to nail chipboard and blocks together
40 mm (1½ in) wire nails to nail hardboard onto formwork
Bricks/blocks
Apart from a separate keystone, you can use the same bricks or blocks that you are using for building the wall to make the arch.

1 Using one of the methods described, draw the shape of the formwork onto the board and cut two with a jigsaw.
2 Cut the square length of wood into six blocks, each 190 mm (7½ in) long, and nail these in place between the two pieces of board.
3 Cut a strip of hardboard to fit the perimeter of the arc and nail it on to the wooden blocks lining the edge of the formwork. This gives a smooth surface over which the bricks are laid.
4 Using the gauge rod, work out the position of the blocks to be laid over the top of the formwork. Avoid cutting blocks by making mortar joints thicker. Mark the formwork as a guide.
5 Before the arch former is made, the wall needs to be built up to the level of the bottom of the arch.
6 Wedges can be used to position the blocks around the former so that lines can be drawn back to the centre of the circle showing the position of the block.
7 Blocks are laid in mortar from either side, checking they have the correct alignment and are level with the face of the former.
8 The last block to go into place is the keystone – here one three courses deep and standing slightly proud of the surrounding blockwork for effect.

7

8

CONCRETE BLOCK STEPS

These instructions are for basic steps. For three steps 1,800 mm (6 ft) wide with 200 mm (8in) risers and 500 mm (20in) treads, you will need:

55 curbstones
110 concrete paving blocks

Foundation/sub-base

35 kg or $^2/_3$ bag (77 lb) cement
90 kg or $2^1/_4$ cu ft (200 lb) sand
140 kg or 3 cu ft (308 lb) aggregate
100 kg or $2^1/_2$ cu ft (220 lb) concreting sand
200 kg or 4 cu ft (440 lb) hardcore

1 Excavate two side brick walls.
2 Wooden formwork is used to form the concrete for the riser curbstones.
3 Concrete is shovelled into the formwork and roughly levelled off.
4 Once the concrete has set (allow three days), remove the formwork.
5 Use a string line to position the curbstones, placed on a mortar bed.
6 Lay all the curbstones.
7 Now shovel in a mixture of small stones and finer granular material.
8 Compact the sub-base thoroughly until it is at the required depth.
9 Shovel fine concreting sand in and compact this with the hand compactor. Lay two screeding rails 60 mm ($2^1/_2$ in) below the finished step height.
10 Screed off the sand; remove rails.
11 Use a block splitter (masonry saw) to cut blocks for filling in small gaps.
12 Lay the paving blocks.
13 Compact sand with the compactor, using wood to protect the blocks.
14 Brush fine sand across the blocks, .
15 Compact to force sand in between the joints and to level the blocks.

1

5

2

6

3

4

7

8

11

14

9

12

15

10

13

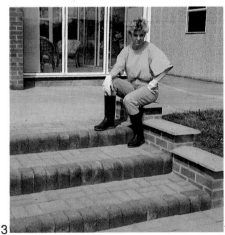

16

DRIVEWAYS

A solid concrete, brick or concrete paving block driveway not only makes a good first impression but also provides a surface on which you can park a car or van. The driveway needs to be especially well constructed with proper foundations. If it is not, the new surface will soon get uneven or cracked and will look unsightly.

Although it is certainly hard work, laying a new drive is a job well within the capabilities of an enthusiatic handyman (preferably with an equally enthusiatic helper), though some specialised equipment will need to be hired, for instance a concrete mixer for solid concrete drives and a plate vibrator and block splitter (masonry saw) for concrete block driveways.

PLANNING
Although the actual siting of a driveway will usually be fairly obvious (typically between the road and the garage or leading to the front door of the house if there is no garage) or you may not even have a choice of position, there are several very important points to bear in mind when choosing the size and the exact location of the drive.

The drive must be wide enough so that the car doors can be opened with sufficient room for people to get in and out and, if between garage and road, long enough so that the garage doors can be opened and the front gates closed with the car in position. In addition, the drive should not slope so much that the car 'bottoms' as it moves from the garage to the drive or from the drive to the road.

For a driveway in front of the house, you will want to ensure that parked cars do not obscure natural daylight and do not obstruct access to the front or back entrances of the house. Ideally, the drive should not be so near to the house that the walls can be stained by exhaust fumes or that fumes waft in through open windows, and should not be too close to the neighbouring houses.

Above: The herringbone pattern of the walls is repeated in the drive. Left: An original circular brick pattern is used for this drive.

MATERIALS
Solid concrete is hard-wearing when properly laid and can be attractive if given a textured finish. Concrete is, however, susceptible to oil stains and although inexpensive is not easy to lay properly, especially on a slope. For information on how to lay a concrete slab, see page 118: a concrete drive

needs to be at least 100 mm (4 in) thick or 150 mm (6 in) if on clay or other soft soil.

Concrete paving blocks give the strength of concrete but can be laid attractively in patterns (see page 80). They are laid on compacted sand with 100 mm (4 in) crushed stone as a sub-base. Fine sand is brushed on to the surface and compacted to 'lock' the blocks together by getting into the joints. No cement or mortar is needed, but blocks must be positioned between firm edgings to keep them in place.

The most common size of concrete block is 200 mm (8 in) long, 100 mm (4 in) wide and 65 mm (2½ in) thick. The four common laying patterns are stretcher bond (similar to that used for a brick wall), parquet (basketweave), 45° herringbone and 90° herringbone. See page 80 for examples.

Asphalt is often used for drives because it resists oil spills. However, it can be expensive to lay and is a job best left to a specialist contractor.

Concrete paving slabs can be used to construct a drive, but the necessary

'hydraulically-pressed' type and the deep foundations needed make laying a drive difficult and expensive.

Bricks can be used for constructing drives as they are quite strong (especially if laid on edge) but they may have to be the frost-free type. They can be laid on mortar, but need proper foundations.

Gravel is an attractive and inexpensive material for a drive and easy to maintain as you simply shovel on more gravel. It also copes well with oil spills, but in time can become untidy. Gravel

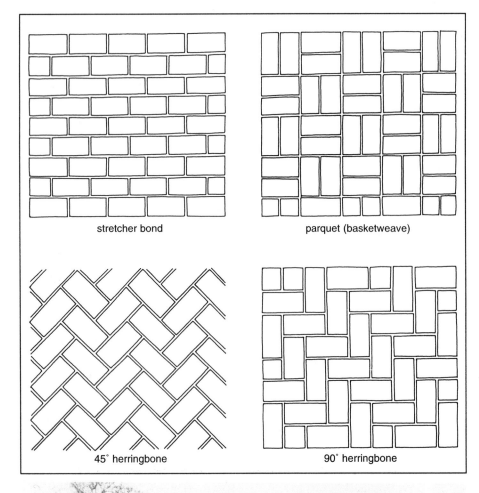

stretcher bond

parquet (basketweave)

45° herringbone

90° herringbone

is best used with other materials – perhaps as an oil trap in a paved or concreted area.

PRINCIPLES
Installing a drive means following some important constructional principles.
• The area to be paved must have a firm, well-compacted base to prevent the paving sagging and/or cracking.
• The drive surface must have a slope to carry rainwater away across and along the surface. If the drive slopes towards the house or garage, a drainage channel must be included.
• Drives which are constructed from bricks or blocks must have proper edging restraint to prevent them from breaking up at the edges.

FOUNDATIONS
Most drives need a foundation of at least 100 mm (4 in) of crushed stone, quarry waste or 'hoggin' (clayey gravel) do not use normal hardcore. The sub-base must be well-compacted. For concrete block drives, this is covered with a 65 mm (2½ in) layer of fine concreting sand which is compacted down to 50 mm (2 in).

DRAINAGE
The minimum drainage crossfall for a drive is 1 in 40 (25 mm m or 3 in/10 ft). If you do not ensure a proper slope, water will collect and may damage house walls. If possible, there should also be a fall of 1 in 100 (10 mm/m or 1 in/8 ft).

The rainwater needs to be disposed of properly. For a large drive draining into the garden or a drive sloping back towards the garage, you will need to incorporate drainage channels to collect it, connected to underground drainage pipes to take it to a soakaway or storm drain not to a drain leading to a sewer, cesspool or septic tank.

Drainage channels can be pre-cast concrete, fibre-cement sections, in situ concrete, bricks or plastic with a metal grid on top.

Left: A complicated but rewarding pattern known as 'hopsack'.

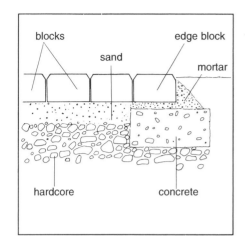

EDGING

When making a brick or concrete block drive, a firm edging, mortared in place, must be provided to prevent the bricks at the sides cracking or falling out. The edging can be the same material as the drive, or pre-cast concrete edging strip. Either way, it needs to be installed with the correct drainage fall and is put in before the main paving material – which makes calculating the exact size of the drive crucial.

Below: A brick drive in herringbone.

SITE PREPARATION

All soil, vegetation (including tree roots) and old drive materials must be removed from the site. For concrete drives, the depth of excavation needs to be 200 to 250 mm (8 to 10 in) below the final finished surface; for concrete block drives around 215 mm (8½ in).

Make sure that the base of the hole has the correct drainage fall from the start so that an even layer of sub-base material can be put down.

TOOLS AND EQUIPMENT

The tools needed for constructing a concrete drive are the same as those needed for laying a concrete slab (see page 118); a compacting machine would be useful for the sub-base.

For a concrete block drive, you will need normal bricklaying tools, but here a plate vibrator and a block splitter (masonry saw) are essential pieces of equipment to be hired.

Below: Using a plate vibrator to compact paving slabs.

Bottom: It is important to protect the finished paving while using a block splitter.

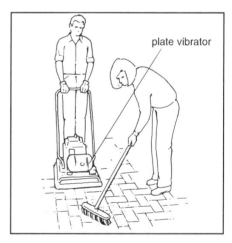

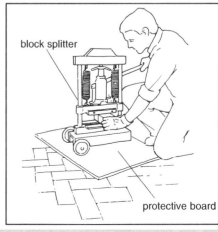

Step-by-step concrete block drive

For a drive 4 m (13 ft) by 8 m (26 ft), you will need 1600 paving blocks (100 x 200 x 65 mm [4 x 8 x 2½ in]) and:

Sub-base/foundation

5½ tonnes or 110 ft³ (5½ tons) hoggin, Type 1 base material or similar
3 tonnes or 70 ft³ (3 tons) sand
67 kg or 1⅓ bags (145 lb) cement
170 kg or 4¼ ft³ (375 lb) concreting sand
280 kg or 5½ ft³ (620 lb) aggregate

Mortar

25 kg or ½ bag (55 lb) cement
110 kg or 3 cu ft (240 lb) builder's sand
13 kg (28 lb) lime
OR 25 ml (1 fl oz) plasticizer

1 Dig out the foundations to the required depth with the correct slope and tamp the soil down with a hand compactor – a large weight on a pole. Do not disturb any pipes or cables.
2 Shovel in the hoggin or crushed stone to a depth of 100 mm (4 in), raking it out so that it is level.
3 The plate vibrator is then used to compact the sub-base.
4 Install the edging blocks and mortar in place onto concrete 75 to 100 mm (3 to 4 in) deep: measure carefully to ensure the edging blocks are spaced to take the block pattern using an exact number of block widths and to make sure they are laid to the correct fall across or along the drive. A 'fillet' of mortar is placed outside the edging to hold them in place. Let the mortar set.
5 The sub-base should be 115 mm (4½ in) below the level of the edging. To estimate the thickness of sand, lay a small area 65 mm (2½ in) deep, place some concrete blocks on it and compact them with timber and a hammer. They should come down to just above the edge restraint. Work out whether you need more or less sand and make a shaped screeding board to use for the correct thickness. Rake the sand before using the screeding board.

Right: The completed drive has been neatly finished off at the edges and around the central drain.

1

3

2

4

5

6 Lay blocks starting at the bottom of a slope or one edge. Lay them on the sand, sliding them down the side of the blocks already in place for a snug fit. If laying a pattern where full blocks will not fit at the edges, leave a gap and continue. Work from the previously laid blocks (kneel on a board) and never from the sand. Cut edge blocks with a hammer and a wide-bladed cold chisel, or use a block splitter (masonry saw) – mark a chalk line on the block for the cut, put it in the splitter and cut. Lay all edging blocks until the whole surface is covered (or about 10 m² or 100 ft²).

Use the plate vibrator to lower the blocks' surface by compacting the sand and levelling the blocks, forcing sand into the joints to secure them. If vibrating a partly laid drive, stay 1 m (3 ft 3 in) away from the laying face or the blocks will be disturbed. Two or three passes are necessary to get the blocks to the correct height; if any crack, replace them.

7 Brush fine joint-filling sand over the drive and make two passes with the vibrator to force this into the joints.

6

7

SEAT AND TABLE

Built-in outdoor furniture simplifies seating for outdoor entertaining, takes up little room, and adds to the value of your home. Instead of having to move chairs and tables outside, the basic equipment is already there. All you need do is add cushions for comfort.

LOCATION

The design of furniture and its location will depend on your requirements. If you want a place to sit and relax, away from normal household activities, you will probably want a simple yet comfortable bench tucked away in a quiet corner. But if you plan to use the furniture for entertaining or for family meals, it will have to meet entirely different needs.

The most common location for this type of furniture is on patios, especially when barbecues are included. Other spots where people congregate regularly, for example paved areas around ponds or pools, are obvious sites for both benches and tables.

Materials

Any furniture left outdoors permanently should be made from weather-proof materials. Brick and stone are certainly very durable and ideal for the basic supporting structure

Wood is a good option for table tops and seats, and it can look very attractive combined with brick. Alternatively, a practical outdoor table can be made by topping a strong, stocky pillar with a smooth, pre-cast concrete slab. Keep the bricklaying to a minimum by building a bench alongside a retaining or screen wall, using the wall to form the backrest of the bench and adding simple timber slats for the seat.

For this simple project, a raft or slab foundation was used, covering the base of the whole area of the structure. This type of foundation is not as deep as a strip foundation, which is used to build walls. Here the foundation was 2,100 x 1,700 mm (6 ft 11 in x 5 ft 7 in) and 100 mm (4 in) deep.

Above: The perfect setting for a relaxed meal outside.

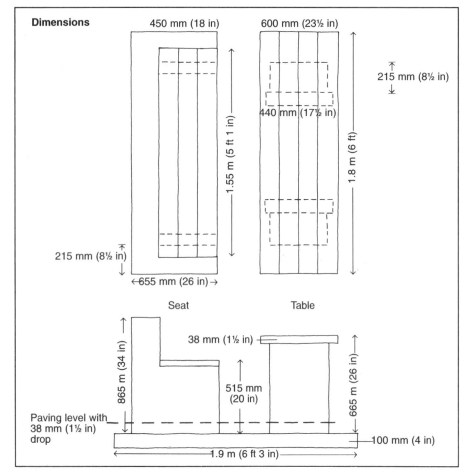

Foundation
75 kg (165 lb) cement
200 kg or 5 cu ft (440 lb) sand
300 kg or 6 cu ft (662 lb) aggregate

Brickwork
410-450 bricks
66 kg (11/2 x 100 lb bags) cement
396 kg or 10 cu ft (873 lb) sand
33 kg (73 lb) lime
OR 66 ml (2 fl oz) plasticizer
11 pieces of wood, 150 x 38 mm (6 x 1½ in) (length for table 4 x 1,800 mm [5 ft 11 in], 2 x 570 mm [22 in]; for seat 3 x 1,550 mm [5 ft 1 in], 2 x 420 mm [16½ in])
22 x No. 8 x 75 mm (3 in) coach screws (screwspikes) (12 for table, 10 for seat)

1 Peg out the area required for your seat and table, allowing an extra 100 to 200 mm (4 to 8 in) on all four sides to accommodate the slab foundation. Excavate to a depth of 100 mm (4 in) – about the depth of a brick on edge.

Make sure your surface is level before you mix the concrete and lay the foundation. Check levels by placing a brick at each corner and using a spirit level placed on a long straight-edge.

2 Mix cement, sand and aggregate in a ratio of 1:2½:3½. Spread the concrete over the entire area, levelling with a spade. Leave the bricks in the corners to keep the concrete surface level.

3 Once the concrete is dry, lay a one-brick wall for the seat. Use a straight-edge and spirit level to keep the back wall level. Check with the builder's square that corners are at 90°.

4 Build up two courses at the corners, using a spirit level to check horizontal and vertical surfaces. Use a gauge rod to ensure brick courses are regular.

5 Start building up the two pillars which will support the wooden table top. It is easiest to work on the bench and table simultaneously, gradually building up all the walls. Stretcher bond is used for these two features which both have wooden strip surfaces. From the foundation level, the seat back is built up to 11 courses, the seat itself to seven courses and the table up to nine

courses. When planning the final levels, remember that two of these courses may be below the final paving.

Strips of wood are screwed together and fitted across the walls for the seat. Thinner brick pavers are used to finish off the top and ends of the seating as the wood does not extend to the edges. The table is built in a similar way, but with an extra piece of wood. The cross pieces are cut to slot in on the inside of the two piers, to prevent the table top from sliding from side to side and to reinforce the seat.

An attractive and useful storage box with a hinged lid doubles as a bench on a compact but much used patio. Large enough to house cushions and other bulky items which might be damaged by rain, it is built on a solid concrete slab (see page 118), and against an existing wall, which is not shown on the illustration. You will require an additional 39 bricks as well as an extra 10 kg of cement and sand for mortar if you need to construct the back wall of a freestanding storage box. Facebricks should be used to build the basic structure, while any good quality timber recommended for exterior use may be used for the lid. If a soft wood (like pine) is chosen, it may be necessary to use thicker slats to prevent any possible buckling.

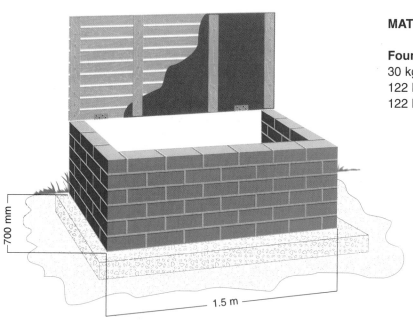

MATERIALS

Foundation
30 kg cement
122 kg sand
122 kg stone

Brickwork
72 facebricks (+ 39 if required)
25 kg cement (+ 10 kg if required)
12.5 kg lime (optional)
100 kg sand (+ 10 kg if required)

Lid
1.5 m x 710 mm x 6 mm sheet exterior-grade plywood
9 x 1.5 m x 70 mm x 40 mm slats
4 x 700 mm x 70 mm x 20 mm crosspieces
15 mm panel pins
36 x 50 mm brass screws
2 brass butt hinges with brass screws and Rawl plugs
waterproof wood glue

1 Measure and mark a 1.6 m x 800 mm area for the foundation. Dig to a depth of 100 mm; then compact and level the ground.
2 Mix the concrete and place over the foundation area. Allow to set overnight.
3 Lay the brick walls of the box using stretcher bond. Allow the mortar to set thoroughly.
4 Meanwhile, assemble the lid. First cut five shallow channels across the width of each of the 1.5 m slats to aid drainage. Then position these lengths, with the grooves

facing upward, on a solid surface so that you have 10 mm gaps between each. Glue and tack the plywood on top using a good quality waterproof wood glue and panel pins. When the glue is dry, position the four 700 mm crosspieces evenly across the ply, so that those at each end are flush with the edges. Glue and then screw through the timber to secure the slats.
5 When the glue is completely dry and the mortar thoroughly set, screw the hinges to the lid and then affix to the wall using screws and Rawl plugs.

PATIO PLANTER

Plain, goodlooking and easy to build, this raised and freestanding planter will add visual interest to any patio. Furthermore, its dimensions are easily altered and it could be increased in size to suit the style and shape of your paved outdoor area. Although this planter can be built on a strip foundation, it is simpler to throw a slab (see page 118), placing bricks on the ground and then removing them to create instant drainage holes once the concrete has almost set. With a structure this size, wastage of concrete is minimal. If building on an existing patio, you will need to chop out some of the bricks to enable water to drain away.

MATERIALS

Foundation
20 kg cement
80 kg sand
80 kg stone

Brickwork
66 facebricks
11 paving bricks
20 kg cement
10 kg lime (optional)
80 kg sand

1 Measure out an area 800 mm x 1 m and peg out. Dig a 100 mm deep foundation.
2 Mix the concrete and, before laying, set two or three bricks in the centre of the proposed structure. Lay the slab and allow the concrete to set. Before it becomes totally hard, remove the bricks.
3 Start laying the bricks using stretcher bond. Create weepholes in the second course by excluding every second vertical joint. Piping can be inserted if more substantial drainage is required.
4 Lay as many courses as required and top with a final course of pavers.
5 If you wish, seal the interior walls of the planter with a bitumen-based product to prevent future discoloration of the bricks by constant moisture.

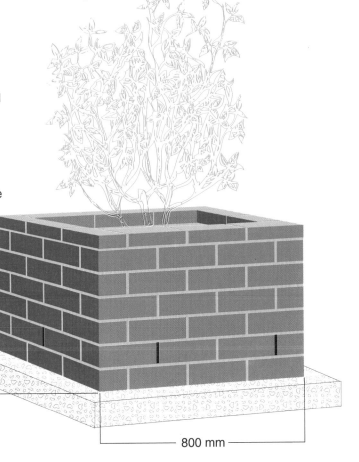

686 mm

800 mm

SIMPLE SEATING

Delightfully rustic seating alongside the house not only provides a resting place, but also adds character to the plain wall. Simple to build, this is a perfect weekend project for the DIYer. These two seats are built from facebrick, but the same design could be rendered and painted. Although quantities specified call for a solid concrete core in each seat, you can save on materials by filling the central gap with sand to about the height of the fourth brick course, compacting well and then topping with concrete.

MATERIALS

Foundations
20 kg cement
80 kg sand
80 kg stone

Brickwork
60 bricks
15 kg cement
7.5 kg lime (optional)
60 kg sand

Woodwork
6 x 125 mm x 22 mm
   x 500 mm for seats
6 x 70 mm x 22 mm
   x 500 mm for back rests
36 x 40 mm brass screws
   with Rawl plugs

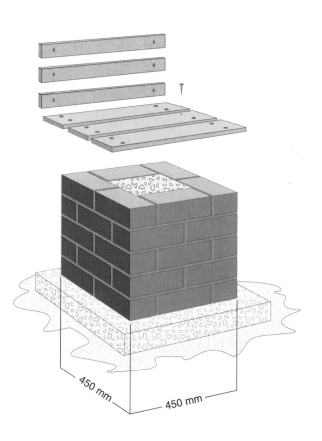

450 mm
450 mm

1 Measure out the two seats and peg the area required for foundations. Dig to a depth of 100 mm.
2 Mix half the concrete and lay the slab (see page 118). Allow to set thoroughly overnight.
3 Build the base plinth using stretcher bond. Leave until the mortar has set.
4 Mix a new batch of concrete and place in the centre of the brickwork. Compact well and level the upper surface.
5 When the concrete is well set, screw the seat timbers to the side walls, using two screws at the ends of each board.
6 Screw the narrow back rest timbers to the adjacent wall, ensuring they are evenly spaced.

CORNER PLANTER

An attractive corner planter not only adds interest to the wall, giving it a more professional finish, but it also allows for visual access, which is particularly important at busy street corners. Built with precast concrete blocks, this design is part of a rendered wall and most appropriate if used around the boundary of a property. As the structure is outside the garden itself, it is advisable to choose shrubs and plants which will not demand much maintenance. Materials specified will allow you to build the wall and planter plus about 3.5 m of wall on either side.

MATERIALS

Foundations
320 kg cement
1 m³ sand
1 m³ stone

Blockwork
408 x 390 mm x 190 mm x 190 mm
  concrete blocks, about 40 halved
  and broken
135 kg cement
68 kg lime (optional)
0.65 m³ sand

Mortar for rendering
320 kg cement
160 kg lime (optional)
1.6m³ sand

1 Mark out the position of the wall and planter as illustrated, leaving the base of the planter untouched.
2 Dig the foundation trenches to a depth of a minimum of 250 mm.
3 Mix the concrete in a cement:sand:stone ratio of 1:4:4 with water and place in the trenches. Compact, level and leave to set overnight.
4 Build the wall and planter using stretcher bond. The planter should be four courses high and the wall itself 12 courses high.
5 Use half blocks and broken pieces to build the capping along the top.
6 Once the mortar has set, render the wall and finish off the capping to create a neat, sloping finish as illustrated.
7 When the mortar has set thoroughly and is completely dry, paint the wall.

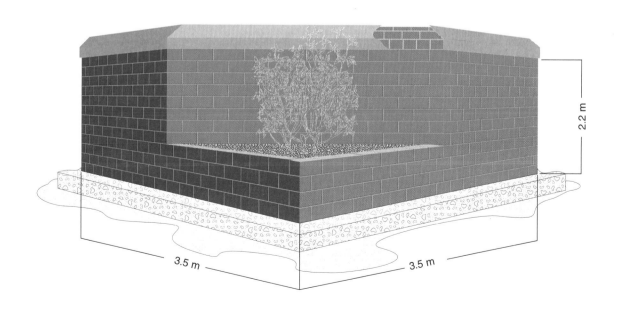

2.2 m

3.5 m   3.5 m

CURVED SEAT AND WALL

This practical screen wall is built on a curve to add character to a patio or utility area. The adjacent seat, which curves alongside the wall, may be used as a resting spot or to display pot plants. Although this design has been roughly bagged with cement to give it a rustic feel, it could also be rendered for a more formal effect, or built with facebricks to match the walls of the house. The seat has been topped with tiles to finish it off; if facebricks are used for construction, paving bricks may be a better option. The materials listed will allow you to build the seat and a 1.2 m high wall which is about 3.2 m long.

MATERIALS

Foundations
70 kg cement
280 kg sand
280 kg stone

Brickwork
437 bricks
24 brick-sized tiles
 (or paving bricks)
150 kg cement
75 kg lime (optional)
600 kg sand

1 Measure the line the wall will follow and peg out the foundations as shown on the illustration. Measure and peg out the area required for the adjacent seat. Dig to a depth of 250 mm. Compact and level the earth.
2 Mix the concrete and lay the foundation for both the wall and seat. Allow the concrete to set before continuing with the brickwork.
3 Lay the bricks for the one-brick wall first, using an English bond with alternate courses of headers and stretchers. Then lay the bricks for the seat. Allow the mortar to set.
4 If desired, mix a small amount of mortar, adding more water than usual, and smear the mixture onto the wall with sacking to achieve a thin, "bagged" finish.
5 Once all the mortar has set thoroughly, top the seat with tiles as illustrated, cutting those at the back to fit. Finally, paint the structure.

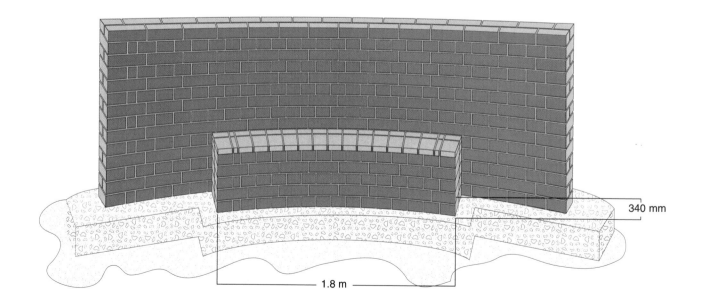

340 mm

1.8 m

PERIOD-STYLE BENCH

An elegant, period-style bench can be constructed in the garden by anyone with basic bricklaying skills. Smoothly rendered with a mortar mix and then painted, it will soon look like a beautifully sculpted piece of garden furniture. This design is built with ordinary bricks, using the simple stretcher bond. The central cavity, which forms the seat of the structure, may be filled with rubble, even though materials listed here call for sand. Whatever material is used must be well compacted before being topped with a layer of concrete, which is skimmed with mortar to create a smooth finish.

MATERIALS

Foundations
100 kg cement
405 kg sand
405 kg stone

Brickwork
207 bricks
50 kg cement
25 kg lime (optional)
200 kg sand

Mortar for rendering
20 kg cement
10 kg lime (optional)
80 kg sand

Seating slab
0.6 m³ sand or fill
15 kg cement
60 kg sand
60 kg stone

1 Choose the position of the seat and peg out a rectangle 2.2 m x 1.2 m. Excavate to a depth of about 150 mm.
2 Mix the concrete in the ratio 1:4:4 and then lay to create a slab foundation (see page 118). Allow to set thoroughly – at least overnight.
3 Build the walls to form the basic structure of the seat, as illustrated below.
4 When the mortar has set, fill the central cavity with sand or fill. Compact well.
5 Mix the concrete for the seating slab and lay over the compacted sand. Leave to set thoroughly.
6 Finally, render the outside walls of the structure with a 1:4 mortar mix, filling in all gaps between the bricks.

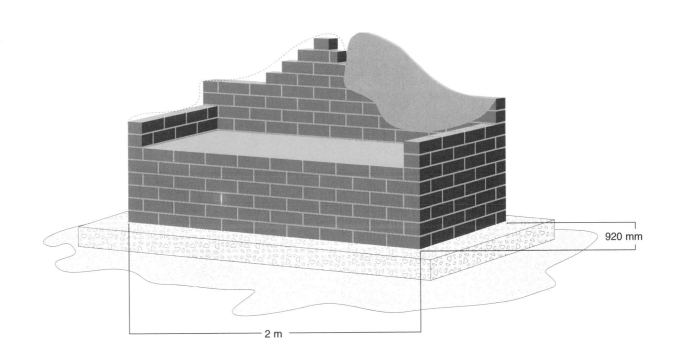

920 mm

2 m

SMART SLATE STEPS

A formal garden staircase, which is a feature in itself, has been rendered and painted and the treads topped with attractive slate tiles to blend with the architecture of a large house. Relatively deep 600 mm treads combine with minimal risers up the slight slope. Although the project specifies 290 mm x 90 mm x 90 mm concrete blocks, the steps may be built with bricks or blocks of a different size. If you do need to adapt the materials, some of the other materials and the proportions may vary. You may also prefer to tile the treads with ceramic, terracotta or quarry tiles. All are suitable provided they have a matt, non-slip finish. Refer back to page 76 for more detailed information on building steps.

MATERIALS

- 190 x 290 mm x 90 mm x 90 mm blocks (some broken)
- 175 kg cement (about 75 kg for foundations and 70 kg for render)
- 50 kg lime
- 700 kg or 0.5 m³ sand
- 300 kg or 0.2 m³ stone
- 100 x 300 mm x 300 mm slate tiles
- 4 x 500 mm x 500 mm slate tiles
- 20 kg cement-based tile adhesive
- 2 x sealed light fittings with conduit (optional)

1 Peg out the 4 m wide staircase, marking the position of the two front pillars.

2 Dig two 490 mm x 490 mm foundation trenches, 50 mm deep, for the pillars, and a 3 m x 190 mm trench of the same depth for the wall which will form the first riser.

3 Mix the concrete using a cement:sand:stone ratio of 1:4:4 and place in the holes. Allow to set thoroughly. If lighting is to be installed, set conduiting in place before placing the concrete.

4 Build the two lower pillars five courses high and lay the two courses of the bottom step in stretcher bond, about 50 mm in from the edge of the concrete.

5 When the mortar has set, cut away the earth behind to form a rough second step.

6 Dig a second foundation trench for the next riser wall and fill it with concrete.

7 Once the concrete has set, fill the gap between this and the front wall and compact the fill so that the surface is about 25 mm below the top of the front bricks. Top with concrete.

8 Repeat this procedure for each riser, building up the side walls at the same time.

9 Build two more pillars at the top of the steps.

10 Use broken blocks to fill in the slope of the walls between the top and bottom pillars. Allow the mortar to set.

11 If light fittings are required, install them or have them fitted now.

12 Render the side walls and risers with a 2:1:8 mixture of cement, lime and sand.

13 When the rendering has set, tile the treads and the top of the pillars. Grout the tiles with a little mortar.

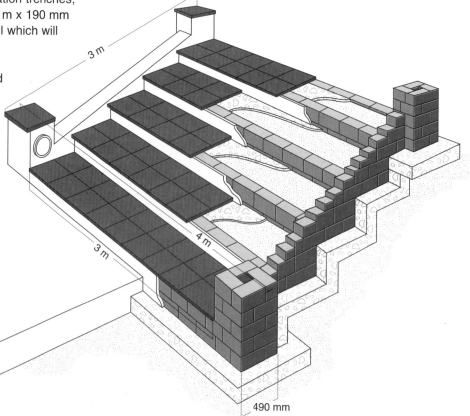

PLANNED FOR PLANTING

A sturdy boundary wall built with concrete blocks incorporates planters in alternate sections of the structure. The wall is constructed between attractive pillars, and the sections which back the planters are stepped back by 700 mm. As this design is imposing in effect, it is particularly well suited to a large property, but could be adapted for just about any location. Materials specified are sufficient for a 6.5 m-long section of wall, as illustrated in the plan.

MATERIALS

Foundations
365 kg cement
1.6 m³ sand
1.6 m³ stone

Blockwork
185 x 390 mm x 190 mm x
  190 mm concrete blocks
60 kg cement
30 kg lime (optional)

365 kg (0.3 m³) sand
brickforce (optional)

Mortar for rendering
150 kg cement
75 kg lime
0.7 m³ sand

1 Mark out the position of the wall as illustrated, with pillars at 3 m centres. Make sure the stepped-back sections are at right-angles to the pillars.

2 Mark the area of the foundations, allowing a width of 500 mm for the wall sections and 1 m x 1 m for the pillars.

3 Dig the foundation trenches to a depth of at least 250 mm.

4 Mix the concrete in a cement:sand:stone ratio of 1:4:4 and place it in the prepared trench. Make sure it is well compacted and level. Leave to set overnight.

5 Mix the mortar in a cement:sand ratio of 1:6, adding the lime if required.

6 Build the first four courses to form the base of the first pillar, using two full blocks as well as a third block split lengthwise in each course. This will make a solid, 800 mm-high base. Use two blocks per course for the rest of the pillar.

7 Build the wall sections in stretcher bond to a height of 8 courses, and the low planter wall to 2 courses. If 390 mm x 190 mm x 190 mm blocks are used, the wall will be about 200 mm thick once it has been rendered.

8 Use half blocks and broken blocks to build the capping on each pillar.

9 Once the mortar has set, render the surface, creating a lip on the top of the wall if you wish.

10 Ideally, keep the rendered surface damp for a few days before painting and planting.

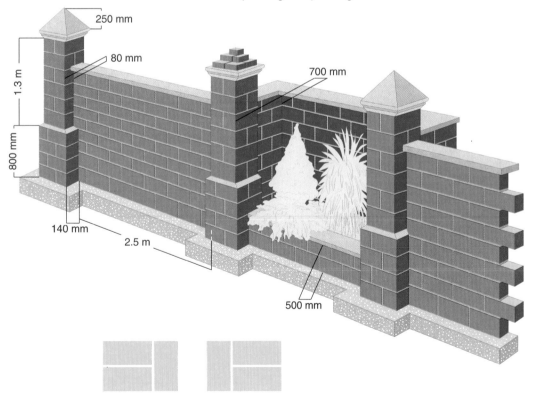

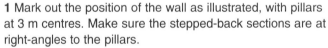

PLANTED STEPS

Expansive brick steps invite one to walk at a leisurely pace from one level to another in the garden. Two 1.5 m x 800 mm planters at the top of the steps, one on either side, are rendered and painted to add contrast and interest to the structure, and also incorporate light fittings. These planters, like the steps themselves, are topped with flat-faced bricks, although pavers could be used instead. The materials specified are sufficient for six steps, rising up a 5.5 m wide slope, but if you wish, the stairway could be extended at either end if the site is suitable.

MATERIALS

Steps
519 bricks
210 kg cement (about 70 kg
  for foundations)
850 kg or 0.5 m³ sand
70 kg lime
360 kg or 0.25 m³ stone
400 kg or 0.3 m³ fill, soil or
  sand

Planters
790 bricks
400 kg cement (about
  140 kg for foundations)
130 kg lime
1 625 kg or 1.2 m³ sand
560 kg or 0.4 m³ stone
2 x weatherproof light
  fittings with conduit
  (optional)

1 Measure out and peg a sloping area about 5.5 m wide and 2.2 m long from top to bottom.
2 At the lowest point, excavate a 5.5 m x 400 mm trench to a depth of about 50 mm.
3 Dig away the bank immediately behind the trench to form a rough step. Then fill the trench with concrete mixed in a 1:4:4 cement:sand:stone ratio and allow to set.
4 Lay a row of bricks 50 mm in from the front of the foundation slab to form a stretcher course.
5 Fill in behind the bricks with soil or sand, leaving space for a 25 mm layer of concrete, measuring 350 mm from front to back, on top. Compact the soil before laying the concrete to form a foundation for the front of the second tread.

6 When the concrete has set, lay bricks to form the tread as illustrated below.
7 Build a two-course wall in stretcher bond to form the next riser so that the top of the first course of bricks is at the same height as the top of the first tread.
8 Repeat steps 3, 5, 6 and 7.
9 Build the third step the same way. Then build the next two steps 3 m wide, centring them on the lower steps.
10 Dig away the slope on either side of the two 3 m wide steps and excavate an area of about 1.4 m x 900 mm to a depth of 50 mm below the top of the third step.
11 Erect formwork to prevent the bank from collapsing.
12 Place a few bricks in the centre of the planter to create drainage holes. Then mix concrete in a cement:sand:stone ratio of 1:4:4 and spread evenly over the entire area to a depth of 50 mm.
13 Allow the concrete to set overnight, but remove the bricks before it hardens too much.
14 To construct the planters, build up one-brick walls five courses high to form two rectangular 'boxes'.
15 Leave a gap in the front of the outer course to accommodate the light fitting, if required. Get an electrician to complete the installation before you go any further.
16 Now build the riser of the top step as for the previous steps.
17 Render the exposed, outer surface of the planters using a 2:1:8 cement:lime:sand mix.
18 When the mortar has set, lay bricks around the top of the planters and along the top tread.
19 Fill the base of both planters with broken bricks and stones, then fill with soil and plant.

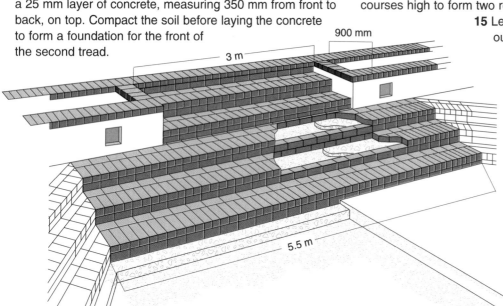

900 mm

3 m

5.5 m

ARCHED ENTRANCE

A charming, arched brick entrance, well within the capabilities of any competent DIY bricklayer, ties in to the boundary wall and incorporates two attractive planters. The generous proportions of the arch itself give the entrance an air of stature, suitable for both small and larger properties. Materials specified for this structure – which could also be rendered and painted rather than built in facebrick – do not include adjacent walls. Any additional brickwork you may wish to construct can be quickly quantified from the instructions provided on page 34.

MATERIALS

Foundation
70 kg cement
280 kg sand
280 kg stone

Brickwork
670 bricks
225 kg cement
112 kg lime (optional)
0.67 m³ (900 kg) sand

1 Peg out the foundations and dig to a depth of 250 mm. Compact and level the soil.
2 Place a few bricks at the base of the planters. Mix concrete in a cement: sand:stone ratio of 1:4:4 and place in the excavated trench. Allow to set partially, then remove the bricks and leave overnight.
3 Build up the walls, leaving a gap as wide as the length of a brick between the single-brick, 24-course-high back wall and the half-brick, eight-course-high front wall of the planter.
4 Build up the arch (see pages 72-75), using formwork made from chipboard and hardboard to support the bricks.
5 Top the front of the planters with a soldier course of bricks and the back wall with a header course.

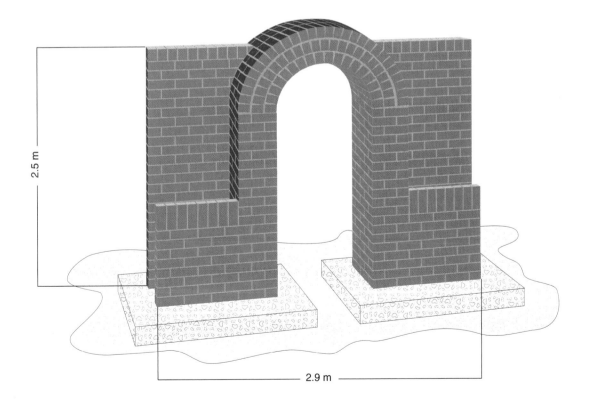

2.5 m

2.9 m

ARCHED PLANTER

This unusual arched planter has been built as a feature in a 2.65 m high garden boundary wall. While the central panel has simply been lightly bagged with a cement/sand slush, the curved wall and surrounding trim have been neatly rendered for effect. Decorated with a precast gargoyle and bowl, and planted with colourful annuals, this design will brighten a dull spot in any garden, big or small. If built on a solid concrete slab and properly waterproofed, it could even be adapted as a pond. Quantities specified do not include brickwork for the adjacent wall or its foundations.

MATERIALS

Foundation
50 kg cement
200 kg sand
200 kg stone

Brickwork
345 bricks
90 kg cement
45 kg lime (optional)
360 kg sand

Render
20 kg cement
10 kg lime (optional)
80 kg sand

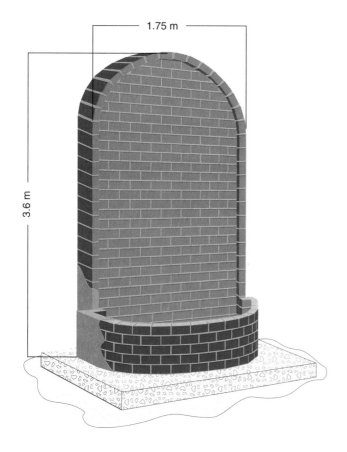

1 Measure and peg out the area required for the planter. Dig trenches for strip foundations to a depth of 250 mm; compact and level the earth.
2 Mix the concrete in a 1:4:4 cement:sand:stone ratio and place in the trenches. Allow to set thoroughly, at least overnight.
3 Unless the structure is to be freestanding, lay the back wall as illustrated, tying in to the garden wall. The first 26 courses require seven bricks in each course; thereafter, use a half brick less in each of the next four courses, and reduce by a full brick in the two top courses. Cut the bricks where necessary to achieve the arched effect.
4 Allow the mortar to set thoroughly. The surrounding trim may then be laid, using bricks on edge. These will protrude at the back and front of the wall.
5 Mix mortar in a 1:4 ratio for the render and finish off the trim and front wall. Add water to what is left of the mix and smear over the back wall with sacking.
6 When all the render has set, paint the structure, then attach a gargoyle and decorative planter bowl, if desired.
7 Fill the planter with soil, and plant.

BUILT FOR ENTERTAINING

This sleek but simple barbecue design incorporates seating on the perimeter of a brick paved patio. Built from facebricks, it has a sophisticated appeal which will suit the more formal garden plan. The pillar on one side may be used as a table, and there is room for storage of wood under the cooking surface. Although the materials specified call for a fibrecement pipe to help remove smoke from the chimney, a metal pipe may be used instead.

MATERIALS

Foundation
130 kg cement
520 kg sand
520 kg stone

Brickwork
514 bricks
50 paving bricks
175 kg cement

85 kg lime (optional)
0.85 m³ sand (including
　0.35 m³ for fill)
650 mm x 114 mm x 75 mm
　concrete lintel
600 mm x 600 mm x 50 mm
　concrete slab
1.8 m x 150 mm fibre-
　cement pipe

1 Measure and peg out the area where the barbecue and seating are to be located. Excavate the ground for a 250 mm slab foundation.
2 Mix and place the concrete (see page 118). Leave to set.
3 Build up the walls as illustrated, using the slab to span the lower section of the barbecue structure. Leave the core of the left-hand pillar and the area below the seating hollow, and use paving bricks for the top course of the pillar.
4 Build the lintel across the front of the base of the chimney. Set the pipe behind the front chimney wall and build into the brickwork. Allow the mortar to set.
5 Fill the hollow areas with sand and compact. Top with paving bricks.

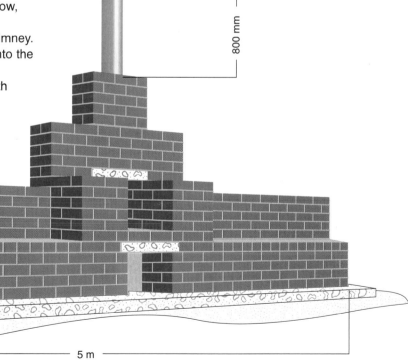

800 mm

1.27 m

5 m

PERGOLA FOR SHADE

Bricklaying skills and a basic knowledge of carpentry are required for this pergola. A simple structure, it is attached to the corner of the house and shades an area of 26.25 m² (32 sq yd). Pillars are made of bricks and plaster. Beams of sawn, planed timber are fixed to the house with truss hangers, so there is no need to knock out any brickwork to attach them. Shadecloth was used as the roof covering, as it filters sunlight, although any awning material could be used.

Materials

384 plaster bricks
210 kg (465 lb) cement
0.65 m³ (¾ cu yd) sand
300 kg (660 lb) stone
20 kg (45 lb) lime (optional)
5 x 3.5 m x 144 mm x 44 mm (11 ft 6 in x 5½ in x 1¾ in) lengths of timber
3 x 3.75 m x 144 mm x 44 mm (12 ft 4 in x 5½ in x 1¾ in) lengths of timber
2 x 3.85 m x 144 mm x 44 mm (12 ft 8 in x 5½ in x 1¾ in) lengths of timber
3 x 2.5 m x 44 mm x 10 mm (8 ft 2 in x 1¾ in x ½ in) cover strips
2 x 3.75 m x 44 mm x 10 mm (12 ft 4 in x 1¾ in x ½ in) cover strips (optional)
2 x 3.5 m x 44 mm x 10 mm (11 ft 6 in x 1¾ in x ½ in) cover strips (optional)
11 m x 3 m (12 yd x 120 in) shadecloth or awning material
12 m (39 ft 6 in) galvanised iron strapping
20 x 100 mm (4 in) coach screws
5 x 50 mm (2 in) truss hangers
10 x 8 mm x 50 mm (⅜ in x 2 in) Rawl bolts
5 x 75 mm (3 in) hexagonal bolts with nuts and washers
26 x 75 mm (3 in) wire nails
heavy-duty staples or shadecloth fasteners

Preparation

1 When building a pergola on an existing patio, remove pavers to accommodate footings for the pillars.

Use a chisel and club hammer to chip away the brick. Where a pillar is to be built on an unpaved surface, remove all vegetation.

Footings

2 Dig four holes as shown in the diagram on page 99, approximately 400 mm (1 ft 4 in) deep and 650 mm x 500 mm (2 ft x 1 ft 8 in) across – they should be big enough to support 2.4 m (7 ft 10 in) high pillars built with three bricks in each course. The corners of the footings should be square.
3 Insert a peg into the centre of each footing to indicate the upper level of the concrete. You will need about 45 kg (100 lb) of cement for the concrete, which you should mix in a cement:sand:stone ratio of 1:3:4.
4 Pour the concrete mixture into each hole to the height of the peg. Divide the strapping into four equal lengths by bending it until it snaps. Bend one end of each length of strapping and sink

4

one into each of the wet concrete footings. Allow the concrete to set for at least 24 to 48 hours. The strapping helps to reinforce the pillars and may be used to hold the pergola beams in place. More substantial pillars will require metal reinforcing rods, and shorter lengths of strapping can be built into the top five or six courses.

The patio before the paving was extended and the pergola constructed.

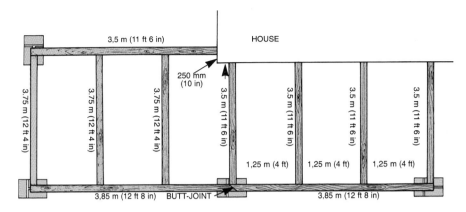

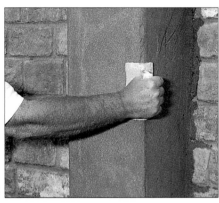

9

Building the pillars

5 Mix cement and sand in the ratio 1:4 for mortar. Lay the bricks so that the strapping extends through the middle of the pillar, with two bricks side-by-side and a third longways at one end. For the next course, alternate the direction of the bricks by laying one to

5

overlap half of the two laid side-by-side and two more to cover the rest of the surface. This help to will facilitate proper bonding. Fill all brick holes and gaps between the bricks with mortar as you work.

6 It is essential to build the pillars so that corners are at 90°, so use a builder's square frequently to check this. Also use a spirit level to ensure that each course is level and the pillars are plumb.

7 Set up corner blocks (see page 47) and a builder's line to ensure that brick courses are even. String a builder's line between the pillars, and use a gauge rod or water level to check that the brick courses and mortar joints are even. For a 2.4 m (7 ft 10 in) pillar, you will need to lay 30-32 courses, depending on how deep the foundation is and how many courses are below the level of the paving.

Plastering or rendering the pillars

8 Once brickwork is complete, allow the mortar to set overnight before plastering. Mix the plaster or render in the same ratio as the mortar (1:4); you will need at least 40 kg (90 lb) of cement. You may have to add lime to improve the plasticity, cohesiveness

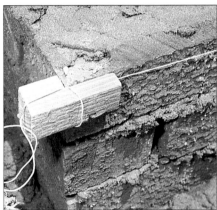

7

and water retention. Using a screed board to hold the mixture, lay on the plaster or render with a plasterer's trowel, applying pressure to make it stick to the bricks. Leave for an hour, then smooth with a plasterer's float.

9

9 Splash a little water on the surface and use a steel float to get a smooth finish. Use a corner trowel to neaten the corners.

10 The plastered or rendered surface should not be allowed to dry out too quickly. Damp it down every now and then with a very fine spray of water for

9

two or three days. Allow it to dry thoroughly before painting.

Positioning the timbers

11 Once the pillars are dry, erect the beams. Mark the position of the truss hangers on the wall. Ensure they are equally spaced and positioned exactly opposite each pillar (see diagram), or the beams will be off-centre where

11

they are attached to the pillars. If the patio is about 7.5 m (24 ft) long, the hangers should be at 1.25 (4 ft) centres. Use a water level to check the height of the truss hangers against the height of the tops of the columns.

12 Drill holes for the Rawl bolts, and bolt the truss hangers to the wall, ensuring that they are absolutely level.

13 Double-check the distance between the truss hangers and the three pillars. If your measuring was accurate, there should be no problems. It is usually wise, though, to buy timber a little longer than required. It is easy to cut a piece off the beam; frustrating to find that the beam is too short.

14 Carefully lower the first 3.5 m (11 ft 6 in) crosspiece into position. One end will slot into the truss hanger and be secured with a hexagonal bolt, while the other will rest on the pillar and be screwed to the abutting beam later on.

17

14

15 Cut one end of each 3.85 m (12 ft 8 in) beam at a 45° angle. Position the first beam so that it is at right angles to the first crosspiece, and that the angled end rests on the middle pillar.

16 Drill holes through the beam into the first crosspiece, and hammer in two coach screws, using a spanner or ratchet to tighten the nuts.

17 Punch a hole in the strapping, wrap it over the beam and nail it down.

18 Position the second 3.85 m (12 ft 8 in) beam to form a diagonal butt joint with the first, and skew-nail the two together.

19 Position the end 3.75 m (12 ft 4 in) crosspiece and secure the two timbers at 90° with coach screws and strapping, as explained in steps 16 and 17.

20 Now secure the last beam to the crosspiece and pillar with coach screws and strapping, and slot the other endinto the truss hanger.

21 Use a spirit level to ensure that each piece of timber is exactly straight and level.

22 Returning to the central pillar, nail the strapping securely over the diagonal butt joint.

23 Secure the three remaining 3.5 m (11 ft 6 in) crosspieces, slotting one end of each into a truss hanger and bolting it, and securing the other end

21

to the beam with coach screws as detailed before.

24 The two remaining 3.75 m (12 ft 4 in) crosspieces are secured at each end with two coach screws.

Finishing the wood
25 If you are going to paint the structure or varnish the wood, do so now. If you plan to paint the truss hangers, remember to coat them with a suitable primer first.

Attaching the awning material
26 Since the timbers are set at about 1.25 m (4 ft) centres, the material will have to be trimmed to about 2.5 m (8 ft 3 in) wide so that the material joins lie along the crosspieces. If you have chosen to use shadecloth, cut it to size with a soldering iron to prevent it from fraying.

27 Wrap one end of the shadecloth around a cover strip or any other narrow length of timber and attach it with tacks, staples or shadecloth fasteners. This will help you to keep it

27

taut and in place. With the cover strip and the fasteners on the upper side of the shadecloth, nail the cover strip across the first three crosspieces, above the truss hangers and as close to the wall as possible.

28 Pull the material taut across the structure, securing it along each of the three beams with staples or fasteners. Use a second strip of timber on the

28

29

other end of the material to help keep the shadecloth in position and to neaten the edge of it. Repeat twice to cover the entire pergola, overlapping the lengths of cloth slightly at the joins. If your pergola fits around the corner of the house, you will have to cut the awning fabric to follow the shape of the wall, and divide one piece of 2.5 m (8 ft 2 in) cover strip into two shorter lengths.

29 Trim the shadecloth neatly along the edge of the timber beam with a soldering iron.

30 When all the shadecloth is in place, you can secure it with additional lengths of cover strip along the joins if you wish.

The pillars have been painted white and the timber black, in keeping with the design and style of the house.

SLATE SOPHISTICATION

This double carport consists of two brick pillars with a wooden roof structure bolted on to the garage wall. Corrugated iron sheeting has been used for maximum protection, while guttering is concealed between the wall and the carport.

MATERIALS

Foundations for pillars
90 kg (200 lb) cement
365 kg or 0.3 m³ (805 lb or 11 ft³) sand
365 kg or 0.3 m³ (805 lb or 11 ft³) stone

Framework
360 facebricks
90 kg (200 lb) cement
50kg (1½ lb) lime
365 kg or 0.3 m³ (805 lb or 11 ft³) sand
extra cement, sand and stone for concrete to fill pillar cavity
2 x 2.4 m (8 ft) reinforcing rods
2 x 6 m x 297 mm x 50 mm (20 ft x 12 in x 2 in) beams
4 x 6.2 m 297 mm x 70 mm (20 ft 4 in x 12 in x 2½ in) rafters

Roofing
corrugated iron sheeting to cover 38 m² (410 ft²)
72 x 350 mm x 260 mm (1 ft 2 in x 10 in) slate tiles

Guttering
1 x 6.2 m (20 ft 4 in) PVC gutter with square channel
1 x 2 m (6 ft 6 in) PVC downpipe
1 gutter outlet
5 gutter brackets
2 stop ends
2 downpipe brackets
1 downpipe shoe
clout nails or screws
precast concrete channel

Fasteners
8 x 200 mm x 80 mm x 80 mm (8 in x 3 in x 3 in) galvanised angle brackets, 3 mm (¹/₈ in) thick
50 x 8 mm (¼ in) coach screws
2 wall plates
10 anchor bolts
clout nails
roofing screws
hoop iron

Paving
1,512 bricks/blocks
1.3 m³ (46 ft³) sand

1 Dig two foundations, 800 mm x 800 mm x 300 mm (2 ft 8 in x 2 ft 8 in x 12 in).
2 Pour concrete into holes and leave to set overnight.
3 Build pillars to 2.4 m (8 ft), building hoop iron into the centre for last five courses. Allow the mortar to set.
4 Bolt wall plates to wall opposite pillars, but slightly lower to allow for drainage slope.
5 Screw angle brackets on to beams at equal intervals, leaving a gap at one end for concealed gutter. Fix beams in place so that they extend over outer edges of pillars, securing with hoop iron.
6 Attach guttering to one of the rafters and fix between beams (see detail illustration and photograph).
7 Working away from the wall, screw rafters in place.
8 Fix roof sheeting to the structure with roofing screws.
9 Use clout nails to fix tiles to outside of beams.
10 Pave the parking area.

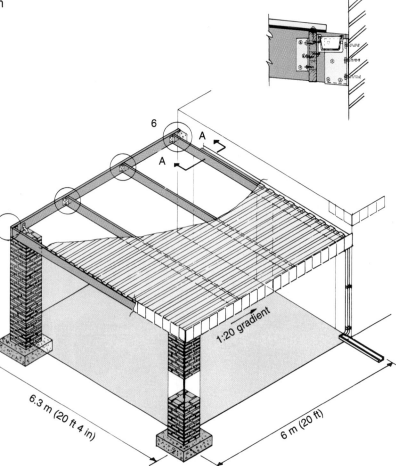

6.3 m (20 ft 4 in)

6 m (20 ft)

1:20 gradient

PORCH PERGOLA

Sturdy brick pillars built on a plinth give form to a simple pergola. While plants form the roof covering, shadecloth would be an alternative. Although a concrete slab was cast to level the ground before paving, this is not included here.

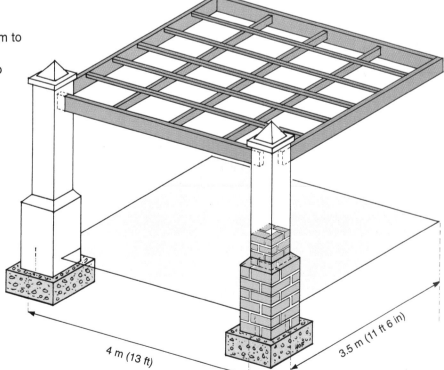

MATERIALS

Foundations for pillars
168 kg (370 lb) cement
680 kg or 0.5 m³ (1,500 lb or 18 ft³) sand
680 kg or 0.5 m³ (1,500 lb or 18 ft³) stone

Pillars
40 x 390 mm x 190 mm x 190 mm (1 ft 4 in x 7½ in x 7½ in) blocks
2 x 2.4 m (8 ft) threaded reinforcing rods with nuts
96 concrete bricks
220 kg (485 lb) cement
0.7 m³ (25 ft³) plaster sand
extra cement, sand and stone to fill in pillars

Roof structure
2 x 4 m x 224 mm x 44 mm (13 ft x 11 in x 1¾ in) beams
2 x 3.5 m x 224 mm x 44 mm (11 ft 6 in x 11 in x 1¾ in) crossbeams
3 x 3.5 m x 144 mm x 44 mm (11 ft 6 in x 6 in x 1¾ in) rafters
5 x 4 m x 44 mm x 22 mm (13 ft x 1¾ in x 1 in) purlins

Fasteners
3 x 12 mm (½ in) Rawl bolts
31 x 12 mm (½ in) brass countersunk screws

Paving
630 paving bricks/blocks
0.6 m³ (21 ft³) sand

1 Dig two foundations, 900 mm x 900 mm x 450 mm (3 ft x 3 ft x 1 ft 6 in) with centre points 4 m (13 ft) apart.
2 Pour concrete into holes and leave to set overnight.
3 Lay blocks to form two 5-course plinths using four blocks per course. Insert reinforcing rod and fill cavity with concrete.
4 Build up pillars using bricks.
5 Attach beam to wall with Rawl bolts.
6 Drill a hole in one end of each crossbeam to accommodate reinforcing rods.
7 Build second beam and crossbeams into brickwork at top of pillar, painting ends with bitumen and slotting the crossbeams on to reinforcing rods.
8 Secure beam to rods with nuts.
9 Skew-nail crossbeams to beam on

pillars. Attach them to beam against wall with a butt joint, using three screws at each end to secure the joint.
10 Fill cavity in pillars with concrete. Plaster pillars once mortar has set.
11 Attach rafters to beams at 1 m (3 ft 3 in) intervals, using mortise-and-tenon joints.
12 Space purlins evenly across rafters and screw into position at each end, and from the top where the purlins and rafters meet.
13 Pave the area.

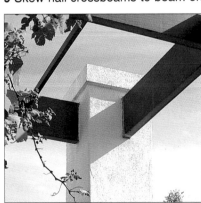

4 m (13 ft)

3.5 m (11 ft 6 in)

WOOD

PART
TWO

Timber is one of the most popular and versatile materials available for garden constructions. It is relatively light-weight, strong and rigid, and has a pleasing appearance. Furthermore, with even just the most basic carpentry skills, it is possible for you to build shelters and simple buildings, decks, steps, fences, play structures, bird houses and aviaries, and a myriad decorative features. For these reasons, it has long been used for construction in the garden.

There are many other reasons for choosing to use wood rather than other building materials, not least of these being the ease of construction and reasonable cost. It is usually quicker to erect a wooden structure and the process is less messy than working with bricks, blocks or stone and mortar. Some wooden buildings are available in kit form, and small utility structures are often supplied in a prefabricated form, just requiring simple assembly. There are countless design possibilities, ranging from traditional types to rustic units which blend harmoniously with the garden environment.

While the most common structures found in any garden are limited to fences, walls and steps, there are

Partial shade is created by a slatted roof.

many more possibilities suitable for 'do-it-yourself' construction, and a large percentage of these are built from wood.

The most obvious examples are pergolas (sometimes referred to as arbours) and walkways, many of which consist of a basic framework made from wood. Either attached to a house or freestanding, these structures may have a solid roof for shelter or be left partially open to the sky. They can be small or large, depending on the size of your garden, and provide ideal support for climbing plants.

A deck is another popular type of timber structure, with more complex variations featuring built-in seating, attractive handrails and sometimes screen walls. Imaginative designs may also incorporate planters, hot-water spas and outdoor storage facilities.

Particularly useful in sloping gardens or hillside locations, wooden decking eliminates the need for traditional terracing which can be expensive and may not suit your lifestyle. It also overcomes the problems of expensive and cumbersome earthmoving and extensive landscaping.

Of course, wood may be used to build a conservatory or sunroom, which will provide you with a welcome transition from house to garden. Similar extensions, using a large percentage of glass, are also popular for hot spas (or whirlpools), which many people prefer to site under cover in the garden.

A 'glasshouse' does not have to be attached to the house; sited beside a swimming pool or tennis court, it can become a haven for relaxation and casual entertaining. This particular method of construction may also be used for a utilitarian but traditional-style greenhouse, designed to trap the sunlight and warmth and protect the plants inside.

A simpler alternative for plant enthusiasts is a straightforward wooden lean-to where pot plants are

sheltered and adequately shaded from sun, wind, hail or snow. Even a freestanding structure can easily be constructed around a very basic framework of wood, using either fibreglass or an awning material like shadecloth or canvas for protection. If space is at a premium, a coldframe takes up even less room.

If you are a bird-lover, a garden aviary or even a raised bird house or covered bird-feeding table for wild garden birds may appeal. Dog kennels, too, may be constructed from wood, and if you live in the country and keep ducks and chickens, it is the most obvious material to use for a simple A-frame shelter. You may want to tackle a more elaborate gazebo with latticework, or a traditional pavilion similar to the bandstands sometimes found in public parks.

For those who are lucky enough to live alongside a lake or waterway, a timber boathouse is a useful project. Another option is a dual-purpose shelter which can be used as a summerhouse as well as for storing movable garden furniture and other items not required indoors.

For families with children, a wooden play structure can be a most rewarding project. Simple swings, sandpits and climbing frames are within the capabilities of most woodworkers. Tree-houses are an all-time favourite, but they must be securely fixed in the branches to prevent accidents. A simple platform built in a sturdy tree will provide hours of fun, and you can erect a small deck around the trunk so that the timber floor doubles as a roof for a makeshift shelter below. It may be necessary to build a step-ladder for easy access.

The simple wooden structures described in this chapter cover most of the above options, as well as timber extensions and additions. You will find various options for a range of utility buildings including garden sheds and outdoor workrooms or studios, although we have avoided buildings larger than 50 m² in size. Also included is a section on building methods to help you adapt these projects to suit the needs of you and your family's lifestyle.

The focus of this section is on timber structures which are practical rather than simply decorative, but there is advice on improving the appearance of an existing structure or one that you plan to build. You will find that a coat of paint or the addition of latticework, wooden cut-outs and carpenter's work, or potted and hanging plants, will give ordinary structures a special charm. The photographs aim to inspire, while the accompanying text gives sound, practical advice and a host of good ideas for you to copy or adapt.

Firstly, plan your project systematically and sensibly; it will enable you to identify your own needs and determine exactly what and where you should build. It will also help you to estimate the cost of the project and decide whether or not professionals should be employed. Refer back to pages 18-19 and 34-35 for detailed information on costing your project and employing professional help.

Various design options are discussed and illustrated, ensuring that your structure will look attractive and will be compatible with the garden plan as a whole, whether it is a decorative gazebo, a children's playhouse (Wendy house) or a purely functional tool shed. In addition, a wide range of flooring and roofing possibilities are considered. Materials are discussed and the relevant tools detailed, along with various basic construction methods which are easy to follow and clearly explained.

There is a section with step-by-step photographs, showing you how to build a range of structures. Although it follows the construction of only one structure – a pole structure – the instructions and illustrations also guide you through a simple method of deck-building, explaining how railings are built, decking slats installed, and how to assemble tongue-and-groove flooring. You can also see how windows and doors are fitted, and how

The sliding doors of this 'glasshouse' may be opened wide on hot, sunny days.

A simple, wooden bird-feeding table.

Reeds clad this delightful hide-out.

a simple roof is erected, plus instructions for making a stud frame panel. These techniques can then be followed exactly when making one of projects at the end of this chapter, or, alternatively, you can adapt them to suit your own design of structure.

In the latter part of this section, there is a series of different plans and projects, together with detailed checklists of materials. Although formal

building plans may be required for these designs (see page 16), these may certainly be used as presented, or adapted and changed to suit your own needs and site.

Whether your intention is to do all the work yourself or whether you plan to employ others to help you, this chapter provides you with an invaluable source of information for a wide variety of outdoor projects.

The essential material for any wooden structure is, of course, timber; the type chosen will depend largely on what you are planning to build. While poles are suitable for pergolas and some rustic structures, most buildings will be constructed from sawn and often planed (dressed) hardwood or softwood. In addition to the timber, you will probably need concrete for foundations as well as the necessary nails, screws and bolts to fasten the various components. If there is glazing to be done, you will require glass; for roofing, you will need sheeting, tiles, slates or thatch (refer back to page 41-43 for detailed information).

If you plan to work or even stay overnight in the wooden structure, internal cladding and insulation materials are essential. See pages 110-111 for a range of cladding ideas.

TIMBER

The exact wood chosen for various garden projects will vary depending on what is available in your area as well as what is best for local weather conditions. In general, the choice is between softwoods and hardwoods, some of which are better suited to particular structures than others. You

A typical example of softwood cladding.

will also need to decide whether you want to use poles or sawn (and sometimes planed or dressed) timber.

Whatever your choice, it is essential to buy wood that is structurally sound and will be durable. Even if you are erecting the smallest shed or lean-to, it is good building practice to select timber treated with preservatives for structural use. Also consider the intended function of the structure and the method of construction to be undertaken. Remember that the workability and nail-holding capacity of different woods vary.

Once you have bought the timber for the project, store it under cover until you need it. It will deteriorate rapidly if left exposed outdoors or in damp conditions. If you have to leave it outside, stack it at least 300 mm above the ground with spacer blocks to aid the movement of air, and cover with plastic or a tarpaulin.

Softwood

Cut from coniferous trees, softwoods are easier to saw and plane than most hardwoods. Trees felled commercially for construction throughout the world include pine, red and white cedar, fir, larch, spruce, redwood and some cypresses. Since different species have different qualities, you will find that certain softwoods are more hardy than others. Redwood, for instance, is durable and renowned for its resistance to decay, while the wood from some quick-growing pines requires frequent maintenance if it is to last for any length of time.

Your choice should always be based on the best quality available at the most economical price.

Hardwood

Generally more costly than softwood, hardwood comes from a variety of broad-leafed tree species. Some of the more common types used in various parts of the world include mahogany, oak, several eucalyptus, ash, elm,

balau and meranti, which is a slightly softer hardwood.

Although many people limit their use of hardwood in the garden to outdoor furniture, several species are particularly suited to deck building.

Even though the classification 'hardwood' is a botanical one and does not refer to the durability, strength or 'hard' qualities of the wood, hardwoods are often tough and very difficult to cut. This means that most need to be pre-drilled when nailing.

Poles

Ideal for pergolas and upright supports of decks and rustic shelters, poles have an intriguing rusticity which makes them suitable for arches, bridges and other structures. While this type of timber may be combined with sawn wood (see below), its versatility should not be underestimated. For instance, if you need flat sections, you can use split poles or even boards cut in a loglap profile. Furthermore, they are suitable supports for thatch or even for some kinds of roof sheeting.

There is usually a choice between poles that have been debarked (and branches removed), and those that have been machined to a smooth surface and reasonably regular size. Poles that have not been machined will taper, quite obviously, from top to bottom, and two poles will never be identical. Even those that have been milled will be slightly irregular in diameter. This characteristic adds a certain rustic appeal, but will not suit all structures.

Sawn timber

Most timber sold commercially for construction purposes is sawn in the mill to form planks, beams, battens, posts and so on. Although rough-sawn timber is widely available, many people prefer to buy it planed all round (PAR) or dressed all round (DAR); this is a bit more expensive, but it has a smoother finish which makes it easier to work with. To finish a garden structure built with PAR (DAR) timber simply give it a light sanding and then oil, seal or paint it.

Waney board, which has an uneven edge with some of the bark remaining, is a less common choice, but one that will cut costs if suitable for your project. If it is available in your area, you may be able to use it to clad a rustic shed or workroom.

The lengths and sections of all timber components must be compatible with the scale of the structure itself. Roof timbers must be chosen with the proposed covering in mind, as this will affect the design of the roof as well as the dimensions of purlins which support roof sheeting, and battens supporting tiles.

Standard sizes do vary, but this is seldom a major issue. In fact most suppliers will always quote nominal sizes, without taking the wastage lost during planing into account.

Timber sizes are given as a guide in the plans later in this chapter; if the exact dimensions are not available, you can have timber planed to size, which can be expensive, or simply use the nearest size available and adapt accordingly.

If your structure requires long pieces of timber you may have a problem, as world supplies of long lengths have become increasingly scarce over the years. An international solution, based on a German invention, is finger-jointed wood, accepted worldwide as a strong and reliable method of lengthening structural timbers in the factory (see page 116). Alternatively, you can buy laminated timber, which is more expensive but considerably stronger and more stable than wood sawn from a single log. It is also reasonably simple to join two lengths by bolting, screwing, nailing or using timber connectors.

If the necessary thickness is not available, you can probably glue and clamp two lengths together. However, do make sure that you use a suitable waterproof woodworking adhesive which will resist temperature changes and moisture.

A timber umbrella on a waterfront deck.

Quality

While timber is graded throughout the world, specific gradings will vary. Certain universal standards do, however, apply.

For instance, all newly felled 'green' timber contains a large percentage of water and the wood must be dried to strengthen it. In factories this is done either in huge kilns or by air seasoning, a method where the wood is allowed to dry naturally. Both processes kill the spores of fungi and destroy pests including termites and beetles, as well as their larvae and eggs. Be guided by the grading; poor grades of wood may still contain a high degree of moisture.

Avoid twisted, bowed or split lengths of wood as these defects can affect the stability of any structure. Sawn wood with an excessively sloping grain should also be avoided as it is more likely to warp, while too many knots, especially hard, dead knots from old branches, are liable to fall out and create points of weakness.

Preservatives

Some wood, such as heart-grade redwood (where it is available), is naturally resistant to fungal decay and infestation, but the best advice to DIY builders is to use timber which has been pressure-treated in the mill. If you do not treat wood adequately it will rot, and insects, termites and other parasites will makes their homes in it and eventually destroy it. On the other

hand, if it is treated according to recognised specifications, the wood will be just as durable and long-lasting as most other materials.

There are three basic types of preservative, coal tar creosote being the cheapest and probably the best known to DIYers. Although creosote is widely available, suitable for outdoor use and useful for coating the ends of posts in the ground, it is highly toxic to plants and causes some materials such as shadecloth (see page 42) to rot. Also, it has an unpleasant smell and cannot successfully be overcoated with paint or another finish. Therefore, before using it, consider whether you might want to paint your structure in the future.

Certain types of organic solvent-based preservatives, including PCP (pentachlorophenol), which is banned in some countries, and TBTO (tributyl tin oxide), are also toxic.

Water-based preservatives are usually colourless and odourless, and can be easily overcoated with a finish. However some of these products, such as CCA (chromated copper arsenate), which is commonly used for pressure- treating poles and roof timbers, give the wood a slightly green tinge. Although CCA can be used outdoors, many of the water-based preservatives (including boron) are suitable only for interior wood. Toxicity levels vary, but any treated wood should never be burnt in an open fire or a barbecue (see page 117).

CLADDING

The majority of garden buildings made from wood require external cladding or siding and, if you wish, internal finishing as well. Although metal was a traditional material for cladding the exterior of timber-frame buildings, it is not commonly used for ordinary garden structures. Instead, wood is a popular choice, and there are various options, ranging from plywood sheeting to strips of weatherboard manufactured in different profiles. The choice of internal cladding is usually limited to either plasterboard or timber panelling of some sort.

While most types can be affixed to the structure on site, some buildings (including sheds, playhouses and even some quite substantial workrooms) are made from prefabricated panels. You may be able to buy ready-made panels, or you can make them by assembling the basic framework in your workshop and nailing the cladding to it before the structure is erected (see page 126).

Plywood

An exterior-grade or weatherproof marine ply (ripped or used in sheets) is suitable for many garden structures. Ordinary plywood or the more

A fort made with poles and rustic timber incorporates a swing and an upper deck.

A colourful pitched pergola.

decorative cladding board, which has false joins to make it look like vertical timber boarding, may be used to panel internal walls and partitions. The basic material is also useful for adding rigidity to pre-made wall panels.

If you wish, you can slice plywood into fairly narrow plank widths and nail them in place so that they overlap one another slightly. This will have a similar effect to weatherboard cladding, as the overlap creates its own angle.

Hardboard

Available in sheets, this man-made board (made of compressed and processed wood-pulp fibre) is favoured in some countries as a wall covering for sheds and barns. Seams may be hidden by nailing battens or cover strips of wood over them to create a more decorative effect.

Particle board

Only exterior-grade particle board is suitable for use as cladding. When properly treated, it has a high resistance to water; it does expand and it is necessary to use a suitable expansion joint filler between boards.

Sawn timber

Ordinary wooden planks may be used to clad a timber-frame structure, although it may be necessary to use battens or cover strip, either internally or externally, over the joins. This is a relatively labour-intensive option, but one which may be used when tongue-and-groove or other overlapping boards are not available. Alternatively, the planks may be affixed to plywood or another sort of panelling.

Trellises and lattice panels made from thin strips of sawn timber may be used for screen walls or to enclose structures which are left partially open to the elements.

Weatherboard

A popular and attractive option, weatherboard is designed so that horizontal boards overlap one another slightly. The profile you choose will affect the visual appearance of your structure. The most common types include traditional shiplap cladding board, a rounded loglap, which gives the impression that the building has been made from logs, and slightly splayed lapboard.

Rounded loglap cladding on this shed creates a rustic, weather-resistant finish.

Shiplap cladding (top) and Waney boards.

Vertical boards

Both tongue-and-groove boards (if sufficiently thick) and V-jointed boards may be used vertically to clad garden buildings. As widths and sizes of tongues and grooves may vary, it is best to buy all your timber from one supplier. Some weatherboard may be affixed vertically, although this not generally recommended.

Fibrecement

Made of a mixture of organic fibres and cement, high-density fibrecement cladding is relatively heavy and so better suited to larger structures. It can be pressed during manufacture to give the impression of woodgrain.

PVC

Although not available everywhere, PVC is a cladding option. It is fixed in the same way as wooden boards and can be used internally and externally.

Plasterboard

Suitable only for internal use, this dry-wall cladding is manufactured with a core of gypsum plaster. Joints should be taped and then skimmed with a mix of gypsum plaster prior to painting.

FLOORING

Wood is often the most obvious flooring choice for a timber structure, but you may prepfer to use a concrete slab (see page 118), brick paving or a ceramic tile surface instead. If the structure is an extension of your house, you might like to continue the flooring used inside.

Timber

Timber is relatively lightweight and easy to work with, and is appropriate flooring for a wide variety of structures including sheds, Wendy houses, workrooms, gazebos, and of course decks. The type of timber used will depend on what is obtainable locally, but the basic choice is between hardwoods and softwoods. Usually hardwoods are more pricey, but are often better suited to exposed decking than a lot of the softwoods which are more readily available.

Both square-edged and tongue-and-groove floorboards are suitable for garden structures. Decking slats may be slightly thicker than internal boards where a very soft wood is used, or where bearers and/or joists are widely spaced. It is best to choose timber that has been planed (or dressed) all round in the factory.

Man-made board

Manufactured in various forms from timber, most man-made boards are cheaper than solid wood.

Both ordinary plywood (made from several very thin layers of wood) and chipboard or particle board (made from bonded fragments of timber) are adequate choices for the internal floors of sheds, playhouses and similar buildings. Waterproof shutterboard (or shuttering plywood) is particularly strong and stable. All these materials should be laid over bituminous felt to prevent damage from rising damp and excessive moisture. Alternatively, the lower surfaces can be painted with a rubberised bitumen sealer.

CONCRETE, MORTAR AND PLASTER

Concrete and mortar, as well as various plasters (renders) and floor toppings, are necessary for foundations, footings and any solid slab floor.

Mortar is used for bricklaying, rendering external walls and screeding concrete floors. Any building that has internal plasterboard cladding may be skimmed with gypsum plaster or with special skimming plaster.

The common components of concrete and mortar are cement and sand. Stone is added to concrete to add strength and give bulk to the mixture. Lime mixed into mortar will improve its plasticity and cohesiveness and aid water retention. This helps avoid cracking once it hardens.

Cement

Although there are various types of cement, Portland cement is most commonly used. Packaged in 50 kg or 40 kg (and sometimes smaller) sealed paper sacks, it hardens when mixed with water and gains its strength by curing, which necessitates being kept damp for a period of time. While it is in storage, cement must be kept dry. Never leave bags outside, and stack them above floor level.

Aggregate

Various aggregates are mixed with cement to form concrete and mortar. Generally, material that can pass

Screeding a floor with mortar.

through a 4.75 mm sieve, like sand, is referred to as fine aggregate, and coarser material (usually crushed stone) as coarse aggregate. Mortar contains only fine aggregate, while concrete includes both forms.

Suppliers of coarse aggregate usually supply what they refer to as single-sized stone. Crushed stone is sieved and natural pebbles screened to size. Gradings may differ slightly, but the most common size used by DIY builders is 19 or 20 mm. Although it is cheaper to buy stone in bulk, it is also available loosely bagged from most shops that stock builders' supplies.

Sand, available from the same sources as stone, is also graded and should contain particles of various sizes. It must be clean and should not contain any clay or vegetable matter. You need fairly coarse or 'sharp' sand for concrete, and softer sand for mixing mortar (used for render and screeds). Bedding sand beneath paving bricks should also be coarse, while that used between the joints should be fine.

Most natural sand is suitable for concrete and mortar. River sand is usually quite clean and free of clay, while pit sand, although well-graded, may have too much clay. Beach sand can only be used if it is thoroughly washed and processed.

Water

Water is a vital ingredient in concrete and mortar, and is not usually measured: just enough is added to the dry materials to make them workable. It is vital to use clean, pure water. Sea water may be used for unreinforced concrete (it will cause reinforcing to rust), but the salt will leave a white, powdery deposit on the surface. A good rule of thumb is that if you can drink the water, you can use it for building.

Lime

Hydrated builders' lime, sold in 25 kg bags, improves the cohesiveness and plasticity of mortar, especially when coarse sand is used in the mixture. Otherwise use a proprietary plasticiser.

Agricultural lime, road lime and quicklime (calcium oxide) are not suitable for this purpose.

Concrete

The properties of concrete depend on the proportions of cement, sand, crushed stone and water in the mixture. The proportions used depend on local conditions and the type of work you are doing, though low-strength concrete is usually adequate for the kind of construction described here. For foundation footings and solid slabs, combine the dry materials in a 1:4:4 cement:sand:stone ratio and add enough water to produce a workable mix (use a higher proportion of cement if you are building a large structure, or if the concrete is to be exposed to the elements). You will need about 230 kg of cement for every cubic metre of concrete (or more if you are making a stronger mix).

Dry mixed materials are available for minor concrete projects, but these are relatively expensive. For larger projects, ready-mixed concrete is often a viable proposition. You will, however, have to order a substantial quantity, and this must be placed as soon as it arrives.

Mortar mixes

Mortar is the conventional name given to various cement, sand and water mixes, and is used for bricklaying, rendering and floor toppings or screeds. Hydrated lime is often added to the mix to make it more pliable.

As with concrete, the proportions of dry materials vary when you mix mortar. You can rely on a cement:sand mix of 1:4 for any bricklaying or rendering required here. Concrete slabs may also be screeded with a 1:4 mix. If you are adding lime to the mortar, combine it in the ratio 2:1:8 (cement:lime:sand).

Plasters

Exterior render (see above) is sometimes referred to as plaster, although the term refers more correctly to gypsum plasters for indoor use only. Mixed with water and applied with a trowel, plaster is used over bare brick, cement render or plasterboard. There are various types, including special finishing or skimming plaster which is also available ready mixed in buckets. Although they can be messy to apply, both gypsum and skimming plasters dry rapidly and create a really good, smooth finish.

INSULATION

Insulation can make the most basic structure habitable. It can also increase the potential uses a garden building can have. There are various insulation materials available, including fibreglass blankets, aluminium foil, treated vermiculite granules and loose fill sold in fibre form. Most may be placed in the ceiling space or fixed into dry-wall panelling. Fibreglass and foil are ideal for garden structures.

Fibreglass

Blankets of fibreglass are useful for both ceiling and wall insulation. Just trim the sheets to size with a utility knife or panel saw, then lay them in the ceiling space, or position them in the walls before the internal cladding is secured. Fibreglass is easy to work with, but it can cause skin irritation so it is best to wear gloves and a mask.

Aluminium foil

Reinforced aluminium foil is manufactured in several grades, sometimes with a plastic vapour barrier on one side. It can be attached directly to both wall and ceiling panels prior to installation. If it is to be positioned once the roof trusses are in place, it should be affixed between the rafters and the purlins or battens with the waterproofing membrane uppermost.

FASTENERS

There is a wide range of fasteners and connectors suitable for use when building wooden structures. Nails are the most common, but screws, bolts and various special connectors are also useful. In addition, you may need reinforcing rods, hoop iron strapping and pieces of angle iron. Wherever possible, use rust-proof fasteners made from galvanised and anodised metal, brass, stainless steel or aluminium.

Nails

Generally sold by weight and length, nails make a quick, strong and

Aluminium foil is an effective material for insulating roofs.

permanent joint provided the correct type is used. Various shapes and sizes are designed for different types and thicknesses of material, so choose the right one. Oval wire nails have an unobtrusive head, making them suitable for the attachment of floorboards, and round wire nails are intended for fairly rough carpentry. Masonry nails fix timber to concrete or brickwork, and ring-shank or twisted-shank nails will secure roof sheeting.

When joining two pieces of wood of roughly the same thickness, make sure the nail goes at least half-way through the second piece; if one section is much thinner, use a nail that is $2^1/_2$ to 3 times the thickness of this piece.

Screws

Screws come in a variety of sizes and gauges. They are generally sold by number and diameter. Head shapes may be raised, rounded or countersunk, and the slot is either straight or crossed in one of three patterns – Phillips, Supadriv or Pozidriv. Common gauges range from no. 4 (which indicates a shank diameter of 2.7 mm) to no. 12 (5.6 mm). Each gauge is available in a range of lengths.

Apart from ordinary wood screws and chipboard screws (which have a deeper thread and do not taper as much), there are special-purpose screws. Coach screws are useful when erecting wooden structures.

They have either a square or a hexagonal head. Sold by diameter rather than gauge number, they are tightened with a spanner instead of a screwdriver.

Bolts

Bolts, in a variety of sizes, are the usual choice for heavy-duty fixing. Coach (or cuphead) bolts have a rounded head and a short thread, while hexagonal bolts often have a thread which extends the full length of the shaft. Nuts and bolts are tightened with spanners. Rawl bolts are a good choice when bolting timber to bricks or concrete, as they expand in masonry to anchor your wood securely.

Staples

Heavy-duty staples are used with a staple gun for attaching awning material to pergolas or plywood to panels. They are 'shot' into place and then hammered lightly until the staple is flush with the surface.

Special connectors

There is a wide range of metal connectors and fastening plates available, including joist hangers, post anchors, pole and truss hangers, angle brackets of various shapes, and spiky nail plates. They are usually made of galvanised or rust-proof metal and most of them are pre-drilled for easy use. See page 30 for more detailed information.

SETTING OUT

Whatever you are going to build and whichever method of timber construction you use, it is essential to spend time laying out the site correctly.

Unless the structure is to be circular or have acute or obtuse angles, it is vital to ensure that all corners are square. This is a fundamental building principle which will help you achieve a professional finish.

With pegs and builder's line or string, mark the perimeter, using a steel square to create a 90° angle at each corner. Alternatively, you can use a larger home-made square, using what is known as the 3:4:5 method. For this, three pieces of wood are hammered together to form a right-angled triangle; the two outside lengths should measure units of three and four respectively (say 900 mm and 1.2 m), while the side which cuts the corners should measure a proportional unit of five (in this case, 1.5 m). If the structure is sufficiently large, it is ideal to measure 3 m, 4 m and 5 m respectively. You can also check the accuracy of your angle with this method, using the steel square and a tape, or by staking the required measurements along the string line and then measuring across the angle. Once you have done this, double-check for square, measuring the layout diagonally from opposite corners; the diagonal measurements should be exactly the same.

Once the basic layout has been established, mark the position of any foundation footings with chalk or flour (which is usually cheaper).

Levels

One advantage of pole buildings is their versatility on sloping ground. These may be structures built on a stick framework or decking, taking the form of a pole platform without sides or superstructure. What you need to establish is the ideal level for the floor and the best position for all the upright supports, avoiding rocky ground.

If you are working on a difficult site, you may require the services of an engineer, but for a gradual slope it is not too difficult to determine these positions for yourself.

Although many professionals use a dumpy level or a transit-theodolite, which is a surveyor's usual tool, the simplest and cheapest way to establish these points is by using a water level (see page 23).

Decide where the upright posts are to be positioned, and where the highest point of the floor structure will be (allowing for joists and bearers), then mark where bearers (or girders) should be secured by using a water level. This is done in the same way as illustrated on page 122, using the highest point as a datum level.

FOUNDATIONS AND CONCRETEWORK

Irrespective of the type of floor your structure has, poles or wall panels must be securely anchored on a solid foundation. This may be a solid slab (see page 118), or individual footings (see page 24). Either way, the depth and dimensions of the foundation must be designed so that the building will be able to withstand all possible loads – weighty materials, wind uplift, rain, hail and snow.

Setting out a structure using the 3:4:5 method.

Upright poles are set in footings and braced in position.

The stilts of this A-frame play structure are securely anchored in concrete.

Footings

If poles or posts are set directly into the earth, the hole (and consequently the length of timber underground) must be considerably deeper than if it is encased in concrete. Furthermore, it is essential to compact the soil at the bottom of the hole to minimise settling.

Although decks are often built on pier footings, with upright posts anchored on to the upper surface of the concrete, this is not recommended for larger structures. This type of footing should be at least 200 mm deep; a tube form, made from cardboard, will enable you to leave a portion of the footing protruding above ground.

Suggested foundation sizes are given in the plans and projects that follow, but these presume you are building on flat and stable ground where abnormal weather conditions are unusual.

If regular frost, snow and strong winds are a factor, all footings must be dug deeper. Numerous tables are available giving figures for greater loads; alternatively consult an expert or professional engineer for advice.

Where a structure is built on sloping land, it may be necessary to embed posts and poles deeper into the ground on the uphill slope for extra strength. The tops of all posts, apart from those at the apex of a roof, will be at the same level, but more timber will be visible at the lowest points under the floor level.

Foundation slabs

If you plan to cast a slab on solid, stable ground, it may be sufficient merely to compact the area thoroughly with a punner prior to pouring the concrete. If the ground is not firm and reasonably level, you may have to create a solid sub-base with sand and hardcore consisting of broken bricks, stones and rubble. This must be well compacted before covering with DPC and pouring the concrete.

The depth of a slab will also relate to the size and weight of the structure it will have to support. While a depth of 100 mm is adequate for a pergola or other light structure, you will need to throw a deeper strip foundation around the perimeter of a slab for a building.

Concretework

The quantities of dry materials recommended for this type of concretework are given on page 112. Use a builder's bucket or clean 25 litre drum to measure accurately; it does not pay to rely on guesswork when mixing concrete.

You can mix the materials with either a spade or a concrete mixer. It is hard work by spade, but unless you have a reasonably large volume to mix, it is not worth hiring a mixer.

To mix by spade, you will need a clean, level surface or a builder's wheelbarrow. Combine the cement and sand first, making a hollow in the centre for the water. Pour in a little at a time, shovelling the materials from the outside to the centre, until they are well mixed and have a soft, porridgy consistency. Add the stone last, with just a little more water if necessary.

When using a mixer, it is advisable to load the stone first, together with a little water. This prevents the cement from building up around the blades. Add the cement next, and then the sand and enough water to obtain a workable consistency. It should not take more than about two minutes.

The concrete mixture must not be allowed to dry out before it is poured. Since dry soil will absorb the moisture from wet concrete, it is essential to dampen the base of the hole before placing the mixture.

It is a simple matter to place concrete in footings; use the back of your spade or shovel to push it firmly into the holes to level the upper surface. The trickiest part is ensuring that the posts remain absolutely vertical.

If you are throwing a slab, you will need a straightedge to compact the concrete, using a chopping action to expel the air. At the same time, level the slab with a smooth, sawing action. Allow the concrete to set, ideally keeping it moist for between five and seven days. This will aid the curing process and the result will be a really strong, solid and long-lasting base for the wooden structure.

It is usually necessary to screed the surface of a concrete floor to give it a smooth finish.

A nail gun is used by the professionals.

A combination square is useful for marking cutting edges.

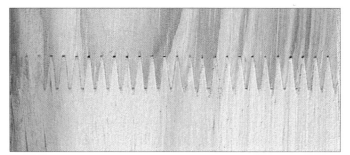

Finger joints are glued at the sawmill (see page 109).

CARPENTRY

Cutting timber and joining it to form various garden structures is reasonably elementary. Nevertheless, it is very important to ensure that the materials you are working with have the correct dimensions. Measure the wood two or three times; cut it once.

It also pays to be meticulous when working out your requirements. If you buy the wrong timber, you could end up having to redesign whatever you are planning to build, or even worse, find that it collapses during the first strong wind. It is usually advisable to buy timber that is a little longer than needed and cut it to size, rather than land up with pieces that are too short and therefore unusable.

If you are uncertain about the optimum spacing of poles, posts and other timbers for your particular structure, local manufacturers or suppliers may be able to advise; otherwise seek professional assistance before you tackle your project (see pages 18-19).

Cutting wood

Although you will find it easier to make a perfectly square, straight cut if you clamp the wood to a workbench, this is obviously not possible when you are sawing timber that has already been erected. You may have to ask somebody to support the other end of the wood. Start the cut in the correct place and then continue sawing in the same line. If you are working with a handsaw, make a small nick in the edge of the wood by drawing the saw towards you. The angle used to work different saws varies slightly (a flatter position is used with a tenon saw), but the movement is much the same. Whether you are using a handsaw or power tool, do not force the blade through the wood; let the blade or the machine do the work.

Working with electric saws does take some practice and confidence. Remember that the narrow blade of a jigsaw cuts on the up stroke, so in order to minimise splintering, place boards and planks right-side down on the workbench.

Drilling

Wood is reasonably soft and easy to drill; the secret is to make the hole in the right place, and to prevent the bit from splintering the wood.

There are various drill bits available, but you will generally use either twist bits or wood bits. For screws with countersunk heads, you will need a countersink, and to make larger holes, a flat bit. Whichever drill bit you use, it must be the right size in relation to the nail, screw or bolt you are using. It is important that pre-drilled holes are the correct depth and that they align with one another. For screws, you will usually have to drill a pilot hole (which is shorter and narrower than the screw) in one piece of wood and a wider clearance hole in the other for the shank. If you are drilling pilot holes for nails, these should also be smaller than the nail itself.

Joining and fixing

Although some gazebo designs might require relatively complex joints and some intricate carpenter's work, most garden structures rely on quite simple joints. Many are nailed together with only simple butt joints.

Where the wood overlaps another piece, a T- or cross-butt joint may sometimes be used, but halving joints are generally more effective. A half-lap joint, where the ends of two lengths of timber are notched so that the pieces slot together, is used either to lengthen two shorter pieces or, if they are joined at right angles, to create a neat corner. A cross-halving joint is ideal for railings round the sides of a deck and for some pergola beams. Mitre joints are used where the ends of timber are cut at a 45° angle resulting in a 90° joint where the pieces abut neatly to form a corner. (See also page 127 for more detailed information on joints.)

Working with saws, nails, power tools, chemically-treated wood and with heavy timber can be potentially dangerous, so it pays to be sensible and to take precautions. If you stay alert and pay attention to what you are doing at all times, you can avert needless accidents.

Clothing

Although there is usually no need for DIY timber builders to don hard hats, boots and gloves, it is important to dress sensibly. Avoid loose clothing or jewellery that could become caught in the moving parts of power tools or machinery, tie back long hair, and wear gloves, boots and so on when necessary. Safety goggles may seem unnecessary, but they are invaluable in certain circumstances. A face mask is also a good idea where the job involves dust and grit, especially if you are sawing or planing wood that has been pressure-treated with toxic chemicals.

Treated timber

While structural timber should be treated with preservatives, there are certain precautions that should be taken when working with it.

• Wear a face mask (see above), especially if you are working in a confined space, as frequent or prolonged inhalation of the sawdust from treated wood can be harmful to you.

• If possible work outdoors so that airborne sawdust can disperse.
• Always wash yourself thoroughly after working with treated timber.
• Sawdust inevitably settles on clothing, so wash it separately.
• Never burn treated timber in an open fire, an indoor fireplace or on a barbecue. The toxic fumes may be dangerous if inhaled and the chemicals can affect food.

Preservatives

When applying preservatives to untreated timber, extreme caution is necessary. Toxicity varies but most preservatives are poisonous to humans, animals and plants, at least until they are thoroughly dry. Some are highly flammable, so do not smoke while working with these chemicals.

Tools and equipment

Always choose the correct tool for the job. If you do not have the right equipment, hire it. Always keep the work area properly illuminated, and clean up after every job. Cluttered spaces and untidy workbenches invite injury.

Power tools

Before using a power tool, check that its voltage requirements are compatible with your power supply. A power source with voltage greater than that specified for the tool can result in serious injury. Also keep

children away from these tools and store them so that little hands are not tempted to use them.

Power tools must be well maintained. Keep them clean and check the cords regularly for damage. It is especially important to keep handles dry and free from grease, and to avoid using these tools in a damp environment or near flammable gases and liquids. If you do not have a helper, use a clamp or vice to hold the timber while working. Always disconnect tools when they are not in use. Remove adjusting keys from tools before switching them on.

Construction and maintenance

All structures must be safe. Make certain that all exposed wood is smooth and that, wherever possible, edges and corners are rounded. This is particularly important where a structure is intended for children. Check the structure regularly to ensure that it is sound, and make sure screws and nails do not protrude. Any rusty fasteners should be removed and replaced if they are in any way hazardous. If repairs are necessary, do them straight away, before the structure deteriorates further and becomes dangerous, and repairs become more expensive. Any rotten or badly split wood should be replaced, and surface areas should be regularly oiled, varnished or painted.

Bridges must be safe, stable and sturdy. Any timber submerged in a pond must not be treated with toxic chemicals.

While the basic techniques used when building wooden structures have been discussed on previous pages, these detailed instructions take them a step further. Basic carpentry skills are illustrated, and the construction methods for a pole structure are shown. These guidelines also incorporate a suspended wooden floor as well as decking, installation of doors and windows, and the erection of a simple roof structure.

Even though the presentation follows the construction of a simple building, these instructions are not intended as a complete project. Instead, they can be easily adapted and used when tackling the full range of garden structures, from the simplest arbour, pergola or cold frame to a more complex greenhouse, utilitarian shed or children's play structures, as shown in the projects and plans which are featured further on in this chapter.

The pole structure illustrates a building method which is ideal not only for sheds and barns, but also for smaller-scale playhouses and even for animal shelters. The roof structure can be adapted for a pergola with a pitched roof, and the deck built as a freestanding feature.

The stud panel, which is shown on page 126, illustrates a method commonly used for garden buildings of all sizes. This is also an approach often suggested for DIY projects. Since the method is easily adapted, assembly of a typical panel is explained.

CONCRETE SLAB

Whether you are casting concrete for foundation footings to support a simple timber structure, or for a solid slab which will form the floor of a garden building to be built from wood or brick, the principles are exactly the same. Of course, if the slab is to act as a foundation, it must be designed and constructed to carry the load of the timber (and any other materials) used. Also, the method of construction will affect the size and type of all foundations and footings used.

This 75 mm thick slab is laid on well-compacted fill. Low-strength concrete (cement, sand and stone mixed in the ratio 1:4:4), which is suitable for most garden buildings, is used.

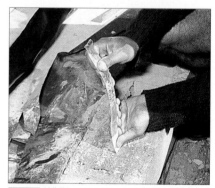

1 Build the foundation walls on concrete and allow the mortar to set. Fill with hardcore and sand, moisten and compact well with a punner, leaving about 75 mm of blockwork above the fill.

2 Spread polythene over the hardcore, overlapping all joins by 100 mm. This damp-proof membrane forms a moisture barrier and is an essential measure to take against rising damp.

3 Working in batches, mix sufficient cement with sand and 19 mm stone in the ratio 1:4:4 and enough water to make it workable. Pour the mixture over plastic to top of blockwork to form the slab.

4 Use a straight-edged length of wood to compact and level the concrete with the top of the foundation walls. If the slab is not square and level, the wall panels will not fit.

5 While you are laying the slab, bend and insert galvanised hoop-iron strapping or steel strips in the concrete (or hollow blocks) at regular intervals around the studs.

Pole-building is one of the oldest and most basic systems of construction. The method demands minimal preparation of the site, even on sloping ground, and structures are quick and easy to erect. Although basic carpentry skills (including experience with power tools and a knowledge of fixing and fastening techniques) will be a help, even an unskilled person can tackle a simple pole structure successfully.

The versatility of this building method creates many design possibilities, and it may be used for a structure of any size. The one illustrated here is only 7.5 m² in area, and has a covered deck 1 m wide and a height of 2 m. This structure is extremely versatile and can be adapted to form a variety of structures, from a potting shed or tool shed to a children's playhouse. A layout of the basic design (page 120) and a drawing of the stud framework (page 122) are also included for convenience.

MATERIALS

Poles or sawn and planed posts may be used as vertical supports. These are embedded in the ground and attached to horizontal timbers which form a framework for the wall cladding (see pages 110-111).

In order to accommodate doors and windows, it is necessary to construct a stud framework to brace the walls. Ordinary, factory-assembled frames are easily installed; however the minimal dimensions of some structures, such as the one shown here, may demand that a smaller-than-usual door is used. The simplest solution is to construct a frame on site using wooden laths.

If relatively weak softwood decking slats are used, these should be quite thick (in this case 110 mm x 35 mm). If a tougher, more resistant wood is used, or if the bearers are closer together, thinner slats can be used.

Although standard bargeboard and fascias may be used to finish the little building, a less expensive and much prettier option is a plywood trim.

1 Mark the layout of the building on the ground using pegs and string (see plan on page 120). This shed measures 2.5 m x 3 m. Use the 3:4:5 method (see page 34) to ensure that all corners are at right angles and the building is absolutely square.

2 If there is a deck, you will need to indicate where this will be located. To do this, string a line 1 m from the front 2.5 m mark, using a builder's square for accuracy. To double-check that the layout is square, measure all the diagonals.

3 Cut as much wood to size as possible. These four bearers are 3 m long, and the five joists which support the floorboards, 2.5 m long. If necessary, trim the wood now, using a combination or try square to mark the cutting line.

4 Although you can use a hand saw, it will be quicker, and the cut will be more accurate, if you use an electric circular saw. As neither the joists nor the bearers will be visible, it will not be necessary to plane the cut ends of the wood.

5 The upright posts will have to be firmly anchored in the ground, preferably in a concrete footing. A good way to prevent any vertical wind lift is to drill a hole and insert a metal rod through the timber a few centimetres from the base.

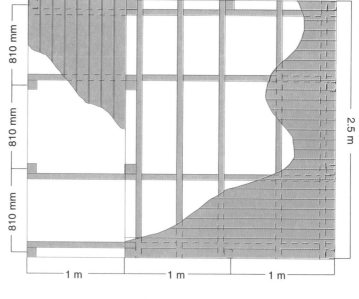

810 mm

810 mm

810 mm

2.5 m

1 m — 1 m — 1 m

6 The holes for the 14 footings should be at least 500 mm x 500 mm x 500 mm in size (see page 115). Dig them all, but only insert the four outside posts, bracing them with battens and bricks to ensure that they are as vertical as possible.

7 Although many people concrete the posts in at this stage, it is easier to keep the structure square and plumb if you start by securing all bearers, joists and uprights. Position the two outside bearers first, using blocks of wood to level them.

8 Use the correct drill bit to bore through the end of each bearer and the base of each of the four upright posts. You will need two suitable coach screws at each point to fasten the timber securely. Tighten the screws with a spanner.

9 It is vital that the outside bearers are affixed at exactly the same height, or your finished floor will be uneven. Use a straightedge with a spirit level placed over it to check. If the ground slopes, one end of the bearers will be off the ground.

10 Now you can position the first joist at the back of the building. Check that it is level and pre-drill holes as before. Use the same length coach screws to secure the joist to the two posts. Then attach the central and front joists of the structure.

11 The next step is to position the remaining upright posts (see step 12) and two inner bearers. This way you will not have to brace the posts. Once these are securely fixed, position the last two joists as shown on the plan and skew-nail to the bearers.

12 The two longest upright posts should be positioned opposite one another, to coincide with the apex of the roof. The four shorter posts should be placed at 810 mm centres at the front of the building, to support the railing and verandah roof.

13 Remove the bracing, but before you go any further, double-check the upper plane of the joists and bearers. Do this at numerous points to make absolutely certain your workmanship is straight and level. It is easier to rectify errors now than later.

14 If you have used sawn (rather than planed) timber, you may have to use a rasp or file to trim, flatten or even out sections of some of the pieces. You are unlikely to need a plane unless the wood is badly bowed; there is no need to sand the wood.

15 Now you can concrete the posts in place. Use a 1:4:4 mixture of cement, sand and stone and place it in the holes with a spade. If all the posts were vertical when they were bolted, the building will be square. Allow the concrete to set overnight.

16 The first decking slat will have to be cut and notched to accommodate the posts. Position it on the bearers, and then draw a line where you are going to cut out. Accuracy is extremely important, so is best to use a combination square.

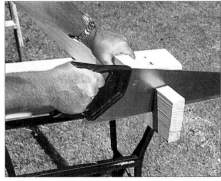

17 The best way to notch timber is with a handsaw and chisel. This gives you better control than with a power saw. Work on a stable surface, like a portable workbench, and use a crosscut saw which is designed to cut across the grain.

18 Although you can use a saw or a chisel to finish cutting the end joint, you will have to use a chisel to cut the back of the notches which will accommodate the two inner posts. Use a hammer to drive the chisel blade gradually into the wood.

19 String a line along one end of the deck as a guide, then secure the slats with anodised nails. Use a block of wood, planed to the width of the gap you wish to leave between the slats, as a spacer. Trim the other end of the decking as shown in steps 22 and 23.

20 Moving on to the inside of the structure, cut the tongue off the first floorboard and nail the board in place with two oval nails at each of the joists. Continue laying the flooring, slotting the tongue of each board into the groove of each previous one.

21 Line up the ends of all the boards at the front of the building. You will need to notch some of these ends to accommodate the posts, and to trim those which lie at the point where the door is to be hung (see plan on page 122).

22 Now you can trim the boards at the back of the building. These must line up with the edge of both the bearer and the upright posts. The best way to ensure that the cutting line is straight is to make use of a chalk line, snapping it between two posts.

23 You can use either a handsaw or a power tool to cut the boards to size. Although you could use a circular saw, it is easier to obtain a really flush cut by using a jigsaw. Otherwise, use a crosscut saw, and follow the line marked previously.

24 Before you affix the cladding, assemble the roof structure. Use a water level to determine the correct height of all the upright posts. The height of the middle posts will be determined by the required pitch; these are 200 mm higher.

25 Once you have measured and marked all the upright posts, you can cut the excess ends off with a crosscut saw; it is too awkward to use a power saw. Note that the two higher posts should be cut at a slight angle to support the rafters.

26 Before securing the beams, cut a notch at the top of each post, in a dimension which will support the rafters. Then, using coach screws, fasten the beams to the uprights, so that the upper surface of each is flush with the newly cut wood.

27 To prevent the two central beams below the apex of the roof from bowing and bending, sandwich a block of wood between them at the centre, and secure with a hexagonal bolt and washer, using a spanner and ratchet to fasten it.

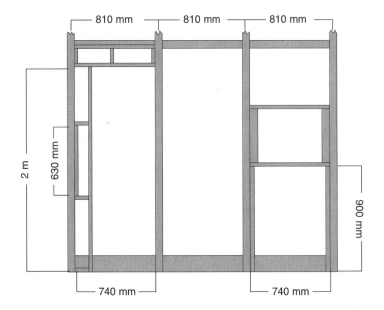

810 mm — 810 mm — 810 mm

2 m

630 mm

900 mm

740 mm — 740 mm

28 You will need eight lengths of timber for the rafters which will have to be cut at a slight angle to ensure that they join properly at the apex. Position a shorter length on the cut-out posts and use a combination square to determine the angle.

29 Mark the same angle for all the rafters, checking before cutting the ends. Drill through the rafter and post, then fasten the wood to form a half-lap joint, using a smaller sized coach screw. Repeat at both ends of each rafter.

30 The rafters are best joined at the apex with nail plates (timber connectors), available in various sizes. Working on the ground, simply hammer a plate on each side of the wood over the join. Alternatively you can make a plywood gusset.

31 Once all the rafters have been positioned and secured, string a line along the apex of the roof. Use this as a guide when measuring and marking where the purlins should be affixed. Remember to leave a space at the apex for the capping.

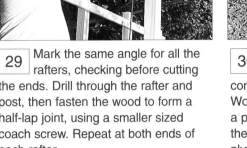

32 Now attach the purlins to the rafters with 75 mm long anodised nails. Use the marks made in step 31 as well as the string line to ensure they are nailed on absolutely straight. If the purlins are crooked, the roofing nails will not be neat.

33 Before you lay the roof sheeting, nail the cladding to the posts. This splayed lapboard is designed to create a weatherproof wall. Use two nails at each post and check your spirit level periodically to see that the boards are horizontal.

34 While the cladding is nailed across the posts on three walls, the front wall incorporates a door and a window. To brace these openings, it is necessary to build a stud framework (see plan on page 122). Secure timber with anodised nails.

35 Studs around the window are nailed to the upright posts, to create an opening exactly the same size as the frame. Although any type of window may be fitted, a PVC frame is one of the easiest to work with as it simply slots into position.

36 Before the window can be glazed, the frame is screwed to the studs. The inner PVC frame is removed and holes drilled through the frame and into the wood. Countersunk brass screws are used to ensure the frame is flush when it is reassembled.

37 When you reach roof height, it will be necessary to notch the cladding around the purlins and cut it to the angle of the rafters. Use a spirit level as a straightedge to mark the cutting line and then saw the timber with a crosscut saw.

38 Buy longer lengths of sheeting than required and cut to size. The flexible corrugated sheeting used here is made from organic fibre, which can be cut with an angle grinder or well-oiled handsaw. Mark a line with a chalk line and cut a straight edge.

39 String lines along all edges of the roof to help you keep the roof sheeting straight. Note that the sheeting must overlap at the joins to ensure that it is waterproof. Align the sheets carefully so that the corrugations overlap exactly.

40 Although it is usually necessary to pre-drill holes for roofing nails, this is not necessary for organic-fibre sheeting as long as you hammer gently. Knock in the nails, using a spirit level and lines to gauge the position of the underlying purlins.

41 The ends of the rafters should line up neatly with the ends of the roof sheeting. Use a carpenter's square to mark this point accurately. Then use a crosscut saw to cut all the excess pieces of timber at the front and back of the shed.

42 The purlins must also be cut so that they are flush with the roof sheeting on both sides. Bargeboard, or in this case a decorative trim, can then be nailed to the ends of the timber. Once again it is best to use a handsaw to cut the wood.

43 Now affix the capping to close the gap between the sheets which cover the two halves of the shed. Capping is supplied in standard lengths and must be overlapped in the same way as the sheeting. Secure with roofing nails along the purlins.

44 Most of the work has been done, and now you can make the railing around the deck. First affix a supporting strut to the shed at the corners of the deck, opposite the two outer posts. Then mark cutting lines on all your crosspieces.

45 As the crosspieces below the rails are angled, the ends of each piece must be cut to form a V at both top and bottom. Use a carpenter's square to draw a straight line down one side of each piece to help you cut in a straight line.

46 Preferably clamp the wood to a portable workbench and use a tenon saw to angle the corners. It is best to cut all the wood before you start assembling the railing. It is also a good idea to check that you have cut the correct angle.

47 Now cut a housing in the centre of each crosspiece so they slot together neatly. It will be slightly angled, depending on the length of the diagonals and where they meet. Mark this position and make a series of cuts halfway through the wood.

48 Chisel out the excess wood from the notch. If the cuts made previously are accurate, you will find that you can simply trim the wood at the base line. Otherwise you will need to pare away the remainder with the chisel blade.

49 The two diagonals should now slot together neatly. There is no need to affix them at this point, although you can glue them if you wish. Once the crosspieces have been secured to the posts and support struts, the railing will be quite sturdy.

50 You can nail or screw the crosspieces into place, but to avoid splitting the wood, it is best to pre-drill the holes. Use the appropriate drill bit and angle each hole. The upper sections are affixed to the posts and lower pieces to the decking.

51 If you are using nails, use ones that are anodised and will not rust. Make sure you hammer them in so that the tops are flush with the wood. It is also a good idea to countersink them with a punch and fill the holes with wood filler.

52 Now fit the top railings over the criss-cross by skew-nailing them to the upright posts on each side. A drilled pilot hole will help to prevent the timber from splitting. Make use of an orbital sander to smooth the edges and round them off neatly.

53 Nail the laths to the inside of the doorway to form a narrow frame along the top and sides, using 50 mm long nails. Then hang the door so that it opens outwards, above the upper surface of the deck. Fit the lock and the handles.

54 The quadrant can now be nailed to the four outside corners of the building using suitable nails. This finishes off the corners neatly. You could also use square lengths of wood or PVC capping for a decorative edge if you wish.

55 Mark the design for your trim on the plywood and cut it out with a jigsaw. Any holes can be made by drilling, using a flat drill bit. Attach it at the front and sides of the structure with 50 mm nails. Also cut out closures for the capping ends from the plywood.

STUD-FRAME PANEL

Simple stud frame structures are often built with prefabricated panels which are bolted together on site. These are simple to make and no special skills are required.

The method illustrated may be adapted for panels of practically any size, and a range of cladding materials may be used. Note that this panel incorporates an optional bracing layer of plywood, which strengthens the structure and improves its insulation qualities.

These guidelines illustrate construction of a typical external panel measuring 3 m x 2.17 m and in corporating a1.14 m x 1.2 m window. You can make it bigger or smaller, depending on your particular design, although the larger the panel, the more studs you will need to ensure a sturdy framework.

1 The framework of the panel is made up with 70 mm x 35 mm PAR (DAR) timber. You will need two 3 m, six 2.1 m, three 1.14 m and one 790 mm lengths, plus two 790 mm x 50 mm x 38 mm supports for the window.

2 Ensure that all panels are absolutely square. Work on a flat surface and use a carpenter's square to check all corners. If you have a large table, affix short horizontal and vertical battens to guide you.

3 Using 100 mm wire nails, join a 2.1 m length of wood to one of the two 3 m lengths. Note how the smaller battens, secured to the table, help keep the woodwork straight and square. Nail all the pieces together.

4 Make sure the gap you have left for the window is exactly the same size as the frame – in this case, 1.14 m x 1.2 m. If it is, you can slot the window frame into place. Wooden, PVC and aluminium frames may be used.

5 Nail or screw the window frame securely into place, depending on the type of frame you have used. Note the two 1.14 m lengths of wood which must be inserted above the top of the window frame to ensure a snug fit.

6 You will need four pieces of 4 mm plywood for the bracing layer; 2 x 930 mm x 2.17 m, 1 x 1.14 m x 860 mm and 1 x 1.14 m x 110 mm for the small section above the window. This should give the structure added strength.

7 Make sure that the plywood is cut accurately and fits neatly over the framework, then use clout nails or round-head nails to secure it firmly to the wood. You can also use heavy-duty staples, inserting them with the aid of a staple gun.

8 Use wire nails to affix the cladding to the plywood, with the first board about 100 mm from the bottom; this allows you to overlap the foundation with cladding on site. Also overhang boards by 70 mm on one side of each corner panel.

Whatever you are going to build, it will be necessary to join separate pieces of timber together. In most instances, relatively simple joints may be used, but it is always essential to ensure that the connection is strong enough to withstand the strains it will be exposed to.

BUTT JOINTS

The simplest of all timber connections, butt joints involve abutting wood without making any special cuts in the wood, such as rebates or tongues. Glue, nails, screws and other fastening devices are used to fix the timbers in place.

Butt joints may be used at a corner or where two lengths of timber meet to form a T. Although a cross-butt joint may be created where two lengths of timber interconnect, halving joints are usually preferable in this situation.

HALVING (OR HALF-LAP) JOINTS

Simple to perfect, neat halving joints are used for many garden structures including the connection of pergola beams to posts. Cross-halving joints are particularly useful where diagonal timbers cross beneath the railing of a deck.

As their name suggests, halving joints necessitate cutting a rebate equal to half the thickness of the wood, usually from both the timbers to be connected. This results in a strong, interlocking join with a flush surface.

With experience, you will find that measuring tools are not necessary to cut halving joints. Simply mark out the cutting lines with the second piece of timber, and remember to cut inside the marked line.

HOUSING JOINTS

Similar to halving joints, housing joints involve only one rebate or groove to support the adjoining piece of timber. These are useful when constructing a stud framework.

MITRED JOINTS

Essentially decorative butt joints, these are found wherever two pieces of wood meet at 45°. Although a standard mitre is not particularly strong, it is a neat joint for many simple garden structures. Alternatively, a mitred halving (or half-lap) joint may be used.

MORTISE-AND-TENON JOINTS

Not common in the average garden structure, mortise-and-tenon joints are sometimes used for pergolas. These involve cutting a rectangular 'mortise' or hole in one piece of timber, and a 'tenon' or tongue to fit into the second. The two lengths of wood then slot together. Although the standard mortise-and-tenon joint is neat, it is not always strong enough.

POLE JOINTS

Even though most structures built with poles do not require elaborate joints, it is useful to know how to adapt methods to fit their cylindrical form. In some instances, poles may be abutted to one another, but simple halving joints are usually a more adequate option, and housing joints are particularly useful where horizontal and vertical timbers need to be connected.

SCARF JOINTS

Used to lengthen timbers, rails, beams and so on, scarf joints are usually glued, clamped and pinned. The simplest kind is made by cutting the ends of both pieces of wood at an angle and attaching them in a straight line This type of joint will be considerably stronger if made with three saw cuts, but they must be accurately marked.

TONGUE-AND-GROOVE JOINTS

Particularly common for floorboards and cladding, tongue-and-groove joints are often found where manufactured timber boards have been used. The tongue fits into the groove, creating a nice, snug finish.

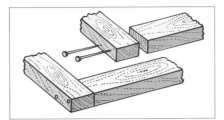
Simple butt joint

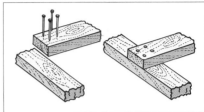
T-butt joint

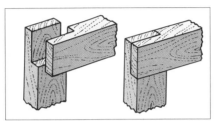
Corner halving joint

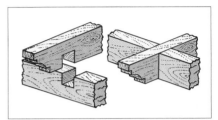
Cross-halving joint

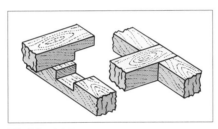
T-halving joint

Mitred halving joint

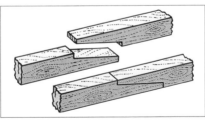
Three-cut scarf joint

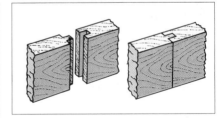
Tongue-and-groove joint

WOODEN PLANTER

While most planters made from wood are simply variations on a basic square or rectangular box, there are numerous ways to enhance the surface area. Try adding timber decoration in the form of raised vertical or horizontal bands. Alternatively, use paint, either as a solid colour, a watered down wash, or to add detailed decoration. The wooden planter shown in the photograph here has been painted and then stencilled with a strawberry design, to tie in with the strawberry plants bedded in the container.

However, do remember that your design does not have to be complicated to be effective – this easy project is perfect for an inexperienced carpenter as it requires few tools and employs simple techniques, and when filled with flowers or shrubs, it will brighten up your patio, balcony or deck enormously.

Materials

28 x 396 mm x 44 mm x 44 mm
   (1 ft 2 in x 2 in x 2 in) pieces of wood
4 x 440 mm x 110 mm x 22 mm
   (1 ft 4 in x 4 in x 1 in) planks
4 x 310 mm x 44 mm x 44 mm (12 in x
   2 in x 2 in) pieces of wood
118 x 75 mm (3 in) wire nails
20 x 50 mm (2 in) wire nails
wood glue
paint or vanish

Preparation

1 Cut the wood to size before you start work. If you do not have a power saw, use an ordinary tenon saw.
2 Place the first four pieces of wood on a flat, stable surface, and use a builder's square to check that the corners are at right angles.

Construction

3 Start gluing and nailing the box together, using the 75 mm (3 in) wire nails. To connect the wood, ensure

that the ends of the pieces of timber overlap each other at the corners. Put wood glue on the surface and push the wood firmly onto it. If the glue dribbles, wipe off the excess.

4 Clamp each corner with a right-angled clamp before gluing and nailing the second and subsequent layers. Predrill the holes to prevent the wood from splitting, making sure nail holes are not directly above each other.

5 Hammer the nails flush with the surface. If the wood is warped, you may have to use sash clamps during the gluing and pinning process to hold the layers of timber together while the glue dries.
6 After gluing and nailing the layers of wood, nail on the base, using 50 mm (2 in) nails. If you have cut the wood accurately, the planks will fit exactly; if not, trim the planks or cut another piece. Insert two nails at the end of each plank and two or three along the two remaining sides of the base.

7 Nail the four 310 mm (12 in) pieces of wood to the base, using the 50 mm (2 in) nails, with their outer edges 44 mm (2 in) in from the edges of the box. These will keep the planter off the ground and enhance the final design.

9 Drill holes in the base of the planter for drainage.

10 Seal the inside of the box with bitumen. This black emulsion waterproofer is simply painted on, but it should be spread reasonably thickly on the wood to be effective. You can also seal the underside of the planter if you wish.

Finishing
8 Fill in nail holes, imperfections in the wood and gaps between the timbers with a wood filler that matches the colour of the wood. Sand the surface when dry.

11 Finally paint, varnish or give the box a coat of diluted emulsion paint for a washed or slightly distressed look. If you plan to display it on your deck, choose a varnish to match the finish of the timber.

Painted and stencilled, the wooden planter is an ideal container for pink roses and strawberry plants.

FENCE PANELS

INTERWOVEN PANELS

This remarkably simple construction creates an attractive basketweave effect between timber poles. The ends of relatively thin horizontal slats, positioned close together, are nailed alternately to the front and the back of each pole. Left to weather naturally, the fence will soon develop a lovely rustic appeal. The materials listed are sufficient for one 2.3 m x 2.2 m panel, and presume you will be using a 1:4:4 concrete mix. Additional adjacent panels will, of course, require only one extra pole each.

MATERIALS

Footings for 2 poles
60 kg cement
245 kg sand
245 kg stone
hardcore and/or soil for fill

Fencing
2 x 3 m poles, 120 mm in
  diameter
22 x 2.2 m x 95 mm x
  15 mm slats (or similar)

Fasteners
88 x 100 mm anodised
  wire nails

1 Mark the position of the fence and peg out the footings at 1.98 m centres.
2 Dig 750 mm-deep footings, 750 mm x 750 mm in size.
3 Brace the poles in position and check that they are vertical.
4 Mix the concrete as described on page 115.
5 Pack the footings about two-thirds full with concrete. When the concrete has set, add enough soil to fill the holes completely. Alternatively, first put a 200 mm-deep layer of hardcore into each hole and then top up with concrete. Leave to set.
6 Before removing the bracing, nail the slats to the poles, alternately bringing one slat to the front of the pole, and then one to the back. Start from the bottom and use two nails at each end of the slats.

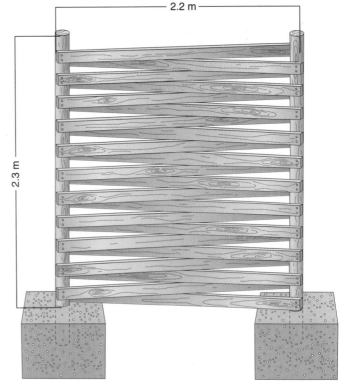

PANEL FENCE

Attractive panels, made by attaching timber slats on the diagonal, are set between recessed, precast concrete posts, to create a good-looking fence which offers privacy and security. A narrow, precast concrete panel is slotted horizontally into place at the base of the timber panels. If precast materials are not available, this design may be adapted for timber posts or masonry pillars. In this case, build a low wall in place of the base panel or position the timber closer to the ground. While the illustration shows two adjacent panels, the materials are sufficient for one panel between two posts.

MATERIALS

Foundations
100 kg cement
405 kg sand
405 kg stone

Framework
2 x 2.35 m x 130 mm x 120 mm precast concrete posts, with 50 mm recesses in both sides
1 x 1.28 m x 200 mm x 45 mm precast concrete panel

Panel
2 x 1.48 m x 70 mm x 20 mm lengths timber
3 x 1.17 m x 70 mm x 20 mm lengths timber
24 x 70 mm x 15 mm slats to fit 2 m², cut to lengths from 300 mm to 1.95 m

Fasteners
144 x 25 mm anodised wire nails
6 x 100 mm anodised wire nails

1 Mark the positon of the proposed fence and peg out the footings at about 1.4 m centres.
2 Mark the 600 mm x 600 mm footings with chalk or flour.
3 Dig the footings to a depth of 600 mm.
4 Brace the posts in position with battens, making certain they are vertical, acccurately spaced and in a straight line. Concrete into position using a 1:4:4 mix (see page 115).

5 Before the concrete sets, slide the base panel into position to ensure the posts are accurately spaced.
6 Check that the concrete is well compacted and leave to set overnight.
7 Working on a flat surface, position the five pieces of timber which will form the framework for each panel, placing the shorter lengths on the inside of the long pieces of timber.
8 Predrill three pilot holes in each 1.48 m-long piece of timber at the point where the shorter lengths are joined to it at right angles.
9 Join the framework together using the 100 mm-long nails.
10 Position one of the slats diagonally across the centre of the panel, and mark the cutting lines at the correct angles. Trim with a tenon saw.
11 Continue to mark and cut all the slats, ending with the shorter lengths.
12 Position the 24 slats across the framework, ensuring the gaps between them are even.
13 Nail the slats to the framework, using 25 mm-long nails at the top, bottom and middle, if necessary, of each slat.
14 Finally, slide the panel into the recesses in the posts (see illustration). If timber posts are used, nail or screw the panel into place. If you have built masonry pillars, bolt the framework to these before affixing the slats.

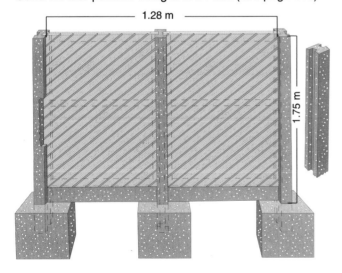

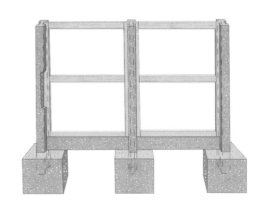

LEAN-TO SHELTER

This shelter would be an attractive and practical addition to any garden, and can be built against a perimeter wall or fence, or against the house itself. It is also extremely simple to construct. The four corner posts are set in concrete to provide a solid framework for the building, and an additional post in the middle of the back wall provides extra support for the waney-edged timber

cladding which helps give the building its rustic appearance. The roof is supported on two sturdy bearers that link the corner posts at the front and back; these are bridged by rafters secured at their top and bottom ends by birdsmouth joints at 600 mm (2 ft) centres.

Tiling battens run across the rafters, and are spaced to match the size of the second-hand clay tiles used for the roof. To prevent any risk of high winds lifting the topmost row of tiles, lead flashing is secured to the top of the rear wall and is dressed down over the ridge and onto the face of the tiles.

Above: Naturally weathered timber and old second-hand tiles combine to create a garden shelter with a rustic look.

You can tailor the size of the shelter to suit the space available in your garden. This building is about 3.6m (12 ft) wide and 1.5m (5 ft) deep from front to back, but you can vary both width and depth as necessary. The overall height is about 2.75m (9 ft) at the ridge and 2m (6 ft 6 in) at the eaves. If you do alter the building's dimensions, aim to keep the roof slope the same as used here – a gradient of about 1 in 2.

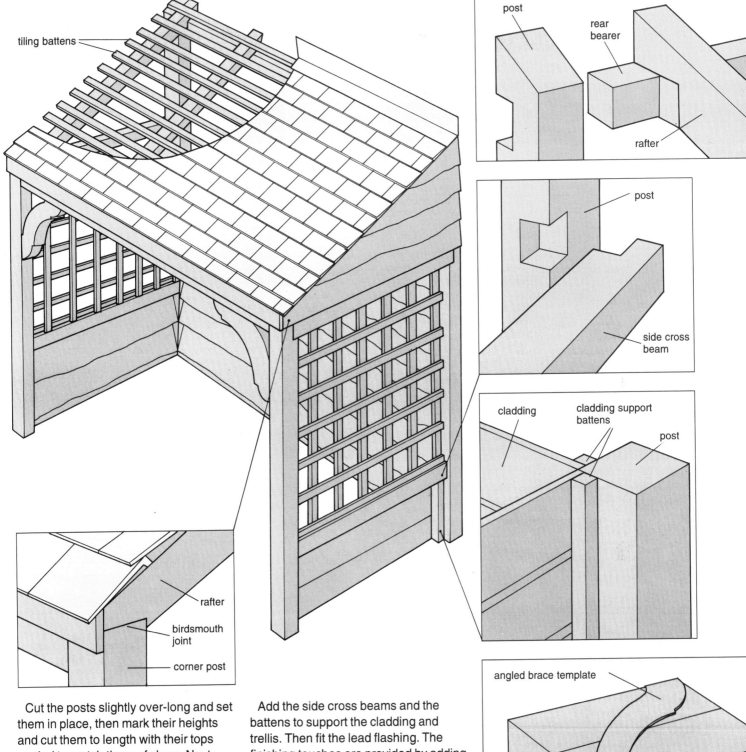

tiling battens

post

rear
bearer

rafter

post

side cross
beam

cladding

cladding support
battens

post

rafter

birdsmouth
joint

corner post

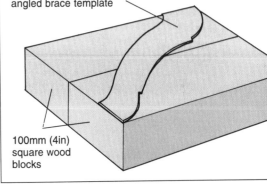

angled brace template

100mm (4in)
square wood
blocks

Cut the posts slightly over-long and set them in place, then mark their heights and cut them to length with their tops angled to match the roof slope. Next, mark out and cut the recesses in the posts to accept the ends of the main cross-bearers and nail these in place.

Add the rafters at 600 mm (2 ft) centres, with the outermost pair set against the sides of the corner posts. Cut birdsmouth joints in each rafter so it sits neatly over the bearers at the top and bottom of the roof slope. Fix the tiling battens at spacings to suit the tiles you are using.

Add the side cross beams and the battens to support the cladding and trellis. Then fit the lead flashing. The finishing touches are provided by adding a fascia board (which could be given a decorative edging) and making the two curved brackets that fill in the front corners. These are made by gluing two pieces of 100 mm (4 in) square timber together with waterproof urea-formaldehyde adhesive, and then marking out the bracket shape on the block, ready for cutting and fitting.

Finish the building with a generous coat or two of preservative stain.

Above: The details to the main drawing show how the frame members fit together, how the tiling and cladding are fixed and how the angled braces are marked out for cutting .

GARDEN GAZEBO

This delightful wooden structure houses birdcages in a pretty garden setting. The gazebo could equally provide shelter for seating and alfresco meals. The basic structure was created with poles, while the roof and railings are made of cut and planed wood. The cut-log floor surface adds a rustic feel, although the surface could be paved instead. This project is recommended for people with sound carpentry skills.

MATERIALS

Foundations for poles
115 kg (254 lb) cement
465 kg or 0.35 m³ (1,025 lb or 12 ft³) sand
465 kg or 0.35 m³ (1,025 lb or 12 ft³) stone

Framework
4 x 2.5 m (8 ft) upright poles, 90 mm (3½ in) in diameter
1 x 560 mm (1 ft 10 in) pole for roof, 120 mm (4¾ in) in diameter
6 x 2.1 m x 70 mm x 45 mm (7 ft x 2¾ in x 1¾ in) timber railings
3 x 800 mm x 70 mm x 45 mm (2 ft 7½ in x 2¾ in x 1¾in) timbers for railing uprights
12 x 1.4 m x 70 mm x 32 mm (4 ft 6 in x 2¾ in x 1¼ in) timbers for railing diagonals

12 x 1.4 m x 32 mm x 22 mm (4 ft 7 in x 1¼ in x 1 in) rafters
8 x 1.7 m x 32 mm x 22 mm (5 ft 7 in x 1¼ in x 1 in) timbers for roof corners
4 x 2.3 m x 32 mm x 22 mm (7 ft 6 in x 1¼ in x 1 in) timbers for roof edges
2 x 3.5 m x 70 mm x 42 mm (11 ft 6 in x 2¾ in x 1½ in) timbers for roof crosspieces
slats to fit 2.6 m² (28 ft²), 70 mm x 10 mm (2¾ in x ⅜ in) in section

Fasteners
wire nails

1 Dig four foundations, 500 mm x 500 mm x 500 mm (1 ft 8 in x 1 ft 8 in x 1 ft 8in).
2 Set uprights in holes and brace. Mix and pour concrete (see page 115). Allow to set.
3 Buy timber longer than specified and cut to fit. First nail railings to poles (see detail photograph) to strengthen structure, notching timber to fit.
4 Assemble roof structure as illustrated, again notching wood and skew-nailing.
5 Finally nail slats on to fit.

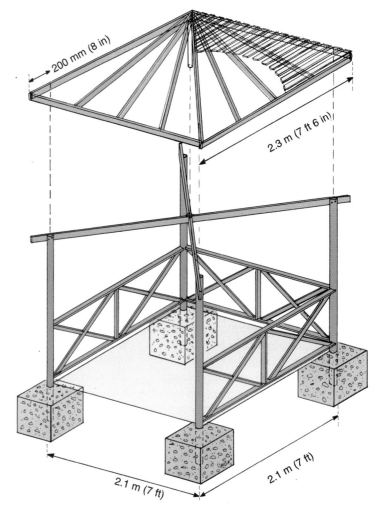

This charming, easy-to-build pergola is the perfect structure to cover a simple barbecue patio. Striped shadecloth shelters the area from the hot summer sun, while brick paving underfoot makes it a practical place for entertaining. A simple bench, easily added to the design, is partially screened by a rustic split-pole railing which can also serve as a climbing frame for creepers.

MATERIALS

Foundations for poles
230 kg (507 lb) cement
930 kg or 0.7 m³ (2,050 lb or 25 ft³) sand
930 kg or 0.7 m³ (2,050 lb or 25 ft³) stone

Framework
6 x 3 m (10 ft) upright poles, 120 mm (5 in) in diameter
1 x 1.25 m (4 ft) upright pole, 120 mm (5 in) in diameter
3 x 3.25 m (10 ft 6 in) beams, 90 mm (3½ in) in diameter
5 x 4 m (13 ft) crosspieces, 90 mm (3½ in) in diameter
3 x 2.3 m (7 ft 6 in) split poles, 45 mm (1¾ in) in diameter
6 x 1.4 m (4 ft 6 in) split poles, 45 mm (1¾ in) in diameter

2 x 3 m x 45 mm x 10 mm (10 ft x 1¾ in x ⅜ in) cover strips
2 x 4 m x 45 mm x 10 mm (13 ft x 1¾ in x ⅜ in) cover strips

Roof covering
shadecloth to cover 12 m² (130 ft²)

Fasteners
12 x 12 mm (1½ in) cuphead bolts with nuts and washers
9 x 10 mm (⅜ in) cuphead bolts with nuts and washers
18 x 8 mm (¼ in) coach screws
clout nails
heavy-duty staples and tacks

Paving
540 bricks/blocks
675 kg or 0.5 m³ (1,488 lb or 17½ ft³) sand

1 Dig seven foundations, 500 mm x 500 mm x 500 m (1 ft 8 in x 1 ft 8 in x 1 ft 8 in) set out as illustrated.
2 Brace poles and pour concrete into holes.
3 Ensure that tops of taller poles are level. Bolt the beams to them, 135 mm (5¼ in) from top with 12 mm (½ in) cuphead bolts.
4 Using 12 mm (1/2 in) cuphead bolts, secure a crosspiece on each side of structure, with an overhang of 200 mm (8 in) at each end.
5 Position remaining three crosspieces over beams at intervals of 730 mm (2 ft 5 in). Secure from above with 10 mm (⅜ in) cuphead bolts.
6 Attach railings with coach screws.
7 Nail sides of shadecloth to the 4 m (13 ft) lengths of cover strip; stretch over structure and staple along crosspieces. Tack to the 3 m (10 ft) lengths of cover strip along sides to neaten (see detail photograph).
8 Pave the surface area.

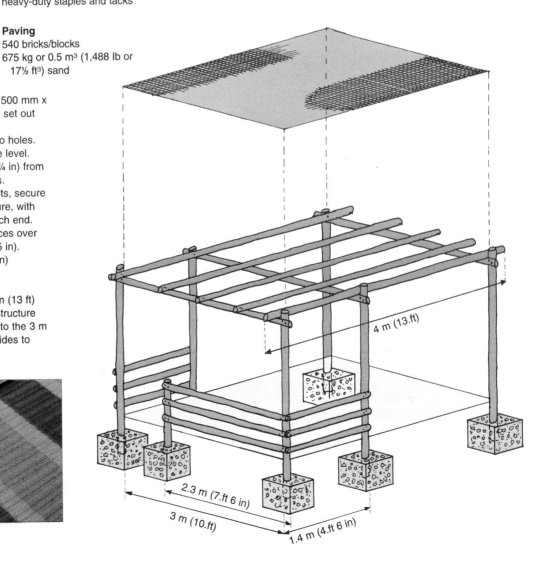

4 m (13 ft)

2.3 m (7 ft 6 in)

3 m (10 ft)

1.4 m (4 ft 6 in)

SIMPLE RUSTIC STEPS

These charming rustic steps are set at the base of a grassy bank and link a stone patio/walkway with a slightly raised garden and are made from timber sleepers and split poles which have been sunk well into the ground. The materials specified will enable you to build four steps set into a similar slope, and a simulated stone slab patio or walkway of 12 m². If you cannot find poles that are long enough to span the treads, simply abut two shorter ones to fit, and adjust the dimensions to suit your site.

MATERIALS
Steps

4 x 1 m x 250 mm x
 150 mm timber or precast
 sleepers
1 x 2.7 m split pole, 90 mm
 in diameter
1 x 2.07 m split pole,
 90 mm in diameter
2 x 1.8 m split poles, 90 mm
 in diameter, for the sides
1 x 1.44 m split pole,
 90 mm in diameter
1 x 900 mm split pole,
 90 mm in diameter

36 x 400 mm split poles,
 90 mm in diameter
78 x 300 mm split poles,
 90 mm in diameter
78 x 75 mm anodised nails

Patio/walkway
0.6 m³ sand
23 x 500 mm x 500 mm
 reconstituted stone slabs
23 x 500 mm x 250 mm
 reconstituted stone slabs
23 x 250 mm x 250 mm
 reconstituted stone slabs

1 Excavate the area of the steps, cutting away roughly to the shape required.

2 Dig a 200 mm deep trench along the front and set thirty 300 mm long split poles in place. Nail the 2.7 m long pole (or two 1.35 m poles) to the back of these, so that the upper surface of all the timber is straight and level. Fill in the excavated soil in front of the step and compact it well.

3 Dig a 200 mm deep trench on either side of the steps, following the slope of the ground. Position the first six or seven 400 mm long poles on either side.

4 Dig another trench at the back of the first tread (which should measure 490 mm from front to back), then set the next row of poles in place to form a second riser. Nail the 2.07 m long pole behind this row as before, fill the trench and compact the fill.

5 Continue, systematically building each tread, making sure the risers are level and well secured from behind. When all the side poles are in place, secure these in the same way. Fill in the treads with soil, leaving 175 mm for the sleepers and a bed of sand, and compact.

6 Spread a 25 mm layer of sand on top of the soil before positioning the sleepers.

7 Top up the area around and between the sleepers with good quality soil before planting.

8 When the steps are complete, level the ground where the patio or walkway is to be sited and compact it well.

9 Spread 25-50 mm sand over the surface and water it lightly with a hose to aid compaction.

10 Lay the slabs in a random fashion, ensuring that they are level.

11 Fill the gaps with good soil before planting.

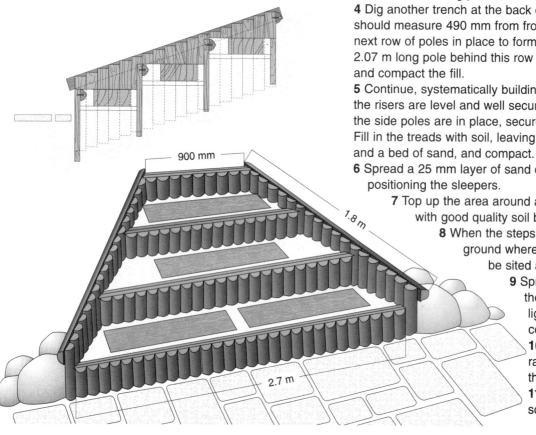

900 mm

1.8 m

2.7 m

WANDERING WALKWAY

Railway sleepers and bricks are cleverly combined to create a slightly winding, gradually stepped path leading to an informal garden. These materials are laid on a concrete slab which is stepped up the slope. Materials listed will enable you to construct a walkway about 5 m long; the number of steps you decide to build will depend largely on the gradient of your site. If timber sleepers are not available, hardwood planks or precast concrete imitation sleepers could be used instead. Although most of the sleepers will stay in place without bolts or screws, it is a good idea to secure those on the treads firmly in the concrete with coach screws.

MATERIALS

230 bricks	535 kg or 0.4 m³ stone
225 kg cement (135 kg for foundation)	11 x 2.3 m x 250 mm x 150 mm railway sleepers
1 180 kg or 0.9 m³ sand (270 kg for bedding bricks)	33 x 100 mm coach screws (optional)
	scrap timber for formwork

1 Mark the line of the walkway and excavate an area 50-100 mm wider than the path on either side and 200 mm deep. Use formwork where the foundation is stepped and overlap the levels of concrete by at least 50 mm.

2 Mix the concrete (materials listed are for a 1:4:4 ratio of cement, sand and stone) and place it over the entire excavated area to a thickness of about 50 mm.
3 If you wish, insert about three coach screws part way into the underside of each sleeper, ensuring that the head and at least half of the screw protrudes from the timber.
4 Before the concrete sets, position the sleepers about 230 mm apart along the path and at the front of each tread and push each one down firmly to level it.
5 Once the concrete has set thoroughly, lay the bricks between the sleepers in the pattern illustrated. Bed each section of paving on enough sand for the bricks to lie flush with the sleepers – about 45 mm. Lay the bricks side by side as shown, cutting some to fit the curves of the path where necessary.
6 Sprinkle a very weak, crumbly mixture of cement and sand (mixed in a 1:6 ratio with a little water) over the surface to fill in any gaps.
7 Spray the walkway lightly with water before this mortar dries.

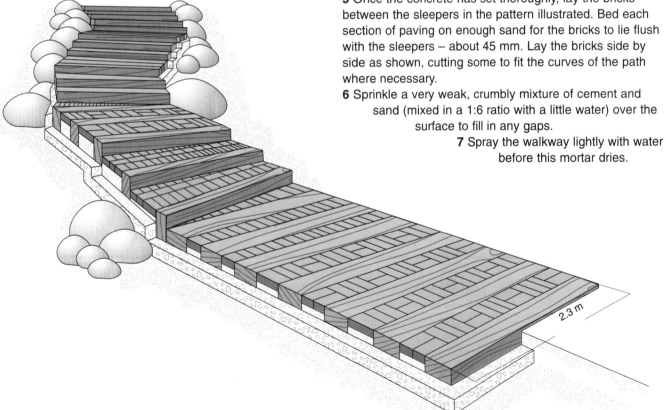

2.3 m

1

2

3

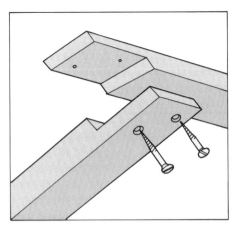

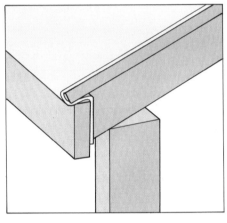

TIMBER SHED

If you construct a garden shed from scratch, you can use good-quality materials and a high standard of joinery to produce a building to last for years.

1 Make up the floor, using 75 x 50 mm (3 x 2 in) joists set at about 300 mm (12 in) centres. Notch the joist ends to accept 50 x 25 mm (2 x 1 in) cross battens that will keep the joists square while you add the decking of either tongue-and- groove boards, plywood or roofing- grade chipboard, nailed to the joists. Set the completed frame in place on its base, with strips of roofing felt under the joists to keep the damp at bay.
2 Make up four wall panels using 75 x 50 mm (3 x 2 in) timber with vertical studs at about 450 mm (18 in) centres and a rail halfway up each panel for strength. Use simple halving joints glued and screwed together. Position door and window frame members to suit the off-the-shelf door and window. The end walls have integral gables, with the angled rafters notched into tops of the wall studs.
3 When the wall frames are complete, stand two adjacent frames in position on the edge of the floor and cramp them together. Drill two holes right through both the corner posts, about one-third and two-thirds of the way up, then bolt the two frames together with carriage bolts. Repeat with the other panels to

complete the shed frame.
4 Fix remaining rafters by nailing to the tops of the side wall frames, and attach the cladding. Cover end walls first, working from the bottom up and cutting the pieces to finish flush with the face of the side frames. Clad these next, letting the cladding overlap the cut ends of the end wall cladding to protect it from water penetration. Treat the end grain of the side wall cladding with preservative.
5 For the roof, fit two panels of exterior-grade plywood or chipboard, screwing each panel to the rafters at 300 mm (12 in) intervals. Lay the first strip of roofing felt in position, taking it over the ridge of the roof if wide enough, and fix with galvanised clout nails. Lay the second strip on the other side of the slope, bringing it over the ridge to overlap the first piece. Cut the felt at the corners of the roof, and fold and tack the overlaps down. Turn the lower edges of the felt over the edges of the roof boards, tack them and fit a fascia board.
6 Fit a gable end cut from wide board or exterior-grade plywood, then finish by glazing the window, hanging the door and applying an overall coat of preservative.

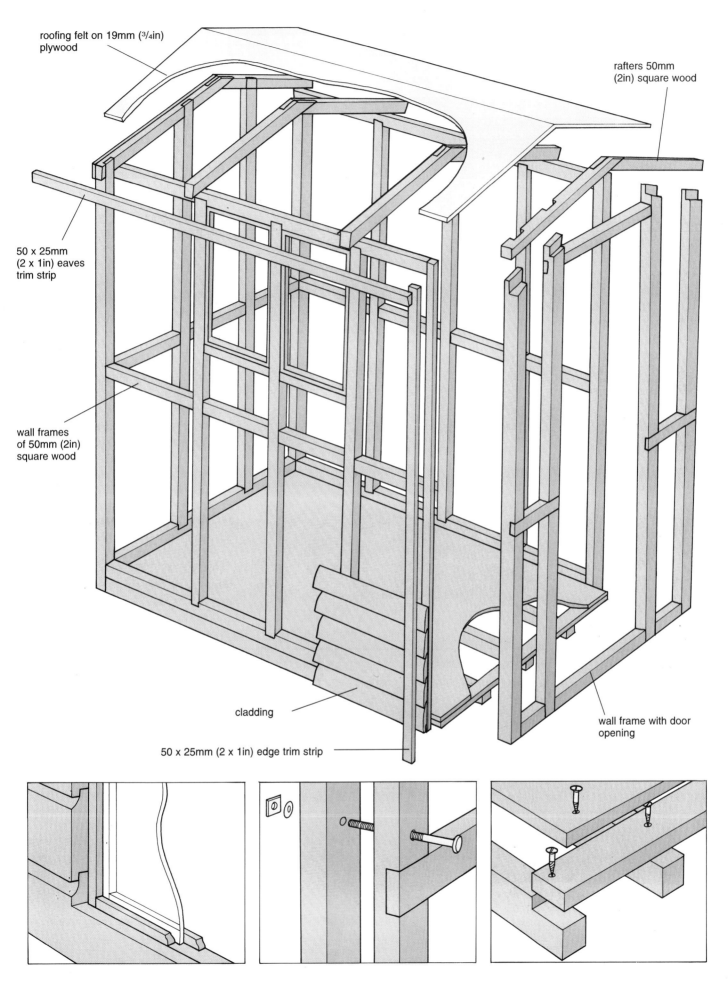

roofing felt on 19mm (³⁄₄in) plywood

rafters 50mm (2in) square wood

50 x 25mm (2 x 1in) eaves trim strip

wall frames of 50mm (2in) square wood

cladding

50 x 25mm (2 x 1in) edge trim strip

wall frame with door opening

If you keep caged birds, you can add a touch of colour to your garden by making them a summer aviary. This has been designed as a mobile unit, so you can roll it into the sun or the shade or indoors as required.

1 Link the corner posts of 50 mm (2 in) square timber at top, centre and bottom by four 50 mm (2 in) square rails with halving joints, glued and screwed .

2 Glue and nail lengths of 50 x 25 mm (2 x 1 in) wood to the outer faces of the top, centre and bottom rails on three sides; leave the back for a full-length panel of 12 mm (in) thick exterior-grade plywood, which is glued and nailed to the posts and rails all round. Another panel forms the floor, glued and nailed to the underside of the bottom rails.

3 The roof is two panels of plywood cut to overlap the eaves and gable ends by 50 mm (2 in). Use a power saw to cut some 50 mm (2 in) square wood lengthwise into right-angled triangles. Glue and nail a length to the upper face of each top side rail as a roof support, and use another length as a ridge board to link the roof panels at right angles. Set the roof panels in place and nail through them into the triangular supports. Cut two gable pieces and nail to the ends of the ridge board and roof supports at the front and back of the structure.

4 Line the door with 38 x 25 mm (1   x 1 in) wood, fitted flush with the front corner posts and horizontal rails. Make up the door. Use 38 mm (1   in) square wood, with halving or mitre joints at the corners, and hinge it to the lining at one side. Add a hasp and staple at the side.

5 Paint the structure. Measure up the length of the three sides of the aviary internally, then cut mesh to the length and height required and make two 90° folds in it on your work-bench. The upper section is in one piece for security. Manoeuvre the section inside the aviary, and start fixing one end to a rear corner posts. Next, staple it to the horizontal side rails, working towards the adjacent corner post. Staple the first fold to the post, then take the mesh across the front to the other front post and finally back to the other rear post. Staple the top and bottom edges to the top and centre rails.

6 Cut panels to fit the two lower side sections and the door, and staple in place. Fit castors.

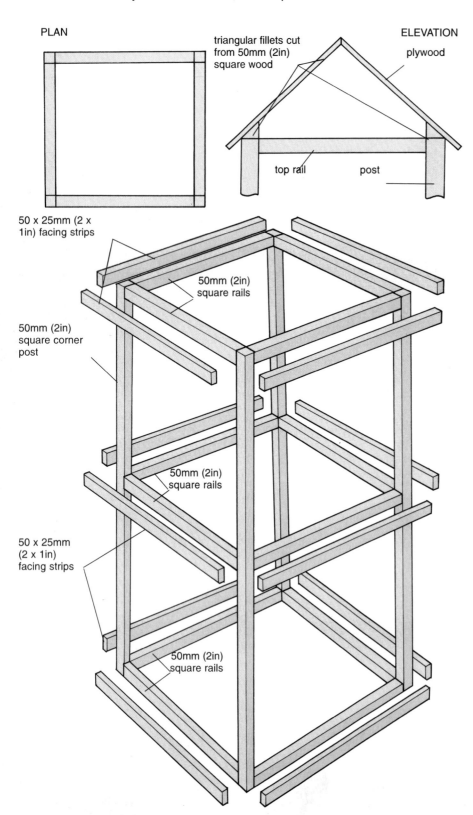

PLAN

triangular fillets cut from 50mm (2in) square wood

ELEVATION

plywood

top rail

post

50 x 25mm (2 x 1in) facing strips

50mm (2in) square rails

50mm (2in) square corner post

50mm (2in) square rails

50 x 25mm (2 x 1in) facing strips

50mm (2in) square rails

5

This simple, wooden platform deck makes an ideal beginner's project. It can be tackled by anybody with just basic carpentry skills and does not require a huge range of tools or equipment. Because it is a small, low-level deck, the framework can be assembled and bolted together before the supporting posts are concreted into the ground.

Although there was only a very slight gradient in this particular garden, the design could also be constructed alongside a house built on a flat plot, or adapted for a much more steeply sloping site.

MATERIALS

For a 5 m x 3 m (16 ft 5 in x 10 ft) deck:

2 x 5 m x 144 mm x 44 mm (16 ft 5 in x 5½ in x 1¾ in) beams

3 x 3 m x 144 mm x 44 mm (10 ft x 5½ in x 1¾ in) beams

10 x 2.5 m x 144 mm x 44 mm (8 ft 2½ in x 5½ in x 1¾ in) joists

6 x 360-600 mm (1 ft 2 in-2 ft) offcuts of wood

8 or more 144 mm x 44 mm (5½ in x 1¾ in) posts

50 x 3 m x 96 mm x 22 mm (10 ft x 3¾ in x ⅞ in) decking slats

72 x 6 mm x 70 mm (¼ in x 2¾ in) anodised self-tapping screws

20 x 10 mm x 90 mm (⅜ in x 3½ in) cuphead bolts with nuts and washers

700 x 50 mm (2 in) stainless-steel nails

50 kg (110 lb) cement

200 kg (440 lb) sand

200 kg (440 lb) stone

Preparation

1 Lengths of timber that are longer than required will have to be cut to the correct size; some cutting can be done before work begins on assembling the deck, but be careful as you will need to double-check some of the measurements for accuracy during construction. If you cannot obtain 5 m (16 ft 5 in) lengths of wood for the framework, then buy shorter pieces and join them together, as shown in Step 5.

2 For a truly professional finish, bevel the top edges of the decking slats with a router. Alternatively, you can order planed wood with 45° bevelled edges to save work.

3 Sand all the timber and give it one thorough coat of sealer before you begin assembling the deck. This is particularly important for sections of wood which will abut other pieces or which will be inaccessible once the structure is complete.

Constructing the framework

4 Using an electric drill attachment and three anodised self-tapping screws at each of the connecting points, drill and screw the two 5 m (16 ft 5 in) lengths to the ends of one of the 3 m (10 ft) pieces of wood.

4

5 If you are joining two shorter pieces of wood to form each of the longer sides of the deck, cut away a block of wood 100 mm (4 in) long and half the width of the beam (22 mm or ⅞ in) from one end of both pieces of timber, so that they slot together to form a lap joint. Holding the two pieces together in position, drill four equally spaced holes where they join. Secure each join with four cuphead bolts.

6 Measure the central point along each of the 5 m (16 ft 5 in) beams and mark with a pencil. Following the instructions given in step 4, connect the central crosspiece to the beams at these points (directly over the join if you have used two pieces of wood to form the longer beam).

6

7 Attach the third 3 m (10 ft) length at the open end of the framework.

8 The joists should be a little less than 2.5 m (8 ft 3 in) long. It is essential, however, to check the distances between the crosspieces before cutting. Since timber frequently bows (particularly in the centre of an unsupported span), the measurements at either end will be the most accurate ones.

8

9 Mark a cutting line on all ten pieces of timber, using a builder's square for accuracy. If the joist timbers are longer than required, the offcuts will be

suitable for the short posts.

10 Cut off the ends with a circular saw. If you are not working with a very hard wood, you may be able to use a handsaw instead. If the ends of the timber have been rough-cut (which is usually the case), it is unlikely that they will be exactly square. Trim both

ends, making sure that your measurements are correct.

11 It is essential that the ends of the joists are sealed before securing them to the beams with anodised screws.

12 If you take the easy option and screw both sets of joists to the central

crosspiece, they will not run in a completely straight line. This is not critical, except that the nails which secure the decking will not be quite in line. If you wish to align the joists, skew-nail the end of one of each pair of joists. Whichever method you use, space the timber at 500 mm (1 ft 7½ in) centres, and check with a spirit level to ensure that they are all level.

13 If the timber bows excessively, you may have to clamp some of the wood in position before screwing it down.

14 Using a combination square, check all timber joins to make absolutely certain that they are at right angles.

Levelling the framework

15 Before you position the posts and concrete them into the ground, you must get the completed framework level. Do this by stacking offcuts under the central beam and by screwing about six short lengths to the inside edges (in the photograph, these are

the upright pieces which you see extending above the top of the framework). Use a spirit level to ensure accuracy.

Positioning the posts

16 For the structure to be stable, it will need to be supported on at least eight permanent posts. To strengthen the deck and stop any sideways movement, position posts on the joins

16

20

21

and as close to the outer corners of the deck as possible.

17 Dig 300 mm x 300 mm x 300 mm (12 in x 12 in x 12 in) holes for the post footings.

18 Bolt the posts to the framework, ensuring that the tops of the posts are flush with the joists. Note that you can utilise the bolts which are already in place at the joins by unfastening and rebolting them.

19 Mix cement, sand and stone in the ratio 1:4:4 and pour the concrete into the holes for the foundation footings. Allow to set thoroughly for 24-48 hours before removing the supports.

21 Nail the slats to the joists, using a 5 mm (¼ in) spacer to space the slats accurately. If you are working with very hard wood, you will have to drill holes for the nails. This is easily done with a fine drill bit.

22 If you wish, you can close the open sides of the deck with additional slats.

Finishing

23 Fill the holes with epoxy or a powder filler mixed with a little sawdust; allow to dry and then sand so that the finished surface is even.

24 Cut uneven edges with a jigsaw, sand, and finally seal or varnish the entire deck.

19

Attaching the decking

20 Position the slats on the joists, working with about six boards at a time. Use a chalk line to ensure that the nails will be hammered in in a straight line along the joists.

The completed low-level deck is a perfect place for weekend entertaining.

BIRD FEEDING TABLE

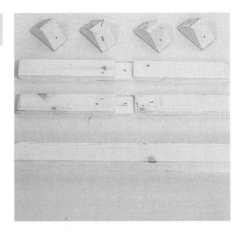

This unusual feeding table is easy to make from a few offcuts of softwood and exterior-grade plywood. It is also ideal for children to tackle, with a little adult supervision. This project can also be made during long winter evenings as it can be built indoors and then moved outside when spring arrives.

The structure is basically a simple hopper that dispenses food – through openings in the sides. It is filled by removing the roof, and the pyramid inside ensures that gravity keeps the food flowing out to the birds.

1 Start by cutting out the feeding table floor a 305 mm (12 in) square of 16 or 19 mm (⅝ or ¾ in) thick plywood. Frame its edges by gluing and pinning on four neatly mitred 317 mm (12½ in) lengths of 30 x 6 mm (1¼ x ¼ in) beading, with their top edges flush with one face of the plywood.

2 Next, prepare the walls. Each is a 200 x 125 mm (8 x 5 in) piece of 12 mm (½ in) thick plywood, with a small door 35 mm (1⅜ in) high and 25 mm (1 in) wide cut into one edge with a coping saw. The top edges of each wall panel are cut away to an angle of 70˚ – a job for a protractor. Glue the four pieces together in sequence so that the face of one piece overlaps the edge of the next as you work round the square. Then glue the assembled walls to the table at a 45˚ angle to its edges.

3 Now you can turn your attention to the roof. Cut two pieces of 12 mm (½ in) plywood measuring 305 x 200 mm (12 x 8 in), and mark up and cut out the two gables – each a triangle with a base length of 175 mm (6   in) and a height of 35 mm (1   in), cut from 19 mm (in) plywood. Plane off one long edge of each roof section to an angle of 70˚ and test that the planed edges meet neatly when a gable end is held against their undersides.

4 Glue the gable ends firmly into place about 25 mm (1 in) from the edges of the roof. Then cut some scrap wood blocks and glue them to the underside of the roof to locate it in place. These blocks should form a reasonably tight fit inside the walls.

5 Finally, make the pyramid to fit loosely inside the house. This is done either by gluing four triangles of plywood together or by shaping a pyramid from a soild block. It measures 110 mm (4   in) square.

6 The stand is made from a 1.4m (4 ft 7 in) length of 50 mm (2 in) square planed timber. It is located in a socket on the underside of the table which has been formed with scrap wood. The feet are two 510 mm (20 in) lengths of 50 x 19 mm (2 x   in) wood, joined at right angles with a cross-halving joint. They are linked to the stand with four triangular braces cut from 75 x 50 mm (3 x 2 in) softwood, which are glued and screwed into place.

7 In windy locations, weight the feet down or dispense with them altogether and set the post in concrete or a fence post socket instead.

Right: Painted green and white, this attractive and easy to make bird feeding table will brighten up any winter garden.

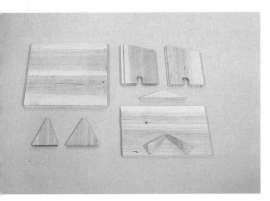

TIMBER STEPS

Any type of wooden deck built above the ground will require a set of steps if you are going to have direct access to the garden or to another level.

Although there are numerous ways to build steps, this project illustrates how to construct the simplest type of timber staircase: steps with an open riser. The same principle may be used for a staircase with a longer span, leading to a higher deck, although handrails would obviously then be required for safety reasons. Should you wish to box in the tread, you will need to use longer cleats along the two stringers to support the riser boards.

Choose wood to match that used in the deck. If you choose to varnish the finished steps, choose a non-slip variety for safety.

Materials

2 x 1.3 m x 220 mm x 36 mm (4 ft 3 in x 8½ in x 1½ in) pieces of wood for the stringers

3 x 1.2 m x 220 mm x 36 mm (4 ft x 8½ in x 1½ in) pieces of wood for the treads

6 x 200 mm x 36 mm x 36 mm (8 in x 1½ in x 1½ in) pieces of wood for the cleats

30 x 60 mm (2¼ in) brass countersunk screws

4 x 8 mm x 110 mm (⅜ in x 4¼ in) coach screws

55 kg (120 lb) cement

225 kg (500 lb) sand

225 kg (500 lb) stone

Preparation

1 Check that the dimensions of the materials specified for this 850 mm (2 ft 9 in) high deck are appropriate for your site. If you are building steps to a deck, the height of the deck will be a major factor in determining the number of steps and, to some extent, the height of the risers.

2 To make the task easier, create a simple profile by nailing two battens together at right angles. The upright length of wood should match the height of the deck (in other words, the

change in level), and the horizontal length should equal the depth of the slope. From this you should be able to work out the optimum number of steps for the site.

3 Even though these steps are made from timber, it is best to concrete the bottom ends firmly into the ground to anchor them and prevent them from becoming unsteady. Having determined where the first step will be, dig two square holes approximately 200 mm x 300 mm (8 in x 12 in) across and 200 mm (8 in) deep.

Construction

4 First cut the stringers to size. These are the lengths of wood on either side of the steps that hold the treads in place. Cut the top of each stringer at the required angle, so that you can abut the stringers to the deck fascia. If the steps lead to a verandah or raised patio, you will have to secure the stringers to a ledger, which must first be bolted secrely on to the patio or verandah wall.

5 Paint the end of each stringer with a coat of bitumen to seal them when underground.

6 Carefully mark the position of the cleats to which the treads will be nailed. In these steps, they are 260 mm (10 in) apart.

7 Use a combination square to ensure that each cleat is straight and level, and secure with the countersunk screws.

7

8 Position the stringer with one end in the hole you have dug, ensuring that the sides are plumb. Attach the top of

5

9

each stringer to the deck with coach screws. Unless you attach it to the fascia before completing the deck, you will have to work from behind the fascia. As an alternative, you can use angle brackets.

9 Mix up the concrete using a cement:sand:stone ratio of 1:4:4 and pour it into the hole. Brace the stringers to hold them in position while the concrete dries.

10 Each tread consists of a 1.2 m (4 ft) length of wood. Position and screw the planks to the cleat.

Finishing

11 Fill all nail holes, then seal or varnish the timber.

10

The finished steps lead to a low-level DIY deck constructed alongside the house.

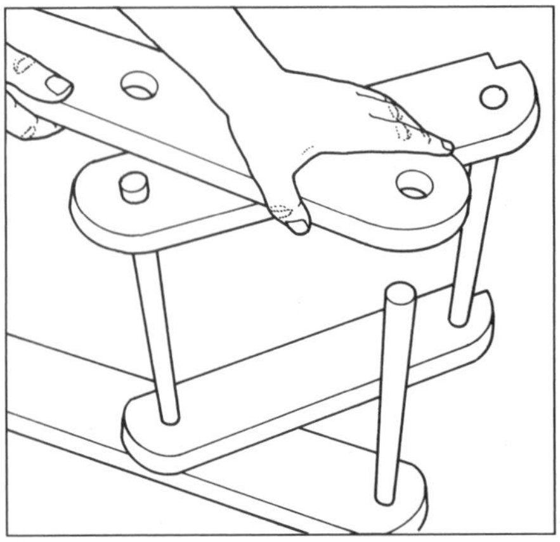

1

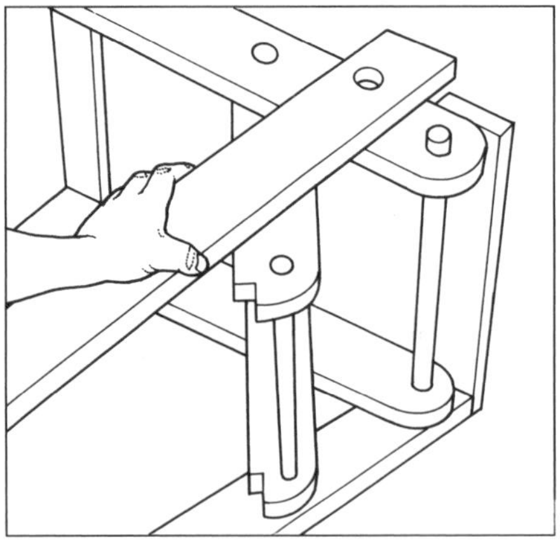

2

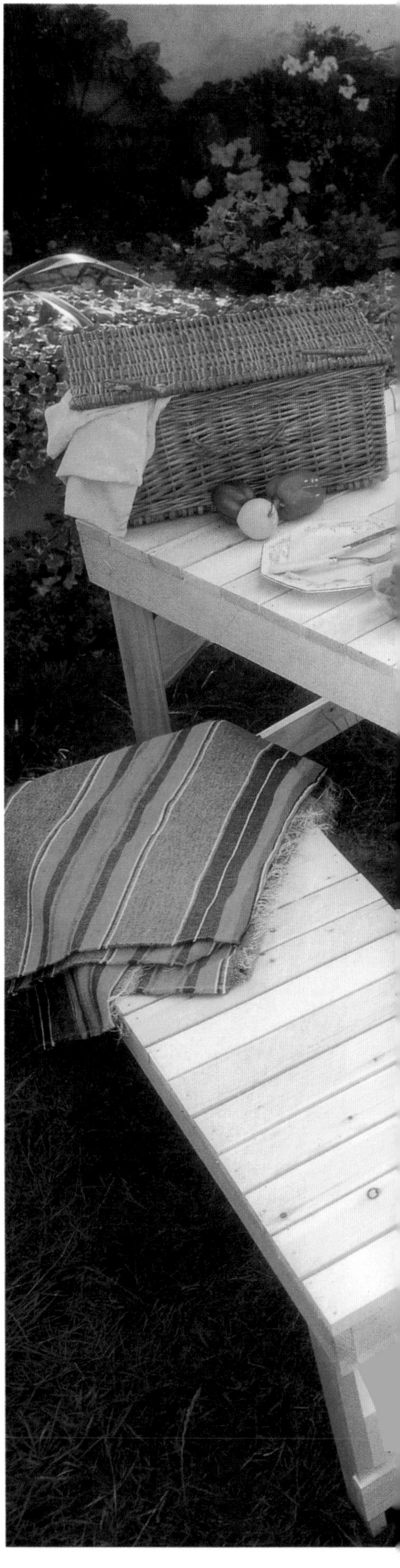

FOLDING FURNITURE

MATERIALS

The table

From 100 x 25 mm (4 x 1 in) wood cut:
15 top slats 750 mm (29½ in) long
2 side rails 1495 mm (58⅞ in) long
2 top end rails 706 mm (27¾ in) long
2 bottom end rails 704 mm (27¾ in) long
4 legs 765 mm (30⅞ in) long
4 leg braces 456 mm (18 in) long

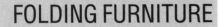

From 25 mm (1 in) diameter dowel cut:
2 top leg bars 750 mm (29½ in) long
2 brace bars 704 mm (27¾ in) long
2 brace bars 658 mm (26 in) long

In addition you will need
2 x 125 mm (5 in) lengths of 75 x 50 mm (3 x 2 in) wood and
2 x 125 mm (5 in) lengths 75 x 38 mm (2 x 1½ in) wood for the leg clamps
2 x 100 mm (4 in) long coach bolts 6 mm (¼ in) in diameter, plus matching wing nuts and washers
8 x 50 mm (2 in) No 8 rustproof countersunk woodscrews

The bench

From 75 x 25 mm (3 x 1 in) wood cut:
15 top slats 400 mm (15¾ in) long
2 side rails 1195 mm (47 in) long
2 top end rails 356 mm (14 in) long
2 bottom end rails 400 mm (15¾ in) long
4 legs 702 mm (27⅝ in) long
4 leg braces 410 mm (16⅛ in) long

You will need 19 mm (¾ in) and 38 mm (1½ in) rustproof (sherardized) oval wire nails, waterproof urea formaldehyde (UF) wood glue and wood preservative.

1 Mark out and cut all the components to length, except the table legs and leg

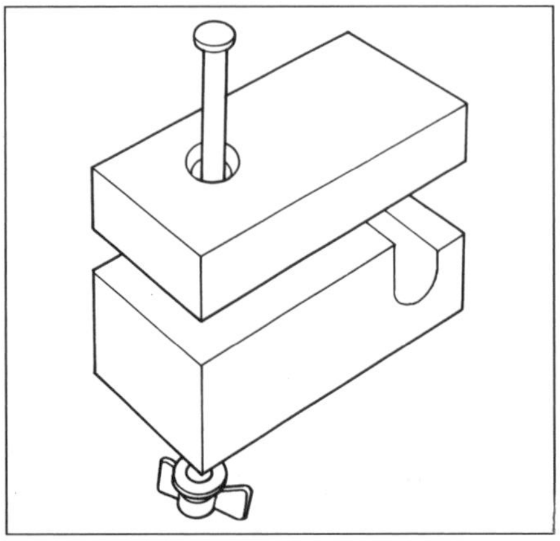

3

braces which should be slightly overlong so the ends can be rounded off.

2 Clamp the table side rails together and drill a 25 mm (1 in) diameter hole through each end of both rails, 71 mm (2¾ in) from their ends.

3 Draw a centre line along one face of each leg and mark off at 48, 53 and 268 mm (1⅞, 2⅛ and 10½ in) intervals. Set a compass on the 53 mm (2⅛ in) mark and scribe an arc from one edge of the leg to the other to draw the shape of the top of the leg. Measure 715 mm (18⅛ in) along the centre line from the top of the arc and square a line across the leg. This is the bottom of the leg. Measure back 50 mm (2 in) from this line and square a second line across the leg. Stand the end of an offcut of 100 x 25 mm (4 x 1 in) wood on the face of the leg so one narrow edge aligns with the second line; draw round it to mark the cut out for bottom end rails.

4 Mark out the other legs, then cut to length, round off their tops, remove the marked cut outs and drill 25 mm (1 in) diameter holes through each leg at the 48 and 268 mm (1⅞ and 10½ in) marks.

5 To make the folding leg braces, cut the four 456 mm (18 in) long pieces that form their sides, mark a centre line along

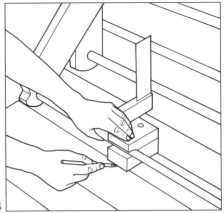

4

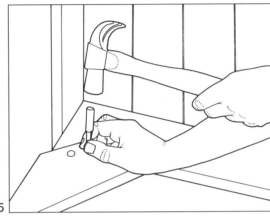

5

each one and make a mark on this 53 mm (2⅛ in) from one end. Draw an arc and round off one end of each brace. Make a second mark on the centre line, 311 mm (12¼ in) from the first mark, and draw a similar arc here, then round off this end too and drill 25 mm (1 in) diameter holes through the braces at both marks. Use a tenon saw to cut a 35 x 22 mm (1⅜ x ⅞ in) notch in one end of each brace; this fits round the table's bottom end rail when the legs are folded.

6 To assemble, glue together the leg braces, with the longer bar protruding equally at each side. Slot these protruding ends into the holes in two of the table legs (1), check they swivel and link the two legs with a bottom end rail (glued and nailed in place) and a top leg bar (glued), checking the latter protrudes equally through each leg. Repeat to assemble the other end of the table, then link the two end frames with the two long side rails and the top end rails after checking that the leg rotates freely (2), and complete the assembly by nailing and gluing on the top slats.

7 Make up the clamps as shown (3). Fit the bolt through the thinner block, then fit the clamp round the leg bar using the washer and wing nut (4). With the leg at

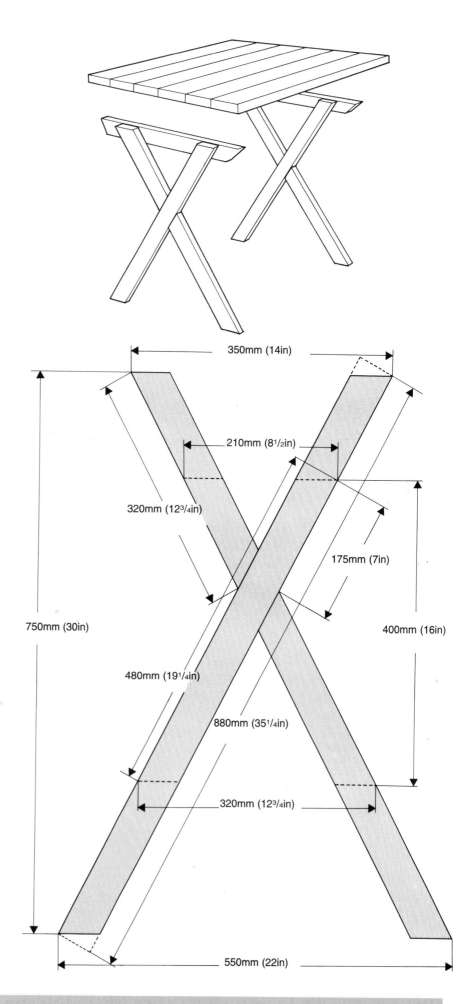

90º to the table top, mark the block position on the underside of the table. Undo the clamp and screw the thinner block to the underside of the table top. The clamp will then secure the leg in both the open and closed positions.

8 To assemble, link the side and top end rails, then add the slats before attaching the legs, the bottom end rails and the angled braces (5). Finish both pieces with wood preservative.

A PATIO SET

This colourful set of patio furniture could not be easier to make. The table top and bench seats are simply planks of wood, set on sturdy X-frame legs to form a solid structure that is heavy enough to stay put even in high winds.

Make up the table top first, to whatever size you like. The table illustrated has a top consisting of eight pieces of 150 x 38 mm (6 x 1½ in) wood, screwed to two 50 x 38 mm (2 x 1½ in) transverse bearers with a narrow gap between each plank to allow rainwater to drain off easily. Countersink the screw holes deeply and fill the recesses with exterior-quality wood filler to remove any risk of rust showing through the paint. Make up the bench seats in exactly the same way.

Next, make up the legs from two pieces of 100 x 38 mm (4 x 1½ in) wood, joined with a cross-halving joint at an angle of 60º. If you do not have a protractor and a sliding bevel, set out the angles. Remember all three sides of a triangle with 60º corner angles measure the same length, and use this to set the pieces at the correct angle. Cut the halving joints with a tenon saw and chisel, check their fit, then drill through the joint and secure it with a coach bolt.

Screw each leg assembly to the outer face of a transverse bearer beneath the table top or seat. Then screw a short length of 50 x 38 mm (2 x 1½ in) wood to the under-side of the top/seats, at right angles to each bearer, to which the diagonal leg braces will be attached. Measure up the required length for each pair of braces, cut their ends at 45º angles, drill deep counterbores for the fixing screws and fix them in position. Finally, sand and paint each item.

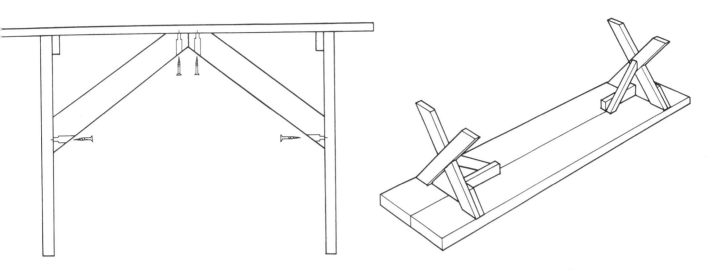

A COLD FRAME

This cold frame is made from tongued-and-grooved softwood cladding, fixed to corner posts, with opening top frames. A router or a set of shaping cutters for your electric drill is invaluable for making this.

1 Cut the 19 mm (¾ in) thick cladding to length – 1169 mm (46 in) long for the front and back, and 578 mm (22¾ in) long for the ends. Glue and cramp the boards together to make up panels to be cut down to the required height – 406 mm (16 in) for the back and 353 mm (13⅞ in) for the front. Mark the ends to be 353 mm (13⅞ in) high at the front and 406 mm (16 in) high at the back, link the marks with a cutting line and saw along it. Bevel the top edge of the front and back panels off to an angle of 20°.

2 Make up the centre strut next from one 578 mm (22⅞ in) length and one 588 mm (23⅛ in) length of 75 x 19 mm (3 x ¾ in) wood, plus one 537 mm (21⅛ in) length of 25 x 15 mm (1 x ⅝ in). Glue and screw the two wider pieces together to form a beam with a cross-section in the shape of a T, aligning them at one end so that the other end of the on-edge piece of wood projects by 10 mm (⅜ in). This stub on the upper end of the strut locates in a vertical blind mortise cut in the middle of the back panel, with the top of the cut-out 44 mm (1⅜ in) below the top edge of the back panel. Glue and screw the 25 x 15 mm length of wood on edge on top of the T-section projecting 44 mm (1¾ in) beyond the lower end of the T-section strut.

3 Cut two 406 mm (16 in) long and two 353 mm (13⅞ in) long corner posts from 45 mm (1¾ in) square wood. Glue and screw them to the side edges of both end panels, and then screw the back and front panels to the posts so the ends of these panels overlap the exposed endgrain of the end panels. Slot one end of the centre strut into its mortise in the back panel, then screw through the front panel into its other end to secure it. Add the top back rail to which the opening frames will be hinged; this is a 1199 mm (47 in) length of 85 x 25 mm (3⅜ x 1 in) wood screwed to the tops of the corner posts and to the centre strut.

4 Cut glazed frames from 25 mm (1 in)

thick wood. The two sides are 572 mm (22½ in) long and 50 mm (2 in) wide, and each has a 9 mm (⅜ in) wide groove cut 12 mm (½ in) deep along its inner edge to hold the glass. The back rail, which is hinged to the top back rail of the cold

frame, is a 538 mm (21¼ in) length of 75 mm (3 in) wide wood, also grooved and with 25 mm (1 in) long tenons cut on each end so the width between the tenon shoulders is 488 mm (19¼ in). The front rail is 588 mm (23⅛ in) long, 80 mm (3⅛

Above: Attractively painted, the cold frame is a practical addition to any garden.

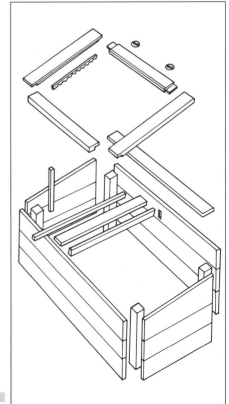

in) wide, with a 50 x 12 mm (2 x ½ in) rebate machined along its length.

5 The top corner has an open mortise joint; the bottom corners are halving joints. The glass oversails the front rail, which overlaps the wall so water drains.

6 Assemble the frames, slide in the glass, measuring 506 x 490 mm (19⅞ x 19¼ in). Secure the bottom edge of the pane to the bottom rail of the frame with glazing springs. Hinge the frames to the top back rail of the cold frame.

SIMPLE ARCH SWING

The earliest rope swings were probably hung from the branch of a tree, and an arch swing suspended from a horizontal beam is the nearest man-made equivalent.

MATERIALS
Hardcore
Concrete (see page 112)

Swing: from planed softwood
2 x 3 m x 100 mm x 100 mm (10 ft x 4 in x 4 in) uprights
1 x 1 m x 100 mm x 100 mm (3 ft x 4 in x 4 in) crossbar
4 x 150 mm x 50 mm (6 in x 2 in) narrow support strips
Eyebolts
Nuts
Nails
Long screws
Rope/swing chain
Nylon rope clamps/chain shackles

Seat: from planed softwood
2 x 550 mm x 100 mm x 25 mm (22 in x 4 in x 1 in) slats
2 x 300 mm x 100 mm x 25 mm (12 in x 4 in x 1 in) support blocks
Foam rubber
Vinyl upholstery fabric
Heavy-duty staples

The beam can be part of an existing garden structure, or you can build a simple free-standing arch consisting of two vertical supports bridged by a horizontal cross-piece. You can even incorporate it in another garden structure such as a pergola if you wish.

This is an easy swing to construct, as all you need are two uprights spaced about 1 m (just over 3 ft) apart, and a well-secured beam spanning their tops to form a sturdy support for the swing. To ensure the structure can withstand the lateral forces that will be imposed on it, the uprights must be set in the ground, secured with concrete.

The crossbar must be thick enough to cope with potential overloading – swing seats often have more than one occupant!

Above: It is important to position swings where other children will not be in danger of being hit.

Cutting the components

The dimensions are for a standard-sized swing, but you can scale them down if you wish.

The two uprights are cut from planed softwood. (Narrower timber 76 mm x 76 mm [3 in x 3 in] will work just as well.) They must be long enough to allow for about 900 mm (3 ft) of their length to be embedded in the ground. The crossbar is cut from the same square wood, and rests on top of the two uprights. It is secured to them by narrow strips of wood screwed to each side of the crossbar and to the sides of the uprights to form a strong support. Two large

eyebolts screwed the crossbar provide supports for the seat ropes or chains.

The seat is made up by screwing the two 550 mm (22 in) lengths of softwood to the two shorter support blocks of the same-sized wood. The seat and the support blocks are drilled at each side of the seat to provide secure fixings for the supporting ropes or chains, which can either pass round the underside of the seat or can be attached to eyebolts.

Making the swing

1 Excavate two 300 mm (12 in) square holes about 1 m (3 ft 3 in) apart to a depth of 900 mm (3 ft) to take the

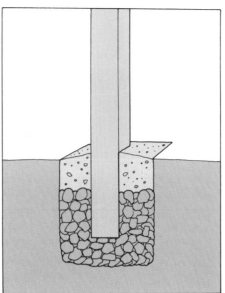

Tighten the nuts fully so the bolts are secure.

5 Attach the seat support ropes or chains to the eyebolts, ready for the seat to be attached. Use proprietary chain shackles or special nylon rope clamps to make the fixings, and test that they are secure.

Making a simple slat seat

6 Glue and screw the timber components together. Drill holes for the support rope – or for eyebolts if you are using chain – through the seat and the support blocks, about 25 mm (1 in) in from the seat corners.

7 Pass rope down through one hole, across the underside of the support

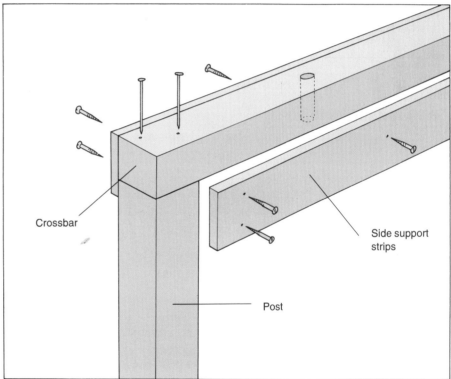

Crossbar

Side support strips

Post

uprights. Set each one in its hole, brace it upright and check it is level with its neighbour. Ram in broken bricks round the base and add concrete to each one. Smooth off the concrete and leave to harden for 48-72 hours (see diagram 1).

2 Nail the crossbar to the tops of the posts. Then add the two narrow support strips, with their top edges level with its upper surface (diagram 2).

3 Drive long screws through the outer face of each strip into both the crossbar and the uprights to secure the crossbar in place.

4 Drill two holes about 500 mm (20 in) apart in the crossbar and attach the eyebolts for the seat support ropes.

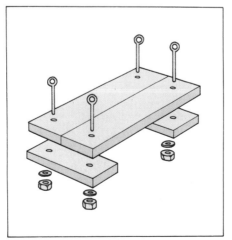

block and back up through the other hole, securing the cut end to the main length of rope with a clamp.

8 Attach eyebolts for the support chains (diagram 3), tightening the nuts before attaching the chain with shackles.

Safety first

Seats can cause a nasty injury if they strike a child. Soften the edges by gluing on pieces of dense chip-foam. Cover the seat with vinyl upholstery fabric, pull it taut across the foam and staple it to the underside of the seat.

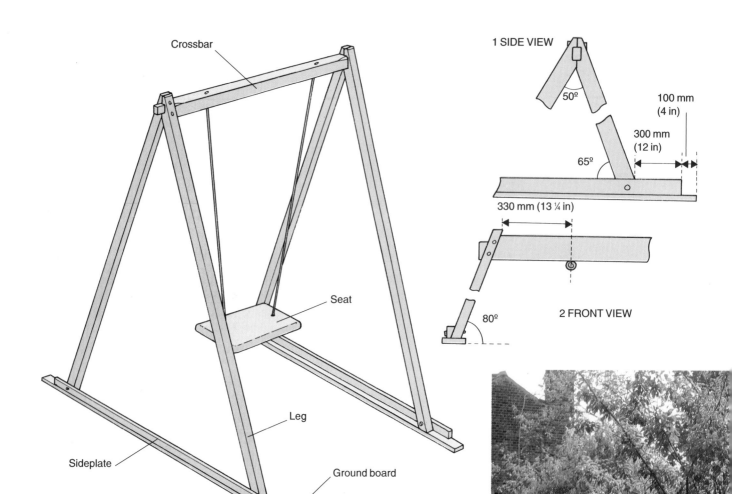

Crossbar

1 SIDE VIEW

50º

65º

80º

330 mm (13 ¼ in)

300 mm (12 in)

100 mm (4 in)

2 FRONT VIEW

Seat

Leg

Sideplate

Ground board

A-FRAME SWING

The traditional swing – the A-frame – is a stable structure. There are two side frames to provide a wide base that resists toppling even when the seat swings high, plus a sturdy crossbar.

Since the only link between the two A-frames is the crossbar, it is essential that the ground boards are fixed down with long metal ground anchors or that cross beams are fitted at ground level to link the ends of the frames together.

MATERIALS

Frame: from preservative-treated planed softwood

4 x 2.7 m x 76 mm x 50 mm (8 ft 10 in x 3 in x 2 in) legs

1.825 m x 100 mm x 76 mm (6 ft x 4 in x 3 in) crossbar

2 x 2.9 m x 50 mm x 25 mm (9 ft 6 in x 2 in x 1 in) side plates

2 x 3.1 m x 76 mm x 25 mm (10 ft 2 in x 3 in x 1 in) ground boards

75 mm (3 in) coach bolts

125 mm (5 in) coach bolts

Eyebolts to attach rope/chain to seat

Nuts and locking washers

Screws

Woodworking adhesive

Rope/swing chain

Panel seat for older children:

1 x 500 mm x 175 mm x 25 mm (20 in x 7 in x 1 in) timber seat board

2 x 500 mm x 25 mm x 25 mm (20 in x 1 in x 1 in) narrow strips to edge seat

2 x 175 mm x 25 mm x 25 mm (7 in x 1 in x 1 in) narrow strips to edge seat
50 mm (2 in) diameter half-round chip foam
Panel pins
Strong all-purpose adhesive
Vinyl upholstery fabric
Heavy-duty staples

Chair seat for smaller child:
From exterior-quality 25 mm (1 in) thick plywood
510 mm x 430 mm (20 in x 17 in) top/arm rest
400 mm x 330 mm (15¾ in x 13 in) seat
310 mm x 200 mm (12¼ in x 8 in) back
2 x 310 mm x 100 mm (12¼ in x 4 in) sides
9 mm (⅜ in) dowel rod
Woodworking adhesive
Chip foam
Vinyl upholstery fabric
Strong all-purpose adhesive
Screws
Leather strap (optional)

You can make the swing with a simple plank seat or, for smaller children, a chair seat with lap strap. In either case you can adjust the height of the seat to suit the ages of the children who will be using it.

Cutting the components
Use planed preservative-treated softwood for making the swing and the basic seat. However, if you decide to make the chair seat, you will need some 25 mm (1 in) thick exterior-quality plywood as well.

Preparing the crossbar
Start by cutting the crossbar to length. You will see from the diagrams (3 and 4 overleaf) that a shouldered tenon is formed on each end, and that this is bolted into matching cut-outs formed in the tops of each of the legs.

1 First mark points on the lower edge of the crossbar, each 65 mm (2½ in) in from the end. Then use a protractor to set a sliding bevel to an angle of 80° and draw a line across the side of the crossbar through each of the two marks. This line represents the angle that will be formed between the legs and the crossbar when the swing is assembled.

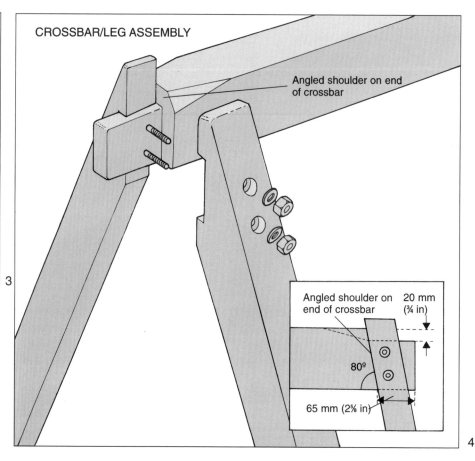

CROSSBAR/LEG ASSEMBLY:
section through joint

20 mm
(¾ in)

75 mm
(3 in) bolt,
nut and
washer

22 mm
(⅞ in)

25 mm
(1 in)

20 mm
(¾ in)

50º

125 mm
(5 in)
bolt, nut
and
washer

3

CROSSBAR/LEG ASSEMBLY

Angled shoulder on end
of crossbar

Angled shoulder on
end of crossbar

20 mm
(¾ in)

80º

65 mm (2⅝ in)

4

2 Next, draw a line on the side of the crossbar at each end, parallel with the top edge and 20 mm (¾ in) below it. This intersects with the 80º-angled line to mark the area of waste wood which must be removed to form the shoulder of the tenon.

3 Once you have formed this shoulder with your saw, use a mortise or marking gauge to mark up a tenon 25 mm (1 in) wide on the centre of each end of the crossbar, as shown in diagram 4, and cut away the waste wood carefully to leave a tenon with an angled shoulder, ready to be bolted in place between the matching shaped cut-outs in the legs.

Assembling the frame

4 Cut the four legs to length. Use a protractor and sliding bevel to mark the cutting angles on each leg. The bottom of each leg is cut to an angle of 65º (diagram 1). At the top a cut is made at an angle of 25º to the edge of each leg, allowing each pair to meet with an angle of 50º between them (diagram 3).

5 Hold the angled top edge of each leg against the side of the crossbar tenon with its side face pressed against the angled shoulder of the tenon.

6 Mark the outline of the tenon on the angled edge of the leg, and then extend the marked lines on to the side faces of the legs so you can mark up a cut-out approximately 13 mm (½ in) deep.

7 Use a tenon saw and chisel to remove the waste wood. (When each pair of legs is brought together, these cut-outs will form a mortise round the tenon on each end of the crossbar.)

8 Check the fit of the joints. Then cramp each pair of legs to the crossbar and drill two 10 mm (⅜ in) holes through the legs and the crossbar tenon as shown in diagram 3.

9 Counter-bore all the holes to a diameter of 25 mm (1 in) and a depth of 15 mm (¾ in), and bolt the joints together using a 75 mm (3 in) long M10 coachbolt (cup-head or carriage bolt) through the upper holes and a 125 mm (5 in) bolt through the lower ones. Use locking washers beneath the nuts so that they cannot work loose.

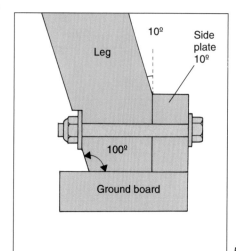

10º

Side
plate
10º

Leg

100º

Ground board

Adding the side plates and ground boards

10 You have already angled the bottom ends of the frame legs to 65º. Now use your protractor and sliding bevel again, this time to draw a line across the bottom face of each leg at an angle of 100º, as shown in diagram 5, to allow the angled leg to stand flat on the ground board.

11 Cut the bottom of each leg to the marked angle. Then chamfer off the outer edge of each leg at right angles to the 100º line so that the side plates can be fitted at right angles to the ground boards; see the cross-sectional diagram 5 again for clarification of this step.

12 Now you can glue and screw the side plates to the ground boards, stand the swing frame on the completed side plate/ground board assemblies and drill a 10 mm (⅜ in) diameter bolt hole through the side plate into the centre of each leg. Bolt the plate to the leg with a 75 mm (3 in) long bolt, nut and locking washer.

Making the panel seat

13 Drill a 10 mm (⅜ in) diameter hole through the 500 mm (20 in) board at

5

each side, 50 mm (2 in) in from the ends, to take the support rope/chain (diagram 6).

14 Thicken the edges of the board by gluing and pinning on the softwood strips all the way round. Glue pieces of half-round chip-foam to the front and to the rear edges of the seat board for comfort and also as protection from accidents.

15 Complete the seat by stapling on a piece of vinyl upholstery fabric, turning it over the foam edges on to the underside. Pierce the fabric over the bolt hole positions and fit the bolts with nuts and washers ready for the support ropes/chains.

Making the chair seat

1 Mark and cut out the components from the plywood using the dimensions and the cut-outs shown in the diagram. Save the off-cut from the top/armrest section to make a drop-in seat (see diagram 7).

2 Make the various cut-outs as shown, then test-fit the back and sides into them.

3 Drill holes for the dowels as shown, and assemble the seat by gluing and

dowelling all the components together.

4 Drill four holes as shown for the eyebolts, fit them with washers and nuts and attach the support ropes/chains (diagram 8).

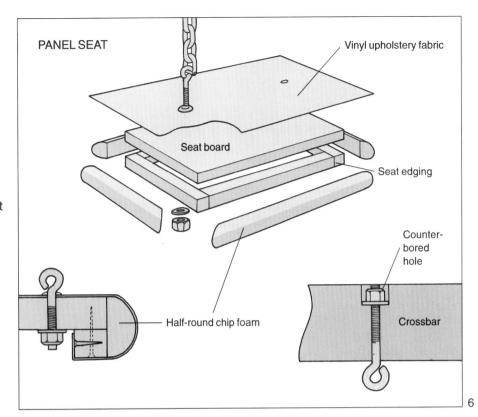

PANEL SEAT

Vinyl upholstery fabric

Seat board

Seat edging

Counter-bored hole

Half-round chip foam

Crossbar

6

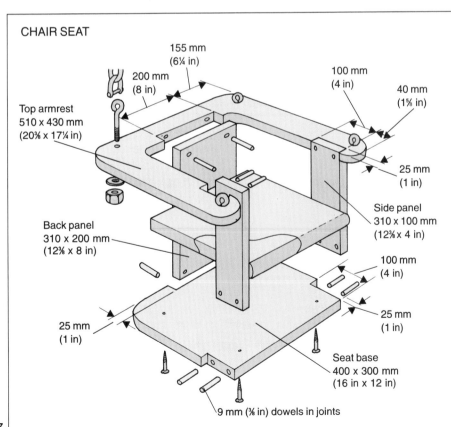

CHAIR SEAT

155 mm (6¼ in)

200 mm (8 in)

100 mm (4 in)

40 mm (1⅝ in)

Top armrest 510 x 430 mm (20⅛ x 17¼ in)

25 mm (1 in)

Side panel 310 x 100 mm (12⅜ x 4 in)

Back panel 310 x 200 mm (12⅜ x 8 in)

100 mm (4 in)

25 mm (1 in)

25 mm (1 in)

Seat base 400 x 300 mm (16 in x 12 in)

9 mm (⅜ in) dowels in joints

7

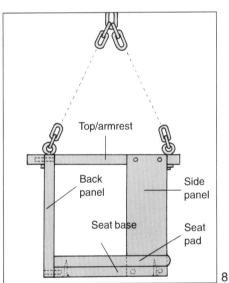

Top/armrest

Back panel

Side panel

Seat base

Seat pad

8

5 Complete the chair by making up the drop-in seat section. Glue some chip-foam to the front edge of the plywood off-cut you saved earlier, cover it with a stapled-on piece of vinyl upholstery fabric and secure the drop-in section by driving screws up through the chair seat into it.

6 For complete safety, fit a leather strap or a length of rope with clip-on shackles and attach it to the front two eyebolts to form a lap restraint.

A SIMPLE FORT

This simple square fort is easy to construct and makes the perfect playground for cowboys and Red Indians or infidels and crusaders, yet it could just as well be a fairy-tale castle.

MATERIALS
Hardcore
Concrete

4 x 100 mm - 150 mm (4 in - 6 in) diameter sturdy corner posts from rustic poles or sawn timber
100 mm x 38 mm (4 in x 1½ in) horizontal rails
100 mm x 38 mm (4 in x 1½ in) intermediate joists
Floorboards from rustic poles or sawn timber
Cladding from rustic poles or sawn timber
Ladder made from planed timber

Ramps: from sawn or planed timber
4 x side bearers
Slats
Slim battens
2 x horizontal braces

Nuts and bolts
Screws

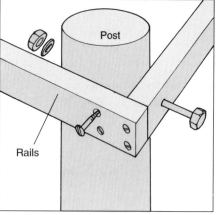

A straightforward design, this easily-constructed fort is built around four corner posts linked by sturdy horizontal rails at four levels to create a two-storey structure. The ground floor is raised, providing a crawl space underneath, and is reached by two ramps. An internal ladder allows easy access to the upper floor, which has castellated walls all round. The wall slats are spaced slightly apart to reduce wind resistance and allow some light in.

Building the fort
Select a level, dry site for the building, and mark out the positions of the four corner posts. The fort shown here is about 2.4 m (8 ft) square and 3 m (10 ft) high, but you can adapt the dimensions and the overall scale.

1 For a structure of this height, set the corner posts in the ground to a depth of about 900 mm (3 ft). Dig each hole to a slightly greater depth, pack the bottom of the hole with some broken brick or similar material to assist drainage round the foot of the post, and stand it in place. Brace it upright with some scrap timber, pack in more rubble round its base and then fill the hole with concrete. Leave to harden for about 72 hours before starting the fort construction.
2 Start attaching the horizontals to the

outsides of the posts, using screws or nut and bolts. Set the first ones about 600 mm (2 ft) above ground level, and the next about 750 mm (2 ft 6 in) above; this second set of horizontals acts mainly to stiffen the structure, but also provides a fixing point for the cladding above the two ramp entry points. Add the third level about 450 mm (18 in) above the second level to form the upper floor, and fix the final level about 300 mm (12 in) down from the tops of the posts (diagram 1).

3 Add two intermediate joists at each

floor level to prevent the boards from sagging, notching them into the perimeter horizontals. Board the ground floor first, then add two short trimmer joists to the first floor framework to form an opening for the ladder (diagram 2). Board the first floor next, trimming the boards round the opening.

4 Start adding the cladding at the corners, butt-joining the two boards in an L-shape. Nail on each length in turn, spacing the slats about 20 mm (¾ in) apart. To avoid wastage, butt-join lengths over the centre of the main

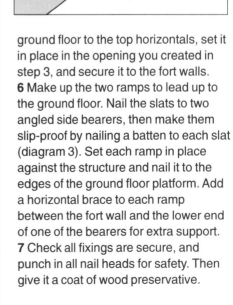

Trimmer joists framing opening for ladder

2

horizontal supports. Leave openings for access to the underfloor void at ground level and for the two ramps that lead up to the ground floor itself. Form the castellations by leaving alternate pairs of boards projecting above the level of the top horizontals.

5 Make a ladder to reach from the

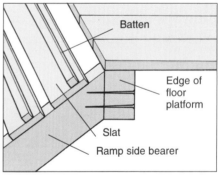

Batten

Edge of floor platform

Slat

Ramp side bearer

3

ground floor to the top horizontals, set it in place in the opening you created in step 3, and secure it to the fort walls.
6 Make up the two ramps to lead up to the ground floor. Nail the slats to two angled side bearers, then make them slip-proof by nailing a batten to each slat (diagram 3). Set each ramp in place against the structure and nail it to the edges of the ground floor platform. Add a horizontal brace to each ramp between the fort wall and the lower end of one of the bearers for extra support.
7 Check all fixings are secure, and punch in all nail heads for safety. Then give it a coat of wood preservative.

SANDPIT AND SEAT

This unusual sandpit and seat is designed to be built round a tree trunk, to provide both an attractive garden feature and a shady area for children to play and adults to sit and keep an eye on them. If you don't have a suitable tree, don't worry! It can also be free-standing and built on any reasonably level part of the garden.

MATERIALS

The dimensions given here are for making a structure 2.7 m (about 9 ft) long and 1.8 m (6 ft) wide. You can of course vary these dimensions to suit the size of your garden if you wish.

4 x 600 mm x 76 mm x 76 mm (2 ft x 3 in x 3 in) short stakes

4 x 900 mm x 76 mm x 76 mm (3 ft x 3 in x 3 in) long stakes

4 x 2.65 m x 152 mm x 25 mm (8 ft 7 in x 6 in x 1 in) side boards

4 x 1.8 m x 152 mm x 25 mm (6 ft x 6 in x 1 in) end boards

4 x 1.75 m x 152 mm x 25 mm (5 ft 9 in x 6 in x 1 in) cross boards

4 x 925 mm x 50 mm x 50 mm (3 ft x 2 in x 2 in) support bearers

18 x 1.8 m x 152 mm x 25 mm (6 ft x 6 in x 1 in) decking boards

6 x 863 mm x 50 mm x 50 mm (2 ft 10 in x 2 in x 2 in) reinforcing battens

12 mm (½ in) thick exterior-grade plywood for lining pit

Gravel

Polyethylene sheeting

100 mm or 150 mm x 25 mm (4 in or 6 in x 1 in) wide planed boards for exterior vertical cladding

Nails

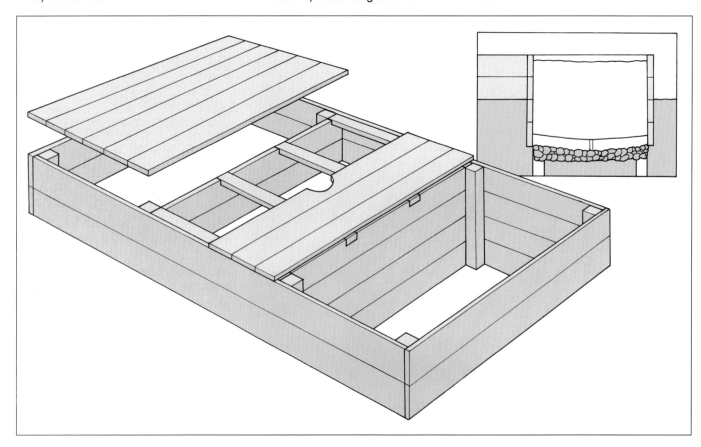

Left and Right: Another example of a dual-use sandpit. This design even allows for parents to use half the sandpit cover for relaxing while their children play.

This structure is built using a variation of the technique used for the above-ground sandpit featured on page 164. The structure is in three sections – the central portion with fixed decking round the tree trunk, one end section with a removable cover and some useful storage space beneath, and the other section dug out to form an in-ground sandpit, again with a removable cover (diagram 1). This design keeps the sand well below the tops of the sandpit walls, and so guarantees that most of it remains inside the pit during even the most strenuous digging sessions.

Assembly

1 Start by setting out the site, marking the eight post positions with pegs. Then sharpen one end of each of the eight posts with four saw cuts. Drive them into the ground with a sledgehammer, checking that they are vertical and that their tops are level.

2 Excavate the hole for the sandpit to a depth of about 300 mm (12 in). Either line the pit walls with exterior-grade plywood, fixed to battens nailed to the corner posts, or use flexible pond liner stapled into place. The former will be more durable than the latter. Fill the base of the excavation with gravel and cover it with perforated polyethylene sheeting or more pond liner.

3 Nail the vertical areas of cladding to the posts as shown, overlapping the external corners neatly, to create the three bays of the structure.

4 Fit the four support bearers across the centre bay to hold the fixed horizontal decking round the tree trunk. Cut notches 50 mm (2 in) wide 25 mm (1 in) deep in the top edges of the topmost vertical cladding boards at each side of this bay, then notch the ends of the four support bearers and nail them securely into position.

5 Fix the horizontal decking to the central bay after making rounded cut-outs as necessary to allow the middle planks fit round the tree trunk. Set the edges of the decking next to the storage area and sandpit back by 12 mm (½ in) from the edges of the vertical boards dividing the areas, so the side edges of the two removable lids can rest on the top edges of the vertical boards.

6 Make up the covers for the storage area and the sandpit by laying the decking boards side by side and nailing three reinforcing battens across the underside of each board. The two end battens should be inset from the ends of the cover boards by 100 mm (4 in), and all three should be inset from the sides of the boards by 25 mm (1 in) at one end and by 12 mm (½ in) at the other (diagram 1).

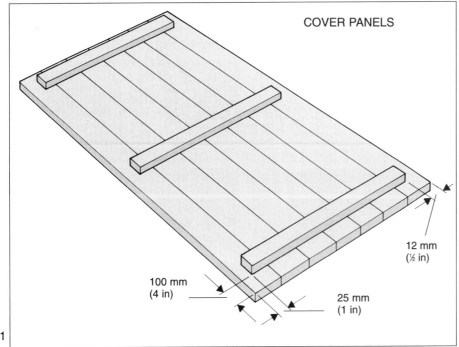

COVER PANELS

12 mm (½ in)

100 mm (4 in)

25 mm (1 in)

1

A RAISED PIT AND SEAT

This attractive sandpit is built above ground and can be set on any firm level surface. The comfortable seat all round helps discourage the spread of sand by providing a surface that can be swept.

MATERIALS
Hardcore
Concrete (see page 112)
8 x 76 mm or 100 mm (3 in or 4 in) sq sawn softwood corner posts
76 mm x 50 mm (3 in x 2 in) sawn softwood rails to link posts
150 mm x 19 mm (6 in x ¾ in) planed softwood planks to clad exterior
Exterior-quality plywood to line pit walls
Short joists
Seat boards as wall cladding
Gravel
Polyethylene sheeting
Sandpit sand

You can use the same boards for cladding the ouside and lining the walls, but 18-20 mm (¾ in) exterior-grade

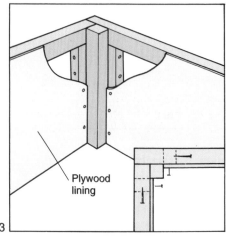

1

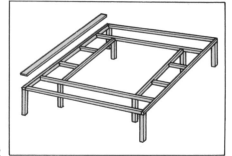

2

plywood would be more durable.
1 If the ground is relatively soft, you can simply drive the corner posts into the ground with a sledgehammer after sharpening them to a rough point with four saw cuts. Otherwise set each post

in a hole dug to a depth of about 300 mm (12 in) and surround it with concrete. Check the post tops are level.
2 Notch the post tops (diagram 1) to accept the support joists. To enable the cladding to be attached, these must sit on edge, faces flush with the post faces.
3 Nail the short joist sections between the joists along the two sides of the structure; this will be covered with planks running lengthwise (diagram 2). These short joists prevent the long boards from sagging.

Rail

Corner post

Plywood lining

3

4 Lay a 50 mm (2 in) deep bed of gravel beneath the pit area and cover it with polyethylene sheeting, perforated at intervals for drainage.
5 Line the walls of the pit next, either with strips of plywood nailed to the posts and inner joists or with cladding boards. Rest their bottom edges on the polyethylene sheeting (diagram 3).
6 Nail the cladding boards to the sides of the outer posts and joists, to build up the external walls of the pit. Overlap their ends neatly at the external corners.
7 Finally, nail the long seat boards in place to their supporting joists and to the post tops, then add the short lengths of board along the remaining two sides of the pit structure. For safety, punch in all the nail heads and smooth off any sharp or rough edges of wood all round the seat area.
8 Fill the pit with sand and get the buckets and spades ready.

Below: This attractive sandpit has been constructed above ground and features a comfortable seat; this also helps to keep the sand off the surrounding lawn.

A PATIO SANDPIT

This stylish sandpit combines a number of excellent design features in one simple project. The sandpit is in-ground, so construction is quite straightforward. It is surrounded by paving, which keeps the sand under control. The slot-in covers camouflage the sandpit when it's not in use, as well as keeping debris and wayward pets out of the sand. Finally, a large parasol can be fitted to the centre post to provide welcome shade on hot, sunny days.

This sandpit is constructed on three levels. The pit itself is a square within a square; the inner part contains the sand, and is bounded by four triangular concrete slabs set in the corners of the larger square to form seats.

MATERIALS
String and pegs to mark the site
Scrap timber for formwork
Hardcore
Concrete (see page 112)

Bricks
Mortar
Plastic sleeve for parasol (optional)
Gravel
Polyethylene sheeting

Timber to make square frame
Slats to make cover panels
Nails

1 Assuming that you are setting the pit into an existing patio that is laid over a sand bed, start by lifting some of the paving slabs or bricks to leave a square recess. Then mark out the central sandpit area with string lines and

excavate the sand and subsoil to a depth of 450 mm (18 in).

2 Excavate the four triangular corner areas to a depth of about 200 mm (8 in), undercutting the edges of the surrounding paving by about 100 mm (4 in). Then peg timber formwork along their long sides and lay a 100 mm (4 in) thick bed of concrete in each corner. When it has set, mortar bricks into the gap between the concrete slabs and the underside of the surrounding paving to stop them from subsiding.

3 Cast a block of concrete in the centre of the sandpit square to support the inner corners of the slatted cover panels (diagram 1). Incorporate a plastic sleeve at this stage if you want to be able to use a parasol.

4 Cover the base of the sandpit square

Above: An ingenious solution when space is at a premium – a sandpit by day reverting to adult use when the children are in bed.

with gravel and a perforated polyethylene sheet and fill it with sand.

5 Make up the four cover panels by nailing slats diagonally to a square timber frame (diagram 2). Size the panels to match the dimensions of the outer sandpit square, and choose the dimensions of the frame timbers to match the depth between the top surface of the triangular concrete corner pads and the surrounding paving so that they sit flush with the patio surface.

Unless you have used pre-treated timber, treat all the panels with wood preservative to protect them from rot and insects.

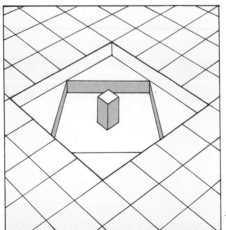

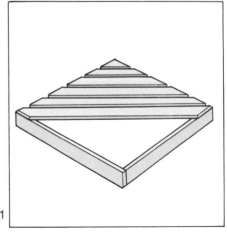

HANGING BARS

If you have neither the time nor the inclination or the skill to construct a fully-fledged climbing frame, your children still need not be disappointed. These rustic hanging bars are so easy to build and will give hours of pleasure.

MATERIALS
Hardcore
Concrete

From 75 mm (3 in) diameter rustic poles
4 x 2.3 m (7 ft 6 in) uprights
2 x 2.4 m (8 ft) horizontals
Smaller poles for angled corner braces
Smaller poles for step up rungs

Hanging bars:
1 m (3 ft) knot-free poles or round
   hardwood mouldings

Fixing bolts
Nuts
Locking washers
Nails

Tyre projects:
Old tyres
Rustic poles
Hardcore
Concrete
Heavy-duty coach screws

Armed with a supply of trimmed rustic poles and the ability to cut some extremely rudimentary halving joints, you can quickly assemble this simple yet sturdy set of hanging bars.

The main framework consists of four uprights and two horizontals, which for strength's sake should be at least 75 mm (3 in) in diameter. If the horizontals are to span a length of more than about 3 m (10 ft), go up a size to poles about 100 mm (4 in) in diameter.

You should start by deciding how big you want the frame to be, especially its height. This will depend to a certain extent on the average size of the children who will be using it; as a rough guide, construct it so that they will have a drop of no more than about 450 mm (18 in) to the ground when they are hanging from the bars with their arms outstretched. An overall length of about

2.4 m (8 ft) and a width of 1 m (3 ft 3 in or so) is ideal for most children and will not take up too much garden space, but you can always make it longer if you have the room.

With any structure from which children could fall, it is wise to provide a soft surface underneath, Here the bars are surrounded by a landing area filled with chipped bark. This is available from DIY and garden centres.

Making the hanging bars
1 Start by cutting the four uprights to length; remember to allow for about 600 mm (2 ft) of their total length to be buried in the ground. Then cut rounded notches about 150 mm (6 in) down from their top ends to accept the horizontals, and make two smaller notches lower down in one of the posts to which a step-up rung will be fitted later.
2 Next, set the uprights in place in holes about 600 mm (2 ft) deep, pack in some

broken brick and rubble and surround them with concrete. Brace each one with lengths of scrap timber so that they stand vertical, and leave the concrete to harden for 48-72 hours.

3 Cut the two main horizontals to length, lay them side by side and mark the positions for the notches into which the hanging bars will fit. Space these at roughly 300 mm (12 in) centres, and cut them out to a rough square shape.

4 Either clamp each horizontal to its posts or get a helper to support it in place while you drill holes through post and horizontal to accept the fixing bolts. Fix each horizontal in place securely with a bolt, nut and locking washer at each end of the frame.

5 Complete the structure by nailing the rungs into their notches, adding the diagonal corner braces and fitting the step-up rung at one end. The braces can be simply nailed in place, but will be stronger and will give extra rigidity to the structure if they are set in simple sawn notches cut into the horizontal and uprights (see the close-up photograph).

Using old tyres

Once upon a time, every child's garden seemed to have an old car tyre suspended by a length of rope from a tree branch or similar support for use as a makeshift swing. Some no doubt still do, but more sophisticated swings have generally taken their place nowadays. However, the humble cast-off tyre can also be used to make some unusual climbing obstacles, in conjunction with some simple supporting timberwork. Because tyres are resilient (if hard) and have no sharp edges, they make remarkably safe pieces of play apparatus.

If you do decide to use old tyres, make sure that they are thoroughly steam-cleaned first in order to remove all traces of oil, tarmac and other materials that could stain your children's hands and skin. It is also well worth scrubbing the tyres thoroughly with strong detergent before bringing them into play.

The two examples here show what can be achieved with a little ingenuity.

The first features a simple three-sided pyramid shape formed by de-barked rustic poles set in a concrete base. The largest tyre acts as a mould for the concrete, while the others are dropped over the top of the poles and then pulled down over them as far as they will go to provide hand- and foot-holds.

The second uses three tractor tyres fixed to the inside of three stout supporting poles. The poles are set in

concrete, and the tyres are secured to them by heavy-duty coach screws through the tyre walls into the posts. For strength, and to stop the tyre walls from splitting, fit two screws at each fixing point and drive them through a piece of scrap metal (see the close-up photo).

Right: Rustic poles and old tyres have been used to make this climbing structure. The bottom tyre is partially sunk in the chippings and forms a join with the concrete.
Above and left: The rungs are nailed into cut-outs in the main horizontals, which are strengthened by angled braces.
Above: Tyres screwed to the pole with a piece of metal to prevent rubber tearing.
Left: An alternative configuration for rustic poles and old tyres.

If you have a large amount of space available in your garden, a relatively inexhaustible source of raw materials at a reasonable price, and above all the time to devote to making your children's dreams come true, then this adventure playground is the project you have been waiting for. It offers children of all ages a marvellous range of outdoor play activities within an elaborate multi-purpose structure, and not only are the various components very simple to construct; they can also be rearranged, adapted and extended to suit any site and satisfy the requirements of the most demanding of children.

As you can see illustrated in the photographs on this and the following pages and from the ground plan overleaf, this adventure playground consists of two main structures – the fort and the hut. Each is built off the ground on sturdy stilts, bringing a third dimension to the variety of games that children can play in, on, around and under each building. There are sturdy steps leading up to deck level in each structure, and a slide that guarantees a quick escape either from the fort at one end of the complex or from the open platform at the other end.

The two buildings are linked together by a novel feature – a chain bridge – which will surely be the site of many a heroic battle for supremacy between the hut-dwellers and the custodians of the fort. However, this is not the only route that attackers of either building could take. The fort can be stormed commando-style via an angled climbing net strung from one of its walls, while the platform next to the hut can be scaled by the agile using a rope ladder suspended from a timber arch.

Of course, the playground is not only the perfect site for every game of attack and defence. It can be an assault course run in a variety of directions, a camp site, a log cabin in the woods, a pirate ship, a private hideaway or simply a series of endlessly enjoyable individual play activities including climbing, swinging, hanging, jumping and hiding.

Construction basics

Each of the two main structures is built in basically the same way. The main elements of the construction are the sturdy vertical corner support posts. These are trimmed and de-barked tree trunks measuring between 100 and 150 mm (4 to 6 in) in diameter, which are set to a depth of at least 900 m (3 ft) and secured with concrete. The floor decks in the fort and hut, and the open platform beyond the latter, are made up of planed planks resting on rectangular sawn timber bearers that are bolted to the corner posts. The walls of each building are formed by nailing split rustic poles (and any other timber that comes to hand) to horizontal rails fixed between the posts, while the hut roof is covered with fencing boards nailed to a simple supporting framework.

Throughout the playground improvisation is the key but safety is the watchword. The entire structure is extremely solid; all the main joints are either bolted or screwed together and all the timbers used are sturdy enough to cope with any imaginable loading they might have to bear. Both the flights of steps have handrails, as does the chain bridge, and all the raised platform areas have walls round them except where jump-off points – next to the rope ladder, for example – require clear access.

The two slides are one-piece plastic mouldings bought from toy or playground equipment suppliers, and the climbing net is of rot-proof polypropylene, securely lashed to its supporting framework. Finally, the entire playground is surrounded by an area of crushed bark to provide a surface that wears well under-foot, drains well in wet weather and provides a soft and safe landing when the inevitable falls occur.

Before you start

As mentioned earlier, you do not have to build this type of outdoor play structure all at once. Its very nature makes it an add-on project; you could start with the fort, build the hut later and add the open platform the following season. Every element is completely adaptable, allowing you to position the steps and slides wherever you like and to add extra features such as hanging rings, swings and the like as the fancy takes you – or as your children insist.

However, before you start building it is a good idea to give some thought to

Right: Children of all ages can enjoy this adventure playground – the perfect site for games of attack and defence.

wood preservation. The underground parts of the posts will be particularly vulnerable to rot and insect attack, and the rest of the structure will of course be exposed to the weather once assembly is complete.

Buy preservative-treated timber if possible; otherwise soak the ends of all the in-ground posts in wood preservative for 24 hours before installing them, and give the rest of the structure a generous coat of preservative once assembly is complete. Pay particular attention to treating cut ends and drilled holes where porous end-grain is exposed.

SETTING OUT THE SITE

Materials
Split poles for perimeter edging
In-ground pegs
Crushed bark chippings

To support posts:
Hardcore
Concrete
Scrap timber

1 Decide how much you plan to build as the first phase of the project, and study the main photos and the ground plan (diagram 1) so you can work out roughly what materials will be required.

2 Choose the site for the playground, clear any vegetation and excavate the topsoil down to a depth of about 150 mm (6 in). Edge the excavation with split poles secured to in-ground pegs to provide a clear perimeter (and to retain the bed of crushed bark chippings which will be laid later on).

3 Mark out the site with pegs to indicate where the main supporting posts will go for each element of the structure, and check everything is roughly aligned and square; total precision does not matter too much so long as the overall impression is satisfactory.

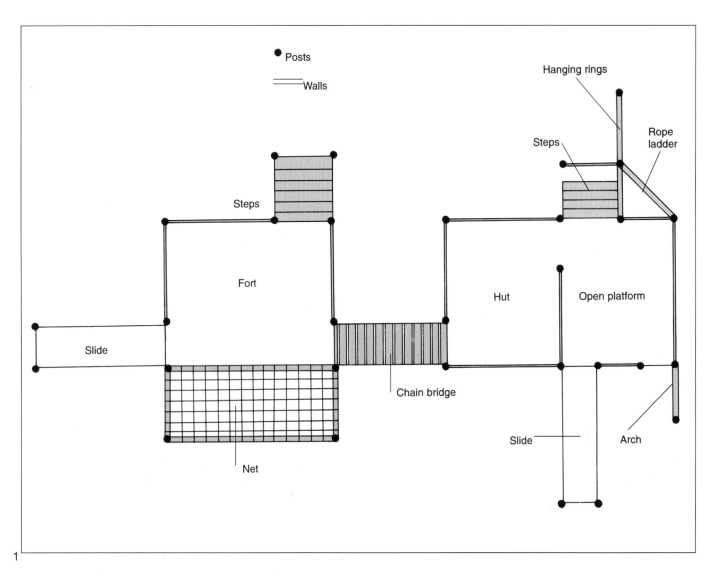

Posts
Walls
Hanging rings
Steps
Rope ladder
Steps
Fort
Hut
Open platform
Slide
Chain bridge
Net
Slide
Arch

1

Securing the main posts

The structure relies for its stability on the main posts. Once these are in place, the construction is quite straightforward.

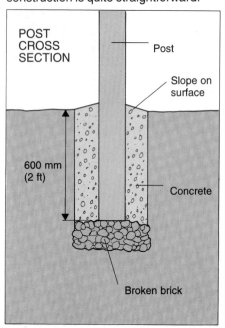

POST CROSS SECTION
Post
Slope on surface
600 mm (2 ft)
Concrete
Broken brick

2

4 For each post, dig a hole 300 mm (12 in) square and about 900 mm (3 ft) deep. Place broken bricks or similar inert material in the base of the hole to help drainage and to keep the post foot dry and free from rot. Stand the post in place and brace upright with scrap timber. Shovel in some coarse concrete, tamp down well and smooth the top at a slight slope to drain rainwater away from the post (diagram 2).

5 Repeat for the other main posts, then leave the concrete to set for 48-72 hours before starting any construction work.

BUILDING THE FORT

Materials
Vertical support posts
Posts at access points
Floor support bearers
Infill wall and floor timbers
Half-round capping rail
Posts for wall cladding

2 x handrail posts
2 x handrails
2 x 76 mm x 25 mm (3 in x 1 in) board to carry step treads
Split logs to form rungs

Slide:
Plastic moulded slide
2 x short posts to support bottom of slide
Angle brackets to fix slide to deck

Climbing Net:
Netting to fit
2 x stout poles for cross pieces
2 x stout poles for side pieces
2 x short supporting poles

The fort is an open, walled platform with access on three sides for the steps, the slide and the bridge. It has a support post at each corner, plus an extra post next to each access point. Five posts project 2 m (6 ft 6 in) above ground, while the posts carrying the net are taller to give climbers something to hold on to.

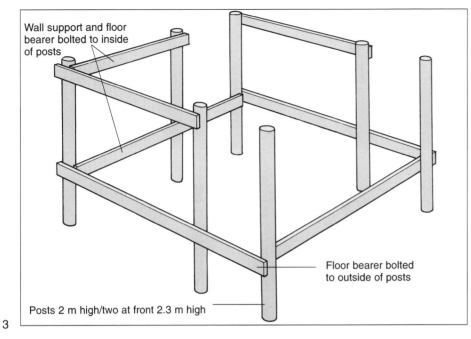

Wall support and floor bearer bolted to inside of posts

Floor bearer bolted to outside of posts

Posts 2 m high/two at front 2.3 m high

3

1 When the support posts are in place, bolt the floor support bearers about 1 m (3 ft 3 in) above ground level. Fix two to the outsides of the main corner posts and the other two (at right angles to these) to the insides of the posts.
2 Bolt or screw similar bearers in place between the corner posts and those next to the access points, level with the post tops, to support the walls round the sides of the platform (diagram 3), and nail on the infill timbers.
3 Nail a half-round capping rail on top of the wall timbers, except along the wall where the climbing net will be, and carefully punch in nail heads for safety.
4 For steps up to the deck, set two short handrail posts in concrete in line with those at the access point and about 1 m (3 ft 3 in) away from the deck edge.

5 Nail two lengths of 76 mm x 25 mm (3 in x 1 in) wood between the high and low posts to carry the step treads, then nail on split logs to form the rungs. Finish the flight off by fixing a handrail at each side.
6 Next, install the slide. Its bottom end rests on two short posts set in concrete; position them to suit the height and length of the slide. Fix the slide securely to the fort deck and the short support posts using screws and angle brackets or fixings provided by the slide supplier.

Making the climbing net (diagram 4)
Rope merchants are listed in telephone directories or try chandlers, boatbuilders or marine supply stores. You can make up a small square of netting yourself by knotting lengths of rope together, although the results are unlikely to be as neat or strong as bought net.

Above: The slide is off to one side and has plenty of space at the end of the chute.

Left: Make sure the handrails are strong enough to take the weight of a child.

7 Make a net frame using four lengths of stout pole. You need two cross-pieces the same length as the width of the fort wall, and two side pieces long enough to reach from the top of the fort wall to the ground at an angle of about 60°.
8 Make a rounded cut-out in the top ends of the two frame sides, and nail the top cross-piece into the cut-outs. Lay the other cross-piece over the bottom ends of the frame sides and bolt it to them. Lash the net to the frame with a series of rope loops (see diagram 4).
9 Position the frame against the wall of the fort and fix bolts through the fort

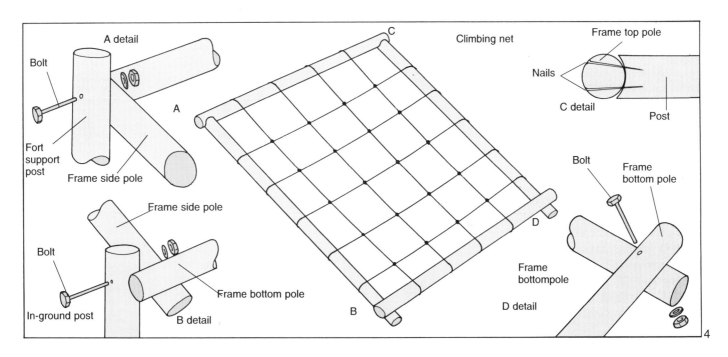

A detail

Bolt

Fort support post

Frame side pole

A

C

Climbing net

Frame top pole

Nails

C detail

Post

Frame side pole

Bolt

In-ground post

Frame bottom pole

B detail

B

Frame bottompole

D

Bolt

Frame bottom pole

D detail

4

corner posts and the frame sides to hold it in place. At the ground end of the net frame, set short supporting posts in concrete and bolt the frame to them.

BUILDING THE HUT

Materials

4 x vertical corner support posts
2 x intermediate posts for access points
Floor bearers
Deck planks for floor
Parallel wall bearers
Wall boards
Long boards for gables
Rafters
Fencing boards for roof

Chain bridge:

2 lengths short chain
Series of 76 mm x 25 mm (3 in x 1 in) planed timber for footholds
2 handrails
Chain shackles with locking pins
Eyebolts

Ladders/Hanging rings:

Horizontal beam
Galvanised steel straps
Extra vertical support post

Left: The climbing net has been fixed at a sloping angle to make it safer and easier for children to use.

The hut construction is very similar to that of the fort (see diagram 5).

1 There are four main corner posts, plus two intermediate posts next to the two access points in the side walls – see the ground plan. The deck is supported on similar floor bearers bolted to the posts about 1 m (3 ft 3 in) above ground level, and the corner posts are linked by parallel bearers higher up to which the wall boards are nailed.

2 Cut longer boards at an angle to form the gable ends of the building, and cut simple rafters to size to support the fencing boards that cover the roof.

3 Cut some of the wall boards short at the top to create rudimentary windows along the rear wall of the hut.

The hut has two open access points in opposite corners. The first is designed to be connected to the fort by the chain bridge, while the latter leads out onto the open platform next to the hut in the completed playground. If you are not ready to build this platform yet, make up a flight of steps leading into the hut.

Making the chain bridge

This is an ingenious construction that is fun to cross. It consists of two lengths of

Above: The chain bridge makes a wonderful alternative entrance to the building.

stout chain suspended across the gap between the fort and hut, to which short planks are secured with nuts and bolts. Two timber handrails are provided at each side for safety; these could equally well be lengths of stout rope fixed between the two structures. Galvanised welded-link chain can be bought from a

chain manufacturer or supplier.

4 Use a hacksaw to cut two pieces of chain long enough to span the gap between the buildings, allowing for a slight droop. Then cut a series of slats from 76 mm x 25 mm (3 in x 1 in) planed timber, and drill a hole about 50 mm (2 in) in from each end of each slat.

5 Attach the slats to the chain links with short bolts and nuts, fitting a locking washer beneath each nut for security. Space the slats about 25 mm (1 in) apart, and leave about 50 mm (2 in) of chain free at each end to attach the bridge to the buildings (see diagram 6).

6 Fix two eye bolts into the floor bearers at each end of the span, and attach the bridge chains to them using chain shackles with screw-in locking pins.

Adding the open platform

You can extend the playground by adding an open platform to the far side of the hut, using the same construction technique as for the fort. The main support posts are positioned as shown in the ground plan to provide two access points to the front – one for the escape slide, the other as a jumping-off point – and two to the rear, one for steps and

HUT FRAMEWORK

Rafters added at each end to support roof (nailed to corner post and each other)

Window

Door

Door

Extra rail to form window slit

Floor and wall bearers fixed as for Fort construction

5

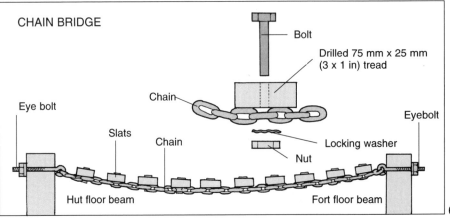

CHAIN BRIDGE

Bolt

Drilled 75 mm x 25 mm (3 x 1 in) tread

Chain

Eyebolt

Eye bolt

Slats

Chain

Locking washer

Nut

Hut floor beam

Fort floor beam

6

the other to allow climbers access to the platform via a rope ladder (see below).

There is direct access to the hut from the platform, and if you built steps to the hut door earlier, it is easy to reposition them so they run up to the rear edge of the platform instead, as shown in the photos and ground plan. Here the flight is partly concealed by planked walls – a purely optional feature.

Ladders and hanging rings

The last features of the playground which you might like to add are a rope ladder at the rear of the open platform, and a pair of hanging rings suspended from a beam next to the rear platform access steps. The rope ladder and rings

Below: Access to the open platform is partly concealed by planked walls.

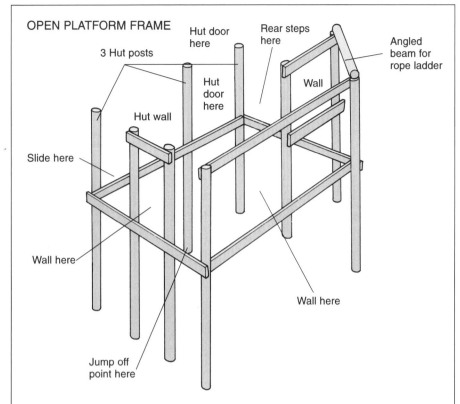

OPEN PLATFORM FRAME

3 Hut posts

Hut door here

Rear steps here

Angled beam for rope ladder

Hut door here

Wall

Hut wall

Slide here

Wall here

Wall here

Jump off point here

7

Above: Secure horizontal beams to the post tops with simple galvanised metal straps.

Left: Make sure that there's plenty of chipped bark for soft landings.

are suspended from eyebolts set in a horizontal beam that is secured to the tops of vertical posts by galvanised steel straps. As you can see from the ground plan, the ladder beam is fixed to the top of two posts forming part of the structure of the open platform, while one extra post is all that is needed to support the beam for the hanging rings.

The safety zone

The entire playground is surrounded with a bed of chipped bark or similar material to provide a safe surface for the children to use.

After edging the excavated site with pegged planks, which should be at least 2 m (6 ft 6 in) away from any likely landing areas, simply spread and rake out the chippings to a depth of about 150 mm (6 in). Tidy the site by re-raking the chippings from time to time, and remember to top up the landing bed with fresh bark chippings as necessary whenever bald patches or hollows begin to appear.

STONE

PART
THREE

INTRODUCTION TO WORKING WITH STONE

No building material has a longer pedigree than stone; after all, the Stone Age was the first recognized period of human culture, and early man used stone not only as a source of invaluable tools but also as a building material of unparalleled strength, durability and versatility. Stone can be used as it occurs naturally, in boulders or random blocks and slabs split and shaped by the forces of nature, or it can be worked into precisely-cut blocks that slot together as snugly as jigsaw pieces. Above all, it offers the infinite variety that only a naturally-occurring material can exhibit.

The earliest use of stone as a building material was probably the casual gathering of loose-lying surface stone to form simple enclosures for defence and to pen animals. It would soon find a use as a paving material for consolidating soft ground, and by Egyptian times records show that it was being used in the design of decorative gardens as well as for the construction of the many meticulously-engineered pyramids and temples of the period. The Greeks and Romans loved their ornamental sacred groves and public gardens, and by the Middle Ages there was a strong tradition of landscape architecture that was to spread across every culture and every

continent. In every case, stone was the predominant structural feature.

Today, stone is as popular as ever for creating a wide range of garden features, from the humblest carved ornament to the most elaborate walls, arches, terraces and steps. No longer are garden landscapers restricted to using just the types of stone provided by the accident of local geology; they can within reason obtain whatever type of stone is required so long as they are prepared to pay for the inevitably high transport costs of one of the densest building materials around.

With this point in mind, perhaps the most significant development as far as garden stonework is concerned has been the growing use of man-made stone products. These are formed by the vibration or compression of selected crushed aggregate to produce walling blocks, paving stones and even ornamental mouldings such as balusters and bird-baths. Not only is the product uniform in size and structural characteristics, unlike natural stone, and therefore easier for the amateur to work

Below: Stone lends itself to all sorts of outdoor uses, either in its natural form or as cut blocks and sculpted ornaments.

with; it is also generally both less expensive and more readily available. But it lacks something: the natural beauty and variety of stone is a quality that even the most ingenious manufacturer cannot hope to copy completely faithfully.

What to build

Whether you choose to work with natural stone or its man-made equivalent, there is a huge range of garden projects to which you can turn your hand.

Walls are an obvious first choice, and there is no finer walling material than stone. Finely-dressed blocks can be

can provide a stunning centrepiece.

Every garden also needs hard surfaces for its occupants to walk on, and stone in its infinite variety is the perfect material to choose for patios, terraces, paths and steps. Large square or rectangular slabs can create paved areas on a grand scale, while the more informal pavers and setts are ideal both for paving smaller areas and for adding detail to larger schemes. Surface colour and texture have an important part to play here too, helping the paving to blend in well with its surroundings.

Stone is also the perfect material to choose for a whole host of other garden features, such as a garden pond set about with rocks, perhaps with a small cascade running into it. Refer to the next chapter on water features for more information. The presence of water allows you to broaden the variety of plants you can grow, and also encourages wildlife to visit the garden.

Lastly, you can use stone for a wide range of other garden projects, too, from rockeries to garden furniture. All are easy – and rewarding – to build and will enhance any garden design. You need few special skills or tools – just the vision to create the effect you want – and the time and patience to put it into practice.

Left: Stone can be split into large slabs for paving, into medium-sized blocks for walling or into smaller setts for paving – here contrasted with rounded cobbles.

Below: Reconstituted regular stone slabs and blocks in the foreground contrast well with the mass of natural stone used for the rockery in the centre of the lawn.

used to create the neatly-detailed formal look, while randomly-shaped pieces can be turned into the most attractive of all garden features, the dry-stone wall, with its rugged natural appearance and plethora of planting pockets. Stone always looks as though it belongs in the garden, especially when it has begun to weather, and is therefore the perfect choice for boundary walls, earth-retaining walls, even low-level planters.

Another stone feature that can look particularly fine is the arch, either as a free-standing feature or contained within a high wall. This is a good test of your skill as a stonemason, and the results

BASIC TOOLS

You will need a selection of basic tools for jobs such as clearing, excavating and levelling sites, setting out projects, mixing, placing mortar and concrete, etc.

The basic excavation tools you will need are a pickaxe and a shovel. The pickaxe has a pointed tip at one end of its curved blade which is used for hacking into and breaking up solid masonry or old concrete, and a spade-ended tip at the other end for grubbing out loose materials so they can be dug out with the shovel. The pickaxe is available with a range of different head weights, commonly 2.2, 3 and 4.5 kg (5, 6½ and 10 lb), and has a strong hardwood handle approximately 900 mm (36 in) long.

When demolishing walls or breaking up concrete, a sledgehammer is a useful alternative to the pickaxe. This has a squared-off head weighing from 3.2 to 6.3 kg (7 to 14 lb), and a handle up to 900 mm (36 in) long.

If you have a lot of demolition work to do or have to break up thick concrete, hiring an electric breaker may speed up the process and save a lot of effort. Breakers are available with a range of interchangeable cutting points (chipping points) and chisels.

A shovel, with either a rounded or squared-off blade, is better than a spade for shifting loose material as the slightly raised sides help retain material on the blade. However, a spade will also be useful for general digging, levelling and other site preparation work.

A tool that is valuable for moving heavy weights, whether you are lifting or placing heavy stone blocks, is the straight crowbar. This is a long steel rod with a point at one end and a chisel blade at the other; to use it you place one end under the object to be moved, position a sturdy fulcrum such as a block of masonry under the bar as close to the loaded end as possible, and apply downward pressure on the other end.

It is likely that you will have to move sizeable amounts of soil, rubble, concrete and stone during the construction of whatever you are creating. It is well worth buying or hiring a sturdy steel contractor's wheelbarrow with a pneumatic tyre; you will soon wreck an ordinary garden wheelbarrow when moving heavy pieces of stone. Make sure you also have a supply of stout planks (scaffold boards are ideal) for use as runways and ramps if you are working on soft or broken ground, to prevent the barrow's wheel from becoming bogged down.

If your project calls for large quantities of mortar or concrete, hire a small electric concrete mixer for the duration of the job. This will save a lot of back-breaking hand mixing, and will also ensure that the mortar or concrete is evenly and thoroughly mixed to the required consistency.

Tools for setting out
The basic requirements here are pegs and stringlines, a steel tape measure and

a builder's square. Make up a supply of tapered sawn timber pegs about 300 mm (12 in) long, and saw a notch all round each one just belo w its top to help retain the strings as you set out your site.

You can make up an accurate builder's square using three lengths of sawn or planed wood. Cut one about 1 m (3 ft 3 in) long and another about 1.3 m (4 ft 3 in) long, and connect them at right angles using a halving joint. Then cut the third piece about 1.6 m (5 ft 3 in) long, and nail it across the other two pieces to form a triangle. Cut off the excess wood from the ends of the angled length.

If you are building dry-stone walls, you will need a home-made device called a batter frame to act as a guide. This consists of four lengths of wood nailed together in a gently-tapered A-shape, with its dimensions selected to match the wall height and its projected thickness at the base and top. It carries movable string-lines that are raised as the wall is built up to keep the wall faces on line.

When it comes to levelling sites, an ordinary spirit level (see Bedding Tools below) is of little use. More versatile is a water level, a length of hosepipe with pieces of clear plastic tube inserted into the ends. The hose is filled with water and corked at each end. Then the tubes are tied to pegs driven into the ground and the corks are removed; the water level in the tubes indicates the true horizontal at each end of the hose.

Bedding tools
A bricklaying trowel is required for working with mortar, whether bedding stones in a wall or laying slabs in a mortar bed. You can use its handle for tamping blocks and slabs into place, but you will find a club hammer better at this; it is also needed for cutting and shaping blocks and slabs.

The other essential tool is a spirit level, to ensure that blocks and slabs are laid truly level. Choose a long metal level for accuracy, and make sure it has end vials to indicate true vertical as well.

Cutting tools
The basic tool for cutting blocks and slabs is the brick chisel or bolster. It is made of steel, measures about 180 mm (7 in) long overall, and has a cutting edge 55 to 100 mm (2½ to 4 in) wide which is ground on both edges. It is held at right angles to the material being cut, and is struck with a club hammer.

The latter, also known as the lump hammer, is a scaled-down sledge-hammer, and has a similar squared-off head weighing up to 1.8 kg (4 lb). It is used for driving carving tools as well.

An alternative to the club hammer for driving masonry chisels and bolsters is the brick hammer. This has a slightly curved head with a square driving face at one end, and a sharp chisel blade at the other, useful for hand-trimming cut edges after the block has been cut.

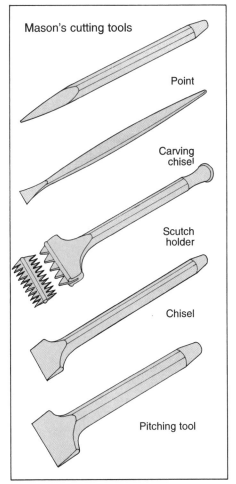

Mason's cutting tools

Point

Carving chisel

Scutch holder

Chisel

Pitching tool

Carving tools
For carving stone, you will need some special mason's carving tools (and a club hammer to drive them). The basic cutting and shaping tool is a chisel, an all-steel construction with a hexagonal cross-section and square-ended cutting blade; it is available widths ranging from 12 to 50 mm (½ to 2 in). The point chisel or punch has a pointed cutting tip, and is used to concentrate the force of the hammer on a small area of the stone during the initial roughing-out of the piece. The pitching tool has a wide single-ground blade, used for removing larger amounts of stone when trimming a piece down to the required size.

For carving recesses, a versatile tool is a mason's scutch holder, a chisel-like tool with a replaceable cutting edge known as a scutch. This is double-sided, and may have plain or toothed edges. It is used after the initial roughing-out. The toothed version leaves a series of furrows in the stone which can either be left as the final finish or smoothed off using either the plain mason's chisel or the wider mason's bolster.

Building tools you will need include:
A spirit level (1), a brick bolster (2), a cold chisel (3), walling pegs (4), a stringline (5), walling line blocks (6), a club hammer (7), a bricklaying trowel (8), a pointing trowel (9), and a hawk (10).

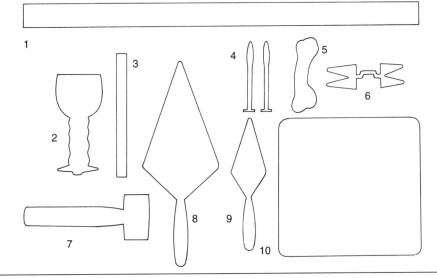

Natural stone

The main stones used for outdoor projects fall into three classes: igneous, sedimentary and metamorphic. Igneous rocks were formed by the cooling of molten magma, while sedimentary stones were created either by the wearing down of older rocks or from accumulations of organic origin. Metamorphic stones are stones that have been changed structurally from by immense heat and pressure.

Granite is the commonest igneous stone. It is extremely dense and hard (and therefore expensive to quarry and cut), highly resistant to pollution, and is almost impervious to water penetration. This makes it ideal as a paving material – usually in the form of small blocks called setts – and for areas of heavy wear, such as steps or kerbs. Most granites are grey or black, but there are varieties with green, red, pink or blue colouring, caused by minerals.

The sedimentary stones are the most widely used for outdoor stonework. They fall into two broad groups, sandstones and limestones. Sandstones consist mainly of particles of quartz, bound together by other minerals such as silica and carbonates and often contain iron ores which give the stone its attractive colouring. This can range from almost white to red, brown and even blue-grey. The best sandstones are very durable, but as a type they tend to weather less attractively than the limestones and can quickly become soiled by atmospheric pollution. Their most popular use is as split flagstones.

Limestones consist mainly of calcium carbonate (calcite), and were formed in one of three ways. Most building lime-

Left: Otherwise, you will have to rely on the smaller stocks of stone held by many builders' merchants and garden centres.

stones are known as oolitic stones, and were formed by the accretion of calcite round small grains of sand or shell, these then being cemented together by more calcite. They were also formed by deposition – the accumulation of organic remains such as shells and animal or plant remains – or by crystallization from solution (stalactites and stalagmites, for example). They vary widely in hardness, although they are generally softer and easier to work than sandstones, making them ideal for carving and general building work. They are, however, attacked by acid rain which initially makes the surface self-cleaning but in the longer term can cause rapid decay of the softer types. Colours range from creamy white (Portland-stone, for example) to light brown.

Since both sandstones and limestones were formed in layers, they have distinct bedding planes which should be reproduced in any structure built with them; they will gradually delaminate if laid with the bedding plane parallel to an exposed face of a wall, for example.

The most common metamorphic stone is slate, formed from heated and compressed clay. This process resulted in a stone that has distinct planes of cleavage, often almost at right angles to the original bedding planes, along which the stone can be split to form slabs of varying thickness. It is strong in tension and compression and has good resistance to moisture penetration, although some types are attacked by acidic pollution, and can be used in blocks as well as slabs for a variety of end uses.

Your choice of stone is likely to depend on what local suppliers stock. Stone surfaces are classified according to the degree of finish they have. The most common terms, in increasing order of smoothness, are: rockfaced; rough picked; fair picked; axed; fine axed; split (riven); sawn or ribbed; sanded; gritted; honed or rubbed; polished (unlikely to be required in the garden).

Man-made wall blocks
Reconstituted stone blocks imitate natural stone and come in a wide range of sizes. The most common measure from 200 to 325 mm (8¼ to 12¾ in) long,

Below: Examples of the wide range of colour and surface texture available, especially in the sandstones and limestones that are the most popular materials for most garden stonework projects.

that some manufacturers make as part of their screen walling block range are about 200 mm (8 in) square and 190 mm (7½ in) tall. Allowing for a 10 mm mortar joint, this means that three pier blocks build up to the same height – 600 mm or just under 2 ft – as two walling blocks.

Paving slabs and blocks

Reconstituted stone paving slabs are mostly squares or rectangles, and come in a range of sizes based on a 225 mm, 250 mm, 300 mm or 500 mm (9, 10, 12 or 20 in) module. To estimate how many slabs will be needed for a project, divide the area to be paved by the area of an individual slab. In practice, however, it is better to design paved areas so they are a whole number of slabs wide and long to minimise cutting. Count the number of rows and how many slabs in each row, and multiply the two figures. If laying mixed slabs of different sizes, draw a scale plan on squared paper and count how many of each size are required.

Some ranges include hexagonal and circular slabs. The former are usually 400 mm (16 in) wide between two opposite parallel sides, and come with matching straight-sided half slabs to allow you to pave square or rectangular areas with them. You will need 55 x 400 mm hexagonal slabs to pave an area of 10 m² (108 ft²). Circular slabs come in several diameters from 300 mm (12 in) upwards, and are intended to be laid as individual stepping stones.

Cast concrete slabs (the cheapest type) are often 50 mm (2 in) thick, while more expensive reconstituted stone ones are usually 40 mm (1⅝ in) thick. They are heavy – a 450 mm² (18 in) slab weighs about 16 kg (36 lb).

Block pavers are generally rectangular, although there are some made in inter-locking shapes to give a less regular look to the surface of the paved area. The standard block size is

75 to 150 mm (3¼ to 5¾ in) wide and 65 to 150 mm (2¾ to 5¾ in) high – the same height as a standard brick. Others in the range are usually multiples of this, which allows you to lay the blocks in a wide range of decorative bonds.

You may also find larger blocks with outer faces moulded to resemble smaller, randomly-shaped blocks. The moulded joints are deeply recessed, and each block may have projecting units at each end for a stretcher-style bond between neighbouring blocks. The result is a stronger wall than one built with simple stack bonding.

To estimate the quantities you need, select the block and use its actual size as a guide. To work out how many blocks are required for one square metre (11 ft²) of single-thickness masonry, add

10 mm (⅜ in) to the actual block length and height to allow for the mortar joint, multiply the two figures together, and divide the result into 1,000,000 (the number of sq mm in a sq m). So, for a 440 x 65 mm block, the sum is: 450 x 75 = 33,750 sq mm, then 1,000,000 divided by 33,750 = 29.63, which means you need 30 blocks per sq m.

Perforated decorative screen walling blocks are made in just one standard size – an actual size of 290 mm (11⅜ in) square and about 90 mm (3½ in) thick, giving a work size of 300 mm (11¾ in) square. You need 11 blocks per square metre of wall. Coping stones usually come in 610 mm (2 ft) lengths – long enough to bridge two of the walling blocks and three 10 mm (⅜ in) mortar joints. The special hollow pier blocks

200 x 100 mm (8 x 4 in) so estimating coverage is easy; you need 50 per sq m (42 per sq yd). Some are as thick as 65 mm (2½ in) or even 80 mm (3¼ in); other light-duty blocks are only 50 or 60 mm (2 or 2⅜ in) thick, and are intended for use as paths and patios rather than for driveways.

Mortar and concrete

The raw materials used to make mortar and concrete are cement, aggregate and various additives that improve the performance or ease of handling of the mix. It can be difficult to estimate materials accurately as they have to be ordered in large quantities for all but the smallest jobs, and waste costs money.

Cement is widely sold only in 50 kg (112 lb) bags, although some DIY shops sell 25 or 40 kg (55 or 88 lb) packs. The mortar and concrete formulae overleaf

are based on standard 50 kg bags.

Sand, both soft (for building or brick-laying) and sharp (for concreting), are sold either in bags or by volume. Bags – either 40 or 50 kg – are convenient for small jobs, but work out expensive for large projects such as laying patios or concrete slabs. For these it is best to order by volume from a builders' supplier or transport company. The smallest quantity most will deliver is half a cubic metre, or about three-quarters of a ton. Remember that a cubic metre is some 30 per cent bigger than a cubic yard.

Aggregate is also sold bagged or loose by volume, and is graded according to the size of the particles they contain – fine if it will pass through a 5 mm (¼ in) sieve, and coarse otherwise. Coarse aggregates for concreting usually have a maximum stone diameter of 20 mm (⅞ in),

although you can get 10 mm (⅜ in) aggregate for fine concrete. A cubic metre weighs nearly two tons, and is a surprisingly large heap when delivered.

Dry mixed materials

You can buy bags of dry, ready-mixed mortar and concrete – usually 25 or 40 kg sizes. The varieties include brick-laying mortar, rendering mix, and fine and coarse concrete. Use them where the scale of the job or their convenience outweighs their comparatively high cost.

Ready-mixed concrete

When ordering ready-mixed concrete, specify the volume you need, what it will be used for, how you will handle delivery and, most importantly, whether there is

Below: Split sandstone is a durable material and ideal for paving projects.

easy access to the site. The supplier will then ensure that the appropriate mix for is delivered.

Mortar and concrete mixes

For mortar, use table 1 to select the mix you need, then use the formula for the mix as detailed under Mix types. For concrete, use table 2. The figures in column 3 of the concrete table are the amounts needed to make 1 cu m of concrete. Note that all mixes should be carefully proportioned by volume, using a bucket.

1: MORTAR MIXES

use	exposure	mix
Walling	Moderate	Mix B soft
	Severe	Mix A soft
Pointing	Moderate	Mix A soft
	Severe	Mix C soft

Mix A

1:½:4 cement:lime:soft sand, or
1:3-4 cement:soft sand plus plasticiser, or
1:2½-3½ masonry cement:soft sand

Mix B

1:1:6 cement:lime:soft sand, or
1:5-6 cement:soft sand plus plasticiser, or
1:4-5 masonry cement:soft sand

Mix C

1:3 cement:soft sand

Working with concrete

You may be using concrete to form foundation strips for garden walls, or to

1 Mix the ingredients dry.

2 Form a central crater.

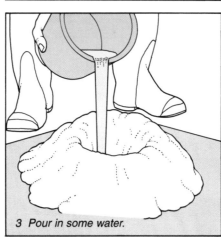

3 Pour in some water.

4 Draw the heap inwards.

5 Turn the mix thoroughly.

6 The correct consistency is smooth and firm.

create a slab as a base for a garden structure. Start by clearing the site of surface vegetation – shrubs, weeds and the like. Then mark out the trench or slab shape with pegs and string, rope or hosepipe as appropriate, positioning your guidelines about 150 mm (6 in) away to allow you adequate room to position the formwork if this is needed to contain the concrete.

Next, excavate the site to the required depth. You can now set the pegs that will support the formwork in position. Use substantial timber – 50 mm (2 in) sq is ideal – and taper one end of the pegs to make them easier to drive in. Hammer them well into the subsoil, and use a

2: CONCRETE MIXES

Use	Proportion by volume		Amount per cu m	Yield per 50 kg bag of cement
GENERAL PURPOSE	Cement	1	6.4 bags	0.15 cu m
Most uses except	Sharp sand	2	680 kg/0.45 cu m	
foundations and	20 mm aggregate	3	1,175 kg/0.67 cu m	
exposed paving	OR All-in aggregate	4	1,855 kg/0.98 cu m	
FOUNDATIONS	Cement	1	5.6 bags	0.18 cu m
Strips, slabs and	Sharp sand	2½	720 kg/0.5 cu m	
bases for precast	20 mm aggregate	3½	1,165 kg/0.67 cu m	
paving	OR All-in aggregate	5	1,885 kg/1 cu m	
PAVING	Cement	1	8 bags	0.12 cu m
All exposed surfaces,	Sharp sand	1½	600 kg/0.42 cu m	
all driveways	20 mm aggregate	2½	1,200 kg/0.7 cu m	
	OR All-in aggregate	3	1,800 kg/0.95 cu m	

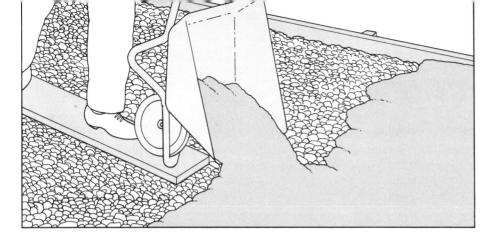

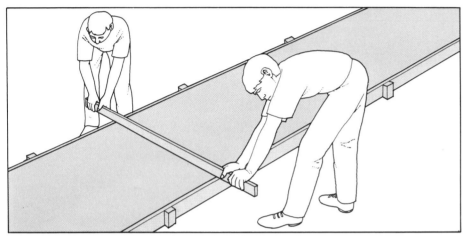

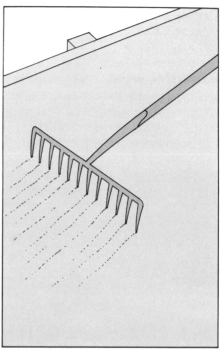

spirit level or water level to set their tops at the desired level for the foundation surface. Nail the formwork planks to the pegs, and check that you have not disturbed them.

Next, put down a level of hardcore. Shovel it out evenly over the base of the excavation to a depth of around 100 mm (4 in) and tread or tamp it down – an old fence post is an ideal tamping tool. Fill obvious gaps and hollows with bits of broken brick or handfuls of aggregate.

To lay the concrete, simply tip it in (1), rake it out level (2) and, with a helper, tamp it down well with a stout beam long enough to span opposite sides of the formwork (3). Use a chopping action first to compact the concrete thoroughly, adding more concrete to any hollows that develop. Pay particular attention to the edges, tamping the concrete down firmly against the formwork. Then finish off with a sawing motion of the beam.

This will give the concrete a slightly rippled finish. For a smoother surface, work over the surface with a soft broom, the back of a clean shovel or a wooden plasterer's float. On large slabs this will mean forming a movable bridge from which you can reach all parts of the surface. The simplest way is to use a ladder with planks laid on the rungs; rest the ladder on piles of bricks outside the

Left: For ambitious projects, like this rock garden, you may need to hire some mechanical help to place the stones.

formwork so the slight sagging as you kneel on it will not touch the fresh concrete surface.

As soon as the slab surface is hard enough not to be marked, cover it with polythene sheeting to prevent it drying out too quickly (it will crack if it does). Weight the polythene down at the edges, and sprinkle sand across it to prevent it ballooning up in the breeze. Leave it on for about three days in colder climates; then remove it, and knock away the formwork. You can walk on it at this point, but you should wait a further five to seven days for the concrete to develop its full strength before starting building on it.

If you are laying a slab more than 4 m (13 ft) across include expansion joints to prevent the slab from cracking. You can incorporate these joints in one of two ways, depending on whether you are using ready-mixed concrete or not.

Below: It is always worthwhile dry-laying paving stones in order to check where the cuts (see right) will be needed.

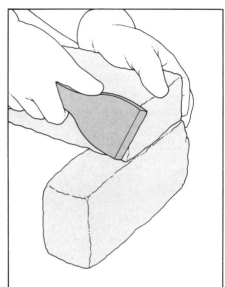

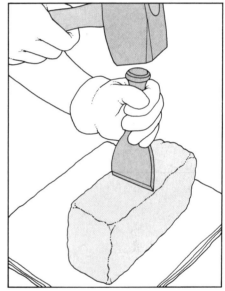

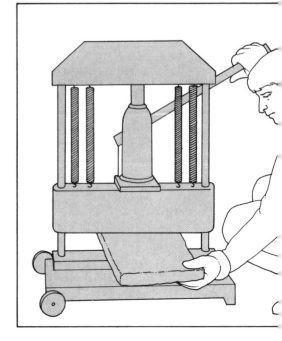

Aim to divide the slab up into two or three equal-sized bays, depending on its size.

With ready-mixed concrete, use hardboard filler strips the width and depth of the slab, held in place with blobs of concrete. The strips should finish level with the top of the formwork, and remain in place once the slab is cast. If mixing your own concrete, simply create the bays with more formwork. Concrete one bay (or the two side bays if you have three) and leave to set; then remove the dividing formwork and fill the remaining bay, simply butting the new concrete up against the edge of the existing bays.

Cutting blocks and slabs

You need a sharp brick chisel or bolster and a club hammer for most cutting work; an angle grinder is useful for cutouts in paving slabs, and a hydraulic splitter will help cutting block pavers.

To cut a natural or man-made stone block, lay it on a thin bed of sand or soil. Score it all round the cutting line with the tip of the chisel (1), then hold the blade upright on the cutting line and strike the chisel firmly with your club hammer (2). Repeat if necessary to split the block.

To cut paving slabs, score a line across the slab and use the chisel and hammer to deepen the cut until the slab splits.

To operate a splitter, mark the cutting line on the face of the slab, place it on the base of the machine with the marked line below the blade, and pull down the lever to 'guillotine' the block in two (3).

DRY STONE WALLS

Dry stone walls have been a feature of the landscape for centuries in areas where stone was plentiful. A well-built dry stone wall will stand for many years, and even a tumbledown one can be quickly restored. The skill in building lies in selecting the right stones to build up a stable, durable and good-looking wall.

WALL STRUCTURE

Since no mortar is used in a dry stone wall, it relies on a sound foundation and careful placement of individual stones for strength. At the base is a layer of

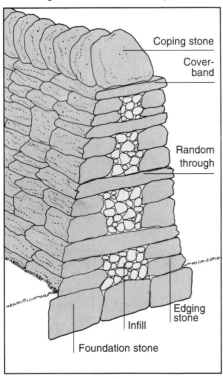

Coping stone

Cover-band

Random through

Edging stone

Infill

Foundation stone

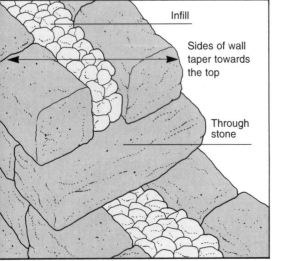

Infill

Sides of wall taper towards the top

Through stone

large, heavy stones set in a shallow trench foundation. Above lies the first course of the wall proper. This is built up as two separate faces, using the largest stones that are available once the foundation has been laid, to a height of about 600 mm (2 ft). The space between the faces is filled with a 'hearting' of smaller stones, and then a course of long 'through' stones is laid so the individual stones reach from one face to the other and bind them together.

Next comes a second course of facing stones, with hearting in between, a second layer of 'throughs' and, if the height of the wall requires it, a third course of facing stones and hearting.

Above and right: If the stones used are small and regular, the structure can be built up safely without through stones, using a similar bonding pattern to that used for a brick wall. Coping stones complete the wall.

Above the final course of facing stones a layer of 'coverbands' is added. These project about 50 mm beyond the face of the wall, and help to bind the top course together; they also prevent rainwater from penetrating the core of the wall, and provide a firm base for the upright coping stones that finish the wall off.

The key feature of any dry stone wall is that each face of a free-standing wall slopes inwards from the foundation up to

the top. This slope is known as the 'batter', and may result in a wall being as much as 900 mm (3 ft) thick at the base and tapering to about 400 mm (16 in) at the top. On earth-retaining walls, the inner face slopes slightly backwards and the outer face has a steeper batter.

Walling materials

When buying stone for your walls from a local stonemason or quarry, he should be able to advise you on the best choice of stone; generally speaking harder, non-porous stone such as granite is ideal, but some limestones and sandstones are also suitable.

Estimating quantities is tricky – you cannot simply count the units as with a brick wall. Stone is generally ordered by the tonne, and you will find that one tonne will build about 1 cu m (35 cu ft) of wall including foundations. It is no bad thing to over-order slightly as carriage is very expensive and you do not want to have to send for a second delivery because you have run short of stone.

If you cannot find – or else cannot afford – natural stone, then the only alternative that looks anything like the real thing is broken paving stone, such as you would use for crazy paving. The broken edges are laid facing outwards

Below: Hammer small pinning stones beneath individual coping stones to ensure that they are securely bedded.

so that they look reasonably natural. One of the big advantage of using this material is that the flat faces of the pieces make it easy to build the wall up evenly in courses, and you can also use slate or similar packing to avoid the appearance that the courses are too close together.

Site preparation

Make sure you have somewhere for the stone to be dumped when it is delivered, and organise one or two helpers with wheelbarrows to transfer it to near where the wall is to be built. Sort the stones into groups of different sizes – large foundation stones, medium-sized stones with at least one square edge for facing, long through stones and smaller infill material. It is a good idea at this stage to set aside the stones that will form the wall coping.

Apart from collecting up the tools and equipment you will need to build the wall – a spade for digging foundations, a club hammer and brick bolster for breaking the stones, a steel tape measure and a spirit level, plus gloves and stout shoes – you should also make up a batter frame to help you build the wall up to a constant and accurate slope. Make two frames from scrap battening (1) and sharpen the feet into spikes so you can set them up at opposite ends of your wall. Link them with a stringline along each face of the wall; you will move this up the frames as the wall rises.

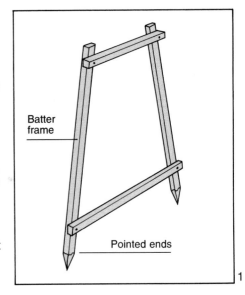

Batter frame

Pointed ends

1

Laying foundations

Mark out the base of the wall, and lift turf or clear vegetation. Dig down about 150 mm (6 in), or until you reach firm, undisturbed subsoil, compacting the soil by stamping or ramming it down firmly (2). In areas prone to prolonged frost in winter, dig even deeper – to a depth of between 450 and 600 mm (18 to 24 in).

Bed in the foundation stones. These should be large and fairly flat, with the squarest edge laid at the face of the

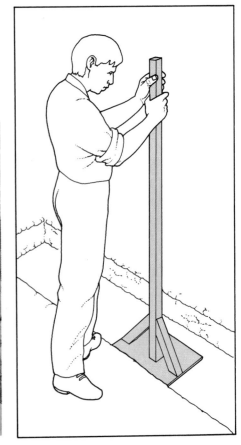

wall. Fit the stones together and fill gaps with smaller stones of the same thickness.

Next, erect the batter frames at each end of the wall. Stand them alongside the foundations and use a hammer or mallet to drive their spiked ends into the ground, ready for the stringlines (3).

Building the wall

Lay a course of medium-sized facing stones on the foundations along each face of the wall, with their squarest edges facing outwards. Check with your stringline, or by 'sighting' across the batter frames, to ensure that the facing stones are set back slightly from the edges of the foundation stones. Use smaller pieces of stones to wedge the larger ones – a process called pinning – so they do not rock on the stone below. These pinning stones should always be

Right: A well-built dry stone wall should need only occasional maintenance .

pushed into position from the inside of the wall so they will not be seen when the wall is complete.

Pack the space between opposite faces with smaller pieces of stone, wedged tightly to ensure the infill is well compacted and will not subside (3). Do not use soft soil for packing; it will soon be washed out by rain, leaving the stones dangerously unstable.

Depending on the thickness of the stone, you may need to add a second or third course of facing stones to bring the wall height up to about 600 mm (2 ft), ready for the first course of through stones. Check each course follows the required slope, and lay the stones so each one overlaps a joint between the stones in the course below it (4, page 193), like stretcher bond in brickwork.

Form ends to the wall by building up a layer of long through stones at each end of the wall structure. Tie the stones into the infill at intervals with a stone laid so it projects back into the centre of the wall, and tilt the stones backwards slightly for extra stability.

Make sure that both faces and the infill are level, then lay the long through stones across the wall. They should reach from face to face for maximum strength; trim any that are over-long using your club hammer and a brick bolster. If you are short of enough stones of the right length, space those you have evenly along the length of the wall and then lay shorter 'half-throughs' between them; they should be long

enough at least to reach to the centre line of the wall. Again, pin the stones inside the wall with smaller pieces of stone so they do not rock, and add infill stones in the gaps between them.

Continue building up the wall to the

required height, adjusting the stringline so you keep the batter constant. A low wall may need just one more thinner layer of facing stones, followed by the layer of coverbands (the final through stones) and the coping. A taller wall (up

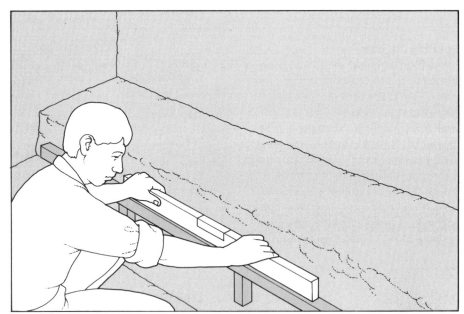

to a maximum of about 1200 m/4 ft – higher walls may be unstable unless built by a specialist) will need another course of facing stones and a second layer of through stones near the top. Complete the pinning and infilling, checking that the top of the wall is level.

Now add the coverbands. These are laid to form a sort of damp-proof course to prevent rain saturating the infill. Lay them with facing edges projecting 50 mm (2 in) beyond the batter slope, and their other edges should mesh as closely as possible with their neighbours like pieces in a jigsaw. Trim stones if necessary to get a good fit, and check that the coverband course is level. Pin any stones that are not perfectly bedded on the top course of the wall, to ensure a stable base for the coping.

If your winters are severe, break with tradition and bed the coverbands in mortar to help reduce water penetration and subsequent frost damage.

Add the coping after adjusting the stringlines (5, page 194). You can use a row of evenly-matched semi-circular stones laid on edge, lay single stones flat on top of the coverband or choose buck-and-doe coping – high and low stones laid alternately to resemble a line of rabbits sitting nose to tail. It is also known as cock-and-hen coping.

Set the stones closely together. With on-edge stones, set them so they all lean slightly in one direction.

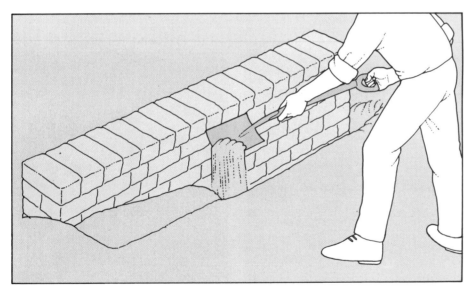

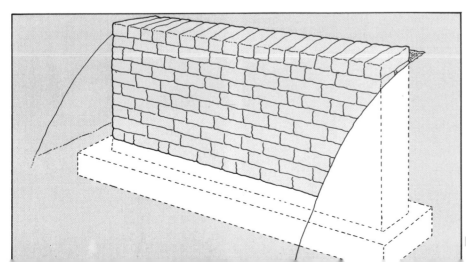

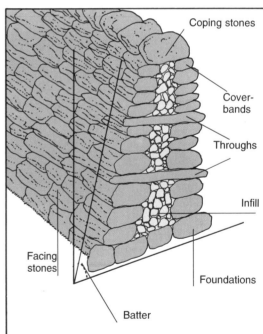

Below: The structure of a dry-stone wall built using irregular sized stones. The most important features are the heavy foundation stones and the long through stones that bind the wall structure together. The facing stones are wedged in place with pinning stones, and the centre is filled with smaller pieces.

Coping stones

Cover-bands

Throughs

Infill

Facing stones

Foundations

Batter

Far left and left: The first step for a retaining wall, whether using random-shaped or regular stone, is to dig out the site (1). Check the base is level (2) and add foundations for high walls. Build the wall up, using mortar to reinforce the bonding between blocks (3). Finish with a coping course (4). Backfill behind the wall (5) to complete (6).

RAISED BED WALL

A simple variation on dry-stone walling can create low walls built for eventual clothing with plants. The wall is built using soil as the 'mortar' between the blocks, creating small planting pockets.

The wall can be built using long garden walling blocks (where available) or pieces of broken paving slab. The former are best for a free-standing wall, with the blocks laid in two parallel rows of stretcher-bond work (end to end, with an overlap of half the block length in successive courses). Link the two halves of the wall with a header (a block laid across the two halves) after every two or three stretcher blocks.

If broken paving slabs are used, build the wall as a cavity construction, with straight edges of slab exposed on the face of the wall and the uneven edges in its centre. The irregularities in the centre can then be filled with packed-in soil.

It must be stressed that walls built in this way should not exceed 900 mm (3 ft) in height, and on no account should they be built as earth-retaining walls unless the blocks or slabs are set on proper concrete foundations and are bedded on mortar, with soil planting pockets only in the vertical joints.

Building the wall

Dig a level trench as the wall footing. Compact it with a length of fence post or similar implement, ramming broken brick or similar material into areas that are soft or have been disturbed. Check the base of the trench is almost level; any minor discrepancies can be made up by increasing or decreasing the depth of the soil bed laid beneath the first course.

Build the wall up course by course, tamping each block into a bed of loose soil about 50 mm (2 in) to compact down to about half its thickness. This works best if the soil is slightly damp. Check each course is level using a straightedge and a spirit level, and raise or lower any stones by adding or removing soil.

If using broken slabs to build the two faces of the wall, set each succeeding course back towards the wall centre by about 12 mm (½ in) so the face of the wall slopes very slightly inwards towards the wall centre as it rises. This will improve the stability of the wall.

Build the wall up course by course to the required height. Because soil is used to bond the blocks, add mortared-on coping stones along the top of the wall to help throw rainwater clear of the wall and prevent it washing out the soil. Push cuttings into the planting pockets.

1 *Excavate the site for the planter, digging down to reach firm, undisturbed subsoil.*
2 *Level and compact it thoroughly.*
3 *Build up the planter course by course, using sieved soil or peat to bed the slabs in place.*
4 *Check the courses are building up level .*
5 *Continue adding courses, sloping the wall face backwards slightly to give the structure extra strength.*

Above: This raised bed has matured over several years to become an attractive feature in an otherwise flat garden. Moss and lichen can be encouraged to grow on the stone by a liberal painting of natural yoghurt or pig dung diluted in water.

If you are about to start work on creating a new patio, renovating or extending your existing one, some careful planning will not only help you to make the best possible use of the site; it will also help the job to proceed in an orderly fashion and with the minimum of disruption. This planning covers your choice of site and materials and enables you to deal with obstacles such as trees and manholes.

First thoughts

If planning a new patio, the first thing to do is to sit down and work out exactly what you expect it to do for you. Will it be used mainly as an outdoor room when the weather is fine, with chairs and a table where you can sit and read, eat and entertain friends? If so, will you want to include features such as a barbecue? Will the furniture be movable or built-in as part of the construction? Will you

need space so that the children have somewhere to play when the lawn is wet? Do you want to include a washing line? Answers to all these questions will help you to envisage exactly what you want in terms of size and features.

Patio materials

At this stage it is also a good idea to start thinking about the sort of materials you want to use, since this will have a direct bearing on your design and planning. The choice is between plain concrete, paving slabs of natural or reconstituted stone, and bricks or block pavers.

Concrete is fairly inexpensive, and can be used to create a patio of any shape or size. Its drawbacks are that the surface is visually uninspiring (although a variety of textured surface finishes can be created), and it is hard work to lay, even if you order it ready-mixed. You will need

quite a lot of site preparation, plus formwork to contain the concrete as it is poured. However, it makes the most durable patio surface if it is well laid, and can always be treated as a sound base for more decorative surface materials.

Paving slabs are the most popular choice. They are available in a wide range of types, shapes and sizes. Natural stone slabs are an attractive choice but are likely to be expensive due to haulage costs. Man-made slabs, though, are relatively inexpensive and are widely available. There are squares and rectangles in a variety of sizes, colours and surface textures – including some very good imitations of natural split stone – which allow you to experiment with exciting layouts. You can also buy inter-locking hexagons, and even round stones that can be intermingled with materials such as cobbles. Laying is easy – either on a sand bed or on mortar over an existing concrete base – but larger slabs can be heavy to handle. The biggest advantage of slabs is the speed with which you can lay even a substantial patio and have it ready for use. The one disadvantage is that it is tricky to lay them in shapes other than rectangles unless you are prepared for a lot of cutting to shape.

Block pavers are a comparatively recent arrival on the DIY scene in certain countries, although they have been used in public works for years. They are roughly brick-sized, so they are easy to handle, and come in a range of colours and textures. Most are simple rectangles, but there are also inter-locking shapes which can look very attractive over small areas. They are designed to be laid over a sand bed with no mortar joints, so they can be placed and levelled very quickly (and taken up again if necessary). Because of their small size, they can also cope with curves and other unusual shapes far more readily than slabs.

Left: Patio surfaces can complement or contrast with the materials used for the house. Here, slate set in mortar is the perfect foil for the house brickwork.

Left: Laying square paving slabs in a spaced-out grid pattern allows grass to grow between them and helps soften the look of an otherwise formal design.

combination of the two), plus building some earth retaining walls to keep patio and garden apart.

If the patio is to adjoin the house, you have to make sure that its finished surface will be at least 150 mm (6 in) below the level of the house damp course to avoid heavy rain splashing back above it and causing damp penetration. If the garden slopes steeply away from the house, you may be able to minimise the amount of backfilling involved by having the patio level well below the DPC, and reaching it by steps from the house. But if the garden slopes up from the house, you need to think about drainage from the patio surface; otherwise your enclosed low-level patio will turn into a pond in wet weather.

Lastly, once you have decided where your patio will be sited and how big it will be, it is time to look at whether there are any obstacles in the way of your plans – things like manholes (which can often be disguised), mature trees (which you may be able to make into a feature of the patio), even existing structures such as paths, steps and clothes lines.

Making detailed plans

For all but the simplest rectangle it pays to make a scale drawing of your proposals before you start the actual construction. This allows you to estimate materials accurately and also to work out precisely how you will overcome any site obstacles.

Work on squared paper to a scale of, say, 1:20 – this means that every 10 mm on your drawing represents 200 mm on the site. If you prefer to work in imperial measurements, use a scale of 1:24 – 1 in on the plan equals 2 ft on the ground. Measure the site carefully so you can draw existing features onto the plan. If the site slopes and excavation and retaining walls will be needed, measure the falls carefully so you can produce sectional drawings as well to indicate precise positions of steps, walls and other three-dimensional features.

If you are intending to use paving slabs, it makes sense to minimise the amount of cutting you by sizing the patio

To get an idea of what is available in your area, visit local suppliers – DIY superstores, garden centres, builders' merchants or concrete manufacturers – so you can see colours and textures 'in the flesh' before making your choice.

Choosing a site

The next thing you should do is decide where the patio is going to go. Nine times out of ten, the automatic choice is to put it across the back of the house, where it acts as a sort of stepping stone between house and garden. However, unless your house faces broadly to the south in the northern hemisphere, or north in the southern hemisphere, you

will not get much sun by siting it here. The solution is to look elsewhere.

For example, by siting it at one side of the garden you will be able to avoid the shadow of the house, and putting it at the bottom of the garden could give you a whole new view of your property. Think too about privacy, especially if you are an ardent sunbather; picking a site that is not too overlooked will do wonders for your peace of mind!

If you're lucky enough to have a flat garden, the actual patio construction will be a strictly two-dimensional affair, but if the land slopes up, down or across your patio site you will have some heavier work to do – excavation, back-filling (or a so that, if possible, it consists of rows of whole slabs. This means that you need to know the size of the slabs. Most are 450 or 600 mm (18 or 24 in) across, but some ranges include half-slabs too to finish rows and, with square slabs, to enable you to stagger joints in alternate rows if you want to. With concrete and block pavers, you obviously have far greater flexibility – a concrete patio can be any size or shape you want, and block pavers are small enough for cutting not to be a major problem.

Now you can draw in the outline of the patio and add details of any other features such as walls, steps or planters. With paving slabs, you can even draw in the individual slabs – useful for estimating quantities, as well as giving you a chance to alter the laying pattern so you can cope with obstacles such as manholes without having to do too much awkward cutting. If you are planning to lay slabs with different textures or colours to create a pattern, now is the time to colour these in – again both to help accurate estimating and to act as a guide when you start laying the slabs.

Coping with manholes

Manholes are one of the most common obstacles when it comes to laying a patio. They are unsightly things at the best of times, and the temptation is simply to pave over them. While frowned on by professionals (and some regional authorities), this is acceptable so long as you take steps to prevent soil or sand from entering the drains and are prepared to lift the paving materials in the event of a blocked drain occurring. This means sticking to loose-laid materials – slabs or block pavers – on a sand bed (and remembering to tell your purchaser what you have done if you ever move house).

As a precaution against sand finding its way into the chamber, you should cover the manhole with a sheet of heavy-duty polythene sheeting, laid so it extends about 150 mm (6 in) beyond the chamber all round. It is also worth giving the manhole cover a coat of proprietary rustproofer before covering it up,

Renovating an old patio

If you inherit an old garden, you may discover an overgrown and derelict area of paving. A mess it may be: however, the one thing that has probably survived intact is the paving itself, and by clearing the area and then lifting and re-laying the old slabs you will be able to create a new patio with all the charm of weathered stone, and at a fraction of the cost.

1 Start by clearing the area of weeds and other foliage that has encroached on it.
2 Working from the edge of the paved area, start lifting individual stones and breaking up any old mortar pointing.
3 If the subsoil is well compacted, re-lay the slabs on pats of mortar. Otherwise use a 50 mm (2 in) thick sand bed.
4 Use square-edged pieces to form the new edge of the re-laid patio.
5 Complete the renovation by re-pointing all the gaps between the stones.

especially if it is made of lightweight galvanised rather than solid cast iron.

Obviously, you cannot do this if you are laying concrete or bedding slabs or crazy paving in mortar. Here there is no alternative but to build up the walls of the chamber so that the cover will finish flush with the patio surface. Disguise its presence by standing a planter on top.

Providing drainage

Any 'solid' patio should have a slight slope to stop rainwater forming puddles on the surface, although this is not critical with slabs and pavers laid loose over a sand bed because water can drain through the open joints. For a patio adjoining the house wall, the slope should be away from the house. Where the patio will be a sunken affair in a sloping garden, you should also incorporate a surface gully at some point near the centre of the patio area and link it to a drain running to a soakaway. You are generally not allowed to drain

Left and below: Reclaimed paving stones have the attractive patina of age that modern paving materials can take years to acquire.

Left: Instead of pointing between the stones, fill the gaps with soil and plant them with small cuttings to encourage spreading ground cover.

surface water into an existing foul water drain or sewerage system.

Working around trees

If you have a mature tree within the area your patio will occupy, aim to lay your paving material no closer to it than about three times the trunk diameter. This will ensure that the tree is not starved of water and will prevent subsequent growth from disturbing the paving. With slabs and pavers, set those round the opening on a mortar bed to prevent them from shifting and to form a neat edge.

Using existing bases

You can generally resurface existing concrete patios by laying slabs or block pavers on top of them so long as raising the surface level by up to 100 mm (4 in) will not cause damp problems in an adjoining house wall. If the concrete is badly cracked, aim to lay your new

surface loose on a sand bed; otherwise so long as it is in reasonably sound condition you can use a mortar bed instead and then point up any of the joints which occur between the slabs.

If you want to extend an existing area of concrete, the weak spot will be the joint between old and new areas. Break up the edge of the existing area and brush on a liberal dose of PVA or latex bonding agent to ensure a strong bond.

Laying a patio

Laying a patio is one of the simplest outdoor projects, and is an opportunity to learn basic building techniques. The actual job does not need a great deal of skill, just your time and effort, both of which are effectively free. Here is how to lay a patio using paving slabs, first on sand and then on mortar.

1

2

3

4

5

6

7

Preparing the base

Unless you are planning to use crazy paving, you will get perfectly satisfactory results by laying your slabs on a sand base about 30 mm to 50 mm (1 in to 2 in) thick: no mortar is needed. However, this base must be flat, with a slight slope away from the house for drainage, and must be properly prepared if you are to avoid subsidence in the future. Most importantly of all, it must not be built up in such a way that the damp–proof course (DPC) in the house wall is bridged. Ideally, the finished patio surface should be about 150 mm (6 in) below DPC level, to prevent heavy rain from splashing back up the wall and causing damp penetration.

This means you will probably have to do some excavation of the patio site, even if only to remove vegetation from the area. If the subsoil is firm, do not disturb it; however, if it is at all loose, you will have to excavate to a depth of about 150 mm (6 in) and lay a 100 mm (4 in) layer of well-rammed hardcore. In this case it is then better to lay slabs on a mortar bed rather than on sand.

You can also lay new slabs over an existing surface – concrete, for example – so long as the finished patio surface will still be at least 150 mm (6 in) below the level of the house damp course.

Estimating quantities

With square or rectangular slabs laid in rows, working out how many you require is quite straightforward so long as you know how big the slabs are; you will need x rows, each containing y slabs – a total of x times y slabs in all. Order a few extra slabs to allow for breakages.

Sand is sold by the cubic metre or yard and parts thereof. To work out how much you will need measure the patio area in square metres and divide the answer by 20. For example, a patio 8 m (about 26 ft) wide and 5 m (16 ft) deep would need 2 cu m of sand.

Laying slabs on mortar

Start by dry-laying the slabs you are using to work out where cut slabs will be needed. Mark your starting point clearly, lift the slabs and the turf and excavate to

Right: The finished patio has a smooth surface that is good-looking, practical and also easy to keep clean.

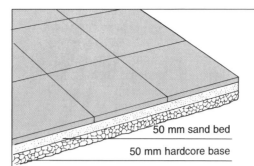

50 mm sand bed

50 mm hardcore base

1 A typical patio cross-section – slabs laid on sand or mortar over hardcore.

2 Excavate soft subsoil, then tip in a layer of hardcore about 50 mm (2 in) thick.

3 Tamp the hardcore down well into the subsoil with a heavy baulk of timber.

4 Check that the hardcore is level by drawing a batten across its surface.

a depth of about 150 mm (6 in) to reach solid, undisturbed sub-soil. Then shovel in a 100 mm (4 in) thick layer of broken brick or coarse aggregate and ram it down to consolidate it. If laying your patio over existing concrete, sweep the surface and remove any loose concrete.

You can lay slabs in a continuous mortar bed, but this increases the amount of mortar. Instead, put down five dabs of mortar, one under each corner and one in the middle, or lay a narrow band of mortar beneath the perimeter of the slab plus one in the centre.

Bed the first slab on the mortar and tamp it down firmly with the handle of your club hammer. Use your spirit level to check that the slab is level in one direction and that it has a slight fall in the other – away from the house if the patio adjoins it. The degree of fall is not critical; the bubble on the spirit level should be just off-centre.

Lay subsequent slabs in the same way, butting them against each other and checking levels. If a slab is too low, lift it and add more mortar before tamping it back. Use spacers for even joints.

Cut and fit slabs as necessary to complete the paved area, laying them in the same way as the whole ones. Make sure that edge slabs have a continuous mortar bed beneath them, and finish it off neatly with your trowel. Mix up some fairly dry mortar for pointing the joints. Fill gaps with mortar if they are too narrow for a cut slab.

To point the joints, cut a sausage-shaped portion of mortar, lay it along the joint and use the edge of your trowel to

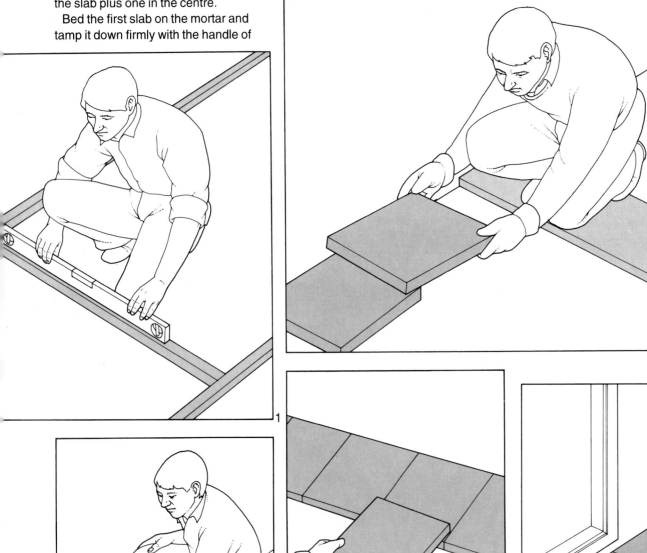

chop it down into the gap. Alternatively, use an offcut of thin board such as hardboard held on edge to press the mortar down. Finish the joint neatly, then move onto the next one. Leave mortar droppings on the slab surfaces to dry, then brush them off; if you try to remove them while wet, they stain the surface.

Laying slabs on sand

1 Begin by marking out the patio area accurately, either by dry-laying slabs or by using pegs and stringlines. Then excavate as necessary – see Preparing The Base, page 202 – and check that the subsoil or hardcore is roughly level. Its surface should be about 90 mm (3 in)

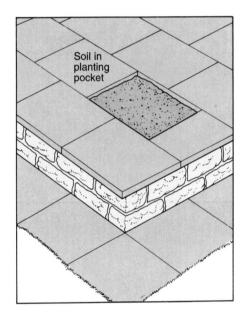

Soil in planting pocket

below the surrounding ground level, so that once the sand bed and the slabs are laid the patio surface will be at the same level as the surrounding ground; it is better to aim for it to be fractionally lower, so you can run a mower along the lawn edge without touching the paving.

If you are worried about weed growth, treat the patio area with a liberal dose of long-acting weedkiller at this stage.

To make it easier to get the sand bed the right depth, place 50 mm (2 in) square battens at intervals across the area to be paved. Then tip and rake out the sand between them and use a long plank spanning the battens to level it.
2 Once you have got a firm, level sand bed, lift the battens and fill in the gaps left behind with more sand.
3 Now all you have to do is to lay the slabs. Start at the edge next to the house wall, kneeling on a plank so you do not disturb the sand bed unduly, and bed the first row in place. As you work, check that each slab is level with its neigh-bour, scooping out or adding sand as necessary, and tamp the slab down gently but firmly with the handle of a club hammer or an offcut of heavy timber.

4 Lay subsequent rows in the same way, sliding each slab into position off the edge of its neighbour in the preceding row rather than standing it on edge and then lowering it to a horizontal position. Aim for closely-butted joints, and check the alignment of the rows as you work.

To cut slabs, refer to page 189.
5 With all the slabs laid, brush some sand and sieved soil into the joints. If the perimeter of the patio will be above the level of the surrounding ground, you need some form of edge restraint to prevent the border slabs from creeping outwards. Bed bricks or garden walling blocks round the edge on a mortar bed, or use lengths of preservative-treated timber – say 75 x 25 mm (3 x 1 in) in cross-section – set on edge and held in place with pegs driven into the ground.

Your newly-laid patio will need little in the way of maintenance. An occasional watering with weedkiller will stop weeds from growing along the soil-filled joints. If any individual slabs show signs of subsidence, simply lift them with your brick bolster and sprinkle a little more sand underneath to restore them to their original level.

Simulated stone slabs may be used to create an attractive patio in a corner of the garden. For this simple project, three different sizes of paver are used to create a random design, giving the area a charming, rustic feel, while pebbles scattered between the artificial flagstones add an interesting finishing touch. A similar effect could be also created with ordinary concrete slabs or real stone.

In the photographs here, the patio is contained by timber on one side, but if you do not plan to have such an edging, excavate to a level which will ensure that the finished surface is flush with the ground.

Materials

For a 3.6 m x 3.2 m (12 ft x 10 ft 6 in) patio:

23 x 500 mm x 500 mm (1 ft 8 in x 1 ft 8 in) slabs

23 x 500 mm x 250 mm (1 ft 8 in x 10 in) slabs

23 x 250 mm x 250 mm (10 in x 10 in) slabs

0.6 m³ (¾ cu yd) sand

40 kg (88 lbs) of 13 mm (½ in) pebbles

Preparation

1 If the patio is not enclosed, peg out the area. Level the ground.

2 If the soil is stable, compact it now; otherwise spread a layer of hardcore to form a solid sub-base before compacting.

Laying the sand base

3 Spread 25-50 mm (1-2 in) sand over the patio area and hose down lightly. The water will help to compact the surface, making it easier for you to level it.

4 Using a spirit level (on its own or placed on a straightedge), smooth out the sand. If the patio is next to a building, the floor surface should slope slightly away from it, and should be at least 150 mm (6 in) below the DPC under the floor slab.

Laying the slabs

5 Start laying the slabs from the furthest corner, leaving a slight gap

between each. There is no particular pattern to be followed – simply place them as you feel they look most attractive, ensuring that you have a good mix of sizes throughout. Tap the stones gently with a rubber mallet to level them. In order to avoid disturbing the sand you have already smoothed out and levelled, it is a good idea to use a couple of slabs as temporary stepping stones.

6 Once all the slabs are in place, stand back and check that you are happy with the configuration you have achieved. If there are large gaps in some places, adjust the stones now for a better fit.

4

3

5

7 Spread the sand over the entire surface and then brush it loosely in between the pavers. Next, hose the area down lightly with water to compact the sand.

Finishing off

8 Finally, spread pebbles over the surface and brush into them place between the stones. Once the pebbles have settled, add more if and where necessary. If you want to give the patio a more informal look, sow some flower seeds between the slabs, water and wait for them to grow.

7

8

A previously unused corner of the garden is transformed by the addition of a flagstone patio.

COBBLED PATIO

4

Regular man-made cobbles or setts can create a delightfully old-fashioned and rustic effect in a small courtyard or enclosed area. The DIY skills required for laying cobblestones are basically the same as for the other types of paving shown in this book, but this is a particularly simple project as their small size makes them very easy and light to handle.

Although the setts were laid in a straightforward grid in this project, they could also be staggered to create a stretcher bond pattern.

Materials
To lay about 10 m² (12 sq yd) of cobbles or setts:
800 x 110 mm x 110 mm x 50 mm (4¼ in x 4¼ in x 2 in) cobbles or setts
0.5 m³ (¾ cu yd) sand
50 kg (110 lb) cement

Preparation
1 Clear the chosen area, making sure that you remove all weeds, grass, stones and any excess soil. Since this example is a courtyard adjacent to the house, there is no need here to set out the site, but it is important to excavate to a depth of at least 200 mm (8 in) below the level of DPC. This will ensure that the tops of the setts, which are 50 mm (2 in) deep, are far enough below the floor level. If hardcore is required, you will obviously have to dig deeper and remove more soil to accommodate it.

2 Compact the surface thoroughly, ensuring that the ground slopes away from the building.

Laying the sand base
3 Cover the area with about 40 mm (1½ in) of sand. Rake and smooth it.

Laying the cobbles or setts
4 If you are laying the cobbles or setts in an enclosed area, start laying them alongside one wall. Tap each cobble or

Bare grass and a small section of badly laid paving do little to enhance a small courtyard.

3

sett gently into the sand bed with a rubber mallet. However, if the patio is not bounded by any walls, first spread a strip of mortar along one side (as described in step 6) to hold the edges in place.

5 Continue laying the cobbles or setts in a straight grid or stretcher bond pattern, as desired. Check the levels frequently to ensure that they are laid as evenly as possible. If any are lower than the others, lift them and put a

little extra sand under them. Even though they are factory-made, artificial cobbles or setts may not be exactly the same size, so the gaps between them will not always be consistent.
6 Wherever the outside edge is not bounded by a wall, you will need to hold it in place with mortar. Use a 1:4 cement:sand mix and spread the concrete with a bricklayer's trowel. Press the cobbles or setts firmly into position.

5

6

7

Finishing off

7 Now make up a dry mixture of cement and sand in the same ratio and brush it into the joints.

8 Sprinkle a little water on to the surface of the patio and continue brushing in the cement:sand mix until all the joints are flush with the top of the paving.

9 Try your best not to leave any traces of mortar on the surface as you work– once it dries it can be very difficult to remove. If you do spot any excess, wipe it off immediately with a cloth or sponge. This may seem a tedious task, but if you try to hose down the cobbles or setts before the mortar has set properly, you will simply wash it out

of the joints. If the cobbles or setts are not made of concrete, remove any excess mortar.

Below: Cobbles or setts transform this small, secluded courtyard and create a charming atmosphere.

STEPPING-STONE PATH

If you do not wish to lay a solid pathway across your lawn, you could lay precast concrete stepping stones to create an attractive and unusual path. However, you will have to make sure you keep the grass growing around them well clipped, or they will quickly become untidy and the effect will be lost.

Since laying a stepping-stone path is simple and reasonably quick, it makes a perfect weekend project, especially for a beginner. The stones are bought ready-made, so no mixing of concrete is required. In the photographs shown here, the pathway provides easy access from the house to a nearby barbecue patio.

Materials

For a 6 m (20 ft) path:
11 stepping stones, 320 mm (12 in) in diameter
25 kg (55 lb) sand

Preparation

1 Lay the stepping stones out on top of the grass, about 200 mm (8 in) apart, and mark around them with chalk or flour.

2 Following the line you have marked, dig out grass and soil to a depth of about 75 mm (3 in). This will accommodate a 25 mm (1 in) bed of sand as well as the thickness of the stepping stone.
3 The surface under the stepping stones must be flat and level. Although it is awkward working in holes, compact it as best you can. A home-made punner or a pole will do the job perfectly well.

Laying the stepping stones

4 Lay a 25 mm (1 in) bed of sand in each hole and compact it.
5 Put the stepping stones in place. The finished surface of each stepping stone should be flush with the lawn. If

they are below the surrounding ground, the grass will probably grow over them quickly. If they protrude above the lawn, people may easily trip

over them. There is no need to cement the stepping stones in place as the earth around them will keep them securely in position.

Right: The completed stepping-stone path leads across the lawn to an adjoining barbecue patio.

1

2

A PATIO PLANTER

An attractive weekend stonework project is this low-level patio planter. You can set it on any firm paved surface as it is light enough not to need foundations.

Use natural stone if or man-made garden walling blocks where each block has its faces and ends moulded to resemble a section of dry-stone walling, and all you do is build up the structure to the required extent and height by bedding the blocks on bricklaying mortar and pointing the joints to match the recesses between the moulded stones. To finish off, use capping blocks moulded to look like traditional on-edge stones used on dry-stone walls.

3

4

5

6

1 Work out the size of planter you want and order the required number of walling and capping blocks. You will also need cement and soft sand (or pre-mixed dry-pack bricklaying mortar), plus a brick bolster and club hammer to cut the blocks, a shovel for mixing the mortar, and a bricklaying trowel and spirit level.

2 Start by laying the blocks that form the first course of the planter, setting them on a mortar bed and checking that they are level. There is no need to point the vertical courses.

3 Add the second course, changing the bonding pattern of the blocks as shown to give the wall additional strength.

4 When you have completed the walls, add the capping stones, setting them on a narrow ribbon of mortar along the centre line of the walling blocks for extra strength. Tap each block so it is level.

5 You will probably have to cut one or two of the capping stones to length to complete the planter. Set the block on a bed of sand and use your brick bolster and club hammer to split the block at the desired position. It should break cleanly along the plane between the individual moulded stones.

6 Complete the planter by setting the capping stone in place. Then leave the mortar to harden for 48 hours before filling the planter with soil and compost.

Right: The finished planter, filled with compost and planted out with variegated ivy and colourful bedding plants.

A SUNDIAL

One of the most attractive small stone features you can add to your garden is a sundial. Apart from being a pleasing object in its own right, it will provide an amusing diversion on sunny days and will become an object of fascination for children who are used to telling the time from more sophisticated equipment.

This project is very simple and quick to assemble, making it an ideal weekend project for beginners. It also requires little in the way of materials or equipment.

The essential ingredients of a sundial are the clock face and the style or gnomon (the pointer that casts the shadow that tells the time). There is

nothing to stop you from making these yourself, using trial and error to get the hour spacings correct on the dial; set the pointer at an angle to the dial equal to the degree of latitude where you live. However, unless you enjoy a challenge, it will undoubtedly be simpler and quicker to buy a ready-made dial and to set it on a column and base of your own design. Dial faces are sometimes available in a variety of metallic and cast resin finishes and are available from some large DIY superstores specialising in garden furniture and ornaments.

The sundial shown here has been mouned on four pieces of stone. The pedestal is formed from two square slabs, one smaller than the other, with smooth top and bottom surfaces and roughly dressed edges. The column is a slightly tapered rough-dressed pillar set on the pedestal, and the dial support is an octagon – a square with the corners cut off at 45º – again with smooth top and bottom surfaces and rough-dressed edges all round.

The dial itself can be surface-mounted on the support. Alternatively, set the face in a shallow circular recess ground into the stone.

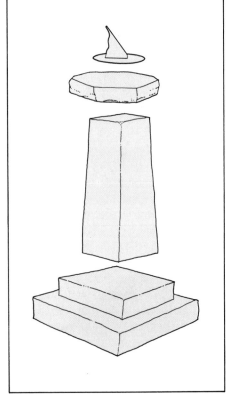

PAVING BY TREES

There may be situations where you want to lay paving in an area occupied by a tree. To avoid depriving the tree's roots of vital air and water, you cannot take the paving right up to the trunk itself.

One solution is to lay the paving units up to a point no closer than about 300 mm (12 in) from the trunk, with a slight slope to encourage rainwater to run into the roots, and then lay cobbles around the trunk to help discourage weeds from growing. Bed the slabs on sand, rather than mortar.

MAKING A ROCKERY

The ideal rock garden is built up in tiers, each smaller than the one beneath it, to ensure that the structure is stable. A rockery needs a good foundation and drainage, especially on a flat site or where the soil is clay. Clay tends not to drain freely, meaning that the rockery becomes waterlogged.

Mark out the shape of the rockery. Do not bother with stringlines; trickling sand around the perimeter of the area is fine.

3

1

2

Remove any turf or vegetation from the site, and excavate to about 150 mm (6 in). Trample the subsoil firmly to create a solid base for the rockery.

With poor-draining clay soils, create a drainage sump beneath the rockery. The backward tilt of the stones will channel water into the centre of the rockery, so dig a hole there 900 mm (3 ft) square and 450 mm (18 in) deep. Fill with hardcore and cover with coarse gravel or upturned turf to prevent topsoil washing into the soakaway and clogging it.

To prepare the bedding material (a mixture of five parts topsoil to one part sand) mix five shovels of soil and one of sand in a wheelbarrow and dump it into the hole until it reaches ground level (1).

Building up the rockery

Select the largest stone (2) to form the keystone of the rockery. It will be too heavy to lift without help, so use a baulk of stout timber and a fulcrum to lever it end over end to the site.

Once the stone is in its approximate final position, look at it from every angle to check its orientation, and to ensure any strata are roughly horizontal. As you adjust its position, swivel it from side to side to settle it into the bedding material. Insert your lever under the front edge to raise it slightly so you can shovel more soil underneath the front and give it a backward tilt. This creates planting pockets above each stone and helps to guide water into the rockery. Compact the soil round the base of the stone, then stand on it to check it is securely bedded without rocking from side to side.

Select two slightly smaller stones next and lay them in the same way either side of the keystone. Set them back slightly to give the front tier of the rockery its desired shape, and butt them up against the keystone. Wedge small pieces of stone into any gaps to help retain soil behind the stones. Tilt each stone backwards, packing soil under its front edge, and consolidate it in position.

Make any adjustments to the first tier, then shovel in more bedding mix behind the stones ready for the second tier (3).

Stamp the bedding mixture down to form a solid base for the next tier before placing the stones. Use large stones near the centre of the tier and smaller ones at the edges (4). Set some stones slightly in front of their neighbours to give the tier a natural appearance and to vary the sizes of the planting pockets. Set the stones with a backward tilt, wedge small pieces of stone between the larger ones to help retain topsoil, and check stability by standing on them.

Add more soil behind the tier to build up height, and create as many further tiers as required. Complete the structure with one or two stones at the pinnacle.

Mix the growing medium – three parts of good topsoil, two parts of compost or peat and one part of coarse sand. Add some bonemeal, mix and spread the mixture over all the exposed soil surfaces of the rockery to a depth of about 75 mm (3 in). Firm it into place ready for planting to begin.

Lay the other stones in the first tier in the same way, tapering them down in size as you work towards the ends of the tier. Check each stone will safely bear your weight as proof it is well bedded.

When planted, water the rockery well. If water runs through gaps between stones, block them with small stone wedges. Spread a 25 mm (1 in) layer of coarse stone chips over all soil surfaces.

NATURAL STONE AND TIMBER FENCING

Rustic timber panels combine beautifully with natural stone pillars. If natural stone is not available in your area, use reconstituted stone blocks. These 2 m-high pillars are 700 mm x 700 mm in size, and the low 10 m-long wall which supports the fencing is 500 mm x 500 mm. If reconstituted stone blocks are used, proportions may be smaller. The slats are cut from rustic timber with bark still attached; any sawn timber may be used.

MATERIALS

Foundations
570 kg cement
1.7 m³ sand
1.7 m³ stone

Wall
stones for 4.5 m³
mortar (amount will depend on size of stones used)

Fencing
4 x 1.6 m upright poles, 90 mm in diameter
3 x 3.2 m x 75 mm x 50 mm support beams
2 x 450 mm x 75 mm x 50 mm support beams
105 x 1.4 m x 95 mm x 22 mm slats

Fasteners
8 x 100 mm anodised wire nails
210 x 50 mm anodised wire nails

1 Set out the foundations, allowing a width of 750 mm for the wall and 1 m for the pillars.
2 Dig a 250 mm-deep trench for the foundations.
3 Mix the concrete in the ratio 1:4:4 and place in the trench.
4 Compact, level and allow to set overnight.
5 Build the pillars and the wall, allowing slightly larger stones to overlap the top of each pillar and so form a natural capping.
6 Set the upright poles vertically in the stonework to a depth of 500 mm, as indicated, to provide a support for the timber.
7 Use a spirit level to ensure the poles are vertical, and brace them in position while the mortar dries.
8 Use the longer nails to fix the horizontal supporting timbers to the upright poles.
9 Then nail the slats to these beams.

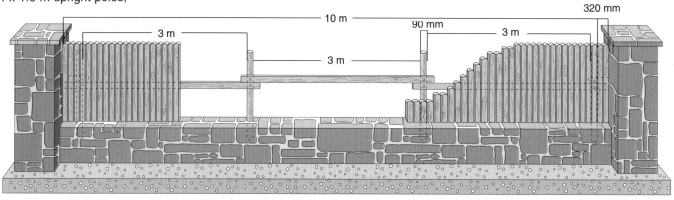

STONE SLAB STEPS

An attractive flight of steps built from dressed stone slabs allows a gradual descent from one level of the garden to another. The lower section of the steps spreads out from a central landing topped with crazy paving. A water feature (not included in the project) adds charm and character. You could continue the stairs across the full width of the area, or you could construct a stepped planter in place of the water feature. A precast pond could also be positioned in between the two lower flights. The stone you use to build the steps will depend on what is available in your area.

MATERIALS

94 slabs of cut stone, average size 300 mm x 200 mm x 100 mm, or stone slabs to cover 8 m²
crazy paving to cover about 2 m²
90 bricks
260 kg cement (175 kg for concrete and 30 kg for brickwork)
1 050 kg or 0.8 m³ sand
700 kg or 0.5 m³ crushed stone
plywood and scrap wood for formwork
2 x precast concrete lamps (optional)

1 Use a profile to establish where the steps will be located. Peg out the area.
2 Roughly excavate the stairway.
3 Construct the formwork in three sections, with treads about 200 mm deep and risers about 100 mm high. Use plywood wherever curves are required. Hammer into place, leaving the central landing untouched.

4 Compact the earth within the formwork. Mix concrete in a ratio of 1:4:4 (cement:sand:stone) and place it to form the foundation slabs for the steps. Level and compact the concrete and allow it to set thoroughly.
5 Excavate the earth between the two bottom flights of steps, using formwork to prevent the bank from collapsing.
6 Dig a trench between the two bottom stairways, 300 mm wide and 100 mm deep, for the foundation of the front wall of the landing.
7 Mix concrete in a 1:4:4 ratio using about 10 kg cement. Place in the trench and allow to set.
8 Build a one-brick wall six courses high in stretcher bond at the front of the landing, leaving drainage holes at the base. Allow the mortar to set thoroughly, then render the front of the brickwork. If you wish to build a water feature, then construction may also take place at this stage.
9 Remove the formwork and backfill the gap behind the wall with crushed stone and soil.
10 Excavate and flatten the earth on the landing. The surface should be level with the base of the concrete which forms the bottom step of the top flight, and the top of the concrete which forms the top step of each lower flight.
11 Mix another batch of concrete and place on the landing. Level and compact it and leave to set.
12 Lay the stone slabs to form the steps, working from the bottom step. If they do not fit exactly, fill in the gaps with mortar or smaller pieces of stone.
13 Lay the crazy paving in mortar on the landing.
14 If you are installing lamps, get an electrician to do the wiring, and then concrete them in position at the top of the steps.

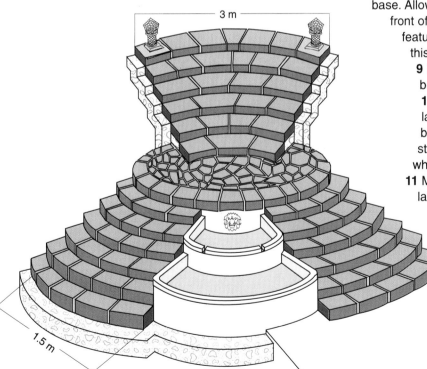

3 m

1.5 m

CARVING A PLANTER

When you have found a piece of stone in an appropriate size, shape and colour, examine it to see which way the 'bed' of the stone runs (see below). Although limestone and sandstone are relatively soft, carving is much easier if you work with the bed horizontal, cutting into it and then hollowing out along it. Set the stone at a comfortable height on a sturdy support; a timber carving table 600 to 750 mm (24 to 30 in) square is ideal.

1 Mark the outline of the recess in pencil on the top surface of the stone. Leave a margin between the cutting line and the edge of the stone of 50 mm (2 in).
2 Using a club hammer and mason's chisel (or a toothed scutch in a scutch holder), outline the recess. Work round the cutting line, chopping downwards first, then lower the tool's cutting angle to 45º to break away the stone within it. Work towards the centre of the recess.

3 As the recess deepens, brush out the stone chippings and dust.
4 Deepen the recess by cutting down the sides to create a smooth bowl. Check the depth of the recess to avoid cutting too deep and cracking the stone or breaking through the base.
5 Either leave the stone with the ridged finish left by the toothed scutch, or smooth off the ridges using a plain scutch, a mason's chisel or a bolster.

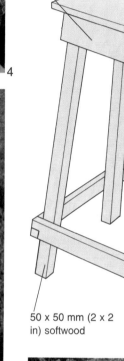

MAKING A WORK TABLE

Use workshop scrap wood and a blockboard offcut to assemble a sturdy carving work table with a comfortable working height. Cut the pieces to length and nail them securely together.

100 x 20 mm (4 x ¾ in softwood)

20 mm (¾ in) blockboard

50 x 50 mm (2 x 2 in) softwood

50 x 25 mm (2 x 1 in) softwood

Left: Working at ground level is always possible, but it can cause back-ache, so a custom-made table (above) is best.

A SANDPIT FOR THE FUTURE

With a little forward thinking you can plan ahead when you build a sandpit as this design can be transformed into a flower bed or garden pond. Your children's demand for a sandpit will not last for ever, and there will come a time when their attentions will turn to more grown-up play activities. At that point it seems a pity simply to have to demolish whatever you created for them; a better solution is to design a pit that can be turned into another feature, and the design shown here is a perfect example.

In its incarnation as a sandpit, it is a gently curved truncated heart shape set at the edge of a block-paved patio. The perimeter of the pit is finished off with a border of stone setts which neatly conceal the heavy-duty polyethylene sheet lining the excavation.

MATERIALS
Coarse gravel
Polyethylene sheeting
Mortar
Stone setts
Builders' sand
Sandpit sand

Assembly
1 To form a sandpit, dig out the shape to a depth of about 300 mm (12 in), keeping the sides of the excavation vertical. So long as the subsoil is firm and well-compacted, the sides should not need any additional reinforcement (diagram 1).
2 Excavate a narrow shelf all round the perimeter of the hole, wide and deep enough for the stone setts to be set in place on it in a mortar bed (diagram 2).
3 Then lay a 50 mm (2 in) deep bed of coarse gravel in the base of the excavation and drape the plastic sheeting over it. Tuck it into the sides, forming neat folds where necessary, and pierce it with holes at intervals across the base of the excavation so that water can drain through it into the subsoil (diagram 3).
4 Trim off excess material round the edge of the lining with scissors or a sharp knife so a narrow strip rests on

the shallow perimeter shelf you cut in diagram 2.
5 Spread a bed of mortar on top of the lining all round and bed the stone setts into place, level with the surrounding paving (diagram 4). Point neatly between them, then fill the pit with sand to a depth that is just sufficient to conceal the lining.

Converting to a pond
When the sandpit's working life is over, you may decide to turn it into an ornamental pond instead.

To do this, you will first have to dig out the sand. Do not waste it, though; use

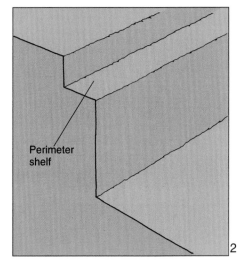

Perimeter shelf

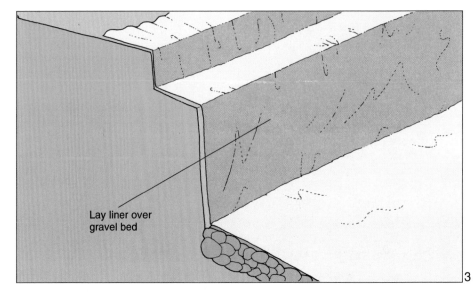

Lay liner over gravel bed

Above: This sandpit can also be lined and used as a pond or a paddling pool, or filled with soil to make a feature flower bed.

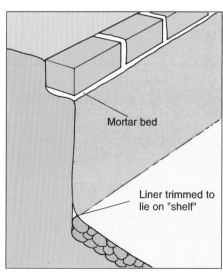

Mortar bed

Liner trimmed to lie on "shelf"

some as top dressing for the lawn, and dig the rest into flower beds to improve the soil texture. Then carefully break away the stone setts and their bedding mortar all round the pit perimeter so you can remove the old lining.

The original hole is not really deep enough for a garden pond, especially if it is to contain fish. Dig out the gravel base you laid beneath the pit lining, and excavate the centre part of the pit to a minimum depth of about 450 mm (18 in); 600 mm (24 in) would be better. Slope the sides of this deeper section gently, leaving a shallower shelf at the level of the original excavation on which to grow aquatic plants.

Line the excavation with damp sand and drape the new pool liner in place. Partly fill it with water and carefully pull out creases in the liner so it conforms to

the outline of the excavation. Then trim excess material from the edge of the liner all round and replace the perimeter setts on a fresh mortar bed to complete.

Converting to a flower bed
If you prefer to turn your redundant sandpit into a flower bed, you have a far easier job than the pond conversion.

Simply dig out the sand, then cut through the liner all round at the point where it disappears beneath the perimeter setts. Lift it out, but leave the gravel bed beneath it in position. Fill the original excavation with good-quality soil and compost, ready for planting out.

An alternative is to turn it into a sunken rockery instead. Bed the rockery stones in place on the bottom of the pit, then add soil and fine gravel and plant it up with alpines.

4

WATER

PART
FOUR

INTRODUCTION TO WATER

For centuries, water has been a source of fascination and inspiration to people of all cultures, making it a common feature of garden design world-wide. This is not surprising since it introduces a magical, sometimes mystical element that is cleansing, cooling and restful. It can also captivate the senses, creating an air of excitement and adding a soothing or splashing sound. Whether your garden is large or small, new or well-established, water can add a pleasing and different dimension.

Ponds, pools and the myriad water features which go with them, are guaranteed to transform the most ordinary gardens, giving them magical and restful qualities. It does not matter what style you decide to follow or what impression you achieve; when you decide to introduce a water feature into your garden, the possibilities are endless. And whether it is created in a

*The water lily (*Nymphaea spp.*) is the queen of aquatic plants.*

formal, natural or a whimsical way, a well-planned water garden will give any outdoor area an aesthetic element which will be appreciated by all.

Generally, water has a tranquil and calming effect, but it will also bring both light and movement into a garden area. A reflective pond will quietly mirror images of plants, buildings and other features, highlighting colours and

encouraging contemplation and a mood of calm, while a water course will tend to shine like a ribbon in the light of the sun or moon. Moving water, on the other hand, will splash and sparkle, producing varying degrees of sound and, often, an exhilarating air of excitement and anticipation.

In this section we illustrate a wealth of contemporary ideas for inspiration. While some projects are influenced by historical approaches, we have tried to present the widest range imaginable. Building methods are discussed, and all the necessary equipment explained.

In addition to the tried and tested techniques and methods used to build ponds and other water features, we have included some innovative and unusual approaches.

Projects range from the simplest water feature, constructed using pre-cast materials, to formal ponds which require more demanding bricklaying

A formal, circular fountain designed as a focal point in a parterre garden and originally laid out in the early 18th Century.

skills. Whether you want to build an elaborate fountain or a simple duck pond, the instructions show you how. Where materials may be difficult to source, alternatives are suggested.

HISTORIC WATER GARDENS
In Egypt water was appreciated as the source of life for civilization, and irrigation systems were established for survival. Water became a prominent component of the renowned pleasure gardens along the Nile. In Ancient Mesopotamia, ponds and running water were a feature of the gardens irrigated by the Euphrates River. In Persia (Iran), where gardens were traditionally identified with paradise, tiled water channels were symmetrical and balanced, and believed to represent the unity of the universe.

Further east, in China, water and rocks represented the Oriental concepts of masculine and feminine, yielding yin and extremely powerful yang. They were the important elements of Chinese landscape architecture and expansive bodies of water were often created.

In Japan, where water is still valued for its tranquillity, ponds have always been commonplace. Even where there was no water, round stones were used to create imaginary rivers of life. Modern Japanese gardeners and landscape architects are renowned for their ability to use even the smallest quantities of water to create beautifully delicate and inspired features.

In Byzantine times, the Romans were acclaimed for their sophisticated water systems, and established magnificent water gardens, which were sometimes copies of the Egyptian designs.

Some of the world's most spectacular water features were devised in 16th and 17th Century Europe. Many of these may be still be viewed in well-maintained Renaissance gardens – at Villa d'Este in Tivoli, Italy, the spectacular Fountain of Neptune and impressive Pathway of the One Hundred Fountains are both celebrated landmarks. In the Austrian Alps at Schloss Hellbrunn near Salzburg, tourists are entertained by the ingenious fountains and 'water games' installed by an archbishop in the 17th Century. And in France, the hydraulics at the Palace of Versailles are marvels, where 1 400 fountains are operated by huge mills and pumps fed by the River Seine.

There are man-made lakes, some in the ancient Orient plus those favoured by English landscape gardeners during the 18th Century. Many of these features were dammed rivers and streams manipulated by gardeners like Capability Brown, to reorganize the landscape and reflect its beauty.

IDEAS AND INSPIRATION
While it is true that few can afford to accommodate the types of ponds, fountains and spectacular features found in the grounds of public buildings and large residences, many of these can serve as inspiration. Magazines and books are another good source, as are established gardens both public and private.

Some nurseries and garden centres arrange regular outings and hold seminars and workshops where

Water trickles over rocks into an attractive, natural-looking pond.

Lush planting softens the edges of a concrete water feature.

amateurs can learn the basics of gardening in general, and often the specifics of water gardening.

Informal ponds, in particular, will reflect nature, and this is where you are assured of getting some of the very best ideas. Look carefully at natural water courses and watch how streams cascade over rocks and boulders or trickle down adjacent surfaces. Observe the natural plant growth and look at how rockeries are formed without the help of human hands. Above all, examine where natural ponds and pools are found. By observing natural water courses, and implementing these features in your garden, you will be able to mirror the beauty of the environment.

PLANNING
Location
Careful thought and logical planning are the key to incorporating a water feature into any garden or patio. The amount of space you have available, gradient, the existence of rocks and established plants will all have a direct

A rustic bridge crosses a man-made waterway lined with river stones.

An attractive concrete-lined duck pond incorporates an island and quaint wooden bridge.

bearing on the layout of your scheme. Local conditions will also influence your design, and soil type may determine the method of construction chosen (see pages 239-247).

You will have to decide the size of your water garden and whether you want a formal feature or something which will blend with the surroundings. Are you planning to keep fish? Do you want to attract other wildlife, like frogs and birds, to the pond? You may simply be looking to plant aquatics, bog plants, water lilies and so on, or to create a pretty cascade with water flowing between different levels.

A vital factor of any water feature is its location. You will find that areas with natural rocks and boulders are often perfect sites, as are slopes where plants will not grow. Unexciting, shady corners may benefit from water features although trees can cause problems when they lose their leaves.

Begin by drawing a scale plan of the garden or area where you plan to construct the water feature. Sketch in buildings, paths or patios and rocks, mounds, hollows, trees and established shrubs. Even if you decide to transplant or remove some plants, a plan is a good starting point. Indicate the direction of prevailing winds and note areas which are shady or sunny.

It may help to sit in the garden or on a patio near to the site you think will be most appropriate. Try to visualise the feature before you start digging holes or building permanent structures.

Then consider the plan in detail. Do you need to incorporate paving around the pond or a rockery to help soften hard edges? Will you need to terrace a slope or build steps to reach the feature? If you are likely to create a muddy trail when walking from the pool, you may have to consider paths.

The choice of materials depends on several factors ranging from basic design to budget. However, it is essential to maintain a visual link with the rest of the outdoor area and any existing theme in the garden.

SAFETY

Wherever there is water in the garden, safety factors should be considered. Toddlers and animals can drown in even the shallowest pool and if a dog cannot get out of the water, it may come to grief.

If you have children and small animals at risk, the simplest solution is to fence in the pond. Unfortunately, this precaution generally spoils the aesthetics of any pool or water garden. Alternatively, think about siting the feature where access is limited; perhaps on a patio approached through doors which can be locked when adults are not present.

The only other solution would be to re-examine your exact needs and choose a feature with a concealed water source or perhaps a very small, shallow pond which can be covered or drained whenever necessary.

The simplest water feature you can choose is a pre-cast bird bath.

An attractive well-planted koi pond established alongside a paved patio.

An unusual three-tiered fountain pours into an informal pond.

Essential tools for bricklaying include a spirit level and corner blocks.

You do not have to be an experienced builder to install a water feature. There are various types of ponds which you can easily build yourself, as well as fountains and smaller features that take the minimum of effort, and very few skills. There are, however, certain basic building principles which should be understood, and several tried and tested methods of construction and installation which will simplify and expedite the projects. It is also invaluable to have a good knowledge of the tools and materials available.

TOOLS

While the tools required for any project will depend on the methods and materials used, there is some basic equipment which all do-it-yourselfers should have at hand. By using the correct tool for the job, you will not only simplify the project, but ensure that all structures are properly built.

Retractable tape measures are the handyman's best friend. A steel tape with a locking mechanism will enable you to set out projects accurately. It is invaluable when checking the depth of an excavated site and when working with wood.

Picks, spades and shovels are essential for excavating in-ground ponds and pools. A pick is

A spade is used for mixing concrete.

indispensable if you are digging hard or heavy clay soil, while a shovel, with its scoop-shaped metal blade, is useful for shifting sand and other building materials. A spade is the most common tool used for digging, as well as mixing concrete, mortar and so on.

Wheelbarrows are an obvious aid when it comes to shifting excavated soil and transporting bricks and other materials. For minor projects and smaller pools, you can use a shallow gardener's wheelbarrow; a builder's wheelbarrow is more practical if you plan to use it for mixing mortar and small quantities of concrete. In any case, it makes sense to buy a good quality barrow with a pneumatic tyre.

Pegs are a practical aid for laying out ponds and watercourses, and for establishing the upper levels around pools. You can buy metal pegs or make inexpensive wooden ones from a stout stick or post.

Compactors are worthwhile items when paving around a pond or pool, or when flattening the interior floor of a sizable water feature. While it is sensible to hire a mechanical compactor for a large project, or if you have to compact hardcore to form a firm sub-base for paving, a homemade punner or ramming tool will be adequate most of the time. To make one, either fill a five-litre (one gallon) tin with concrete and set a pole in the centre, or nail a solid block of wood to the end of a post and use this to flatten and compact the soil.

Levels of various kinds are used for just about every project. First on the list of requirements is a spirit level which will help you ensure that everything from brickwork and paving to bridges and fountain features are flat, level and vertical. These fundamental instruments usually have two vials for both horizontal and vertical use. There are various sizes available, but 1.2 m (4 ft) is a handy length. If the spirit level is not long enough, place it on top of a straight-edge so that it can reach across the pond. Compact carpenter's squares also incorporate spirit level vials.

A *dumpy level* is a useful aid when levelling the ground around the perimeter of a large water feature from a given datum point (the known level), or for determining drainage levels. It is set up on a tripod a short distance from the pool, and a staff or pole, which has been inserted in the ground at the edge of the excavation, marked to indicate the level required. One

Although relatively expensive, a dumpy level is a very useful tool.

A water level can be made fairly easily with inexpensive transparent tubing. To work efficiently, it is vital to ensure there are no air bubbles in the water.

person looks through the lens, which incorporates a spirit level vial, and visually lines up the datum point on a series of pegs inserted around the perimeter. A second person marks off the pegs to show where the surrounding surface should be. Since these professional tools are expensive, it makes sense to hire rather than buy.

A *water level*, which one of the least expensive tools, is invaluable. Working on the principle that water finds its own level, it has a multitude of uses. A level of this kind will enable you to accurately mark the surface area around the water, from a known datum point. All you need is a length of flexible transparent tubing and some water. When working alone, you can attach each end of the tube to a post and check the levels in this way; or ask a helper to hold one end in position and then move the other end of the tubing yourself, to establish the true horizontal level at other points.

Homemade corner blocks are ideal for keeping courses level when laying bricks. These are made by sawing a groove in L-shaped pieces of wood. Builder's line or string is then wound around two blocks (see illustration) which are then slotted onto each end of the brickwork.

The simple water level is invaluable.

Squares, made to form an exact 90°, are essential for checking corners. A *builder's square*, usually made of steel and larger than a normal mathematical set square, is the most common tool used for any building project. When laying out rectangular and square

A corner block and line in position

You can level a circular pool by placing a spirit level on a straight piece of wood. Make sure all the outer pegs are level first.

A trowel is essential for bricklaying.

ponds a homemade square is useful. This can be nailed together using three lengths of wood to form a right-angled triangle in the ratio 3:4:5. The timber should not be warped, and you must be able to handle it with ease. Three lengths of 900 mm, 1.2 m and 1.5 m (3 ft, 4 ft and 5 ft) work well.

Carpenter's squares (or try-squares) usually with one wooden and one metal side, sometimes have a spirit level vial for accuracy.

Straightedges are straight, even lengths of wood or light metal. A straightedge is one of the most important items in a tool kit and is used for all kinds of projects.

Trowels are essential for building a brick or concrete shell. A *bricklayer's trowel* is for spreading mortar, jointing slabs, and levelling small areas of concrete. A smaller trowel may be used to neaten joints in the facebrick walls of a pool, although special pointing trowels are available; or you can use a piece of metal. *Rounded trowels* are useful for smoothing the in-side of rendered ponds.
A *rectangular-shaped plasterer's trowel* is used to apply render or plaster to walls, and to float the surface of a plastered wall or floor screed when a very smooth finish is required. *Angle trowels* are invaluable for neatening inside and outside corners of plastered ponds, and the supporting piers for stepping stones.

Notched trowels are utilised for tiling.
A *wooden float* is usually used to smooth the wet render after it has been laid on.

Hawks, which are used by most artisans, are useful for holding render and mortar when rendering or bricklaying. These tools, also known as mortar-boards, have a handle which is more convenient than the piece of flat metal or board usually chosen by most handymen.

Cutting tools are required for many projects. You will need a pair of sharp, general-purpose *scissors* to trim plastic liners, an *angle grinder* or tile-cutting machine for finishing an edging or stepping stones with tiles, and a saw to cut wood. A *bowsaw* is useful for sawing logs and wooden poles, and a tenon (or back) saw, for most other small jobs. A *hack-saw*, also be used for cutting metal, is favoured by many DIY enthusiasts. An *electric jigsaw*, which will cut both straight and curved edges, is indispensable for the wooden bridge on page 280.

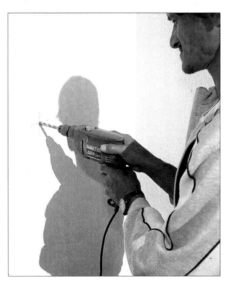

It is imperative to use the correct bit with your drill, depending on the material you are drilling.

The chisel end of a brick hammer or a brick bolster with its wide blade, will enable you to cut bricks.

Hammers are tools which most people have. The most useful is an ordinary *claw hammer*, designed for both

knocking in and extracting nails. A hefty *club hammer*, used in conjunction with a *wide-bladed cold chisel* (brick bolster), or the chisel end of a brick hammer, may be used to cut bricks. A *rubber mallet* has a heavy rubber head, and is useful for tapping paving bricks, blocks and pre-cast slabs into position.

Screwdrivers and spanners are used for attaching some fountain fixtures and fittings to walls. Various *spanners*, including flat, socket and ring types, are required for tightening nuts and bolts, while screwdrivers are, of course, used for fastening screws. You can buy a set of screwdrivers, in different sizes, with both flat blades and cross-point drivers (for Phillips, Pozidriv and Supadriv screw heads). A *spiral ratchet screwdriver*, with interchangeable blades and drivers, is a good investment.

Drills are not generally important for the construction of ponds and pools, although you will need one if you are incorporating wooden features or affixing a wall-mounted gargoyle on a fountain. Most DIYers will already have an electric drill which is more versatile than a hand drill (wheel brace), and you will be able to use it for a wide range of additional tasks. There is a large assortment from which to choose, but those with a variable speed are generally recommended. Models with a hammer action will enable you to drill into concrete, bricks and timber. Before you can use your drill, you will need a selection of masonry bits for drilling into brickwork and concrete, and a choice of wood bits for making holes in timber.

Sanders There is not much sanding to be done when building water features, and a sheet of a suitable grade sandpaper combined with a little physical effort, will usually suffice. However, both belt sanders, which will level slightly rough wood, and orbital sanders, for finishing, will prove invaluable if you are building wooden bridges or erecting decking. A carborundum stone is effective for smoothing the edges of cut tiles.

Polyethylene is an inexpensive material which can be used to line ponds.

MATERIALS

Bricks and mortar, rocks and concrete, clay or even a simple plastic liner can all be used to build attractive water features. Various pre-cast units may be used as fountains, and there are many ready-made ponds available which can be simply sunk into the ground. Timber may be utilised for bridges, decking and jetties, and there is a wealth of other materials available to surface the surround of your pond or pool. Various factors, including your building skills, budget, and the finished effect you want to achieve, will all influence your choice.

Flexible liners

Various kinds of flexible liners are invaluable for the waterproofing of ponds and pools. Not only may they be used for just about any size or shape of pond, but also to establish a bog garden or even to line a cascade or waterfall.

Polyethylene is the most inexpensive type of flexible liner which, although widely available, is much maligned because it punctures relatively easily and deteriorates when exposed to the sun's ultra-violet (UV). Commonly used for damp-proofing various parts of buildings, it is manufactured in various colours and different gauges. Black sheeting contains carbon which inhibits the effect of UV light and therefore increases its lifespan, making this colour the obvious choice for ponds. Fortunately, black pools also look more natural.

Since it is an accepted fact that exposed polyethylene will become brittle and eventually degrade, it is best to lay pavers around the perimeter of the pond so that they overlap the water slightly, providing some protection from the sun. Also keep the pond topped up so the liner is constantly under water.

While it is quite possible to line a pond with relatively thin, 250 micron polyethylene, there is no doubt that 500 micron will last longer; and some experts even advise using the thicker plastic as a double layer.

Recycled polyethylene should be rigorously avoided as it does not have the strength of virgin plastic.

A cross-laminated, high density polyethylene, may be used with rubberised asphalt, which acts as an adhesive, to join (or even patch) this type of plastic. It is manufactured in sheets for waterproofing various parts of a building.

PVC or vinyl sheeting, commonly used to line swimming pools, is the second option. Normally considered more UV stable than polyethylene, it is most commonly manufactured in either blue or black.

As it can be heat welded in the factory, PVC is suitable for quite large pools, and is sometimes packaged in kit form.

Like polyethylene, PVC may be punctured by sharp objects, and it is also affected by the sun. Although PVC itself does not stretch, the addition of plasticisers during the manufacturing process makes some PVC liners relatively elastic. This makes it easier to gradually smooth out crinkles and wrinkles as you fill the PVC-lined shell with water.

Laminated PVC, which may be produced in tarpaulin grades, incorporates textile reinforcing which gives it strength. Although it is commonly used as a pond liner in Britain, this application is not customary throughout the world.

Woven polypropylene, another type of plastic, is quite long-lasting and may be used to line ponds. More commonly used for erosion control, this matting material may be draped in the excavated hole and then coated with a rubberised bitumen sealer to make it completely waterproof. Unlike other liners, it cannot be used for ponds unless it is sealed.

Butyl rubber is undoubtedly the most expensive flexible liner, but one which the experts say is highly resistant to puncturing and degeneration as a result of UV rays. Normally black in colour, it is said to have a life expectancy of at least 50 years.

Although it has various applications, butyl rubber has been used for over half a century to line canals and reservoirs in some countries. If it is used for a pond, it should be at least 0.75 mm (1/32 in) thick.

EPDM, an ethylene propylene polymer, has replaced butyl in some places. A cheaper rubber, it is UV-resistant and considered long-lasting.

Rigid liners
The most common materials used for construction are fibreglass,

For concrete, the cement and sand are combined first (top) and then they are mixed with water, before the aggregate is added.

fibrecement and various thermoplastic materials. Glassfibre reinforced cement ponds are a relatively new invention; small features are moulded into various shapes, while panels may be used together with a thermoplastic or butyl rubber liner.

Fibreglass (glassfibre reinforced polyester) may be moulded to any configuration. Made by bonding several layers of glassfibre with polyester resin, these pools may be made in virtually any colour. They are invariably the most expensive option in this category of pond.

Fibrecement may also be moulded to virtually any shape. Although there is a wide selection of plant containers, there are few configurations of pond, and the material is not common in all countries. Made from organic fibres, cement, and sometimes a small percentage of asbestos, fibrecement is lighter than pre-cast concrete, but considerably heavier than fibreglass.

Thermoplastic shells are made from a variety of related materials including PVC and polypropylene. Numerous different designs are manufactured.

Glassfibre reinforced cement (GRC) is a relatively new product. While it is only available from specialist outlets and actual methods of manufacture may vary, this is an effective material, not only for natural preformed ponds, but for very realistic fake rocks as well. Moulded to form panels, it can be used to support a vinyl-lining.

Concrete
This material has a multitude of applications. It is used for foundations, to build some pool shells, arched bridges and footings for wooden decking set in the water. It is also useful for supporting paving around the edge of ponds (see page 245).

Although it will be reasonably impermeable if a waterproofing compound is added to the mixture, concrete shells should also be rendered (see page 235) and coated with polyurethane or a bituminous waterproofing compound.

Various grades of concrete are used for different projects, depending on their type and magnitude. Watertight walls and pond foundations should be built from a high-strength 1:2:2 mixture of cement, sand and stone. Adjust this ratio to 1:2:1.5 if you are using the smaller-sized aggregate.

Bricks and blocks
Made from burnt clay or pre-cast concrete, bricks and blocks may be used for the walls of formal pools and,

if you wish, for the surrounding paving. Both types come in a range of colours from charcoal to terracotta, and the laying procedure is the same.

If you are building walls, your immediate decision will be whether to render the brickwork, to use low-maintenance facebricks or reconstituted stone blocks and to leave the walls unrendered.

Whatever you decide, you will need mortar, made with cement and sand, for bricklaying and possibly for jointing paving bricks or slabs. If you decide to render (plaster) your brickwork, cement and sand will be required for the render mixture.

Note that while it is usually considered good building practice to add hydrated builder's lime to render to improve its plasticity and help prevent future cracking, this should be avoided when building ponds. Lime is toxic and can kill fish and other creatures. You can, if you wish, add a non-toxic plasticiser to the mixture to make it more cohesive. A waterproofing additive will make the render coat more impervious to water (see page 237).

Although swimming pool builders frequently use marble plaster mixed 1:3 with white cement to give the shell a nice, smooth waterproof finish, this is an expensive and therefore infrequent option for fish ponds. Marble plaster is usually available in 25 kg (50 lb) bags.

If you decide not to coat the rendered pond with bitumen, it is best to fill and empty the feature several times before introducing plants or fish, to get rid of any traces of toxic lime (from the cement). Neutralizing chemicals may also be used.

Pre-cast concrete materials
Various pre-cast materials may be used when constructing water features.

Pre-cast concrete products, which range from ordinary paving slabs to ornamental fountains, can be extremely useful when constructing water gardens and features.

When paving around the perimeter of a pond or pool you can choose from concrete bricks, plain slabs and even interlocking units. Particularly popular are pavers, flagstones and setts (sometimes called cobbles), as well as imitation sleepers and fake log slices, all of which are made from reconstituted stone. Compressed or vibrated in moulds, these simulated stone products have an attractive appearance and are especially well suited to the more natural type of water feature.

Pre-cast fountains may be as plain or ornate as you wish, although those incorporating statuary are frequently used as a focal point in formal pools. Simple bird bath designs, manufactured from fibrecement as well as pre-cast concrete, may also be used as fountains. The majority of concreteworks incorporate pipework in the mould to adapt them if necessary, while fibrecement is generally easy to drill into (see page 258).

Fake fibreglass or GRC rocks are also useful when building a water feature. They are considerably lighter than the real thing, and may be used to camouflage the pond edge, to hide pumps, filters and so on, and even to construct rockeries for waterfalls.

Stone

A suitable material for use both in and around water features, stone comes in various guises. While boulders are the ideal choice for rockeries, natural and even reconstituted (or simulated) stone slabs are a common paving material around ponds and pools. A raised pond or bridge may be constructed from cut stone, and stepping stones created with reasonably flat rocks.

When it comes to paving, an advantage of using man-made products is that they are reasonably regular in shape and size and therefore easier to lay. However, natural stone will blend with the environment more easily. Flagstones are relatively expensive and often difficult to find, but irregular pieces of cut stone or slate may be laid as crazy paving around ponds.

Another alternative is to use cobbles or setts. Traditional setts were made from granite, and you can now buy concrete 'cobbles', which are flatter and more regular than water-worn stones taken from river beds.

A small but classical fountain is set in a shallow, circular pool.

For Japanese style, pebbles and crushed stone or gravel are the perfect complement for water. Use these materials to create a beach alongside the pond, or to camouflage the concrete or plastic liner in the water. Your local garden centre should stock these, although stone and gravel may also bought from aggregate suppliers .

If you do have access to local stone from a nearby quarry, this is usually the best option for rockeries, as it will help to create a most authentic effect.

Tiles

Suitable for patio surfaces and formal pool surrounds, tiles may be used around the edge of a pond or on top of stepping stones (see page 276). Since glazed tiles become extremely slippery and therefore dangerous, use those that are intended for outdoor use and do make sure that they have a matt finish. Terrazzo, terracotta and quarry tiles are all suitable. If yours is a formal pool and your budget allows, you could always consider punched

A charming little pond, brimful with water plants, on a tiled patio.

(rather than polished) marble tiles which are non-slip.

Timber

Although not the most common material used to construct ponds and pools, timber should not be overlooked. Most hot tubs, which like spas are fitted with a filter, heater and jets, are constructed from timber (Californian redwood for instance), so there is no reason why this material should not be used for ponds.

Wooden wine barrels make attractive and watertight containers. Like hot tubs, they are made from timber which is resistant to rot and which swells when wet. Note that barrels which are not used for winemaking will usually have to be sealed to make them watertight.

Hardwearing railway sleepers may be used to line the sides of a pool, or to build the entire structure. However, these will not be waterproof unless the interior surface of the pond is sealed with bitumen or fibreglass, or the excavation is first covered with a flexible liner.

Of course, timber is also a useful material for those special features which add the finishing touches to any water garden: bridges, adjacent decks, gazebos and jetties are all easily constructed from either poles or planks. Even though wood tends to get slippery in wet weather, it may be used as a flooring material for adjacent patios and as an edging for your pond.

Timber decks are particularly well suited to water gardens as the material blends well with the environment. While decking may be used successfully on both flat and sloping ground, to create terraces or simply to extend over a pond, a charming ploy is to allow water to flow under a deck to create the impression of a much larger feature than really exists.

Where part of the supporting structure of decking (or a jetty) is in the water, additional steps must be taken to ensure it is safe. You will have to treat wood that will remain submerged and piling may be required to anchor it securely. If necessary, consult an engineer who will design the foundations of the structure.

Wood can be bought as poles and split poles, or as sawn timber which may be rough-cut or planed all round (PAR). In addition, laminated beams, manufactured by gluing strips of wood together under pressure are available. These are usually expensive, but very stable and come in fairly long lengths.

While knots are unavoidable in various types of wood, it is best to avoid planks and boards with large knots as these can affect the strength of any structure.

Whatever you are building, it makes sense to use a wood that will last, and it is vital that the timber used for bridges and decks will not warp and split when it comes in contact with water. Although your choice will be limited to what is available in your area, you will find that hardwoods are generally more resistant than softwoods. One exception is Californian redwood, a softwood which is valued for its resistance to decay and infestation.

Some of the most popular species of hardwood include oak, which is attractive, strong and versatile; Philippine mahogany, another particularly durable wood; and, in hotter climates, balau, a fine-textured timber noted for its strength and durability and karri, a tough eucalypt which originated in Australia.

Nowadays, most sawn timber is treated with either organic or water-based preservatives, and is impregnated under extreme pressure in the sawmill. The actual chemicals used vary and some may be toxic to fish. However, a thick coating of hot tar or bitumen will protect the wood and seal in the poisons.

Although hardwood poles (which may be machined to size) are often dipped in creosote which is an oil distilled from coal tar, softwood poles like pine are more commonly treated under pressure with a water-based preservative like chromated copper arsenate (CCA). This may give the wood a slightly green tinge. While it is essential to buy timber that has been treated against infestation and rot, do investigate the poisons involved. Creosote is highly toxic and should be avoided.

Whatever wood you decide to use, store it indoors if at all possible. If not, it is advisable to stack it level at least

300 mm (1 ft) above the ground and to protect it with plastic or a tarpaulin to prevent it getting wet and warping or rotting before construction of your project begins.

Metal

Although metal is often used to build public bridges, it is not common for ordinary gardens. In some situations, it can be used if combined with wooden slats. Apart from nuts, bolts, screws and other connecting mechanisms made from metal, reinforcing will also be required for some ponds and supporting wall structures. Although ordinary chicken wire (with its characteristic hexagonal mesh configuration) may sometimes be used, a more sturdy weld mesh is more frequently recommended. Sold in a roll, it can be cut to reinforce irregular shapes.

Since water is a constant factor, it makes sense to use metal that will not rust. Stainless steel, aluminium and galvanized or anodised metals are all suitable materials.

Waterproofing materials

There are various ways to ensure water features will be impervious and it is advisable to familiarise yourself with the full range of waterproofing methods before you begin.

Both flexible and rigid liners are waterproof, while concrete and brickwork are porous. Rendering the internal surface will make it reasonably watertight, especially if a waterproofing additive is included in the mix. There are several types available and it is important to follow the manufacturer's instructions to obtain good results.

Although not a common choice for ponds, one of the finishes for modern-day swimming pools is marble plaster which gives the shell a smooth, waterproof skin. Made from white cement and granular marble dust (mixed with water in the ratio 1:3), marble plaster is more expensive than ordinary render and known to be adversely affected by certain environmental conditions. Like any plaster, it must be sealed or treated

with a neutralising chemical if you wish to keep fish.

Another possibility is to build a concrete or brick shell and to then make it watertight with a flexible liner or more costly fibreglass which is coated onto the surface in situ. The latter option, which may also be used to seal timber, is recommended where boulders and rocks are to be incorporated in the pond design.

Bitumen is one of the most common and least expensive sealants used by pond builders. Since it is black, it gives the pond a natural appearance. Choose a rubberised product which is water-based and non-toxic. Even if the pool has been rendered, this multi-purpose waterproofing compound is worth using as it will also prevent toxic lime from seeping into the water.

Moisture-curing polyurethane, available in different colours, including blue and black, may also be used to waterproof ponds. Products

Below: An unusual pool under construction was built with hand-packed concrete which was marble plastered prior to lining it with loose-laid bricks.

developed for use in tanks and dams containing drinking water and fish are tough, chemical resistant and non-toxic. You may need a specific primer, and may have to leave the pond to cure for a few days before filling it with water.

Various paints suitable for swimming pools may also be used. These may be either rubber-based, epoxy-based, vinyl-based, or acrylic.

Where holes have been drilled in walls to accommodate electric cables, use a suitable silicone sealer to prevent leaks.

Above: Silicone sealer is successfully used to seal around an electric cable.

QUANTIFYING AND COSTING

Before you begin building or installing your water feature, it is sensible to ascertain exactly how much it is going to cost. While many of the items required may simply be priced at the source of supply, some materials will have to be quantified for the specific project before you can calculate costs.

You will need to order slightly more of certain of the items to allow for waste and breakage. In the step-by-step projects, quantities have been rounded off where appropriate. An additional percentage has not been included.

Flexible liners

Unless your pool is a reasonably regular shape, you will find it necessary to buy very much more liner than you actually need to form a blanket over the excavation. Unfortunately, there is very little you can do about this waste.

For minimum waste, it is essential to ascertain the dimensions of various liners during the planning stages. The maximum width of polyethylene varies, depending on the gauge; the thinner the sheeting, the wider it may be. While some types of sheeting can be joined, be cautious, it may not last. EPDM, for instance, is very difficult to bond. PVC can be heat welded in the factory, so although you cannot join it yourself, you may be able to order a custom-made pool liner to fit.

Another solution is to find out what is readily available in your area, and, if necessary, adapt the size of the pond to suit the liner you have chosen.

To ascertain how much material you need, draw the pond roughly to scale, and measure its length and breadth at the longest and widest points. Decide how deep it will be, and add twice the depth, plus a bit extra for around the outside edge, to both the length and the width. Rather buy too much material than run short later.

Concrete

To work out the quantities of cement, sand and stone required for your concrete mix, it is necessary to estimate the total volume of the foundations and/or the concrete shell, using the simple mathematical calculation: total area x thickness. Since most pool walls are fairly low, a 100 mm- (4 in-) deep foundation trench is usually quite adequate, while a concrete shell will be at least 80 mm (3 in) thick. Remember that the length and width of foundations are always slightly greater than the dimensions of the wall or structure it supports.

Presuming you are mixing cement, sand and crushed stone in the ratio 1:2:2, you will need about eight pockets (400 kg/880 lb) of cement and 810 kg, (0.6 m³/21 cu ft) each of sand and aggregate, as well as sufficient water to produce a workable mix, for every 1 m³ (35 cu ft) of concrete.

Bricks, blocks and tiles

Brick sizes vary slightly, but most are about 222 mm (8¾ in) long, 106 mm (4 in) wide and from 50 mm (2 in) to 75 mm (3 in) thick; the thinner bricks are for ordinary domestic paving. Blocks used for building and slabs for paving are less standard; these sizes depend on the individual manufacturer.

When calculating the number of ordinary bricks required for a wall, it is safe to assume you will need 55 for each square metre of half-brick walling (46 bricks per square yard), that is 106 mm (4 in) thick. For every square metre of brick paving, you can count on using as many as 45 pavers (38 per square yard).

Alternatively, simply estimate the surface area of each building unit and the approximate area of your proposed wall or paved surface; divide the first figure into the second and you will immediately know how many to buy.

The easiest way to quantify pre-cast blocks or slabs and tiles, is to calculate the area of a single unit and then divide this into the total area to be paved. If you are using flagstones or pavers of varying sizes, the simplest solution is to add together the areas of each kind and use equal numbers of every sort of paver.

Stone

Unlike man-made products which are of standard sizes and reasonably easy to quantify, it is more difficult with rocks and stones, and you may have to enlist the help of professionals.

The availability of natural stone directly affects its price. If you are fortunate enough to have rocks and boulders on site, these will cost you nothing. If there is a quarry in your area, it is advisable to get rocks directly from there. Although transportation can be costly, it is likely to amount to less than if you were to buy from your local garden centre or through a professional landscaper.

Stone is classified according to its finished surface: it may be rockfaced, rough picked, axed, split or sawn.

Mortar

The quantity of mortar required for bricklaying depends on the cement:sand ratio, and the size of the brick or block you are using. Since a reasonably strong 1:3 mix is recommended for this type of work, you will need about one pocket of cement and 155 kg (340 lb) of sand for every 150 bricks in a half-brick wall.

The same mix may be used for render, and, if it is spread evenly to approximately 10-15 mm (about ½ in) thick, the above quantity will render about 7 m² (75 sq ft) of wall.

Timber

Standard sizes of timber are reasonably universal, although you will find some variation from suppliers to supplier. In general, metric sizes are simply conversions from the imperial system which was established in Britain many years ago. In Europe these measurements have been rounded off, while in certain other countries, including South Africa, the exact conversions are still used.

When ordering timber, it is not essential to buy the dimensions identical to those specified for projects, provided they are similar. It is more sensible to purchase what is available at your local sawmill or timber merchant than to have the wood specially planed to size.

Similarly, the lengths you purchase will often be longer than those required, particularly if you can cut two or three pieces to size from one plank or beam. It is always worth doing a little arithmetic beforehand in order to minimise waste.

CONSTRUCTION METHODS

The materials chosen to construct your water feature will determine the construction methods used. If you do not have the necessary skills, you may want to hire an artisan to assist you, or even employ a contractor to do the work. Always ask for references and check with previous clients before deciding to use outside services.

Setting out

Before you do anything else, it is necessary to mark out the position of your water feature. Whether you are building a raised pool or sinking a pond into the ground, peg out the area, or outline its proposed position with a hose-pipe, rope or chalk.

The simplest pond to set out is an irregular one which is to be sealed either with a flexible liner, concrete, clay or bentonite. Here accuracy is not essential, providing you maintain the basic size and shape you have used for estimating materials.

Aluminium silicate and soil are mixed thoroughly during the sealing process (clay puddling).

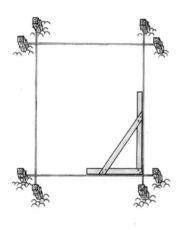

A square made from three lengths of wood in the ratio 3:4:5 is useful for setting out rectangular and square pools.

When utilising a rigid shell, you can place this on the ground and draw around its perimeter. If it has a symmetrical shape, place it upside down so the lip is included in the layout; otherwise stand it upright and simply allow for any wider areas.

For a rectangular or square pool, it is essential that corners are at right-angles. A reliable way of doing this is to use what is known as the 3:4:5 method. A home-made wooden square (see illustration) is helpful here,

especially if the pond is small; or you can use a steel builder's square and a tape to check for accuracy. First of all, the two diagonals must be identical when measured from corner to corner. Check this and then, working from one corner, measure 300 mm (1 ft) and 400 mm (1 ft 3¾ in) along the two adjoining outside edges. Mark these points with pegs and check the distance between the two pegs. It should be 500 mm (1 ft 7¾ in). Repeat at the other three corners.

To set out a circular design, you can use a 'compass' made with pegs and string. Simply knock a peg or stake into the centre of the proposed pool

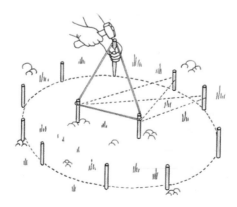

A circle is marked out with a single peg and string, but for an oval shape use pegs and a loop of string. Use additional pegs to demarcate the shape.

area and attach a piece of string to it, the length of the radius. Attach the end securely to a second peg or stick, pull the string taut and then scrape it around in a circle to mark the circumference on the ground.

An oval shape is marked in a similar way to a circle. Two stakes are driven into the ground and a piece of string is attached to them to form a loop (see illustration). Pull the string taut and stick a peg in the ground at the furthest point. Repeat several times around the perimeter, so indicating the basic outline. Note that the closer the pegs are to one another, the more circular the shape will be.

Installing liners

No building skills are necessary to install liners in the ground, although it is vital to ensure that the upper edges of the pond are level. If one side is higher than the other, this will be obvious once the pool is full. A spirit level set on a straightedge will enable you to check the surface around most ponds. A post set absolutely vertically in the excavation will enable you to pivot the straightedge and so check levels at different points around the perimeter; a method which is particularly useful for a circular or oval shape. If the pond is very large, you may have to use a dumpy level (see page 231).

Flexible liners are particularly simple to fit. Regardless of which material you are using, the liner is draped into the hole so that the centre sags on the ground. The edges are secured with bricks or stones around the perimeter and the pond filled with water.

As you fill the pond, you can straighten out some of the creases and folds. The success you have will depend on the material you are using. Butyl rubber is probably the most flexible liner available; and PVC tends to stretch into the excavated shape more easily than polyethylene.

It is not necessary to trim the liner to the shape of the pond until it is full. Trimming is done with sharp, multi-purpose scissors, leaving 300-500 mm (1 ft-1 ft 8 in) around the edge. Tuck the edge of the liner into the soil and place rocks or slabs around the edge; or secure by paving over excess liner.

Some people advocate lining the excavated hole with a layer of soft sand before installing the flexible liner. This step is only really imperative on a stony site; usually any twigs, stones and other sharp objects which could damage the liner once it is filled with water, should be removed before the liner is fitted.

Rigid liners may be installed both below and above the ground, but you will have to build a supporting wall of some sort around a raised pond.

For below-ground ponds, installation for all types of rigid liner is basically the same as for the project on pages 48-49. It is necessary to dig a hole slightly larger than the shell and ensure that the base of the excavation is flat and smooth. Use a spirit level and a straightedge, and ensure you bed the shell with the lip below the surrounding ground, otherwise you will not be able to hide the rim with edging.

Once the liner is in position, shovel sand or soil between the walls of the shell and the sides of the hole. It is a good idea to bed the liner on a layer of well compacted sand. If the design you choose includes a plant shelf, the excavation must allow for this. Care should be taken to backfill and compact thoroughly so that it is stable.

A raised pond should be set on a flat

A pre-cast fibrecement pond installed in a sloping garden has been cleverly camouflaged.

surface before the space between the liner and the wall is backfilled to maximise rigidity and stability.

While you can backfill with mortar or a dry cement and sand mixture, the high alkalinity of cement may eventually lead to the deterioration of materials like fibreglass.

Working with concrete
Concrete pools may be hand-packed or made by pouring the mixture between shuttering. Whichever method is chosen, there are certain basic principles which should always be followed regarding the mixing, laying and curing of concrete.

Concrete was used to build this dual-purpose pool which may also be used for swimming.

hollow in the centre. It is not necessary to measure the water; use a garden hose to pour it into the centre very slowly, shovelling and turning the dry materials as you do so. It is best to add water bit by bit, scooping the mixture from the outside to the centre, until it is soft and workable, but not runny. Add the stone last, with more water if the concrete mix is too dry.

If you decide to use a concrete mixer, the above procedure is reversed, with the stone and a little water being added first to prevent the mortar clogging the blades. Then add the sand and cement with more water to obtain the correct consistency.

Placing concrete in foundations directly against the ground, can result in some loss of moisture. To minimise this, dampen the soil in the foundation trench first, and allow the water to soak in before laying the concrete.

Once placed, the concrete must be well compacted or vibrated to get rid of all air bubbles. With a straightedge or wooden beam, use a chopping action to compact and a sawing motion to level. Check the surface with a spirit level to ensure it is absolutely flat.

When handpacking concrete to form an irregularly shaped pond, use a slightly drier mix and to angle the sides slightly outwards to prevent the mixture from sliding to the base. Use some sort of reinforcing to hold the mixture in place and strengthen the

If you are building a large pond with concrete, it is advisable to consult an engineer for advice on the stresses that the pressure of water will create.

Batching is essential for mixing concrete in the correct ratio. For DIY projects, the simplest and most effective way to batch materials is by volume, using the same size container for each component. Fill the vessel flush with the rim and, ideally, use a whole sack of cement for each batch.

When employing unskilled labourers, make sure that the correct ratios are used. A common mistake is the assumption that 1 bag of cement mixed with three, four or six wheelbarrow loads of sand is a 1:3, 1:4 or 1:6 mix. This is wrong, since a

builder's wheelbarrow can hold about two 50 kg (110 lb) pockets of cement and you will end up with a mixture which is far too weak for pool construction. If you are using a waterproofing additive, follow the manufacturer's instructions carefully.

Mixing concrete takes effort rather than skill. For small projects, it is common to mix by hand, in which case you will need a clean, hard surface, or a wheelbarrow. Never mix directly on the ground as water will be absorbed from the concrete and soil will contaminate it; and do not be tempted to mix on existing paving as it is very difficult to clean.

Start by mixing a batch of sand and cement together and then form a

Bitumen products are often used to seal concrete ponds.

A man-made water feature incorporates cascades and pools. Various water-loving plants, including Cyperus papyrus give it a natural charm.

shell. Weld mesh (or even galvanized chicken wire) is commonly used to line the excavation, ideally with spacer blocks made from cast mortar or timber, set between the soil and the mesh to help ensure that the reinforcing stays in the centre of the concrete so that the shell is evenly strengthened. Most reinforcing mesh comes in a roll, to be cut it with a hacksaw and bent to fit the shape.

While the framework of a hand-packed swimming pool should be 150 mm (6 in) thick, 80 mm (3 in) is adequate for most ponds. In cold climates with frost, thicker shells with extra reinforcing are recommended.

To ensure the finished edges of the pool will be at the same level on all sides, mark a constant height with pegs around the perimeter before you start the concretework. Use a water level to check their height.

The procedure of handpacking concrete is basically the same as throwing a foundation, although you cannot use a straightedge for compacting and levelling the material. In this instance, it is best to use a

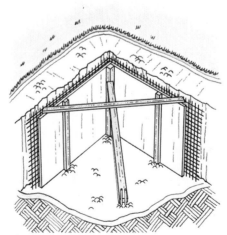

With shuttering, concrete is cast in situ.

round trowel, stamping the concrete to expel the air and level the surface with a float to smooth it off (see pages 268-269). Remove pegs before concrete sets and smooth over the holes.

Shuttering is sometimes used in the construction of formal pools with vertical concrete walls. This is an especially useful method on a sloping site, or where a raised pond is required. It is also essential for the construction of concrete bridges.

The first step is to cast a slab (see Foundations, below) or, in the case of a bridge, strip foundations on either side of the water. Once this has set, construct a strong, rigid formwork using timber boarding braced with wooden battens. The shape of the formwork, or shuttering, will determine the configuration of your structure. As the formwork must be removed after

A delightful little brick pond incorporates a circular planter around its perimeter.

the concrete has set, it is sensible to oil it lightly before pouring the mixture.

Position the reinforcing prior to erecting the shuttering, and only remove shuttering after approximately 14 days, when the concrete is well set.

Curing is needed for concrete to gain its maximum strength. Since it is the water which starts a chemical reaction causing the cement to harden, it is vital that sufficient moisture remains present in the newly cast material. It is important that the temperature of the concrete does not fall below 10 deg C (50 °F). To aid curing, the concrete should be sprayed now and then with water; and in cold weather, it should be covered with sacking or black polyethelene to insulate it.

It takes about 28 days for the concrete to gain most of its strength; but, provided there is some moisture present, it will continue to strengthen for several years. It is important to realise that concrete does not get strong by drying out. In fact, if it is allowed to dry out too quickly, it can crack or even crumble.

Since 'ponding' water on the surface of newly-laid concrete will actually help it to cure, you can quite safely fill a pond after about 48 hours.

Finishes for the concrete shell range from render or plaster to waterproof bitumen. If these are disregarded, your pool will probably leak, even if you have used a waterproofing additive in the concrete mixture. At the very least, a slurry of cement and building sand should be rubbed over the surface. The koi pond featured on pages 268-269 was rendered and then coated with a rubberised bitumen sealer. Other waterproofing possibilities are mentioned on page 237.

Another factor to consider is that the inherent lime content of the cement, can be harmful to plants, fish and animal life. If you do not coat the internal surface with a sealant, you will have to drain the water from the shell once or twice to rid it of any impurities. Each time you fill the pond, leave the water to stand for a couple of days so that it absorbs the lime residue. A commercially-available chemical lime neutraliser can also be used.

Bricklaying and stonework

Foundations are essential for all ponds and pools constructed with bricks, blocks or stone. While the required dimensions will vary depending on the height of the wall and other factors, a depth of 100-200 mm (4-8 in) is ample. It is normally a good idea to cast a slab foundation which acts as the base of the pond as well as the support for walls.

The weakest spot in a pool built this way is where the floor joins the walls.

As a safeguard, especially in deeper ponds, set reinforcing in the concrete and build this into the brickwork.

Laying bricks is not difficult, but it is vital to recognise the importance of the principles of square, level and plumb. A brick structure that does not stand upright will look odd, and may leak.

The tools required for a professional finish are detailed on pages 230-232, and the method of setting out a pond is described on pages 239.

Practise using a trowel, as this tool is used throughout bricklaying. You will need it to spread the mortar, to butter the bricks and bed them firmly into place, and to scrape off excess mortar.

Once the foundation has set, mix the sand and cement together with water in the same way as for concrete (see page 238), but without adding the coarse aggregate. The mixture should be reasonably thick and porridgy, and pliable enough to work with.

Lay mortar in a strip along the foundation where the brick wall is to be placed, and use a trowel to create an uneven furrow down the centre. Since the first course of bricks is the most important of all, string a builder's line to check it is straight. A steel builder's square can also be used.

Begin bedding bricks in the mortar, ensuring you have an even 7-10 mm (¼ in) joint between each. You can fill the joints after bedding the bricks, but it is easier to butter one end of each brick as you go. Do this by lifting a blob of mortar with the trowel and squashing it onto the short side of the brick. Slide the brick into position and then tap firmly with the handle of the trowel, to bed and level it.

Before starting on the second course, check that the bricks you have already laid are level (see page 230). From this point, corner blocks and a line may be used to keep each course straight; and a gauge rod, to ensure that mortar joints are even (see pages 231-232). A spirit level should be used frequently to check both horizontal and vertical brick surfaces.

Another critically important building principle to remember is bonding. If the load of the bricks is not properly distributed, even a low wall can collapse. There are various different bonding patterns. The most common is stretcher bond, formed with each brick overlapping the one below by half.

Use the trowel to scrape away excess mortar. This is important when using reconstituted stone or facebricks, although it will still be necessary to use a pointing tool or piece of metal to neaten the joints when building is complete.

Stonework is similar in many ways to brickwork. However, stone may be laid randomly or in courses with a regular horizontal joint and irregular vertical joint (cut stone).

A dry stone wall, built without any mortar, is only suitable to camouflage a rigid shell set above the ground.

To simplify waterproofing, it makes sense to aim for as even an internal surface as possible. For this reason, cut (or dressed) stone is an obvious option (refer to the Stone chapter).

Rendering is a useful skill, as many brick structures are finished this way. The internal shell of concrete and stone pools may be rendered with a cement/sand mix. The mortar mix – the same as that used for bricklaying – should preferably contain plasticiser to make the material more pliable and easier to spread over the surface.

It is applied to the brickwork or concrete shell with a rectangular or rounded trowel and pressed down so that it will adhere. The trowel is then used to scrape it flat before it is smoothed with a wooden float. In hot weather, splash a little water on the render as you work. Finally, corner trowels are used to neaten edges and both internal and external corners.

External plaster or render must be kept damp in exactly the same way as concrete, to ensure it cures and does not crack. It may, however, be painted with a rubberised bitumen within a relatively short period of time.

Tiling and paving

Two options for a pool surround are tiles or paving. The basic principles involved are much the same for all these related materials, although the preparatory work does vary from project to project.

Tiles must always be laid on a solid base, and you will therefore first have to throw a concrete slab. If you are going to bed them with a cement-based tile adhesive, you will have to screed the surface with mortar. Some tiles, including the terracotta type, may be laid on a bed of mortar set directly on the concrete.

After approximately 72 hours, once the screed has set hard, mix the tile adhesive according to the manufacturer's instructions. This product is spread with a notched trowel which forms ridges to aid adhesion, and the tiles are then pressed firmly into place.

An attractive pre-cast concrete fountain.

A formal fountain mounted on a plastered wall features fish and a gargoyle.

A formal brick pond with planters.

A steel square and a straightedge will enable you to lay tiles at the required angle, and spacers (made of plastic or metal) will guarantee equal joints. Use either a line of string to mark the edge and secure each end under loose tiles or bricks. A rubber mallet is the best tool to tap the tiles so that they are level. Use a spirit level to check that the upper surface is flat. If any of the tiles are lower than the others, spread extra adhesive on the base of the unit.

Laying tiles on an adhesive layer is less messy than laying them on a bed of mortar. However, in both cases, these materials should be wiped off before they dry and stain the surface.

Grouting is done after about 48 hours, when the adhesive is dry or the mortar has set. Use ready-mixed grout or mix the powdered type with water, according to the manufacturer's instructions, and spread thickly over the joints. Wipe any the excess off immediately with a sponge, especially if you are using very porous tiles.

Tiles that have been laid on mortar can be grouted with a 1:3 cement and sand mixture. When mixed with water, it should be fairly dry and crumbly. A small pointing trowel may be used to fill and smooth the gaps. Again, wipe off excess mortar immediately.

Paving may be laid on concrete, but it is quicker and cheaper to lay bricks, blocks and slabs on sand. If the ground is unstable, you will need to excavate 100–200 mm (4 in–8 in) for a sub-base of crushed stone or gravel before spreading the sand. This should be thoroughly compacted.

When laying any form of paving directly on the existing ground surface, remove all vegetation before compacting. The layer of sand should be no more than 30 mm compacted to 25 mm (about 1 in), and should never be used to level uneven ground. Smooth it with a straightedge before laying the bricks, allowing a slight slope for drainage (see page 228).

Fill the joints between pavers with sand or a weak mortar mix. A rubber mallet is useful for tapping the pavers into place.

The recommended cement:sand mix for jointing clay bricks laid on sand is 1:6, while a slightly stronger 1:4 mix should be used when jointing pavers, flagstones and setts made from concrete, or clay bricks which have been laid on a concrete base. Either brush the material in dry and then spray the surface lightly with water; or alternatively, use a trowel to fill the gaps with a crumbly mix.

Cutting tiles and bricks can be a wasteful business. Using a bolster and brick hammer is relatively simple, once you get the knack. Place the brick on the ground, ideally on a thin bed of sand, and use the chisel end of the bolster to score the surface on all sides. Position the bolster on the cutting line you have made and tap the handle end firmly to break the brick. Another method is to score a cutting line with the chisel end of a brick hammer, and then continue tapping around this line until the brick breaks.

When tiling, special cutting machines which score and break the tile are useful. Thick quarry and terracotta tiles should be cut with an angle grinder using the appropriate disc.

Edging and coping

The principles involved when laying any kind of edging are dependent largely on the materials used. For instance, grass may be allowed to grow right up to a clay-puddled pond, but it is inadvisable as an edging for a liner pond where any erosion of the bank could be disastrous. Tiles or brick paving look beautifully sophisticated laid around a formal, symmetrical pool, while rocks, stone slabs and even timber will be more appropriate if used to edge a natural pond. A coping will only be necessary around raised pools, to finish off the supporting wall.

Edging around any water feature is one of the final tasks. There are various options and, except for raised decking erected alongside the water, it is important for all types of edging and surround to be laid on a soil bed that

A simple fish-pond, designed for koi, and set in a sheltered Oriental-style garden, has a character-istic stone edging around its perimeter.

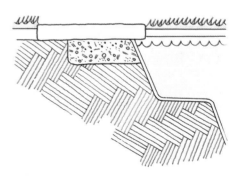

Lay paving slabs on a concrete foundation to prevent the edges of the pond from collapsing.

Grass has been allowed to grow to the edge of this natural pond, constructed to encourage wildlife to visit the garden.

is sound and well compacted.

Although not essential, a collar of concrete laid around the perimeter of the feature will stabilise the edging. If bricks are used as an edging around pools they should be securely set in mortar to ensure they do not loosen.

Slabs, bricks and tiles may be laid to overlap the edge of the water slightly to hide the shell and, in the case of polyethylene and PVC, protect it. By sloping these away from the water slightly, excess water and mud can be prevented from washing into the pond.

When laying the edging, a common problem is that excess mortar falls into the pond. The lime in the cement damages plants and can kill fish. It is essential to clean the shell before filling the pond. If it is already full of water (which will be the case if you have fitted a flexible liner), drain and clean it before introducing pond life.

Coping will finish off any raised pond or pool. Various materials are suitable, including paving bricks, tiles and simulated stone slabs. Either match the coping to the wall or use a contrasting material. Most materials will be cemented into place, although it may be necessary to bolt timber to stabilise it. The upper surface of stepping stones may be finished in exactly the same way.

Woodwork

Only the most basic carpentry skills are needed for the average water garden project. You will need to know how to cut and join timbers, and which connectors to use to secure them. There is no need for elaborate joints in garden structures, and most of the time you can rely on the simplest arrangement which may be nailed, screwed or bolted. Refer back to the Wood chapter for further details.

Cutting timber across the grain is the normal procedure for this type of woodwork. This may be done with a tenon saw, hand-held power saw or a circular bench saw, which is what most professionals would use. Secure the timber to get a clean cut, preferably by clamping it to a workbench. You will usually saw the ends of beams, railings, etc perfectly square; when you mitre corners, however, it will be necessary to make an angled cut.

Joints are essentially simple. The main intention is to keep them neat, safe and secure. Even a reasonably large deck can be built with ordinary butt

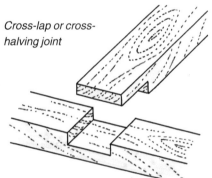

Rudimentary carpentry skills were all that was required to fashion this effective fountain feature made from well-sealed railway sleepers.

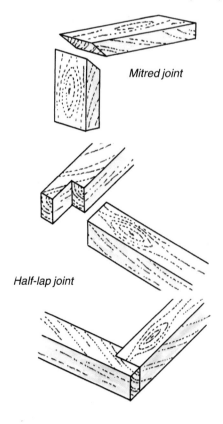

Mitred joint

Cross-lap or cross-halving joint

Half-lap joint

may be used. The secret is knowing which item to use where.

Wood screws are the most common choice for carpentry and it is important to choose the right one for the job. Coach screws, with a hexagonal head, are tightened with a spanner and are useful for garden structures. Most screws are partially unthreaded, but self-tapping screws have the thread right up to the head, giving a better grip. They often used to secure decking and handrails for bridges. Self-tapping screws can be screwed directly into softer woods, but to prevent the wood from splitting, drill a pilot hole, thinner than the screw first.

Where timber is attached to masonry or brickwork, special expansion bolts (Rawl bolts) are invaluable. Hexagonal bolts, which, like coach screws, are tightened with a spanner, and cuphead or coach bolts, may be used to affix heavy beams and upright timbers.

Nails are easily hammered into timber, but they sometimes pull out easily. Longer, thicker nails are more secure than short, thin ones, although take care not to split the wood. Ideally, a nail should be more than double the thickness of the wood you are fixing. To strengthen the join, first glue the two pieces of timber. Dovetailing the nails, by hammering them in at an angle, will help prevent the wood from twisting. Ring shanked nails have a good grip and may be used when fitting decking slats

When nailing very hard woods, drill a small pilot hole first; and when nailing soft timber, it is best to blunt the tips of the nails to prevent wood splitting.

The cheapest nails and screws are made of steel, but will rust unless anodised, galvanized or coated in some other way. If ordinary steel is used, countersink screws below the surface and fill up to surface level with a filler. Hide nail heads by prising up a sliver of wood before hammering in the nail, and glue the wood back in place.

Finishes applied to timber are varied. Treat wood with a preservative and protect it from excessive weathering by oiling, varnishing or painting. The common choices are wood dressings and water-repellent finishes that soak

joints (where two pieces of wood are joined without any fancy cutting), some of which may overlap to form a T- or cross-lap joint, and other elementary connections. These include lapped joints, to lengthen pieces of timber, and half-lap joints where two pieces of wood are cut out to slot together to form a flush surface. Both half-lap and mitred joints are used for neat corners.

Securing the connections is quite easy, and a variety of nails, screws and bolts

An unusual water feature flows across the brick-paved driveway.

a plughole can be well sealed with silicone, this will always be a particularly weak point which could result in leakages. Unless the draining water is led right away from the pond by underground pipework, the water will inevitably erode below the structure and may cause it to collapse.

Another problem is excess water which overflows in rainy weather. In severe instances, the sides and banks of a pond tend to erode and fish may be swept out of the pond.

In high rainfall areas, it is sometimes advisable to install an overflow system of some sort to cope with all the excess water. The simplest is a pipe or channel which leads to a gulley, French drain, or even a bog garden.

A severe drop in the water level is also damaging. Not only can it affect fish and plants, but if you have used a polyethylene liner, prolonged exposure to sunlight will cause rapid deterioration. If bentonite was used, the exposed surface may crack unless

into the wood, and various tinted varnishes which add a depth of colour

FINISHING OFF

Once your water feature is complete, you may connect the electrics, fit the pump and perhaps a filter. It is sensible to make sure you have paid attention to drainage around and are familiar with its maintenance.

Drainage

Wherever there is water, drainage is an inevitable factor.

Unfortunately, a disadvantage of a water garden established where water occurs naturally is that you are likely to have muddy, boggy areas around the pond, at least when it is rainy. In fact, if any pool overflows during wet weather, this will inevitably result in mud.

A solid edging and adjacent paving will minimise potential problems. The surface should slope away from the pond very slightly, to allow for water run-off. Where an adjacent patio abuts the house, the paving must always slope away from the building. The finished surface should be at least 150 mm (6 in) below the damp-proof course (DPC) of the house, or below the internal floor level.

If grass is grown right up to the water, you may be faced with erosion of the bank. While this is not a problem with bentonite or clay ponds, which seal themselves, mud will slide into a rigid shell and flexible liners may start to collapse.

One solution is to establish a bog garden around the perimeter of the pond, but access to the water will be limited. Alternatively, dig a trench around the water's edge and fill it with stones or gravel to create a French drain and conceal it with plants.

Drainage holes are seldom included in ponds nowadays; and they should, in any case, be avoided. Even though

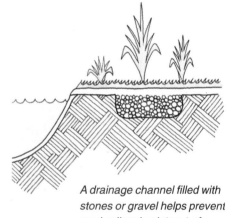

A drainage channel filled with stones or gravel helps prevent mud collapsing into a turf-lined pond.

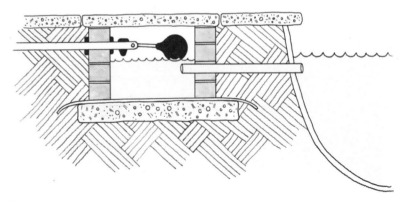

PVC pipe links the reservoir and pond; a ball-valve regulates the water flow.

the water level is raised.

If the level drops, either top-up the pond with a hose-pipe, or install an automatic top-up system to maintain a constant water level. The most common method is to use a ball valve similar to those found in toilet cisterns. Set to the correct level, it automatically allows water fed through a pipe from the mains to fill up the pond. You may want to hide the ball itself under a wooden platform or beneath a fake GRC or fibreglass rock. Alternatively, the ball valve can be set in a small reservoir tank next to the pool, and camouflaged with a paving slab. This operates like the cistern itself, feeding the water to the pond through a pipe.

There can be restrictions on connecting pools to the mains water supply, so check with your local authority first.

Pumps and filters

Water and electricity do not mix, and new installations and modifications should be overseen by an electrician. It is important to check the official regulations applicable to electricity in the gardens in your area. In some countries only low-voltage supplies may be used near water and a transformer may be required.

If the pump is connected to a household electrical circuit, you will often be protected by an existing circuit breaker or trip switch. However, you may need

A selection of pumps, fountain accessories and adjustable-flow fountain heads (right). Transparent flexible and black semi-rigid tubing are also pictured.

to install one of these units on a separate circuit to detect deviations or leakage in outdoor current.

Many electrical appliances for use in and around water features can be safely installed without professional assistance. Electric cables are easily protected in conduiting (or armoured cable), which can be buried underground. Specially designed weatherproof boxes enable you to plug in submersible pumps outdoors and operate fountains with a switch.

If you are unsure of your capabilities, consult a qualified electrician.

Pumps are essential for the circulation of water, so if you install a fountain, waterfall or cascade, this will be an important piece of equipment.

There are two main types of pump – submerged or housed on the surface. Your choice depends largely on the volume of water involved. While a small pump will be adequate for most fountains, you will require a more powerful unit for a large water feature with waterfalls and flowing streams.

The pump output (described in litres or gallons per hour) will be specified on the packaging. Do not choose one that is too powerful, as excessive turbulence churns up dirt, making the water murky. When installing a fountain, it is important to ensure the water head is compatible with your

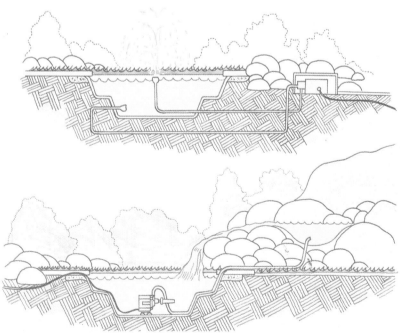

Surface and submersible pumps are used to recirculate water and operate fountains.

design – the water head being the distance between the maximum fountain height and the pond water level. The pump should be capable of spurting water to the required height.

Submersible pumps are generally simple to install and operate, and an added advantage is that they do not have to be primed. Most have a strainer on the inlet to prevent fish or floating debris from being sucked into the moving parts. Fountain jets are often fitted directly to submersible pumps and some are sold with interchangeable jet fittings.

A submersible pump can be used to operate a fountain in a large pond, but do consider accessibility. If the strainer requires cleaning, you should not have to wade into the water. Instead, site the pump near the edge of the pond, on a ledge or loose-laid bricks, and run a pipe to the jet in the centre.

These units are completely sealed and attached to a cable which can be plugged into an appropriate waterproof box. This box is, in turn, connected to the internal electrical system. Conduits and cables can even be run from the pump directly into the house and plugged into an internal wall socket. In very cold climates, where freezing temperatures are experienced, the pump should be removed from the water in winter.

Surface pumps, including those for swimming pools, are expensive and can be noisy, but they are often the only option for larger water features.

Pumps should be located near the pond, preferably just below the level of the water and housed off the ground in a waterproof box. Alternatively, cover the unit with a fake, hollow rock.

Some surface pumps have to be primed manually, but self-priming models are available. If a pump will not prime, or if it loses its prime while running, check whether there are any leaks in the pipes leading to the pump, whether the impeller is broken or the pump seal is faulty. The pump operates by drawing water from the pond through a strainer and suction pipe – these could be blocked or the water level in the pond may have dropped.

A certain amount of plumbing is

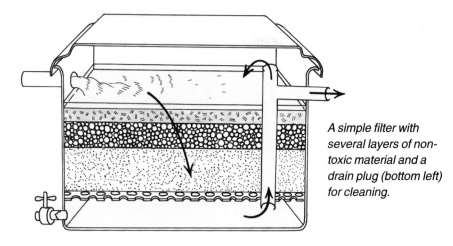

A simple filter with several layers of non-toxic material and a drain plug (bottom left) for cleaning.

inevitable with any pump and it is important to use non-toxic fittings. Plastic is usually the safest option.

Filters, like pumps, may be housed outside the pond or submerged in the water. Generally though, the external type is preferred as these are more reliable and easier to keep clean.

Just as swimming pool filters are used with a pump, so too are pond filters. A major difference though, is that swimming pool filters rely on chemicals for effective sterilization of the water. A pond filter is used to keep the water clear and to rid it of harmful

waste materials including dead plant matter, fish excreta and uneaten fish food. A relatively simple mechanical filter will sieve out dirt, waste and algae and it can be run sporadically as needed. A biological filter allows natural organisms to flourish, helping to break down decaying plant material and fish excreta.

The simplest biological filter is a box (sometimes made of fibreglass) which contains various filter media. The more advanced varieties consist of several chambers with valves, and make use of the usual filtration material.

The size of the filter depends on the

A hollow fake rock has been used to hide the filter.

Concealed lighting effectively highlights this attractive water feature.

Adjustable spotlights illuminate an elaborate moving water feature at night.

volume of water in your pond and the number of fish it contains. If the filter does not have the required capacity, it will not keep the water clean. When installing the filter, follow the manufacturer's recommendations on the flow rate. If it is too high or too low, the filter will not operate efficiently.

A new filter will take several weeks to mature and it is best to wait a while before introducing fish (particularly koi). Once running, the filter should only be disconnected for cleaning. Maintenance does not take long, but should be done regularly to prevent a build-up of waste.

Lighting

Lighting relies on electricity and is subject to the same concerns as pumps, but there is no doubt that water gardens benefit from illumination. Effective garden lighting improves security and safety.

Methods of lighting various objects and areas in the garden range from direct illumination, which casts a strong spot or single beam, to a selection of decorative uplighters and assorted lamps.

When deciding how to light your outdoor area, consider function. For instance, general lighting is best reserved for patios, and floodlights for tennis courts and driveways. Paths, steps, and bridges should be lit with safety in mind. Visitors need to see where they are walking and confusing shadows from partly-concealed decorative lighting can be hazardous. It is essential that fittings are positioned in such a way to avoid light shining directly into people's eyes.

It is best to combine several types of lighting, perhaps making use of free-standing lamps for walkways, spotlights to add interest to plants, and uplighters to highlight a waterfall or cascade. Another option is to make use of underwater lighting from within the pond, for example, to emphasise a fountain. Special submersible lights are necessary for this purpose.

Fittings chosen for gardens in general, and water features in particular, must be manufactured for outdoor use. A sealed unit which can be exposed to all weather conditions is essential. While this sounds limiting, there is a wide range available, from wall-mounted carriage lamps to spots attached to stakes which may be anchored in the ground.

Whatever you choose, make sure the fitting is in keeping with the style of your garden. There is little point in achieving a beautiful effect at night, if the light looks ugly during the day. Run-of-the-mill units should be hidden beneath foliage or behind rocks.

Installation should usually be carried out by a professional, although there are DIY kits (or similar fittings) which can be easily positioned without any help at all. Most include spotlights on spikes for sticking in garden beds. Like many pumps, the whole system is plugged into a waterproof box linked to the existing electrics. Proper outdoor cable should be used. This should preferably be threaded through conduiting before being buried in the ground. Wherever two lengths of flex are joined, the connection must be protected with a waterproof coupling.

Lighting which is near or attached to the house will usually be part of the internal electrical arrangement. These lights are simpler to install than new fittings in the garden, which have to be

FLOWING URN

An ordinary ceramic urn, originally manufactured for pot plants, makes an attractive water feature ideal for a compact border bed or small corner of the garden. It takes up very little space, is simple to construct and introduces both the soothing, relaxing sight and sound of gently trickling water to your garden.

Although a variety of containers may be used, a shaped vessel is preferable. You will need to provide or construct a reservoir of water which is hidden beneath the urn. It is essential that this is designed to accommodate the necessary pipework which will enable the water to flow back under the container.

Note that the diameters given for this project relate to the upper openings of containers.

Materials

urn approximately 250 mm (10 in) in
  diameter, 430 mm (1 ft 5in) high
container approximately 560 mm (1 ft
  10 in) in diameter, 310 mm (1 ft) high
plastic pot, 200 mm (8 in) in diameter,
  180 mm (7 in) high
1 x 600 mm x 12 mm (2 ft x ½ in)
  semi-rigid tubing
1 x submersible pump, with 1.4 m (4 ft
  6 in) water head
waterproof sealant (see step 1)
river stones

Preparation

1 The first step is to ensure that any pre-cast container you plan to use as the reservoir is absolutely waterproof. If necessary, plug up any holes and then seal the interior surface.

The reservoir used here is a planter sold for small cacti displays. Made from fibrecement, it has been manufactured with a hole in the base for drainage. It makes an ideal shape for this feature, as the upper diameter is considerably wider than the base which, in turn, is the same size as the plastic pot. It is also quite simple to fill any drainage hole with a two-part epoxy putty.

2 Having decided where to site your flowing urn feature, place the waterproof container upside down on the ground and mark its upper diameter with flour or chalk.
3 Dig a 310 mm (1 ft) deep hole on the position marked. If you are using a similar-shaped container, try to slope the walls to avoid unnecessary excavation.

Installation

4 Place the container in the hole you have dug and then use a spirit level across the top to check that it is level. Fill any gaps with soil and compact it down firmly.

5 Carefully cut a hole in the bottom of your plastic plant pot in order to accommodate the pipework. Put the pump on the base of the waterproof container and then place the pot upside down over it.
6 The urn used must also be waterproof, except for the hole you need for the pipework. Seal any other holes with epoxy putty (see step 1) and allow to dry thoroughly. Paint the container at this stage, if you wish. The one featured in the photograph has a rag-rolled finish in toning shades of terracotta.
7 You will need to drill a hole carefully in the bottom of the urn with a 16 mm (⅝ in) diameter to accommodate the tubing which has a 12 mm (½ in) bore. Push the tubing through the hole so it extends almost to the top of the urn. Use some more two-part epoxy putty to keep it in place and to seal around the tube.

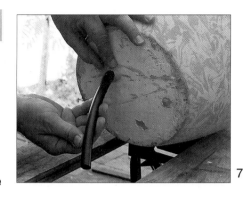
7

8

8 Position the urn on the plastic pot so that the tubing extends through it, and join the tubing to the pump connection. Make sure that both the pot and urn are level.

Finishing off

9 Fill the bottom container with water and place some river stones around the feature to disguise the arrangement below. Note that some of the rocks will inevitably be positioned in the reservoir.
10 Fill the urn with water, connect the power and switch it on to start the water flowing.

8

Water trickles and flows over the edges of the urn onto the rocks below. With time, moss and algae will collect on both rocks and container.

DECORATIVE POND

7

Although many small water features look artificial, it is possible to create a natural-looking pond on a very small scale which is ideal for a small garden. The pond featured here has the appearance of rock but you can choose any simulated stone product, perhaps to complement other stone features in your garden, or even a small fibreglass shell. In some places, thermoplastic liners are manufactured to look like simulated rock. Check your local DIY stores or garden centres to see what is available in your area.

Installation is simple and a small water feature like this can be completed within just a few hours. The secret is to sink the pond into the ground so that it looks as though it has occured naturally, and then to plant right up to the rim of the feature with suitable water-loving plants.

Materials

For a pre-cast pond with a maximum diameter of 740 mm (2 ft 6 in):
A suitable pre-cast shell

Preparation

1 It is essential that the ground into which you sink your pre-cast pond is absolutely level. You can rectify slight undulations with soil dug out from the hole, but a pond this small is not suitable for sloping or uneven ground.

Installation

2 Dig a hole slightly larger than the shell, taking the irregular shape into account. Use a spirit level to check that the base of the hole is completely flat and level.
3 Place the shell into the hole and make sure it is level. If necessary, use a long, straight-edged piece of wood under the spirit level.
4 The next step is to backfill around the pond and to compact the soil, filling all visible gaps so that it sits firmly in place.

Finishing off

5 A rock-faced pond like the one shown here, does not require an

edging. It will look more natural, however, if you plant right up to the edge with groundcover.If you are using a shell which is not as realistic, you can edge the pond with simulated stone slabs or smallish rocks to hide the rim.
6 Fill the mini-pond with water to enjoy the effect you have created.

Within a few hours the transformation is complete. The ground cover has been re-established around the pond which is just big enough to support a few goldfish and floating aquatic plants.

2

3

PEBBLE FOUNTAIN

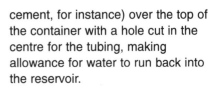

Pebble fountains, like the one photographed here, make simple yet effective garden displays. They do not take up much space, so may be sited in even the smallest garden area; alternatively, you may wish to include one as part of a much larger and grander landscaping scheme.

You can site a pebble fountain in lawn, although it will be easier to maintain if it is located in a garden bed. Alternatively, you can sink the reservoir prior to paving a patio and incorporate it as a permanent feature of the patio.

Materials

container approximately 560 mm (1 ft 10 in) in diameter, 310 mm (1 ft) high
plastic pot, 200 mm (8 in) in diameter, 180 mm (7 in) high
1 x submersible pump, with 1.4 m (4 ft 6 in) water head
1 x 350 mm x 12 mm (1 ft 2 in x ½ in) semi-rigid tubing
epoxy putty (optional)
fountain heads (optional)
outdoor cable and conduit (optional)
river stones
rounded pebbles

Preparation

1 You will need to build or install a reservoir to hold water below ground level. You can construct this with bricks and mortar and then render and seal it with bitumen or polyurethane, or simply sink a watertight container in the ground. A bowl-shaped planter made from fibrecement was used here, so the drain hole in the centre of the base had to plugged with epoxy putty.

2 Decide where the water feature is to be built and then either peg or mark out the area with flour.

3 If you are working in a lawned garden, remove sods of turf to use elsewhere in the garden and dig a hole to the same shape as your chosen container.

Installation

4 Lower the container into the hole and use a spirit level to check that that the lip is level. If it is not, remove the container and rectify.

5 Place the pump in the container and fix the semi-rigid tubing onto the outlet. Cut a hole in the centre of the plastic pot and position it upside-down over the pump. This will enable you to contain a greater volume of water in the reservoir than if stones were packed around the pump itself. It is also a good idea to drill three or four holes in the sides to allow the water to flow more easily between the pot and the reservoir.

6 Now pack some of the river stones around the plastic pot to disguise it and to create a surface on which the pebbles can sit. Trim the tubing with a sharp knife to the required height. Alternatively, you could set a grid or piece of water-resistant board (fibre-

cement, for instance) over the top of the container with a hole cut in the centre for the tubing, making allowance for water to run back into the reservoir.

7 Finally, pack the pebbles over the river stones, covering a wider circumference than that of the hidden bowl.

Connecting the fountain

8 You will, of course, need to plug the submersible pump into a power socket. If the feature is in the garden,

The pebble fountain has been sited in lawn next to an attractive garden bed.

some distance from the house, you will have to bury cable underground.

9 When the pump is operated with a fountain head fitting, a jet of water gushes up into the air like a geyser.

10 If you wish, you may slot a different fountain head onto the tubing in order to change the effect altogether. The dome- or tulip-jet is always a favourite for pebble fountains.

9

10

WALL-MOUNTED FOUNTAIN

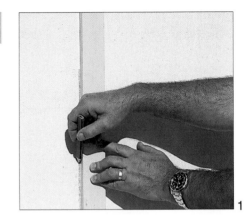

Pre-cast, wall-mounted fountains are available in a wide variety of designs and sizes from garden centres and large DIY stores. They can be much lighter that you might think simply from looking at them. Most are based on classical designs, often featuring lions (as shown here) or angels. They are reasonably straightforward to fit and can add an air of old-fashioned elegance to any garden.

Some, like the one featured here, are supplied in two parts, but assembled as one unit, while others, also consisting of an ornamental outlet and catchment container, are secured to the wall at two separate points. Some are moulded as a single unit, with a head of some kind and a basin.

While the basic installation is the same for all designs, the pipework of a two-part fountain will have to be embedded in the wall as illustrated in the Pond with Planters shown on pages 272-273. Apart from the fountain itself, minimal equipment and materials are required for this project, making it suitable for beginners. Do note, however, that the number and size of screws and other accessories may very well alter according to the

particular design of fountain that you choose for your garden.

Materials
pre-cast fountain for mounting on a wall
4 x No. 8 x 50 mm (2 in) screws
4 x M8 Rawl plugs
1 x 1 m x 10 mm (1 yd x ⅜ in) flexible tubing
1 x submersible pump, with 700 mm (2 ft 4 in) water head (or less)
outdoor cable and conduit

1 Decide exactly where your fountain is to be mounted and mark a vertical line on the wall using a carpenter's pencil and spirit level for accuracy.
2 Now use a retractable tape to measure the point where the top (or bottom) of the fountain will be positioned. This particular fountain will be affixed about 200 mm (8 in) from the top of a 1.8 m- (6 ft-) high wall. Measure the full height of the mould and mark the position of its lowest point on the wall.
3 Before you attach anything to the wall, mark where the top of the basin will be positioned on the wall. Since it is essential that your container is absolutely straight, alwaus use a spirit

level rather than relying on your own judgement.
4 Pre-drill two holes in the basin, using the appropriate bit for the material you are working with – in this particular case, a masonry bit. Also make absolutely certain that the drill bit is the correct size for the screws you are using.
5 Attach the basin to the wall, double-checking that it is absolutely level.
6 Insert the tubing through the lion's mouth, ensuring there is sufficient to extend to the pump below.
7 Screw the top panel to the wall as before. Make certain the bottom connects snugly with the basin and

An uninteresting expanse of wall at the end of a raised patio.

5

6

that the sides are perfectly vertical. Since there is a slight gap between the panel and the wall, you can ease the tubing into position so that it protrudes between the two sections of the fountain. Make absolutely sure there are no kinks in the tubing or the water will not be able to flow properly.

8 Using a sharp utility knife, trim the tubing so that it does not extend beyond the lion's mouth.

9 Attach the pump outlet and tubing.

10 Now fill your fountain to the required level with water.

7

Above: Proof that even the simplest wall-mounted fountain can add charm and instant ambience to any patio, however plain and ordinary.

11 You will need to plug the pump into a nearby power point to operate the fountain. There are several different ways of doing this (see page 249 for more information).

9

BIRD-BATH FOUNTAIN

This project proves that even the simplest bird bath can make a pleasing and versatile water feature, while attracting wildlife to the garden at the same time. While most bird baths are made from pre-cast concrete, this particular one was moulded from much lighter fibrecement and then painted to look like marble. Fountains like this are widely available at garden centres and larger DIY stores in a number of differnt sizes and styles.

You will find that most bird baths are suitable for fountain use, and that many manufacturers of pre-cast products will convert them for you by simply inserting a pipe or tubing through the stem.

Since it is a free-standing unit, this fountain has been set in a large bowl. If a catchment bowl is not supplied with the bird bath, use any suitable watertight container, or secure the fountain to a plinth in a pond. Secure it properly to make sure it does not fall over. Note that the pump which activates the various water jets is hidden in the base of the hollow stem of this bird bath.

Materials
pre-cast bird bath and bowl
water-resistant paint (optional)
1 x 520 mm x 12 mm (20 in x ½ in)
    flexible tubing
1 x submersible pump, with 700 mm (2
    ft 4 in) water head
fountain heads
outdoor cable and conduit

Preparation
1 Unless your bird bath has already been converted into a fountain, the first step will be to drill a hole in the centre of the upper dish to accommodate the pipework. Remember that 12 mm (½ in) tubing has an exterior diameter of approximately 16 mm (⅝ in), and the hole should therefore be wide enough to accommodate this. You must also use the correct drill bit for the material you are drilling.

2 Push the tubing through the bottom of the supporting stem and the hole you have drilled in the dish or bowl of the bird bath. Secure it in position with a suitable two-part epoxy putty and, when this is dry, seal the upper surface with silicone or something similar.

3 If you want to paint the bird bath, or give it an appropriate paint finish such as marble, do so now. Make sure that the paint is water-resistant and, if you plan to stock the pond or collecting bowl with fish or plant life, that it is also non-toxic. Rinse the surface thoroughly before filling.

4 Establish the position of the nearest electrical connection and take the necessary steps to ensure you can operate the fountain safely once it has been installed. You will need a sealed power point close to the fountain, or a waterproof cable which runs into the house. If required, enlist the assistance of a qualified electrician to ensure safety.

Installation
5 Having decided where your fountain is to be located in the garden, check that the site is absolutely level by using a spirit level. You will find this is probably the case with an existing hard surface such as a patio. If you are placing it on an established lawn or in a garden bed, any uneven earth will have to be removed. If it is to be

1

set within an existing pond or pool, you may have to drain away the water and then build a plinth with bricks and mortar. Alternatively, you may be able to simply set it on bricks or blocks. If there is any danger of instability, you will have to cement the fountain firmly in place.

5

6 Using a sharp utility knife, trim the tubing which extends out of the dish. Make sure, however, that you leave enough exposed to attach the various fountain fittings.

6

7 Remember that the power of the pump chosen should be compatible with the height of the bird bath; for instance, a pump with a water head of 700 mm (2 ft 4 in) is suitable for this 500 mm (1 ft 8 in) high design. When attaching the pump, you will probably have to trim the other end of the tubing

The fountain feature has been positioned under a tree to attract birds.

before joining it to the outlet. If the tubing is not the correct diameter for the outlet, you may have to use a reducer of some sort.

8 Now you can fill the catchment bowl with water.

Operating the fountain
9 Before you activate the fountain, decide which jet type you want and slide it onto the pipe.

10 Your pump can now be plugged into a power point and switched on. Sit back and enjoy the different patterns

9

The pipe spurts without an additional jet.

A dome-shaped jet makes a pretty effect.

JAPANESE FEATURE FOUNTAIN

This Japanese-style fountain, modelled on a traditional shishi odoshi, enhances a small pebble garden planted with a selection of grasses, bamboo and suitable shrubs. There is nothing to stop you erecting the fountain so that the water from the bamboo pipes flows into an appropriately designed koi pond, thereby continuing the eastern theme.

The unusual green colour of bamboo will fade to the more characteristic golden brown as it dries, creating a natural effect that complements the simple elements and shapes of this delightful fountain.

Materials
5 kg (11 lb) cement
20 kg (44 lb) sand
1 x 1 m x 80 mm (3 ft 3 in x 3¼ in) length bamboo
2 x 600 mm x 80 mm (2 ft x 3¼ in) lengths bamboo
3 x 450 mm x 80 mm (1 ft 6 in x 3¼ in) lengths bamboo
1 x 260 mm x 10 mm (10 in x ⅜ in) galvanized hexagonal bolt with nut
8 washers
2 m (6 ft 6 in) natural fibre rope string (optional)
1 x 1.5 m x 10 mm (5 ft x ⅜ in) flexible tubing

Preparation
1 This Japanese-style fountain can be incorporated with the previous project. First you should remove the grass around the reservoir of water. Then follow steps 1–4 for the Pebble Fountain (pages 254-255).
Assembling the bamboo feature
2 If you have cut your own bamboo, you will now have to saw it to size. Do this with a tenon saw, cutting off an angle of 45º at one end of both the 450 mm (1 ft 6 in) and the 1 m (3 ft 3 in) lengths of bamboo.
3 To work efficiently, you will have to ensure that there is a natural joint in the longest piece of bamboo, just ahead of where it is bolted (see

illustration). Additional joints between this one and the angled end will have to be drilled out (using a wood drill bit) so that the weight of the water will cause the pivoted bamboo to see-saw gently. You may also have to drill into the second angled segment to feed through the tubing.
4 Drill holes in the remaining two 450 mm (1 ft 6 in) lengths, approximately 100 mm (4 in) from the top, and a hole in the 1 m (3 ft 3 in) length at a point about halfway. Also drill one of the 600 mm (2 ft) lengths to accommodate the tubing (see illustration below).
5 Bolt the three pieces of bamboo together as illustrated, sliding 4 washers between each piece to create two even gaps.
6 Cut holes in the two 600 mm (2 ft) lengths of bamboo to support the shorter horizontal length. These should be 150 mm (6 in) from the top of each one and the same diameter as the bamboo it will support (in this case

Pebbles, grasses, ferns and the Japanese bamboo fountain create character and interest.

80 mm or 3¼ in). Install the fountain, by tying the three pieces together temporarily with string.

Installing the bamboo feature

7 Dig two foundation trenches measuring 250 mm x 250 mm x 150 mm (10 in x 10 in x 6 in), and position the bamboo so that the smaller horizontal section of the fountain constantly feeds the one below it with water. The longer, lower, pivoted side has a see-saw action which should spill into the pebble reservoir, while the pieces that are tied together act as a faucet. Use a spirit level to check that the four bamboo posts are standing absolutely upright. **8** Now mix the cement and sand in the ratio 1:4 and add water until it is smooth and porridge-like. There is no need to add stone, as this is a lightweight structure, although you can if you wish. Lift the cement mixture with a spade and pour it into the two trenches. Compact it with the back of the spade. Double-check that the posts are still straight.

9 Place the pump in the reservoir bowl with one end of the tubing fixed to the outlet pipe. When the cement has set, push the tubing through the one 600 mm (2 ft) post. Lead the power cable to a waterproof socket box or lay underground conduit. If necessary, consult an electrician for assistance at this stage.
10 Replace the string with more sturdy, more attractive rope. Do this by crossing two pieces over on one side and securing with a reef knot. Use string to neaten the ends if you wish.

While you are doing this, use a spirit level to check that the horizontal faucet is straight.
11 River stones and pebbles are now set in position over the reservoir, as with the pebble fountain, except that you may want to spread the pebbles further, rather than creating a circular feature.

Finishing off

12 Fill the reservoir with water and plant around the feature with grasses, ferns or miniature bamboo.

3

8

PRE-CAST FOUNTAIN FEATURE

2

5

Perhaps the most popular fountains are those which comprise a pre-cast pond and some kind of ornamental structure with pedestal which sits in it and stands against a wall. Like the Bird-Bath Fountain featured earlier on pages 258-259, these are easy to erect and the huge variety of designs now available make them suitable for most applications.

Although many of the pre-cast versions are free-standing, several designs can be placed against a wall, which makes them a particularly good choice for the smaller garden or townhouse patio. There is, of course, nothing to stop you installing this type of fountain in a pond or in the garden itself, although you may first need to establish a solid and level surface to accommodate it.

Once you have installed the fountain, you can make more of a feature of this part of the garden by painting or decorating the surrounding wall. In the fountain shown here, the supporting wall has been stencilled with a realistic latticework design, complete with climbing plants growing through and around it.

Materials
pre-cast fountain (pond, pedestal, bowl and gargoyle)
cement-based adhesive
heavy-duty hook with Rawl plug
1 x 1.7 m x 10 mm (5 ft 6 in x ⅜ in) flexible tubing
1 x submersible pump, with 1.4 m (4 ft 6 in) water head
outdoor cable and conduit

Preparation
1 Before you do anything else, make sure you have access to a suitable power point.
2 Decide where you want to erect the fountain and, if necessary, measure the distance from each end of the wall, to ensure it will be centred. If you are building a solid base for the fountain, it is essential to first mark the position of the pond.

3 The next step is to ensure that the surface beneath your fountain is absolutely flat and level. If your paving or hard surface slopes, you will have to build a low plinth with bricks and mortar, or with concrete cast in situ. Slight imperfections in gradient can be rectified with a little mortar, held in place with shuttering while it dries.
4 Many pre-cast concrete fountains are made to accommodate and therefore hide the pipework in the centre of the pedestal, if it is freestanding, or behind the bowl, as is the case with this particular design. If necessary, make a groove by cutting carefully with an angle grinder. It is important that the tubing does not kink anywhere and thus prevent the water from flowing freely.

Installation
5 Position the pedestal in the centre at the back of the pond and use a spirit level to ensure that it is completely vertical. Pre-cast products may be slightly uneven, which adds to their charm, but can make installing them rather more difficult. As each section of the fountain balances on the piece next to it, you must ensure that the pedestal is straight.

6 If you find that the pedestal is not perfectly straight and upright, you can rectify this by lodging small chips of stone under the base when you cement it into its permanent position. To do this, you can use either a strong, dry-cement screed or a cement-based adhesive. Only a small quantity is

The pre-cast concrete fountain, supplied in four sections, is to be erected alongside a wall.

required, and it should be a relatively dry mixture.

7 Smooth the edges of the adhesive with a trowel and check that the top of the pedestal is level. Allow to dry thoroughly overnight.

8 Once the pedestal is secure, the scalloped bowl can be cemented into position. To ensure that the water overflows into the pond and does not splash onto the surrounding paving stones, the bowl is set so that it tips forward very slightly. Nevertheless, the back of the container must be level, as this, in turn, will support the spurting gargoyle above.

9 Since this fountain is designed to be erected against a wall, the gargoyle must be securely attached in some way. This one is made to hang and you will have to drill into the wall and bolt a heavy-duty hook in position. By using a hook, rather than a straight bolt, you will allow the top panel to fall forward slightly which will, in turn, affect the flow of the water.

10 Before you hang the gargoyle above the bowl, position the plastic

tubing behind the fountain structure so that it fits snugly into the groove behind the scalloped bowl. Remember to allow sufficient tubing to protrude above this container so that you can push it through the gargoyle's mouth to allow water to cascade down.

11 Now hang the gargoyle on the hook, pushing the length of tubing carefully through the hole from behind. If it is too long, you can trim it to the correct length with a sharp utility knife so that it finishes flush with the gargoyle's opening.

12 Fill the bottom pond with clean water. You can also pour a little water into the scallopped bowl to facilitate the flow.

Operating the fountain

13 First, check that the pump has the correct water head for your fountain. Connect up the tubing to your pump as previously described and then plug the pump into the power point provided. Finally, switch on the fountain and enjoy the soothing trickle of water.

Terracotta pots and a stencilled trellis with wisteria add the finishing touches.

PRE-CAST POND

This type of pond is undoubtedly the simplest and most foolproof of all to install, as the pre-cast shell guarantees instant results. The designs available and materials used to manufacture the shell will differ in various areas, but the principles involved in sinking one of these ponds remain the same.

Since most are manufactured in irregular shapes, pre-cast shells are commonly used to create informal ponds. The secret of making them appear natural is to disguise the most obvious man-made finishes, and to hide the edges.

The pre-cast fibrecement pond featured here has a kidney shape and is approximately 270 mm (10½ in) deep, with a flat, level base. The reconstituted stone paving slabs positioned around the edge look less contrived than most other materials and cover an area of approximately 1.2 m² (13 sq ft).

Materials

For a 1.1 m x 1.8 m (3 ft 7 in x 6 ft) pond:
1.75 m² (18¾ sq ft) kidney-shaped pre-cast shell
18-20 x 250 mm x 250 mm (10 in x 10 in) paving slabs
50 kg (100 lb) sand
50 kg (100 lb) sand (optional)

Preparation

1 Decide where you want to sink the pond and place the shell upside down on the spot. This will enable you to incorporate the lip when you mark the outline of the shell with chalk, lime or flour (see page 239). A word of warning, however: if the pre-cast pond you are installing has an irregular shape, you will have to set it right-side up or you will end up with a mirror-image and the shell will not fit.

Excavation

2 Put the shell aside and dig out the soil to the full depth of the pond plus the thickness of the proposed surround; in this case 310 mm (1 ft). It will be easier to place the shell in position if you make the hole just a little wider than you have marked. If there is a shallow end, excavate that section first and then dig out the soil, gradually working your way towards the deeper end.

3 When excavation is complete, make sure that the base of the hole is absolutely level and that there are no stones, small rocks, plant roots or undulations which will prevent the shell from sitting firmly on the ground. If the earth is very stony, you can lay a shallow bed of sand (about 20 mm (¾ in) is more than adequate) over the top of the soil to cushion the weight of the pond. If this is necessary, you will have to excavate the hole slightly deeper in order to accommodate the layer of sand.

Placing the pond

4 Place the shell in the hole and use a spirit level to check that it is perfectly straight and properly aligned. You may need to remove the shell and add or scrape a little soil away in places to make it even.

5 The surround will sit on the lip of the pond, which should now be a little below the original ground level. Place the paving slabs around the pond and mark their approximate positions. Next, remove the surrounding grass and soil to a depth of about 65 mm (2½ in) in order to accommodate the paving slabs.

6 Use some of the soil originally excavated to backfill the gap between the sides of the shell and the hole. Compact this area and the newly dug section around the perimeter of the pond. If the pond has moulded shelves for plants, take care to backfill under these areas properly in order to support them. Do not worry if the interior of the pond is soiled, this is one occasion when you do not want it to look pristine as it will help to disguise its man-made appearance.

7

10

9

Paving the surround

7 Carefully deposit a layer of clean building or river sand around the excavated and compacted edge of the pond. This should be approximately 25 mm (1 in) thick once it has been compacted.

8 Smooth the surface of the sand with a long, straight-edged piece of wood. For more efficient drainage, it is prudent to allow the top of the surrounding paved surface to slope very slightly away from the actual edge of the pond.

9 Lay the paving slabs on the sand without mortar. Press them firmly into place and make use of a spirit level to check that the surface of the edging as a whole is flat.

10 Fill all gaps between the slabs with soil and then plant with a ground cover which will thrive in the moist conditions. Pebbles or stones pushed between the slabs can also look very attractive.

Finishing off

11 Make sure the interior of the pond is clean before filling it with water and stocking with a selection of water lilies, aquatic plants and fish.

Below: Suitable for even the smallest patio, this pond transforms what was previously a neglected corner of the garden.

LINER POND

The size and shape of a pond is a matter of taste, but experience shows that the minimum size to produce harmony between volume of water, plants and fish is 4 sq m (40 sq ft). The depth should be 380 to 450 mm (15 to 18in) for small to medium-sized ponds; 600 to 750 mm (24 to 30 in) for larger ponds (over 10 sq in or 100 sq ft). Build in shelves 230 mm (9 in) wide and deep around the edge for plants.

The pond shown here is constructed using a heavy-duty liner: for this, the sides of the pond should slope by approx- imately 20° – 75 mm (3 in) inwards for every 230 mm (9 in) of depth. To calculate the size of liner you need, take twice the maximum depth and add this to both the overall length and overall width of the pond, irrespective of the actual shape.

Simple shapes with sweeping curves are best: avoid narrow necks, promontories, bays and inlets.

1

2

3

4

Base
100 kg or 2½ cu ft (220 lb) builder's
  sand
Black plastic liner

Surround (600 mm [2 ft] wide)
5 sq m (50 sq ft) paving materials
40 kg or almost one bag (88 lb)
  cement
80 kg or 2 cu ft (176 lb) sand

1 Lay a hosepipe or rope to mark the pool's outline. Start excavating, cutting inside the marked outline to allow for final trimming later.

6

7

2 Cut out the shelves for marginal plants around the edges and trim the edges back 50 mm (2 in) to allow for the overlap of the edging stones.

3 Insert short wooden pegs 1 m (3 ft 3 in) apart around the edge of pond and level with a spirit level. It is vital that the top of the pond is horizontal as the water will show any discrepancies.

4 After trimming and excavation, check the depth and width of the marginal shelves. Inspect the inside for stones or roots which could damage the liner.

5 Place a layer of sand 12 mm (½ in) thick all over the excavated area, filling any holes. Smooth the sand down – at the top, make sure it is level with the marking pegs and then remove the pegs and fill the holes with sand.

6 Loosely drape the liner into the hole with an even overlap all around with stones or blocks at the corners and on the sides. Start filling with water.

7 As the pond fills, ease the stones off at intervals to allow the liner to fit snugly into the hole. Some creases are inevitable, but can be removed by stretching and fitting as the pond fills.

8 When the pool is full, cut off excess liner, leaving a flap 100 to 125 mm (4

8

9

to 5 in) wide. This can be temporarily secured to prevent slipping by driving some 100 mm (4 in) nails through it.

9 Rectangular pools can be edged with pre-cast regular paving: curved ponds are better finished with broken stone flags or concrete paving stones. Lay the edging stones on a mortar of one part cement to three parts sand, and remove the temporary nails.

10 The pond should be emptied and refilled before planting and stocking with fish, especially if mortar has been dropped in during construction. Add fountains, lights and other ornaments.

10

Roughly formed with concrete, this pond was designed to accommodate and display koi. It is 500 mm (1 ft 8 in) deep, the minimum required for these ornamental fish, and a biological filter has been fitted. This pond incorporates attractive man-made rocks around the perimeter. If similar fake rocks are not available, a more conventional rockery could be assembled and constructed.

Materials

For this 6 m² (65 sq ft) pond:
1 x 3 m x 3 m x 6 mm (9 ft 10 in x
   9 ft 10 in x ¼ in) reinforcing mesh
250 kg (550 lb) cement
0.45 m³ (16 cu ft) sand
300 kg (8 cu ft) stone
waterproofing additive (optional)
15 l (3 gal) rubberised bitumen sealer
   (depending on brand)

To build the rockery (optional)
2.5 m x 76 mm (8 ft 2 in x 3 in)
   galvanized metal pole
wire mesh
glassfibre reinforced cement (GRC)
   rock panels OR rocks
mortar
immersible pump, with a water head
   compatible with the rockery height
biological filter
pipework and connectors (dependent
   on configuration of rockery)
outdoor cable and conduit

Preparation

1 Decide where you want the pond and mark it out with a hose or rope.
2 Knock pegs into the ground around the perimeter of the pond at intervals of about 500 mm (1 ft 8 in). These enable you to establish the level of the ground surrounding the pool.
3 Before you start digging the hole, establish a datum point which will enable you to mark the height of the proposed finished surface around the pond. Do this by hammering in one of the pegs inserted into the highest level of ground, so that its apex is at the correct height. Then use a spirit level to accurately adjust all the other pegs

so that their tops are even. If you have a dumpy level (see page 11), you can speed up and simplify this operation. You will need to work with a helper.

Excavation

4 The excavation of this pond is exactly the same as all the others. However, it is more important to slope the sides slightly because of this particular method of construction. Make sure the pegs remain in position even once the hole has been dug.

Reinforcing

5 Once the hole is ready, line it with the reinforcing mesh; this steel reinforcing will make the pond more stable and help to stop it from cracking. Since this is an informal pool with an irregular shape, it will be necessary to cut some of the mesh to get it to fit. You can do this without too much effort if you use a hack-saw or bolt cutters. Bend and then push the ends you have cut into the soil to keep it in position. To ensure an even thickness of concrete, it is useful to insert small chips of brick to form spacers between the mesh and the earth.

Concrete

6 Working in batches, mix together a total of three bags of the cement and approximately 300 kg (600 lb or 8 cu ft) each of sand and stone; the correct amount of waterproofing additive (based on the manufacturer's instructions) and just enough water to make the concrete pliable. Mix only as much as you can place in two hours.

7 If you are incorporating a rockery, throw a concrete slab at one end of the pond to form a supporting shelf. If you (or a landscaping specialist) are using GRC panels, it will be necessary to embed a metal pole in the centre of the slab to brace and support them. Note that a feature made with natural rocks will require more space than one made with panels.
8 Shovel the concrete mix into the hole and use a trowel followed by a float to smooth the surface.

2

8

9 The completed concrete shell should be about 80 mm (3 in) thick. Make sure that the upper lip is level with the top of the pegs previously inserted around the circumference of the pond.
10 Use a spirit level and a water level (see pages 230–231) to check that the upper surface of the shell is level. You can also use a dumpy level, but these are cumbersome and considerably more expensive. (However, do consider hiring one for a really professional job.)
11 Allow the concrete to set for at least 48 hours.

Plaster or render

12 You will need a good, strong render mix to finish the pond. The remaining cement and sand will give you a 1:3 mix, which is recommended not only for ponds, but for reservoirs and swimming pools as well. It is a good idea to add a waterproofing agent to this too. Use a round trowel like those employed by pool builders to render the pond. Then take a damp sponge and smooth the surface.

9

12

Pump and filter

13 Install all pipework and fit any electrical connections before you finish the pond. While guidelines are given on pages 249-250, the factors involved are variable and DIY builders without adequate experience should seek help from an electrician and possibly a plumber. The pump used here is an immersible one, while the filter is hidden above ground, behind the rock feature. The 32 mm (1¼ in) tubing

The enchanting water feature, complete with waterfall, is now the focal point. In addition, now that all the paving bricks have been removed, lush plants and an attractive fake sleeper pathway which leads to the front door of the house, add to the picture.

from the pump is routed up behind the rockery with connectors. The pump will then discharge water into a pre-cast bowl which spills into the pond.

Rockery

14 Construct the rockery on the concrete shelf behind the pond. The lightweight panels are wired and welded to the metal pole in a simple, manner. Wire mesh is then attached between the panels, to cover all gaps.
15 Using the same 1:3 render mix, the mesh (or chicken wire) is completely covered with a roughly rendered coat. This mixture is trowelled on and then manipulated so that it blends with the moulded GRC panels.

14

16 When the render is dry, the feature is spray painted in stone colours.

Sealing

17 Although the waterproofing agent added to the concrete and render will ensure a fairly waterproof shell, it is best to give the interior of the pond at least two coats of rubberised bitumen sealant. The emulsion product used here was diluted for the first coat and applied full strength for the second.

Finishing off

18 When the bitumen is dry, fill the pond. Plant the area around it, and allow all water plants to become established before introducing koi.

15

FORMAL FACEBRICK POND

A formal, reflective pond need not necessarily be large. Provided a portion of the water surface is kept clear of plantlife, even the smallest pond can have dramatic, reflective qualities. This design, which was built with just 150 bricks in a single weekend, is raised above the ground and is deep enough for both fish and aquatic plants. By restricting plantlife to water lilies and potted papyrus (*Cyperus papyrus*), a good expanse of water is still visible.

The inside surface of this pond was painted with four coats of rubberised bitumen sealer to make it watertight. You may, if you wish, render the walls as well as the concrete floor before sealing to help to guarantee it is impervious and will not leak at a later date (see page 244). Other waterproofing possibilities are mentioned on page 237.

Materials

For a rectangular pond, 1.9 m x 1.2 m (6 ft 4 in x 4 ft):
125 facebricks
25 paving bricks
175 kg (385 lb) cement
435 kg (0.4 cu yds) sand
250 kg (550 lb) stone
waterproofing additive (optional)
20 l (4½ gal) rubberised bitumen sealer (depending on brand)

An old tractor tyre, without its inner ring and used as a sandpit, provides a play area but does little to improve the garden.

Preparation

1 Peg out the required area of the pond and string a line between the pegs. Then dig out the soil to a depth of about 300-400 mm (1 ft-1 ft 4 in). Reserve the soil for use in another garden project.

Concrete

2 Now for the arduous part of the project. Mix the concrete in the recommended ratio 1:2:2 (cement:sand:stone) and roughly line the bottom and sides of your excavated hole, levelling the concrete mixture with a spade or trowel. For this pond, you will need almost two bags of cement for your concrete. If you wish, you can add a bonding compound (waterproofing additive) to the concrete mixture to improve the waterproof qualities of the pond, but always follow the manufacturer's instructions carefully.

3 Use a trowel to get the surface reasonably smooth (see page 232), taking care to level the upper rim which will form a foundation for your low brick walls. Leave the concrete to set for at least 24 hours before tackling the brickwork.

Brickwork

4 Lay out the first course of bricks to ensure they fit and then mix mortar in the ratio 1:3 (cement:sand). You will need approximately three-quarters of a bag of cement (37.5 kg or 82 lb 8 oz) to lay all the bricks, but only mix as much mortar as you can use in a two hour session.

5 Now you can begin laying the bricks in the usual way (see page 243 or refer back to the Brick chapter). Remember to check frequently with a spirit level to ensure that they are level and plumb. Use a builder's square to make certain all four corners of the pond are completely at right angles for a good end result.

6 Corner blocks and a line will help you to keep the brickwork straight and level. Check your work for accuracy regularly - do not wait until you have finished your bricklaying before checking it is level and square. Since you are laying light-toned facebricks, it is very important to clean off all excess mortar as you work and before it has a chance to dry. Scrape the trowel carefully upwards against the brickwork to do this.

7 Continue to build up the walls until you have five courses, then top this with paving bricks to finish it off neatly. You could also use tiles, or larger paving slabs which would overlap the wall slightly.

8 To achieve a really good, even finish, use a piece of metal or a jointing tool to rake out a little of the mortar between the bricks. Allow the mortar to set overnight.

6

10

Sealing

9 It is essential that the concrete base of the pond is rendered. To ensure the pond is watertight, you may also need to render the inside walls, but for this you will have to increase the quantities of materials listed on page 270. Ensure that the render is about 15 mm (½ in) thick.

10 Once the render has set thoroughly, the next stage is to paint on the rubberised bitumen sealer, polyurethane or any other suitable pond sealant you choose to use. Follow the manufacturer's instructions provided on the can carefully and thin down the first coat of sealant if required.

Filling the pond

11 When the bitumen is dry the pond can be filled with water. You can add interest to the pond by placing river rocks on the bottom and grouping plants around them. If necessary, set pots on bricks or flat-topped rocks to achieve a good balance of plant life in the pond.

The completed pond has been incorporated into a paved patio where grass would not grow. Additional plants around the adjacent tree trunk add to the lush and now tranquil surroundings.

POND WITH PLANTERS

Imaginative design and creative thinking will enable you to build more elaborate formal ponds which incorporate planters and fountain features. This enchanting formal koi pond combines the benefits of a reflective water surface with the sight and sound of water. The ingenious fountain spillway was custom-made from glass.

The design includes four planters, one of which accommodates a submersible pump. A biological filter is housed above the height of the fountain, behind the back wall, to allow the water to flow out automatically, with gravity. The front section of the pond is deeper than the back section to provide for the needs of the exotic koi. Quantities given presume you are building against an existing wall. If not, you will need more bricks, cement, sand and stone.

Materials

For a pond with measurements as shown in the illustration:
862 facebricks
850 kg (1 875 lb) cement
1.45 m³(1.9 cu yd) sand
0.6 m³ (0.7 cu yd) stone
waterproofing additive (optional)
15 l (3¼ gal) rubberised bitumen sealer (depending on brand)
3 m x 40 mm (10 ft x 1½ in) semi-rigid tubing
2 elbow connectors
1 x submersible pump, with 5.5 m (18 ft) water head (pumps 70 l or 15 gal per minute)
1 x biological filter with 4 400 l (968 gal) capacity
1 x 350 mm x 700 mm x 10 mm (1 ft 2 in x 2 ft 4 in x ⅜ in) sheet fibrecement (or similar material)
1 x 700 mm x 160 mm x 10 mm (27½ in x 6¼ in x ⅜ in) glass or perspex
1 x 700 mm x 60 mm x 10 mm (27½ in x 2¼ in x ⅜ in) glass or perspex
3 x 80 mm x 40 mm x 10 mm (3¼ in x 1½ in x ⅜ in) glass or perspex, with one end splayed to 50 mm (2 in)
silicone sealer

Preparation

1 Peg out the pond according to the dimensions shown below in figure 1, but allowing an additional 100 mm (4 in) on all sides for the foundations. Then excavate the hole to a depth of about 350 mm (1 ft 2 in). You will have to dig out an additional 650 mm (2 ft 2 in) of soil from the front rectangle which is deeper.

Concrete

2 For this pond you will need 8 bags of cement for the concrete, which should be mixed in the ratio 1:2:2 (cement: sand:stone), with a waterproofing additive if you wish. Throw a strip foundation for the walls of the planters, and for a dividing wall between the two sections of the pond (see area indicated by dotted lines in figure 1). Note that the dividing wall extends from the base of the lower pond to the base of the upper one.

3 You should throw slab foundations for both ponds and the small planter which will contain the pump. Build the dividing wall as described on page 243. Allow time for the mortar to set and then fill any gaps behind the wall with soil and compact well.

4 Now you can throw the slab foundations using a straightedge to level and compact the concrete as described on page 242. Use a spirit level to check your surface, then allow the foundations to set for at least 24 hours. Note that there is no concrete on the base of the three additional planters.

Brickwork

5 As this is a fairly complex design, it will help to lay out the first course of bricks without mortar before you start laying. You will need about 300 kg (660 lb) cement for the mortar which should be mixed in the ratio 1:3 (cement:sand).

6 Lay the bricks in the usual way (see page 243) in stretcher bond, remembering to use the correct levelling tools (see page 230). Checking will be necessary to ensure that the structure is properly built. The front section of the pond comprises brick walls which are eight courses high (excluding the coping), with only a single course above ground. The back planters are nine courses high, with six extending above ground level, while the two small planters are only four

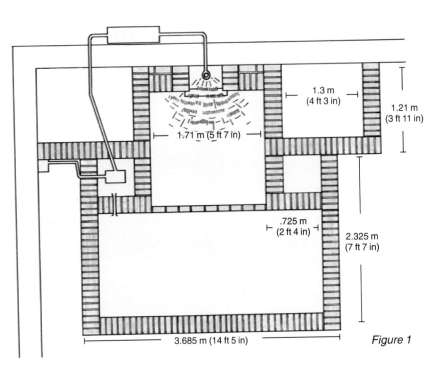

1.3 m (4 ft 3 in)

1.21 m (3 ft 11 in)

1.71 m (5 ft 7 in)

.725 m (2 ft 4 in)

2.325 m (7 ft 7 in)

3.685 m (14 ft 5 in)

Figure 1

courses high. Leave a couple of unmortared gaps in the wall between the main pool and pump compartment for the free flow of water. Also leave a small gap to accommodate the pipework which leads to the filter.

7 Lay the bricks on edge as a header course so forming a coping on top of the walls. Note that this particular design incorporates a double course of coping bricks on the inner wall of the small planters (see figure 1).

8 Rake out the joints and allow the mortar to set.

Fountain

9 Lay the bricks for the fountain feature according to figure 2. Two piers, about 650 mm (1 ft 2 in) apart and measuring 540 mm x 340 mm (1 ft 9 in x 1 ft 2 in) are built up six courses in stretcher bond.

10 Place the sheet of fibrecement over the gap between the two piers and build up a further two courses, with a half-brick course spanning the opening to create a weir. The finished fountain construction is slightly lower than the surrounding planter walls.

11 Make up the fountain spillway by gluing the five sheets of glass or perspex together with a clear silicone sealer (see figure 3). When the

An unusual formal koi pond with planters and an intriguing spillway fountain adds life and interest to a brick paved patio.

structure is thoroughly dry, lay it across the front of the opening and then lay the coping as indicated in figure 1.

Pipework and wiring

12 Knock two holes in the wall behind the pond so that you can lead the pipework from the filter to the fountain and the pump. Push one end through the hole you previously left in the one small planter. Do not connect the pipe to the pump until the interior surface has been rendered and sealed with bitumen.

13 To enable you to lead the power cable unobtrusively from the pump, drill a hole in the side wall of the same small planter.

Plaster or render

14 The floor of the pond, including the planter which will house the pump, and the internal walls may now be rendered. Mix 150 kg (330 lb) cement with 0.3 m³ (10 cu feet) of sand and add sufficient water to make the mixture pliable. Include a waterproofing additive and plasticiser in the mix if you wish.

15 Working from the back wall, lay on the plaster or render with a plasterer's trowel, applying pressure to make it stick to the bricks. Work in sections, smoothing with a plasterer's float once

it has settled, and using corner trowels to neaten the corners. Note that the render applied here is about 20 mm ¾ in) thick.

16 At the same time, render in the pipework where it enters and exits the various walls.

Sealing

17 Allow the smoothed render to set for at least 24-48 hours before painting on a rubberised bitumen sealer or any other suitable sealant, according to the manufacturer's instructions.

Pump and filter

18 The bitumen does not take long to dry, and then you can place the pump in its own compartment and connect it to the loose pipe. Connect the other end of the pipe to the filter, which should be positioned above the fountain spillway.

19 Remove the electric plug from the pump and take the power cable through the hole previously drilled. Replace the plug and connect it to an external socket in a waterproof box. Seal around the cable with silicone sealer.

Finishing off

20 When the sealant is completely dry, you can fill the pond with water and plant the additional structures.

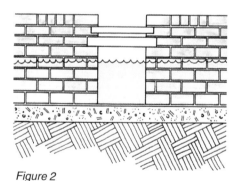

Figure 2

10 mm (⅓ in) thick glass

160 mm (6⅓ in)
60 mm (2⅓ in)
80 mm (3 in)
40 mm (1½ in)
700 mm (2 ft 3 in)
50 mm (2 in)

Figure 3

COOL POOL

This water feature may be constructed as a freestanding structure or built into a wall. Although this one was built using precast concrete materials, the illustration will enable you to build it with bricks. As the pool must be waterproof, you should use stronger concrete and mortar mixes than those specified for ordinary garden structures. Avoid using toxic lime, especially if you plan to stock the pond with fish. You may incorporate corbels at the sides instead of the low side walls, and top the three-brick-high front wall with swimming pool coping instead of a rendered lip. The wall-mounted fountain is an optional feature to add movement to the pond. Any fountain-head or gargoyle may be used and this can spurt directly into the pool or into a bowl set on the lip.

MATERIALS

Foundation
375 kg cement
0.55 m³ (750 kg) sand
0.55 m³ (750 kg) stone

Brickwork
570 bricks
160 kg cement
480 kg sand

Render
175 kg cement
waterproofing additive (optional)
525 kg sand

Fountain and accessories (optional)
Precast fountain-head or gargoyle
2.2 m tubing, 12 mm in diameter
2 elbow connectors, internal diameter
 12 mm
Submersible pump with
 1.8 m water head
Outdoor cable
 and conduit

1 Measure out the area required for the structure. Peg and excavate a 475 mm deep trench to accommodate a 250 mm deep foundation and two brick courses. Compact the base.
2 Mix concrete in a cement:sand:stone ratio of 1:2:2 and place in the trench. Level and compact it; allow to set well.
3 Build up the brick walls and side pillars according to the illustrations, using a 1:3 cement:sand mix. The first nine courses of the back wall are double courses; from the shelf upwards, build a half-brick wall. If precast materials are to be used, secure them with mortar.
4 When the mortar has set, fill in the upper section of the trench with soil.
5 Chase a channel in the wall for pipework. Chip out with a cold chisel to a depth of about 20 mm.

6 Route the cabling to the pond, either through the pond wall or over the edge. Seal with silicone if necessary. Run the cable to an outside weatherproof box and connect to the electricity supply.
7 Cut off two 100 mm lengths of tubing and join them to the longer length with elbow connectors. Push into the channel and allow them to extend at either end.
8 Render the entire structure, creating lips and indentations as required.
9 Once the rendered surface has set thoroughly, attach one end of the pipe to the pump and push the other end through the hole in the fountain-head.
10 Paint several coats of rubberised bitumen or any other sealant onto the inside of the pond, following the manufacturer's instructions.
11 Paint the rest of the structure.

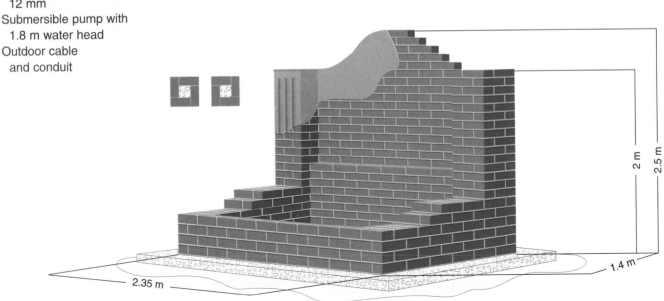

2 m

2.5 m

1.4 m

2.35 m

SPLASHING WATERFALL

A charming, natural-looking waterfall links two ponds constructed at different levels of a sloping garden. Both ponds were built with concrete and then plastered, and a series of rocks cemented into place around the edges to hide the structure. Plants further soften the effect.

The rocks which form the course of the waterfall, have been secured onto the concrete steps between the ponds. As the concrete has been made impervious, there is no need to waterproof the rocks. Materials quantified are for the waterfall only, and not the ponds.

Materials

120 kg (265 lb) cement
245 kg (0.25 cu yd) sand
245 kg (540 lb) stone
waterproofing additive
large rocks and boulders
10 m x 20 mm (11 yd x ¾ in) semi-rigid tubing
1 x submersible pump
outdoor cable and conduit

Preparation

1 Mark out the chosen position of the rockery and cut three steps into the slope. The dimensions of each step will depend on the size of the boulders you have, as well as the slope. Although instructions are not given here, you should also mark out and prepare for construction of the two ponds at the same time.

Concrete

2 Concrete the surface of the collecting pond first, then start working from the bottom of the rockery. You will need to mix the cement, sand and stone in the ratio 1:2:2 with waterproofing additive and water. Be sure to use sufficient additive or the waterfall will leak.
3 You will need at least three large, flat-topped rocks for the rockery, and so it is inevitable you will require assistance to lift and position them. Lay about 100 mm (4 in) of concrete on the lowest step, compact with a straightedge and,

while the mixture is still wet, place the first rock in position (see illustration), so that it slopes forward very slightly.
4 Concrete around one end of the rock and lay another 100 mm (4 in) of the mixture along the second step. Set the second rock in position, sloping it in the same way as before. Repeat this procedure, using the smallest rock at the top.
5 Finally concrete smaller rocks into place along the edges of the rockery and around the perimeter of the ponds.

Pump

6 The pump may be concealed in the collecting pond and cables run to a waterproof box or the nearest plug point. Make sure it is accessible so that you do not have to wade into the water to remove it for cleaning or repairs. If necessary, consult a qualified electrician at this stage.
7 Connect the tubing to the pump and run it underground to the top pond, and lead it into the water about 500 mm (1 ft 8 in) from the apex of the waterfall.

Not only does a waterfall look attractive in the garden, it also increases the oxygen level in the pond which is advantageous for both fishes and plants.

Cross-section of the waterfall constructed on three tiers.

SIMPLE STEPPING STONES

Designed to allow access from the garden to a stairway built alongside the house, these stepping stones are topped with non-slip marble tiles. Supporting piers 500 mm (1 ft 8 in) high have been made with bricks and mortar, while the surface matches adjacent paving and is level with it. For convenience, one stepping stone abuts the stairway, but this is not essential.

Although the finish here is essentially formal, the basic step-by-step instructions may be adapted for just about any man-made stepping stones. Materials and DIY instructions for the pool are not included in this project.

Materials

This project allows for construction of five rectangular stepping stones approximately 800 mm x 320 mm (2 ft 8 in x 1 ft) equally spaced across a 2.24 m (7 ft 4 in) wide pool.

288-315 bricks
12½ x 320 mm x 320 mm (1 ft x 1 ft) tiles
125 kg (275 lb) cement
390 kg (0.3 cu yd) sand
waterproofing agent (optional)
15 litres (3¼ gal) rubberised bitumen sealer

Preparation

1 You will need a solid foundation for the stepping stones. For this reason it is best to build your pond with bricks and mortar or to construct a concrete shell as described in previous projects (see pages 270 and 272). It is possible to build stepping stones in a liner pond (see figure 2), but there is a real danger that you will puncture the plastic during construction.
2 Allow the concrete shell or foundation to set before you start laying the bricks.
3 If you are building stepping stones in an existing pond, drain the water first and scrub the inner shell to get rid of algae and other plant growth.

Brickwork

4 Measure out the position of the stepping stones and mark these on the concrete with chalk or loose bricks.
5 Mix cement and sand in the ratio 1:3, using two bags of cement. For each pier measuring approximately 800 mm x 320 mm (2 ft 8 in x 1¼ in) you will need 48 to 63 bricks. If fewer bricks are used you will need to fill the central cavity with hardcore or concrete before the tops can be tiled.
6 Lay the bricks as shown in figure 3 with additional bricks in between them if you wish. Make absolutely certain that the corners are at 90°, using a builder's square to check this frequently. Every brick course must bond with the next, so allow the bricks in each successive course to overlap those below by half (see figure 1).

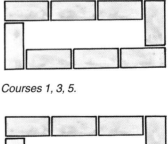

A stepping stone is attached to the stairway.

7 For 500 mm (1 ft 8 in) high piers, you will need to build up six courses of brickwork. Using corner blocks (see page 231) and a builder's line as you work will help you to ensure that each course of bricks is even and straight. If the upper level of the stepping stones is not even, you will find it difficult to walk across them, so also use a gauge rod to maintain equal mortar joints.

Plastering or rendering

8 Once you have completed the brickwork, allow the mortar to set for at least 24 hours. Your plaster or render should be mixed in exactly the same ratio as the mortar used previously. You can add a non-toxic plasticiser (see page 234) to make the mixture more cohesive, but do avoid lime, especially if you plan to stock your pool with plants or fish. It is also a good idea to add a little waterproofing agent to the mixture.

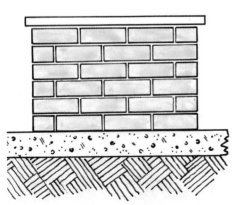

Figure 1 One of the project stepping stones.

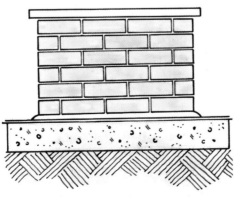

Figure 2 Stepping stone on flexible liner.

Courses 1, 3, 5.

Figure 3 Courses 2, 4, 6.

9 It is best to use a screed board to hold the render mixture while you work. Lay the render on with a plasterer's trowel, applying pressure so that it sticks to the surface. When you have roughly plastered all six of the piers, go back to the first one and smooth its surface with a plasterer's float. Use a corner trowel to obtain neat corners.

Tiling

10 If you plan to use an adhesive to set the tiles in place, you must wait for a few days until the render has set. Alternatively, you can use a little of the plaster/render mix used earlier, in which case you will not have to wait before putting the tiles on top of the piers, but work carefully or your handiwork could be ruined. Instead of the usual tile adhesive, simply spread a little of your mixed render on the back of the tiles, using a notched trowel to form ridges to aid adhesion. Push them carefully into place and then knock them gently with a rubber mallet to level them into position.

11 If you are using the size tile specified, you will need 2½ tiles for the top of each pier, which means there will be some tile cutting to do. The simplest way to do this is with a tile-cutting machine. First mark the cutting line with a pencil and then score the surface of the tile. Bring the handle of the machine down firmly to cut the tile. If you are using reconstituted stone or quarry tiles, you will have to use an angle grinder.

12 If you used a tile adhesive to set the tiles, allow this to dry before grouting the joints. Alternatively, rub a little of the plaster mix into the gaps between the tiles.

Finishing

13 Do not allow the plaster/render coat to dry out too quickly, especially in hot weather. Dampen it down with a fine spray of water from the garden hose once or twice a day, for a few days, to help it to cure thoroughly.

14 Seal the supporting piers of the stepping stones with a rubberised bitumen sealer or suitable polyurethane at the same time as you seal the pond shell.

Marble tiles give the stepping stones a sophisticated finish which complements patios.

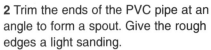

6

7

Small patio features often benefit from the addition of potted plants. This mini-cascade is no exception, and look-alike planters have been used to contain both water and plants. Although the receptacles may be made of various materials, they should be geometric and regular in shape. Sizes may be different to those illustrated, provided they fit together attractively. Those which hold water must be absolutely waterproof, while the planted containers should have holes for drainage.

For extra interest the planters and troughs have been painted and then stencilled with a decorative pattern. If you wish to do this, then use a paint suitable for outdoor use.

Materials

4 x troughs 600 mm x 600 mm x 200 mm (2 ft x 2 ft x 8 in)

2 x planters 380 mm x 380 mm x 380 mm (1 ft 3 in x 1 ft 3 in x 1 ft 3 in)

2 x planters 380 mm x 380 mm x 580 mm (1 ft 3 in x 1 ft 3 in x 2 ft)

48 bricks

1 x 200 mm x 12 mm (8 in x ½ in) semi-rigid tubing

1 x 1.5 m x 10 mm (5 ft x ⅜ in) flexible tubing

5 x 100 mm x 16 mm (4 in x ⅝ in) rigid PVC pipe

1 x submersible pump, with 1.4 m (4 ft 6 in) water head

Preparation

1 Carefully seal the drainage holes in three of the troughs with a two-part epoxy putty.

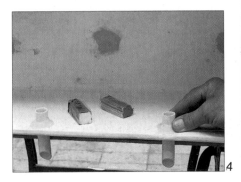

4

2 Trim the ends of the PVC pipe at an angle to form a spout. Give the rough edges a light sanding.

3 To accommodate the pipe, you will need to drill holes in two of the sealed troughs, 25 mm (1 in) below the rim and at 200 mm (8 in) centres apart. In the fourth trough (which is to be used as a planter), drill one central hole for the PVC spout. Presuming you are using PVC with a 16 mm (⅝ in) bore, all these holes should be about 20 mm (¾ in) in diameter.

4 Position the five pieces of pipe in the holes and secure with epoxy putty. Make sure the spouts are all level otherwise the water will not flow through them evenly.

5 When the putty is dry, you can paint the troughs if you wish. Decorate the planters at the same time. Add the stencilled pattern at this stage too.

Installation

6 Place the loose bricks as indicated to provide a stepped support for the troughs. If you are using containers with different dimensions, this arrangement will have to be altered. Make sure the bricks are secure and level.

7 Now you can position the water troughs on the bricks, with the spoutless container on the ground. Use a spirit level lengthwise on each one to ensure they are level. It is easier to make adjustments now than when they are full of water.

Fitting the pump

8 You will probably need to drill a 16 mm (⅝ in) hole in the bottom of the top trough so that you can push the semi-rigid tubing through it and into the top spout. Join the other end to the flexible tubing, which is, in turn,

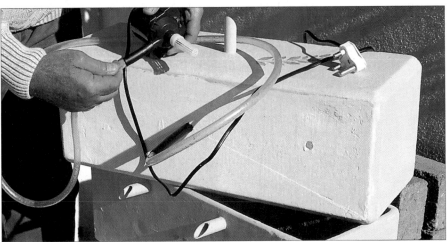

8

attached to the pump.

9 When you position the top trough, make certain that the tubing falls through the gap in the bricks so that you can lead it out through one side. Carefully position the pump in the bottom trough.

Finishing off

10 Now you can position the planters, with the highest two at the back and the shorter two at the front. Once they are planted, you will be unlikely to notice the plastic tubing leading from the troughs.

11 Fill the troughs full with clean water and plug the pump plug into a suitably waterproofed outdoor socket, or into the nearest indoor socket. Switch on the power and enjoy the soothing sound of gently trickling water.

The corner of an ordinary patio lacks life and vitality.

The cascade water feature adds colour and interest to the patio, inviting one to linger a little longer.

WOODEN BRIDGE

A simple wooden bridge can be both practical and attractive, adding to the appeal of most water gardens. This bridge has been dsigned to ford a narrow stream running through the garden, but it could also be used as an access route across ponds. If you wish to make the bridge much longer, consider whether you will need to add supporting piers below it to help take the weight.

The design shown here incorporates straightforward handrails and a slightly arched walkway. As the handrails are fairly high, take care when children are crossing over the bridge. A properly treated softwood bridge, like this one, will give you many years of pleasure in the garden, although one constructed from a hardwood will be more resistant to both rot and weathering.

The walkway of the structure featured here was made from inexpensive pine split poles planed to form planks which are slightly rounded on one side. Since these are not standard in all saw mills, the materials list specifies ordinary planed planks of the same size which can also be used. All the timber used should be planed all round (PAR) and treated; you may need to adapt timber dimensions slightly, depending on what is available in your area.

Materials

1 x 3 m x 150 mm x 50 mm (10 ft x 6 in x 2 in) length timber for bearers
6 x 900 mm x 76 mm x 38 mm (3 ft x 3 in x 1½ in) for uprights
22 x 600 mm x 70 mm x 22 mm (2 ft x 2 ¾ in x ¾ in) walkway planks
4 x 900 mm x 76 mm x 25 mm (3 ft x 3 in x 1 in) handrails
6 x 70 mm (2¾ in) wire nails
12 x 70 mm x 6 mm (2¾ in x ¼ in) galvanised coach screws
16 x 50 mm x 4 mm (2 in x ⅛ in) cross-head screws
88 x 40 mm (1½ in) ring shanked nails or self-tapping screws

Preparation

1 The first step is to cut all the required timber to size and make sure you have sufficient screws and nails for the project. Also gather together all the tools you will require for assembling the bridge..

2 While most of the lengths are straightforward to cut, the two bearers, which are sawn from a 3 m (10 ft) long piece of wood, must be curved, and this is a little more complicated. Mark out the first bearer by knocking two nails partially into the wood 1.5 m (5 ft) apart, slightly in from one end and from the bottom edge to facilitate cutting. Now measure the central point between them and knock in a third nail here, just in from the opposite edge. Next, bend a thin strip of pliable wood between the nails to enable you to draw a curve with ease. Draw a second curved line 75 mm (3 in) below

A stream meanders through the garden.

this, making sure the width of the bearer is even throughout. You can use additional nails to support the strip of wood if you wish.

3 Using a jigsaw, cut along the lines you have drawn. Do not cut the length of wood in half as you will need the overlap in the centre.

4 Now use the first bearer as a template for the second bearer, drawing around it to mark your cutting line, and then cut out.

Construction

5 Nail two straight lengths of timber to the underside of each bearer. These will act as temporary supports and will be removed once the structure is complete. Note that neither these

6

8

10

lengths of wood, nor the nails, are included in the list of materials as you can use scrap wood. Use ordinary wire nails and any suitable scraps of timber.
6 Turn one of the bearers on its side and position three of the uprights as indicated, with 150 mm (4 in) of each outer one extending below the bearers. These extensions can be set into the ground later for added stability. The bottom of the central upright timber should be flush with the lower edge of the curved bearer. Make sure all three lengths of wood are absolutely straight and parallel with one another, before knocking in wire nails to hold them in place. Check again that they are vertical, and then secure with two coach screws at the base of each upright. It helps to use a batten under the uprights to support them while you are working; this piece of wood does not, however, form part of the structure.
7 Repeat the procedure described in step 6, using the second bearer and all of the remaining uprights to assemble the other side.
8 With the temporary slats still nailed to them, position the two bearers upright on a flat surface 600 mm (2 ft) apart. Nail the planks to the upper surface of the bearers with ring shanked nails; or use self-tapping screws (which are also hammered in).
9 Measure the six upright posts and trim them to the desired height with a jigsaw. You will achieve a good balance if the centre lengths are 700 mm (2 ft 4 in), and the outer ones about 830 mm (2 ft 9 in) at their longest point which includes the 150 mm (4 in) extensions. Then trim the upper ends of the upright posts at a slight angle (see illustration above right) with either a jigsaw or tenon saw, so that the two handrails will fit snugly to them.

10 Using the 16 Phillips head screws and an appropriate screwdriver, attach the handrails securely to the six upright posts. Take care to ensure that the upright timbers remain completely straight and do not lean.

Finishing
11 Sand rough edges, rounding the ends of the handrails if you wish, and remove the temporary slats. Finally, apply a sealer following the manufacturer's instructions.

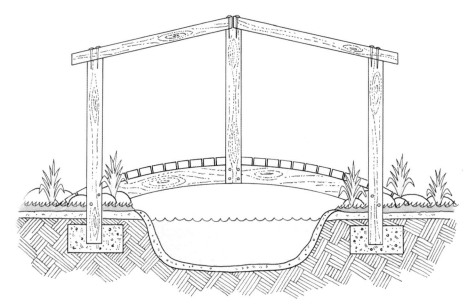

The bridge is both functional and attractive.

Aggregate
Fine or coarse, this is added to cement and water to give bulk to concrete and mortar mixes. The usual forms are sand (fine) and crushed stone (coarse).

Auger
Machine or hand tool used to bore holes in the ground.

Bargeboard
Timber used to neaten the edge of a roof at the gable ends of a building.

Basketweave
A pattern used when laying block pavers, consisting of pairs of blocks laid at right angles to adjacent pairs.

Batching
Method of measuring materials for one batch of concrete, mortar or render.

Batten
Lengths of timber commonly used as part of a roof structure.

Beading
Narrow moulding for neatening edges.

Beam
Squared timber used horizontally at the base of a roof structure and supported at both ends.

Bearer
Large supporting beam or girder used at the base of a floor structure.

Bitumen
Tar-like substance used to protect and waterproof timber.

Blinding layer
A layer of sand used to cover a base of hardcore or crushed stone.

Bond
Method used to strengthen and hold brick walls together. Bricks are laid in various patterns to form different bonds.

Bore
Hollow part of piping; term used in relation to internal diameter.

Buttering
Technique used to apply mortar or adhesive to tiles or bricks.

Butyl rubber
A synthetic rubber used to line ponds.

Capping
Covering manufactured to protect the apex of pitched roofs.

Chicken-wire
Wire netting with a hexagonal mesh, traditionally used to fence-in chickens. Useful for DIY concrete ponds.

Chipboard
A man-made constructional board formed by binding wood chips together with resin. Exterior-grade board is essential if to be used outside.

Cladding
Material used to cover and finish the timber framework of dry walling. There are types suitable for inside and out.

Cleat
Wedge of wood attached to the stringers of a staircase to support treads of some step designs. Longer cleats are also used when attaching panelling to internal walls.

Clout nail
A galvanised nail with a large flat head, mainly used to fix sheet roofing materials.

Coach bolt
A long, round-headed bolt with a plain shank threaded at one end to accept a nut, used to bolt wooden frameworks together.

Cobble
Rounded stone used to form a path, patio or road surface. Man-made cobbles are usually regular in shape and more like setts (see below).

Concrete
A mixture of cement, sand, crushed stone or gravel and water used for foundations, steps, paths, etc.

Coping stone
Flat or ridged stones used to weatherproof the top of masonry walls. A coping can also be formed by a course of blocks laid on edge.

Course
A continuous row of bricks. Several courses form a wall.

Curing
Keeping concrete or mortar moist to ensure a chemical reaction which gives it strength as it hardens.

Damp-proof course
A layer of impervious material built into a brick structure to prevent damp rising into it from the ground.

Datum point
A known point which is utilised to attain levels; for instance around the upper surface of a pond.

Dry wall
A timber-framed wall which, unlike conventional brick and block walls, does not involve any 'wet' work (bricklaying, etc.) during construction.

EPDM
Relatively inexpensive rubber made from an ethylene propylene polymer.

Facebrick
Clay or concrete brick manufactured for use without plaster.

Fascia
Timber used to neaten the back and front of buildings at the ends of rafters; this is the surface to which gutters are usually affixed.

Fibrecement
Material composed of cement, organic fibres and sometimes a small percentage of asbestos, which can be moulded to form pond shells, fountain features and pot plant containers.

Flashing
Waterproofing which seals the joins between the roof and protrusions.

Float
Process used to smooth floor screeds or rendered walls.

Formwork
Shuttering used to form a profile which holds wet cement in situ.

French drain
Drain filled with hardcore to allow water to drain through.

Galvanise
Method used to coat iron with zinc to stop it from rusting.

GRC
Glassfibre reinforced cement used to mould architectural features and various products including fake rocks.

Gypsum plaster
An internal plaster finish, containing hydrated calcium sulphate, used on both bare and rendered walls. Certain gypsum plasters (e.g. cretestone) are used to skim ceilings and plasterboard.

Half-brick wall
A brick wall equal in thickness to half the length of a standard brick. A one-brick wall is built with two rows of bricks which are laid end to end, so that the thickness equals one brick-length.

Hardcore
Various materials including broken bricks or stones used to improve drainage or compacted to form a well-drained sub-base beneath concrete.

Hardwood
Botanical classification identifying broad-leafed species of trees.

Header
Brick laid with face at right angles to the wall. Also head or short side of a brick.

Herringbone bond
Pattern for laying blocks. Each block is laid at right angles to its neighbour, and overlaps by half the length of the block.

Jointing
Method used to neaten the joints in brickwork where facebricks are used.

Level
Flat horizontal plane.

Marbelite
A mixture of white cement and granular marble dust used to plaster the internal shell of swimming pools.

Medium-density fibreboard (MDF)
Constructional board made by bonding wood fibres with resins. Exterior grade board must be used outside.

Mortar
Mixture of cement, sand and water used to bond bricks when building a wall or other structure.

pH
Degree of acidity or alkalinity of water, measured on a scale from 0-14.

Pier
Thicker section of masonry built at wall ends and along its length for support.

Piling
Post driven into soft sand to support a structure. For pile foundations, holes are bored into the ground and filled with reinforced concrete.

Plaster
Protective coating applied to bare brick or cement block walls. Some refer to plaster as a cement and sand mixture (see render), in parts of the world it refers only to gypsum plasters.

Plumb
Flat, vertical plane.

Plywood
Constructional board made by bonding thin plies of wood together. Exterior grade is essential if to be used outside.

Pole-building
Term used for construction using a framework of posts set in the ground.

Polyethylene
Polymerized material, including polythene, often referred to as 'plastic'.

Post anchor
Metal base set in a concrete foundation to anchor timber posts.

Prime
Procedure used to make some pumps start working. Certain surfaces must also be primed before being painted.

Punner
Ramming tool used to compact earth or hardcore.

PVC
Abbreviation for polyvinyl chloride, a thermoplastic made from a polymer of vinyl chloride.

Rawlbolts
Heavy-duty expanding bolts used to attach timber and other materials to brick and concrete surfaces.

Render
A coat of mortar (also referred to as 'plaster') applied to exterior walls. There are various rendered finishes; smooth stucco is probably the most common.

Sand, sharp or soft
The fine aggregate in concrete, mortar and plaster, sand is graded. Coarse or sharp sand is used in concrete, and soft building sand in mortar. Plaster sand may contain extra lime.

Screed
A smooth mortar layer spread over concrete to create a flat surface.

Sett
A small block of stone (traditionally granite) used for paving.

Shuttering
Framework of wood or steel, erected as a temporary support for concrete to be cast on site.

Softwood
Botanical specification identifying conifers.

Stretcher
Bricks laid with sides in face of wall. Also refers to the long face of a brick.

Stud
Vertical post of timber-frame houses and panelling.

Stud frame
Framework for dry walling or partitions made with studs and rails.

Water head
The height a pump can spurt from the surface of the water in a pond or pool.

Aquatek
33 Bruce Grove
North Watford
WD2 5AQ
Tel: 01923 246312

B & Q plc
Portswood House
Hampshire Corporate Park
Chandlers Ford
Eastleigh
Hants
S05 3YX
Tel: 01703 256256
(Branches throughout the UK)

Blagdon Water Garden Products Ltd
Bristol Road
Bridgwater
Somerset
TA6 4AW
Tel: 01278 446464

Brick Development Council
Woodside House
Winkfield
Windsor
Berks
SL4 2DX
Tel: 01344 885651

Building Centre Group
26 Store Street
London
WC1E 7BT
Tel: 0171 637 1022 (technical advice)
Tel: 01344 884999 (useful literature)
Also in Bristol, Glasgow and
Manchester

Do-It-All
Falcon House
The Minories
Dudley
West Midlands
DY2 8PG
Tel: 01384 456456
(Branches throughout the UK)

Great Mills Retail
RNC House
Paulton
Bristol BS18 5SX
Tel: 01761 416034
(Branches throughout the UK)

Harcross Timber and Building Suppliers
1 Great Tower Street
London
EC3R 5AH
Tel: 0171 711 1444

Homebase Ltd
Beddington House
Wallington
Surrey
Tel: 0181 784 7200
(Branches throughout the UK)

Jewson Ltd
Intwood Road
Cringleford
Norwich
NR4 UXB
Tel: 01603 56133
(Branches throughout the UK)

Onduline Building Products
Eadley Place
182-184 Campden Hill Road
Kensington
London
W8 7AS
Tel: 0171 277 0533
(organic-fibre roof sheeting)

Surrey Water Gardens
Clandon Park
Clandon
Nr Guildford
Surrey
Tel: 01483 224822

Texas Homecare
Homecharm House
Parkfarm
Wellingborough
Northampton
NN5 7UG
Tel: 01933 679679
(Branches throughout the UK)

The Water Gardener Magazine
9 Tufton Street
Ashford
Kent
TN23 1QN
Tel: 01233 621877

Travis Perkins
Lodge Way House
Lodge Way
Harlestone Road
Northampton
NN5 7UG
Tel: 01604 752424
(Branches throughout the UK)

Waterworld
Kingswood Nurseries
Bullsmoor Lane
Enfield
EN1 4SF
Tel: 01992 761587

Wickes
120-138 Station Road
Harrow
Middlesex
HA1 2QB
Tel: 0181 863 5696
(Branches throughout the UK)

CONVERSION CHART

To convert the metric measurements given in this book to imperial measurements, simply multiply the figure given in the text by the relevant number shown in the table alongside. Bear in mind that conversions will not necessarily work out exactly, and you will need to round the figure up or down slightly. (Do not use a combination of metric and imperial measurements - for accuracy, keep to one system.)

To convert	Multiply by
millimetres to inches	0.0394
metres to feet	3.28
metres to yards	1.093
sq millimetres to sq inches	0.00155
sq metres to sq feet	10.76
sq metres to sq yards	1.195
cu metres to cu feet	35.31
cu metres to cu yards	1.308
grams to pounds	0.0022
kilograms to pounds	2.2046
litres to gallons	0.22

INDEX